"[*Edith Wharton, Willa Cather, and the Place of Culture*] demonstrate[s] exemplary scholarship in [the] blending of close literary analysis with historical and biographical insights."
—CATHERINE MORLEY, *Tulsa Studies in Women's Literature*

"The parallel careers and lives Olin-Ammentorp explores here shape a stunning synthesis of the biographical, the cultural, and the literary. Wharton and Cather, together here, capture the modernist moment. While the two never met, their writing defined, this book well shows, the place of culture through the culture of place."
—ROBERT THACKER, coeditor of the *Willa Cather Review*

"*Edith Wharton, Willa Cather, and the Place of Culture* dispels oversimplifications that have positioned Cather and Wharton as opposites. In rejecting such traditional characterizations of the two, Julie Olin-Ammentorp beautifully demonstrates that they are in fact comparable and complementary. If the book stopped here it would be truly valuable, but it goes further, exploring concepts such as place, culture, home, and even that most elusive of ideas, beauty.... Olin-Ammentorp develops provocative rereadings of texts we thought were familiar."
—JANIS STOUT, author of *Willa Cather: The Writer and Her World*

"A splendid meditation on place, culture, and beauty. Olin-Ammentorp takes the reader on a journey of discovery through the lives and works of two beloved American authors, demonstrating that, although they may seem to inhabit different worlds, in fact the two share many crucial concerns. With a particularly sensitive attention to language, the book is filled with rich insights and nuanced readings of both Wharton and Cather, and it builds a convincing argument about the centrality of beauty and of place in the lives and writings of both."
—IRENE GOLDMAN-PRICE, editor of *My Dear Governess: The Letters of Edith Wharton to Anna Bahlmann*

"*Edith Wharton, Willa Cather, and the Place of Culture* is a game changer, opening up the ways we look at two of the most famous American writers (male or female) of the early twentieth century. Olin-Ammentorp combines a masterly grasp of the big picture alongside the nuance and detail of close analysis and invites new ways of thinking about the writers' interconnectedness, their sense of place, geography, culture, beauty, and language.... [This] will be a touchstone reference text for a whole new generation of scholars."

—LAURA RATTRAY, author of *Edith Wharton and Genre: Beyond Fiction*

"That Wharton and Cather lived lives seemingly so different yet so profoundly parallel makes for an endlessly compelling analysis. This work also speaks more broadly to the careers and global interests of women writers whose experiences of place, travel, geography, nationality, and postwar identities shaped their careers in ways distinctive to the early twentieth century.... Clearly the product of deep knowledge, this work promises to contribute to comparative studies; to studies that focus on geography, place, and travel; and to literary interpretations of both authors' works."

—MELANIE DAWSON, author of *Edith Wharton and the Modern Privileges of Age* and past president of the Edith Wharton Society

EDITH WHARTON,

WILLA CATHER,

AND THE PLACE

OF CULTURE

EDITH WHARTON, WILLA CATHER, AND THE PLACE OF CULTURE

Julie Olin-Ammentorp

UNIVERSITY OF NEBRASKA PRESS | LINCOLN

© 2019 by the Board of Regents of the University of Nebraska. Portions of chapter 4 were previously published in "Girls from the Provinces: Wharton's Undine Spragg and Cather's Thea Kronborg," in *Edith Wharton's The Custom of the Country: A Reassessment*, ed. Laura Rattray (London: Pickering and Chatto, 2010), 127–41 (reproduced with permission of Informa UK Limited through PLSclear); and "Coral Hicks: Edith Wharton's 'Heiress of All the Ages,'" *Letteratura d'America: Rivista Trimestrale* 37, no. 164 (2017): 27–47. All rights reserved.

The University of Nebraska Press is part of a land-grant institution with campuses and programs on the past, present, and future homelands of the Pawnee, Ponca, Otoe-Missouria, Omaha, Dakota, Lakota, Kaw, Cheyenne, and Arapaho Peoples, as well as those of the relocated Ho-Chunk, Sac and Fox, and Iowa Peoples.

First Nebraska paperback printing: 2025
Publication of this volume was assisted by the Le Moyne College Committee on Research and Development.

For customers in the EU
with safety/GPSR concerns, contact:
gpsr@mare-nostrum.co.uk
Mare Nostrum Group BV
Mauritskade 21D
1091 GC Amsterdam

Library of Congress Cataloging-in-Publication Data
Names: Olin-Ammentorp, Julie, 1959– author.
Title: Edith Wharton, Willa Cather, and the place of culture / Julie Olin-Ammentorp.
Description: Lincoln: University of Nebraska Press, [2019] | Includes bibliographical references and index.
Identifiers: LCCN 2018049387
ISBN 9781496203243 (cloth: alk. paper)
ISBN 9781496244604 (paperback)
ISBN 9781496216885 (epub)
ISBN 9781496216892 (mobi)
ISBN 9781496216908 (pdf)
Subjects: LCSH: Wharton, Edith, 1862–1937—Criticism and interpretation. | Cather, Willa, 1873–1947—Criticism and interpretation. | Culture in literature. | Place (Philosophy) in literature. | Literature and society—United States—History—20th century.
Classification: LCC PS3545.H16 Z754 2019 |
DDC 813/.5209—dc23
LC record available at https://lccn.loc.gov/2018049387

Set in Arno Pro by Mikala R. Kolander.

For Warren, Jane, and Wilkie,
who have traveled to so many Wharton
and Cather places with me.

CONTENTS

List of Illustrations	ix
Acknowledgments	xi
Introduction: Wharton, Cather, Place, and Culture	1

PART 1. CONTEXTS AND INTERSECTIONS

1. The "Literary Aristocrat" and the Plainspoken Pioneer	25
2. The Land of Letters, the Kingdom of Art	70

PART 2. THE PLACE OF CULTURE

3. New York City: Beauty, Business, and Hothouse Flowers	105
4. The West: Provinciality, Vitality, and the "Real" America	145
5. The Idea of France	193
6. Questions of Travel and Home	258
Notes	305
Bibliography	345
Index	367

ILLUSTRATIONS

1. Illustration of Wharton and Cather among other authors, April 24, 2015 — 33
2. "American Novelists Who Have Set Art Above Popularity," 1921 — 41
3. Wharton in procession of honorees at Yale, 1923 — 43
4. Cather portrait from *Yale Alumni Weekly*, July 5, 1929 — 43
5. Letter to Wharton from Cyril Clemens, August 8, 1936 — 47
6. Wharton at desk, 1931 — 71
7. Cather at desk, ca. 1900 — 71
8. Map of Wharton's and Cather's New York City — 107
9. Cather on horseback in the Southwest — 167
10. Wharton on donkey in Santorini, Greece, 1926 — 167
11. Map of Wharton's and Cather's Paris — 200
12. Cather in Leon Bakst's studio in Paris, 1920 — 202
13. Wharton with Teddy Roosevelt's sons and others, 1918 — 219
14. G. P. Cather with his regiment, commanded by Theodore Roosevelt Jr. — 219

15. G. P. Cather in uniform	221
16. Newbold Rhinelander in uniform	223
17. "Inquiétude"	233
18. & 19. Indefatigable travelers	261
20. & 21. At home in France	301
22. & 23. "Good eating and good talk"	302

ACKNOWLEDGMENTS

Without the help and encouragement of many people, this work would never have taken form. I am grateful for my many fine colleagues at Le Moyne College. Within the English Department Ann Ryan and Julie Grossman read portions of the manuscript and offered invaluable advice; thanks also to Maura Brady, Michael Davis, and Chris Warner. Other Le Moyne colleagues have also been instrumental, including John Langdon, Irene Liu, Holly Rine, and the late Mary MacDonald. I am also grateful to my students, who regularly confirm my sense of the ongoing importance of Wharton and Cather, and especially to the Secret Cather Club, Sean Abrams, Emily Powers, and Brandon Sisson. At Le Moyne's Noreen Reale Falcone Library, my thanks to Wayne Stevens, Inga Barnello, and our former librarian, Kelly Delevan. Eileen Familo, faculty secretary extraordinaire, provided crucial help with manuscript preparation.

   I greatly appreciate the collegiality of many Wharton and Cather scholars. Irene Goldman-Price expertly read portions of this project at crucial stages; Alan Price shared enthusiasm and research finds. Donna Campbell, Jennifer Haytock, Laura Rattray, and Virginia Ricard all provided assistance, as did Anne Schuyler at The Mount. Many Cather colleagues have generously shared their knowledge, including Thomas Gallagher, Cristina Giorcelli, John J. Murphy, Tracy Tucker, and the collective knowledge of 5 Bank Street. Special thanks to Richard Harris, Andy Jewell, and Robert Thacker, all of whom helped in myriad ways, as did Diane Prenatt and Elaine Smith, who kept me going with Cather conversations from Red Cloud to Rome. Beyond these scholarly circles, my dear friends Linda Pennisi and Lisa Suhair Majaj kept me grounded in the wider world. Finally, I owe a vast debt to the late Elsa Nettels. My mentor and friend for many years, she commented on my work, including the early stages of this project, with insight and wisdom.

Le Moyne College has supported this work in several ways. From 2007 through 2010 I held the Francis J. Fallon, S.J., Fellowship, which provided a course release and funding for conferences and research travel, allowing me to explore ideas of place. Le Moyne also supported my work through sabbaticals in 2010 and 2015. The Research and Development Committee provided a grant for research at Yale's Beinecke Library and an additional grant to cover some costs associated with the book; a Harriet O'Leary grant allowed me to travel to the Society for the Study of American Women Writers conference in Bordeaux, France, in July 2017.

Other individuals and institutions have provided support and permissions. I am grateful to Erin Greb, who worked patiently with me as she created the wonderful maps for this book. Many thanks to Peter Pennoyer for permission to use his photograph of Edith Wharton with his grandfather, James Russell Parsons, and two of the Roosevelt sons during the Great War. I am grateful to Edward Sorel for permission to use his brilliant drawing of Harold Bloom being scrutinized by an instantly recognizable Wharton and Cather; Alison Lenert at Condé Nast kindly provided a digital copy. My thanks to the following: Ilaria Della Monica at the Villa I Tatti; the Harvard University Center for Italian Renaissance Studies for permission to quote from Wharton's letters to Bernard and Mary Berenson; Harriet Shapiro, Erin Schreiner, Carolyn Waters, and the staff at the New York Society Library; Mary Haegert at the Houghton Library, Harvard University; AnnaLee Pauls at the Firestone Library, Princeton University; Pamela Pierce of the Theodore Roosevelt Center at Dickinson State University; Emma Florio at Chicago's Newberry Library; Mark Branch at the Yale Alumni Magazine; and the staff at the Yale Collection of American Literature at the Beinecke Library. For permission to use images and photographs, my thanks to the Archives and Special Collections, University of Nebraska–Lincoln Libraries; the Art Institute of Chicago; the Lilly Library, Indiana University; the Nebraska State Historical Society, Lincoln, Nebraska;

and the National Willa Cather Center, Red Cloud, Nebraska. These people and institutions made research a pleasure. At the University of Nebraska Press, many thanks to my editor, Bridget Barry, her assistant, Emily Wendell, and to Sara Springsteen and Bojana Ristich for their help and their patience.

Finally, I am grateful for the support of my family. My late father, David Olin, enthusiastically read everything I have written; my sister Susan Olin has cheered me on, consulted on matters literary, bibliographical, and cartographical, and generously proofread the manuscript. My husband, Warren, has encouraged me over many years and many conversations; our daughter, Jane, proved a thoughtful reader of Cather and an expert research assistant; our son, Wilkie, provided an observant eye and inspired me with his own example of diligence in research. Warren, Jane, and Wilkie were integral parts of the making of this study, traveling with me to places as various as Lenox and Nice, Santa Fe, Aix-les-Bains, and Clermont-Ferrand, and providing insight and good humor along the way. It is to them that I dedicate this book.

EDITH WHARTON,

WILLA CATHER,

AND THE PLACE

OF CULTURE

INTRODUCTION

Wharton, Cather, Place, and Culture

If Miss Wheeler had half a chance she would be an actress of merit. But she has not had the chance. She was a raw Kansas City girl, who had never even seen any of the greatest acting, put down to hard work just when she should have had time to develop and study. She puts great sincerity and tenderness into her words, but she is utterly crude and even her elocution is faulty. I wish Miss Wheeler had been born further east. Geography is a terribly fatal thing sometimes.
    WILLA CATHER (quoted in Slote, *The Kingdom of Art*)

I don't want to read the "Life"! It always saddens me to read of those starved existences, (starved, I mean, compared to what they might have been in England or France—anywhere where there is a dust of ideas in the air.) I feel as sad as I do when I read Emerson's Journals, & think of the rich & dramatic lives of his European contemporaries.
EDITH WHARTON, letter to Bernard Berenson, February 22, 1930

WHARTON, CATHER, AND PLACE

Despite their status as two of the most important American novelists of the first half of the twentieth century—the first and second women to receive the Pulitzer Prize for the novel and the first and third women to receive the honorary Doctor of Letters degree from Yale University—Edith Wharton and Willa Cather have rarely been studied together.

On the contrary, critics and academics seem to have conspired to keep them at a safe distance. Wharton is often perceived as a New York "literary aristocrat," while Cather is usually thought of as the midwestern chronicler of the lives of ordinary people.[1] These depictions, though partly valid, rely on huge oversimplifications of their work and neglect the fact that in many ways the lives and the works of these two authors demonstrate significant complementarity and continuity. Wharton and Cather both portrayed the American scene from the Civil War through the Gilded Age, the Great War, the Jazz Age, and into the Great Depression. Both depicted wealth and poverty, upper-class and working-class characters, urban and rural scenes, men and women who die for a lack of beauty, and characters who will do anything to succeed. As the critic Merrill McGuire Skaggs said, "Sometimes books talk to each other."[2] Wharton's and Cather's books carry on complex and fascinating conversations which have been little listened to.

When we pay attention to the nature, extent, and intensity of the conversations between Wharton's and Cather's works, we realize that their fictions align not only in terms of characters and issues but also in the worlds the authors inhabited. The same places often appear in their lives and works; New York City, Paris and other regions of France, and—surprisingly in Wharton's case—the American West were crucially important to both. Far from being mere coincidences, these confluences demonstrate that Wharton and Cather shared a deep concern with the United States and American issues, including perplexing questions about the nature of American culture itself—if, indeed, there can be any single or unified concept of American culture. Paradoxically, if there is any defining aspect of the United States, it may be its vastness and variety, which contribute to the common and nearly reflexive geographic categorization of Wharton and Cather as "eastern" and "western"—a categorization so pervasive that the deep affinities between the two authors and their works have rarely been acknowledged. Yet when we read their works carefully and when we plot their lives and works onto the same maps, the continuities and the complements emerge, and we find that the oeuvres of both authors offer the same fundamental and searching analysis of American culture and its limitations.

First and foremost, *Edith Wharton, Willa Cather, and the Place of Culture* offers, I hope, new and deeper understandings of the lives and works of two of the greatest American authors of the first half of the twentieth century. At the same time, this study entertains a wide range of questions. What, after all, makes an American author American, and in what sense are Wharton and Cather, different as they are perceived to be, both American? Is the part of the country we think of as the "West" somehow more "American" than the region we think of as the "East"? What are the deep connections between American and other literatures and cultures, particularly European literature? These are questions that have haunted all of what we call "American literature," from Washington Irving to Ralph Waldo Emerson to Nathaniel Hawthorne, or for that matter from the Puritans, Spanish explorers, and original Native Americans to current transnational American authors like Naomi Shihab Nye, Jhumpa Lahiri, and Junot Diaz.

This book also addresses questions about critical practice and particularly about the ways in which common critical categories shape and thus limit the terms in which we think. It began as a general comparative study of Wharton and Cather; as I delved deeper into their works and realized their intersections in place, their common interest in the nature of American culture, and the powerful connections between place and culture in their work, I knew I had my work cut out for me. "Culture" is certainly a common concept in literary and historical studies; its very malleability as a term is both a strength and a challenge. "Place" as an analytic category, however, is far less common. To many, "place" may seem a simple "fact" of literature, a variation on "setting"; what more is there to say? Alternatively it may run deep, as it does in analyses of southern culture in southern literature, or it may serve as a net to catch many things—stories, novels, films about a given place—with the net for some places catching relatively few fish and the net for others (New York City, for instance) catching so many that it may well burst. Following the cues provided by Wharton and Cather, I hope to illustrate that place as an axis of organization is an underused but powerful tool, encouraging us to think in ways that are historically, geographically, and literarily valuable.

From my interest in the meeting of place and culture emerged a third, equally difficult term: beauty, perhaps the most intractable of all. Since the modernist period and particularly since the work of cultural critics like Michel Foucault, "beauty" has been a suspect concept. Cultural critics have argued persuasively that there is no such thing as "beauty" per se; it is, rather, a social construct created to further privilege the powerful. Given this understanding critics have often retreated to the relatively safe term "aesthetically pleasing" and have sometimes substituted the term "taste," which acknowledges that any idea of "beauty" is shaped by a multitude of factors. Indeed even as I am challenging the retreat to terms like "aesthetically pleasing" and "taste," I also accept them. One person's or culture's idea of the aesthetically pleasing is not the same as another's, nor should it be. Yet to all of us the "aesthetically pleasing" is important, just as places we live in and visit are important. Even in the twenty-first century, "we do not live in an abstract world of 'airy nothing' but rather in a world of tactile realities";[3] we live in particular homes (which most of us strive to make "aesthetically pleasing"), which are located in particular cities, towns, or landscapes; many people strive to live in a place they find *beautiful*, to avoid the word no longer.

While this book is, first and foremost, a comparative study of Wharton and Cather, it is also, I hope, one that will encourage criticism focused on place and culture, including the role of beauty. These are essential categories in the lives of most people; they should be in criticism as well. In drawing attention to matters of place and culture in this study, I hope to broaden the kinds of meaningful discussions we can have about literature and the ways we think about American literature in general.

THE SPATIAL TURN

Literary studies in general have varied in the amount of significance they have given to place. "Setting," situation in time and place, is one of the most fundamental of literary categories, yet it is often treated as trivial, a quiz-question aspect of fiction needing no further investigation. At a foundational level, the lack of attention to place has its roots in the literary formalism of the New Critics of the 1930s, who stressed the internal coherence of literary works, not their relationship to the historical and geographic worlds they portrayed or from which they emerged. If place mattered at all, it was primarily as an abstraction in which certain events unfolded; it had little to do with the deepest elements of the text, much less with actual locations. Many twentieth-century theoretical approaches, even those newly attuned to culture, politics, and history, have been more attuned to space as an abstract concept than to specific places.[4]

Yet the spatial turn that has occurred in many academic disciplines allows us to recognize and discuss the importance of place, including its importance in literature. The spatial turn has deep roots, reaching back to the Roman concept of the *genius loci*, or spirit of place, "whereby a tutelary spirit presides over a particular landscape."[5] Within academe the spatial turn has its roots in the work of Henri Lefebvre, Raymond Williams, and Michel Foucault;[6] another powerful force in this movement has been Yi-Fu Tuan's 1974 *Topophilia: A Study of Environmental Perception, Attitudes, and Values*, which reconceptualized the field of geography, arguing for the profound connection between place and human culture in a range of disciplines. Philosophers and cultural critics have discussed the relationship between place and human experience in works like those of Carter, Donald, and Squires, *Space and Place: Theories of Identity and Location* (1993), and J. E. Malpas, *Place and Experience: A Philosophical Topography* (1999). This movement has continued to gain momentum and provide new perspectives, with recent work building increasingly on Mikhail Bakhtin's concept of the chronotope (literally, time-space), articulated in his essay "Forms of Time and of the Chronotope in the Novel." In literary works, Bakhtin argues, "Time, as it were, thickens, takes on flesh, becomes artistically visible; likewise, space becomes charged and responsive to the movements of time, plot and history."[7] Similarly, Bertrand Westphal's *Geocriticism: Real and Fictional Spaces* (2007) has set the stage for various studies in which, in the words of his translator Robert Tally Jr., "the geocritic orchestrates a number of different points of view" to reexamine and reconceptualize our concepts of specific spaces and places.[8] Such studies, however, often emphasize time rather than space. Bakhtin, after coining the term "chronotope" and pointing out "the inseparability of space and time," states bluntly that "in literature the primary category in the chronotope is time," and often it is time, not space (or that yet more concrete category, place) that draws the most attention.[9] Edward Said observed that "after [Georg] Lukács and [Marcel] Proust, we have become so accustomed to thinking of the novel's plot and structure as constituted mainly by temporality that we have overlooked the function of space, geography, and location."[10] Westphal himself points out that space (and place) are often displaced, as it were, by an analysis of time: "'Time was aristocracy' while space was 'only a rough container, a plebeian frame for time.'"[11]

While I frequently track chronology in some detail and acknowledge that places exist in time as well as in space, my own emphasis in this study is on place rather than on time. Seeing the conceptual intersections between Wharton and Cather led me to my interest in place in their works, which ineluctably led me back to larger questions of culture; in analyzing and interpreting these issues, I have found clues to the map of my work in both literary studies and studies of place. One touchstone of my work is the principle articulated in *The Spatial Turn* (2009). In their introduction to this important collection, the editors and geographers Barney Warf and Santa Arias explain: "The spatial turn ... involve[s] a reworking of the very notion and significance of spatiality to offer a perspective in which space is every bit as important as time in the unfolding of human affairs, in which geography is not relegated to an afterthought of social relations, but is intimately involved in their construction. Geography matters, not for the simplistic and overly used reason that everything happens in space, but because *where* things happen is critical to knowing *how* and *why* they happen."[12] "*Where*," in short, is essential to *how* and *why*.

Within the field known as "the spatial turn," theorists distinguish between space and place. Space is, generally speaking, wide open and unshaped by humans; one thinks of "the wide open spaces of the West" or, even more broadly, of outer space. In contrast, "place is space that has been given meaning and borders" and is shaped by humans.[13] (Cather provides a nice example of the distinction in *My Ántonia*: Jim Burden's initial response to Nebraska is that "there was nothing but land: not a country at all, but the material out of which countries are made."[14] He sees Nebraska as a space, not a place.) Like space, place provided a new axis on which knowledge could be organized. This gave rise to several influential studies, including William Cronon's *Changes in the Land* (1983), the first study of environmental history, which proceeds not by analyzing a particular event or person but by tracking change in a single place in New England. Similarly Simon Schama's *Landscape and Memory* (1995) studies the relationship between place, history, and wide-ranging mythologies in locations as different as Poland and Yosemite. Schama introduces the concept by citing his childhood reading of Rudyard Kipling's *Puck of Pook's Hill*: "Apparently, there were some places in England where, if you were a child . . . , people who had stood on the same spot centuries before would suddenly and inexplicably materialize. With Puck's help you could time-travel by standing still."[15] The concept of intersecting place, time, and culture was one Cather also appreciated: on a postcard from Rome she wrote to her sister Elsie that "if one listened long enough the fountains [of Rome] would tell one more even than Puck of Pook's Hill knew, for it was here that modern Europe was made."[16]

In concert with the emphasis on place, maps have gained a new prominence. Peter Barber, map librarian at the British Library, has written that in the wake of widespread navigational systems like GPS, cartography suffered a devaluation. Yet "having been lost to Geography, maps became available to other disciplines. . . . Academic historians of all types . . . and literature specialists began to take an interest in maps and to find that they offered perspectives on their subjects that were not possible from other sources."[17] A work like Malcolm Bradbury's 1996 *Atlas of Literature* attests to readers' interest in the detailed geographic relation between literature and place; Rebecca Solnit and Joshua Jelly-Schapiro's recent *Nonstop Metropolis: A New York City Atlas* (2016) makes the infinite possibilities of mapping visible, as the authors create and comment on twenty-six different maps of the city, each emphasizing a different aspect of its history and culture. Wharton and Cather, too, write about characters who create their own "individual maps" of particular places.

If the spatial turn has come with relative ease to European scholars, who can often, by standing in a single place, quite literally see layers of history before them, it may be more of a challenge for Americans, at least non–Native Americans.[18] As Wai-Chee Dimock has written, Americans, as members of a "young nation," are often "largely indifferent to the history of the world" and frequently see the past as irrelevant, and unconnected to, the present.[19] To most Americans, as Dimock points out in one example, the destruction of Baghdad's Iraqi National Library in 2003 had nothing to do with the Mongols' destruction of it in 1258, while Iraqis saw it "as yet another installment of that long-running saga."[20] With some obvious exceptions—Philadelphia's Independence Hall and Gettysburg battlefield, for instance—Americans are often far less conscious of history than people in many other cultures, and for that very reason they are often struck by the visible presence of the literary and historical past if they visit Europe's cities and landscapes. American tourists to Bath, for instance, may be surprised to see the ongoing presence of Jane Austen's world in sites referenced in her novels and in various museums and markers; in the famous baths themselves, they may stop to appreciate the visibility of many layers of history, going back to the Roman and Celtic worlds. Similarly cities like London and Paris are full of historical markers commemorating significant sites. In contrast, the difficulty of seeing the historic and literary past in the United States is clear to readers trying to trace Wharton or Cather in New York. Thanks to the voracious American appetite for change, much of the New York these writers depict has been lost, despite the fact that their New York is relatively recent, far closer to us in time than New Amsterdam or pre-contact Manhattan, known as Mana-hatta (or hilly island) to the local Indian populations. Wharton's birthplace on West Twenty-Third Street is now a Starbucks; the building she and her husband lived in at 882–884 Park Avenue is gone. (Even those street numbers are no longer in use.) Cather's early residence on Washington Square South has been replaced by multi-story buildings, and the home on 5 Bank Street that she so enjoyed was demolished decades ago. To be sure, small plaques commemorate Wharton's birthplace and 5 Bank Street, but to "see" Wharton's and

Cather's New York, one needs to be armed with a good map—and an excellent imagination.

In 1956 Eudora Welty asked, "What place has place in fiction?"[21] The question is still relevant. Often broad cultural forces reiterate that actual place does not matter. In 2003 Michael Kowalewski wrote that "regional art and identity have never seemed stronger in American society, yet there is a nagging suspicion that they may be increasingly peripheral in ... postindustrial economies that run on global flows of information and capital. ... Increasingly large numbers of Americans feel less tied to and less aware of the places in which they live."[22] As the world has become increasingly global, it may be not only less local but also less attuned to specific places. The novelist Annie Proulx remarked in 2008 that the "deep landscape novel, in which the story that unfolds can only happen because of *where* it happens, is rarely written" today.[23] Yet in creating such works herself, Proulx is one of a long tradition of American writers who have believed in the importance of place. In 1929 Sinclair Lewis stated, "The scene of a story is the environment affecting the character, and that scene ... is as much a part of the protagonist's character and development as his heart."[24] He emphasized the importance of a novelist's knowing his or her setting personally and intimately: "One can express adequately only a scene which one knows by the ten thousand unconscious experiences which come from living in it."[25] Welty also declared her belief in the centrality of place: "It is by the nature of itself that fiction is all bound up in the local. ... Fiction depends for its life on place."[26]

Some critical traditions have dismissed place or simply left it by the wayside. Yet place matters deeply in the literatures of a number of cultures: for instance, "The sense of place always dominates in Ireland," Bradbury observes.[27] In American literary criticism many scholars of regional literature have called special attention to the links between the fictional landscapes and the geographical ones that inspired them. In recent decades critics have picked up the tradition of Alfred Kazin's 1988 touchstone volume *A Writer's America: Landscape in Literature*, including Charles Crow, *A Companion to the Regional Literatures of America*, and H. L. Weatherby and George Core, *Place in American*

Fiction: Excursions and Explorations. Perhaps more than any other literary approach, ecocriticism has been attentive to place, focusing on the relationship between writers and the natural world. Cheryll Glotfelty has also asked whether place should be added "to race, class, and gender" as "a new critical category," observing that some "ecocritics have studied the environmental conditions of an author's life—the influence of place on the imagination—demonstrating that where an author grew up, traveled, and wrote is pertinent to an understanding of his or her work."[28] This principle is crucial to understanding Wharton's and Cather's writing about place.

Using place as an axis of organization for thinking about Wharton and Cather demonstrates the limitations of reflexive geographic labeling, highlights the proximity of the authors' lives and fictions, and points to their shared concerns. A simple but salient example is the role played by New York City. Although it is Wharton who is usually associated with New York and thought of as a New York author, Cather lived there far longer. Wharton was born in the city but left it at age four and did not return until she was ten; after that she lived in and out of the city when she was in the United States, summering in Newport, Rhode Island, and later at The Mount, her home in western Massachusetts. She spent the vast majority of her adult life in Europe, traveling there for several months every year during her early married life and living in France from 1907 until her death in 1937. In contrast, Cather moved to New York in 1906 and lived there until her death in 1947, when she died suddenly in her apartment at 570 Park Avenue—only a few blocks south of where the young Mrs. Wharton had lived. Timelines remind us that, paradoxically, both authors lived for a relatively brief period in the places with which they are most associated. Except as a very small child, Wharton rarely lived in New York for more than a few months at a time; Cather lived in Nebraska for only thirteen years, from her family's arrival there in 1883 until her departure for a job in Pittsburgh in 1896. Her association with Red Cloud, frequently thought of as her home town, is even briefer. Her family moved there in 1884, and she left a scant six years later, in 1890, to attend a year of preparatory school in Lincoln before beginning at the University of Nebraska. New York

City figures prominently in the works of both, as we will see in chapter 3. Such facts challenge the dominant perception of Wharton as a New York author and even of Cather as a Nebraska author; thinking of these authors in terms of a single place distorts our view of them.[29]

The spatial turn, then, reorients us to the importance of place. As Mary MacDonald states in her introduction to *Experiences of Place*, "A place is a locality or a physical environment, a space which human beings have converted into a meaningful habitation. Place, however, means more to us than a physical location.... It is also a poetic and aesthetic conception" and can even be "a political strategy."[30] The anthropologists Pamela Stewart and Andrew Strathern articulate a multi-dimensional view of place, differentiating (in Graham Dawson's summary) "three zones": first, the "material environment" or physical place itself; second, the "meanings and associations ... attached to the place," or "cultural landscape"; third, "an internalized sense of place formed from personal memory interwoven with elements of cultural landscape," or "inner landscape of the mind."[31]

All three levels play a role in this study. I am interested in geographic place and the material and cultural environments in which Cather and Wharton lived and set their works. Particularly in discussions of New York City and Paris, specific addresses play a role; the maps in chapters 3 and 5 allow readers to visualize these easily. In other parts of the argument, place as "cultural landscape" is the foremost concern. The "West" and "France" are such large cultural concepts that detailed maps are not as useful, yet remembering that cultural concepts are deeply rooted in particular geographic places helps us focus on important strands in the works of both authors. Finally, and on several levels, places often create or mirror "inner landscapes of the mind." As individuals, the minds of Wharton and Cather mirror the landscapes that shaped them; as writers, they also project their inner landscapes onto the page. Their characters, too, shape and are shaped by experiences, expectations, and even readings about landscape and sometimes project their own inner landscapes onto the geographic landscapes they perceive. The same may be said for readers, who come both to places and to literary depictions of place molded by their own experiences;

readers may also find that their "inner landscapes" as well as their perceptions of actual landscapes are profoundly shaped by the written word, including Wharton's and Cather's descriptions of place.

Wharton and Cather critics have, generally speaking, somewhat different records on their attention to place. Cather critics have been attentive to place in her works. Indeed Warf and Arias's statement that "geography matters... because *where* things happen is critical to knowing *how* and *why* they happen" was anticipated decades earlier by Cather's first biographer, E. K. Brown, who wrote in 1946 that "Cather had always understood that a person's relation to a place might be as valuable to him... as any relation he might have with other persons. What happens in one place could not happen in just the same way in any other."[32] Critics have taken Cather's observation that "geography is a terribly fatal thing sometimes" as a central principle in her writing, and several collections emphasize the relationship between Cather and particular places, including John Swift and Joseph Urgo, *Willa Cather and the American Southwest*; Ann Romines, *Willa Cather's Southern Connections*; Robert Thacker and Michael Peterman, *Willa Cather's Canadian and Old World Connections*; and Merrill Skaggs, *Willa Cather's New York*. If "Willa Cather and Nebraska" seems conspicuously absent from this list as a separate title, it is only because commentary on Cather's relationship to Nebraska is an integral part of so many different studies of Cather and her works.

Wharton's work has not benefited from quite the same extended attention to place as Cather's, perhaps because critics may assume that the settings of many of her fictions, including New York and Paris, are more familiar than Cather's Nebraska or New Mexico. Yet Wharton's biographers—R. W. B. Lewis, Shari Benstock, Eleanor Dwight, and Hermione Lee—have all thoughtfully reflected on her relationship to the places she lived; her relationship to Europe has been studied extensively in the last two decades, beginning with Katherine Joslin and Alan Price's *Wretched Exotic: Essays on Edith Wharton in Europe*. Critics have also paid attention to the role of specific places in her works, including Spain and Morocco, and have fruitfully drawn attention to the social geography of New York in works like *The House of Mirth* and

The Custom of the Country.[33] Wharton's choice of locations may seem less distinctive than Cather's, but it is always equally specific. Her use of the Hudson River Valley as a setting for her late novels *Hudson River Bracketed* and *The Gods Arrive*, for instance, is simultaneously symbolic and rooted in history, as we will see in chapter 4.

Yet the ways in which Wharton's and Cather's thinking about place intersect and the larger patterns emerging from their geographic thinking have not been commented on. For instance, while critics have often quoted Cather's remark that "Geography can be a terribly fatal thing," no one has connected this statement to the fatality of place in Wharton. In *The Age of Innocence* Newland Archer's fate is determined by the fact that he lives in New York; Ethan Frome is frozen into his life in western Massachusetts. *A Son at the Front* is Wharton's most vivid illustration of Cather's remark about place. In this work the parents of a twenty-five-year-old American chafe at the fact that their son has been mobilized to fight in World War I; George Campton was, by chance, born in France. George's father fumes, "If only the boy had been born in America! It was grotesque that the whole of joy or anguish should suddenly be found to hang on a geographical accident."[34] George eventually dies of wounds received in battle; geography can quite literally be fatal.

Even when not deadly, geography is still a powerful force, strongly affecting an individual's access to culture. In the first epigraph to this chapter, Cather asserts the power of the connection between place and culture when she writes that Miss Wheeler might have been an "actress of merit" had she been "born further east" and had greater opportunities to learn her art. Surely Cather had her own literary opportunities, or lack of them, in mind as she wrote this remark. When writing her memoir, *A Backward Glance*, Wharton offered a similar remark. In a letter to her friend Mary Berenson, an American expatriate living near Florence, she wrote, "*Please* send me 'by return' some advice as to how to write my own 'Life,' for I'm hopelessly stuck, & feel how much easier it wd [would] have been if I'd lived in Florence with picturesque people instead of stodging in New York!"[35] While this might seem a minor complaint—certainly Wharton managed to draw her early childhood in New York quite picturesquely in *A Backward Glance*—it reflects the same awareness of the link between place and opportunity. Writing to Bernard Berenson, Mary's husband, Wharton explained that the relation between culture and place was anything but minor. Declining to read a biography he had recommended, she explained, "I <u>don't</u> want to read the 'Life'! It always saddens me to read of those starved existences.... I feel as sad as I do when I read Emerson's Journals, & think of the rich & dramatic lives of his European contemporaries."[36] For Wharton America was the culturally starved place Henry James had described in his study of Nathaniel Hawthorne: "One might enumerate the items of high civilisation, as it exists in other countries, which are absent from the texture of American life, until it should become a wonder to know what was left. No State.... No sovereign, no court ... no palaces, no castles, nor manors, nor old country-houses ... ; no literature, no novels, no museums, no pictures."[37] For Wharton the United States was as starved as the Midwest Cather had depicted in early stories such as "A Wagner Matinée" and "The Sculptor's Funeral." Miss Wheeler's range was limited by her western birth, Emerson's by his in New England.

PLACE AND CULTURE

For Wharton and Cather, then, place was integrally connected to issues of culture. Yet even this statement needs explanation, as the terms "place" and "culture" are simultaneously broad and flexible. "Place," which functions as both a noun and a verb, is usually a noun in this study, an indicator of a specific location, such as New York City, or a broader, more conceptual category, like the West. As a noun, it also refers to status, as in the phrase "the place of culture." Yet it is also a verb, and as I write about "placing" the works of Cather and Wharton side by side, I hope that the reader may at some moments imagine physically placing their fictions and concepts on a desk or table, the better to visualize their similarities. "Culture" is an even more complex term. Generally speaking, the word's nineteenth-century meaning referred to the world of art, music, literature, and so on—the "culture" to which Matthew Arnold referred in his influential 1899 study *Culture and Anarchy*, which, as its title suggests, argued the centrality of culture in creating and sustaining civilization. Wharton and Cather grew up in this world and continued to value culture in this sense. Yet it was also during their lifetimes that the word "culture" changed. As Richard Millington has noted, in the works of the early twentieth-century anthropologist Franz Boas, "the concept of 'culture' is broken free from its static and honorific association with the refined arts that signify genteel cultural authority. Rather than representing what 'civilized' European nations have and 'primitive' people lack, *culture* refers . . . to the . . . ways distinct communities construct meanings for the individual lives that unfold within them."[38] Yet "culture" also retained its older meaning, referring to what is now sometimes distinguished from general or popular culture with the designation "high culture." This study uses "culture" to refer both to the "high" culture Wharton and Cather valued and to "the ways distinct communities construct meanings." Given Wharton's and Cather's concern with "the place of culture" in American society, I chose to use that phrase in my title. But "the culture of place," the ways in which national or regional communities establish values, underlies "the place of culture" and is equally a concern.

If place and culture were integrally linked for Wharton and Cather, so culture was integrally linked to issues of beauty. Boas's redefinition of "culture" may have freed the concept from its limiting definition as "the arts," and surely it was a good thing that in doing so, Boas "helped dismantle the narrative of cultural, class, and racial superiority dear to embattled late-nineteenth century elites."[39] Yet Wharton and Cather were deeply connected to the world of the arts that was somewhat devalued when "culture" came to have its broader meaning. Both authors were influenced by the work of Walter Pater, who in *Studies in the History of the Renaissance* reminded his readers that life is short; we are all "under sentence of death."[40] Given this, he argues, the best course is "in getting as many pulsations as possible into the given time"; the best way to achieve this is to pursue the "great passions," which provide a "quickened sense of life. . . . Of such wisdom, the poetic passion, the desire of beauty, the love of art for its own sake, has most. For art comes to you proposing frankly to give nothing but the highest quality to your moments as they pass, and simply for those moments' sake."[41]

In Pater's famous formulation, "To burn always with this hard, gem-like flame, to maintain this ecstasy, is success in life."[42]

In his 2007 work, *Only a Promise of Happiness: The Place of Beauty in a World of Art*, Alexander Nehamas examines the long philosophical debate about the value of beauty, including its decline in status between Pater's day and our own. Turning to the classical roots of aesthetics, he remarks that Plato admired beauty unambiguously, seeing it both as valuable in itself and because it leads to desire—first to physical desire and then to desire for higher forms of beauty, including a love of the beauty of wisdom itself—that is, philosophy. Yet by the late 1800s, as Nehamas writes, "Beauty had long ago ceased to go hand in hand with wisdom and goodness; it had eventually come to be, as it is to most of the world today, largely irrelevant and often opposed to them."[43] The eminent Victorian art critic John Ruskin, Nehamas notes, "had to acknowledge the breach between beauty and morality," and "the twentieth century gradually came to doubt beauty itself."[44] Once beauty became morally suspect, high art of the twentieth century turned away from it: "Philosophy disavowed it and relegated the beauty of human beings and ordinary things ... to biology and psychology, to fashion, advertising, and marketing."[45] In the influential school of thought articulated by Pierre Bourdieu, art itself is suspect, little more than "a means of acquiring and exercising power."[46] A major part of Nehamas's project is to rehabilitate the intellectual respectability of beauty and to argue for its importance not merely in the lives of the elite or in locations such as art museums and national parks but in everyday life.[47] Echoing Pater, Nehamas remarks that beautiful things matter because they "quicken the sense of life, giving it new shape and direction" and argues that the worth of beauty "lies no further than itself: it is its own reward."[48]

Like the shift in the term "culture," the transition from beautiful art to art that disavows beauty, from the admiration of beautiful things to the suspicion of them, occurred in the period in which Wharton and Cather were writing; both, as we will see, wanted to reclaim "culture" and "beauty," however hard to define these concepts had become. Yet in spite of their admiration of older societies more dedicated to art, they were also concerned that such societies might lack a certain vitality that they saw as essentially American—even if that energy was all too often dedicated solely to business and material interests. The balancing of these elements—of place and culture, energy and beauty—is integral to their work.

Part 1 of the book, "Contexts and Intersections," is composed of two chapters that establish this study's literary foundations. Chapter 1, "The 'Literary Aristocrat' and the Plainspoken Pioneer," establishes the proximity of Wharton's and Cather's lives, interests, and careers. The chapter discusses the long-ingrained perception of difference between the two authors, examining its historical roots and its current manifestations. Yet during their own lifetimes, Wharton and Cather often shared the stage, publishing in many of the same magazines and receiving many of the same honors. Far from living in separate worlds, Wharton and Cather shared influences, acquaintances, friends, and, later, biographers. The final section of chapter 1 discusses their relationship with each other as writers. Wharton's work, especially *The House of Mirth* and *Ethan Frome*, was important to Cather in a range of ways, sometimes even as an example to be rebelled against. Wharton, who was also aware of Cather, may have found the younger author's success troubling in some instances; in others, she may have borrowed from Cather's work.

Wharton and Cather shared profound similarities in their understanding of literature and their experience of place, the topics of chapter 2, "The Land of Letters, the Kingdom of Art." For both, literature was nearly a geographical location in itself, a place both welcoming and potentially dangerous. The similarities in their ways of thinking about the literary world are less surprising when we delve into their profoundly similar beliefs about great fiction and what it should accomplish. Both had roots in the works of the French naturalists, admired many of the same writers, and were influenced by Henry James. Biographically, their deep sensitivity to the culture and aesthetics of place came from parallel experiences of displacement as pre-adolescents, which would shape some of their earliest fictions and influence them throughout their lives. Both their published fictions and their personal letters show the interweaving of reading, writing, culture, and place in their works.

Part 2, "The Place of Culture," is composed of four chapters. Chapters 3, 4, and 5 focus on the intersection of Wharton's and Cather's lives and works in New York City, the West, and France, exploring the cultural meanings of these places in their works and the ways in which these meanings are in dialogue. Chapter 3, "New York City: Beauty, Business, and Hothouse Flowers," reveals the cultural conversation between Wharton's *The House of Mirth* and Cather's "Paul's Case." The two works resonate deeply, pointing to the same concerns about American culture, concerns realized in the very geography of New York City. Critics of these works have both sympathized with Lily Bart and Paul as victims and faulted them for their failure to toughen up; I argue that through these remarkably similar characters Wharton and Cather point to the American overemphasis on sheer moneymaking and the concomitant undervaluing of beauty. Wharton's and Cather's ongoing concern with this issue is reflected in their analogous treatment of it in two fictions from the early 1920s, Cather's "Coming, Aphrodite!" and Wharton's *A Son at the Front*.

Chapter 4, "The West: Provinciality, Vitality, and the 'Real' America," shows the underlying similarity of Wharton's and Cather's concerns with American culture in their attitude toward the West. Initially this similarity seems counterintuitive: Wharton's creation of western characters such as Undine Spragg, the protagonist of *The Custom of the Country*, seems cruelly parodic; the western settings in novels like *Custom* and *Hudson River Bracketed* are thin in comparison to Cather's nuanced and complex portrayals. Yet Wharton and Cather both wrote consciously against the rise of the hypermasculinized "western," even as the rising popularity of America's newly mythologized West gave Cather's fame a boost. Further, a comparison of Wharton's *Custom of the Country* and Cather's *The Song of the Lark* shows surprising continuities between these works and their western heroines, including an admiration of their western vitality. Rereading Wharton's later fiction, especially her two-volume Künstlerroman, *Hudson River Bracketed* and *The Gods Arrive*, with an eye on the West brings forward some surprisingly positive points. Although Vance Weston, her western protagonist, has his human flaws, he also possesses a uniquely American energy and freshness of vision that allow him to be an artist.

Chapter 5, "The Idea of France," argues that France and French culture also formed a crucial part of the lives and works of both novelists. Like many others of their era, Wharton and Cather admired France, finding in French culture a possible solution to the problem posed by New York: if in the United States business repeatedly trumped art, in France they saw a culture in which beauty was valued in daily life. All the more appalling, then, was the advent of World War I, which threatened the very existence of France and led them to write their war-related novels, Cather's *One of Ours* and Wharton's *A Son at the Front*. Reflecting a deep understanding of French perseverance during the war, their novels provide a perspective unusual in American fiction. Both authors also believed that France could be a positive influence on the United States, with Wharton urging Americans to focus not on "what America can teach France" but on "what France can teach us."[49] Yet, paradoxically, it was not Wharton, who lived in France for decades, but Cather who used her fiction to bring the muse of French culture into her patria in the pages of *Death Comes for the Archbishop*.

Chapter 6, "Questions of Travel and Home," focuses not on a single place but rather on a tension between places: the pull between the desire to see the world and the need for a place that feels like home. Wharton and Cather were indefatigable travelers who sought travel beyond the mere tourism represented by guidebooks. Yet both expressed a visceral need for a home place, and their works often portray characters whose lives are troubled by their fundamental rootlessness. Still, neither author endorsed any conventional view of family and home in their works; on the contrary, they repeatedly challenged such views. Moreover, in a world changed by World War I, they found that their experiences as travelers offered them important alternative perspectives. Seeing life in the 1920s as ever more harried, materialistic, and "brok[en]," to use Cather's term, they sought connection and meaning. For their final, unfinished novels, Wharton's *The Buccaneers* and Cather's "Hard Punishments," both chose locations where place and culture were integral; portraying characters who have suffered painfully, they focus on the beauty of place and the wonder it evokes as elements essential to meaningful survival.

In their works Wharton and Cather asked questions about American character, American culture, and whither the nation was tending, including questions about the role of "high" culture. A century after the publication of some of their most famous works, America remains a place in which there is tension between those who believe America's *raison d'être* is business and profit, and those who do not question the importance of prosperity but who also believe that a nation's culture must be more than its GDP. In 1897 Cather wrote that Charles Stanley Reinhart, an internationally renowned sculptor from Pittsburgh, had been "born in a purely commercial town"; at his funeral she repeatedly heard, "Reinhart dead? Oh, yes; his brother is a fellow of some means.... Stanley never amounted to much."[50] The elevation of profit over art was, she implied, an American tragedy. In 1963—the midpoint between the publication of works like *The Song of the Lark* and *The Custom of the Country* and our own day—John F. Kennedy reiterated Cather's views, stating that "this country cannot afford to be materially rich and spiritually poor"; he remarked that he was "look[ing] forward to an America which will not be afraid of grace and beauty."[51] Yet very little seems to have changed since Kennedy's speech. On the contrary, such matters have recently become only more urgent, with the proposal to eliminate the National Endowment for the Arts and the National Endowment for the Humanities in spring 2017 bringing such issues into the limelight. As one commentator put it, these agencies offer "tangible, official, institutional evidence that the society represented by the United States government is one concerned not merely with commerce and power but with ideas and values"; they are "potent reminders [that] many things, including artworks, can and should be made, preserved, or shared for reasons other than profit."[52] Lacking a commitment to anything other than profit, we are, in the words of another commentator, in danger of "succumb[ing] to the shallowness of a purely commercial civilization."[53] The persistence of these issues suggests that they have been insufficiently addressed or reminds us that questions that seem to have been answered do not necessarily remain answered. Perhaps particularly as Americans, a people who value the new, we fail to learn from our history.

In a 1919 letter Wharton asked, "How much longer are we going to think it necessary to be 'American' before (or in contradistinction to) being cultivated, being enlightened, being humane, & having the same intellectual discipline as other civilized countries? It is really too easy a disguise for our shortcomings to dress them up as a form of patriotism!"[54] Such remarks have sometimes struck readers as snobbish and impossibly *grande dame*, Wharton at her elitist worst. Today they may instead strike us as relevant, even prescient, and the dismissal of them as a symptom of the very problem she describes. Seeing a concern with enlightenment, intellectual discipline, and humanity as elitist is surely a profound error. As Kwame Anthony Appiah, former president of the Modern Language Association, noted in 2017, Matthew Arnold "reserved his particular disapproval ... for the nexus of money and machinery he identified with industrialism and ... for those who would trivialize culture as a badge of class privilege."[55]

A concern with beauty, central to Wharton and Cather, has often been written off as elitist. Americans in general often shrug off discussions of beauty, at least as a public concern. Writing of his decision to move to France in 1995, Adam Gopnik remarks that when he and his wife told friends that they wanted their son "'to grow up someplace where everything he sees is beautiful,'... we realized that the moment our backs were turned our friends' eyes were rolling."[56] A concern with beauty is sometimes, as Appiah remarks, "loftily shunned as corruption." But, he adds, "resistance isn't always a matter of matching a political gesture with a political gesture."[57] Writers like Audre Lorde and Alice Walker have reminded readers for decades that poetry is not a luxury, and that quilts and gardens attest to the need for beauty in everyday life.[58] As Roz Chast has written of New York's High Line Park: "It's surprisingly beautiful and satisfying, and its construction and existence is profoundly optimistic about people: that everyone—not just the 'elite'—is in need of beauty and wonder."[59]

Appiah has written that "the invention of literary studies" meant, among other things, that "the critic became a cartographer, mapping out from on high the territories where writers found themselves.... Critics likewise, assuming the mapmaker's placeless vantage, sought to see forces and patterns imperceptible to the writers they acted on."[60] I disagree with Appiah's claim that critics are "placeless"; even if they are unaware of doing so, critics always write from a specific place and perspective. Yet his distinction between the critic who maps territory from on high and the writer who, like the pedestrian, sees details visible only from the ground, is illuminating. In this study I sometimes survey the terrain of Wharton's and Cather's works from a bird's eye perspective, and at others I walk through their writings at ground level in order to notice and explore details, even details at the level of the individual word. By doing both, I hope to trace crucially important confluences in the works of these two brilliant and thoughtful writers.

PART 1

Contexts and Intersections

1

THE "LITERARY ARISTOCRAT" AND THE PLAINSPOKEN PIONEER

> Unfortunately surface differences—as the word implies—are the ones that strike the eye first.... We must dig down to the deep faiths and principles from which every race draws its enduring life to find how like in fundamental things are the two people whose destinies have been so widely different.
> EDITH WHARTON, *French Ways and Their Meaning*

THE MEETING THAT NEVER TOOK PLACE

Edith Wharton and Willa Cather never met. But to anyone interested in these authors and their works, it is enticing to imagine how they might have gotten along had they met—perhaps as mature, successful novelists in the late 1920s or during Cather's 1930 trip to France, where Wharton had been living since 1907. It is entirely possible that the two women would not have hit it off. Wharton, who maintained energetic lifelong friendships with many people, is also known to have been stiffly formal, even cold, on occasion. Cather, although she had interviewed celebrity writers as a journalist and, during her career as an increasingly prominent author, had become friends with many important authors and musicians, was also a private person. Further, she may still have harbored vestiges of her youthful insecurities about being "provincial"—insecurities that meeting "Mrs. Wharton" might well have stirred.

A certain degree of underlying tension would have been particularly likely if they had met (as they probably would have) at one of Mrs. Wharton's two homes in France—the Pavillon Colombe, a villa located just north of Paris in the town of St. Brice-sous-Forêt, if it had been a summer meeting, or Sainte Claire le Château in Hyères, on the Mediterranean coast, if it were winter. Wharton might well have been her chillier self to the younger writer, whom she referred to, in her only known written comment on Cather, as "the lady with the blurry name," and whom she may have seen as a real-life version of one of her own characters, Undine Spragg, a parvenue from the West who invades New York.[1] If this had been the case, Wharton might well have conveyed it through her manner, however subtly, and Cather might well have responded by becoming a bit defensive.

Yet by 1930 both were confident of their abilities, the authors of novels that had achieved popular success and critical acclaim; both had received honorary doctorates from Yale University, as well as the Pulitzer Prize for the novel, among many other honors. They shared many interests; perhaps most important among these were their love of literature and their devotion to the art of fiction. If the visit had gone well, they might have spent hours discussing ways to craft a character or shape a plot, topics on which, as we will see, their views were remarkably similar. So were their views on literary modernism: both disliked it. The theater, poetry, paintings, and music—all were arts that fascinated them both. There was much else they could have discussed, including their mutual friends and acquaintances Sinclair Lewis, F. Scott Fitzgerald, and Zona Gale, a novelist little remembered today. Their shared love of France could have provided hours of discussion, as could their dislike of New York City. If they had been lucky enough to sit outside in one of Wharton's beautifully designed gardens, the conversation might easily have turned to their shared love for plants and flowers.[2] Eventually they might have discussed their views of the state of American culture, which concerned them both deeply.

We will never know, of course, how this hypothetical teatime would have proceeded. It would doubtless have been a polite meeting, but the odds are good that it would have been neither a big success nor a dismal failure. One trait the two great writers shared was that both were fundamentally very private people. Especially in their later years, it could take some time to get beyond the persona each showed to the world, although those fortunate enough to see beyond that persona found a warm and enthusiastic personality. They might well have kept the encounter civil but short, and then said a formal goodbye. Afterward each would have returned to her own privacy: Wharton to her library and Cather to a good hotel nearby—both, in all likelihood, to enjoy a good dinner and then, in the evening, to write letters about the meeting to their friends.

THE ARISTOCRAT AND THE POPULIST

Popular perceptions, like history, seem to have conspired to keep the two authors apart. Despite the increasingly complex critical analyses of both authors in recent decades, they are often still seen in the terms in which influential early critics defined them. Wharton is still often seen as "our outstanding literary aristocrat," the New York chronicler of an East Coast American aristocracy, while Cather is frequently thought of as the Nebraska author of novels "redolent of the Western prairie" that "pulsate with the life of the people."[3] These thumbnail portrayals function as shorthand for two of the most significant issues that have kept the works of these authors apart: not class and race, as has often been true in literary studies, but class and place—social class and geography, which are directly related to a broad swath of cultural issues and to wide, even semiconscious, myths about America and Americanness.

Vernon Parrington was the critic who in 1921 dubbed Wharton "our outstanding literary aristocrat," and although it may sound today like a compliment, the moniker was meant to dismiss her and her work as irrelevant, passé, and questionably American. In his review of her 1920 novel *The Age of Innocence*, Parrington remarked, "With her ripe culture, her clear and clean intelligence, her classical spirit, her severe standards and austere ethics, Mrs. Wharton is our outstanding literary aristocrat."[4] Yet his conclusion was that despite the novel's literary accomplishment, "it doesn't make the slightest difference whether one reads the book or not."[5] Wharton's choice to depict the "little clan of first families" in New York, to "open [her] doors ... only to the smart set," and to live with "windows [that] open only to the east, to London, Paris, Rome" means that she has wasted her art on "insignificant material" and on "rich nobodies."⁶ Parrington concludes that "there is more hope for our literature in the honest crudities of the younger naturalists, than in her classic irony; they at least are trying to understand America as it is."⁷ As we will see in more detail in chapter 4, questions of literary subgenre—the tension between realism and naturalism—and inherent "Americanness" are imbricated with those of gender, class, and place (and, in this instance, with underlying attitudes toward age). Parrington's "younger naturalists" attempting to "understand America as it is" were obviously not writing about New York aristocrats looking eastward toward Europe. In remarks such as these, Parrington led the critics who, in the 1920s and 1930s, charged Wharton with being out of touch with her home country and with what mattered in a world changed by World War I.

Paradoxically, since Parrington wrote his review a century ago, his dismissive moniker for Wharton has come to epitomize her in ways that have also been seen as positive. "Our literary aristocrat" is not repellant but appealing to Americans, many of whom have become increasingly fascinated with the rich, famous, and quasi-aristocratic. Certainly part of the staying power of the idea of Wharton as "literary aristocrat" is that in many ways, the shoe fits. Wharton, who traced her ancestry back to the early Dutch settlers of New Amsterdam and a Revolutionary War general, belonged to "Old" New York. During her extended travels in Europe as a child and adolescent, she socialized with many people, including members of the French aristocracy, as she chronicled in "Life and I," a brief memoir never intended for publication. As an adult, she lived in France from 1907 until her death in 1937, keeping company not only with its literary and political elite but also with countesses and princesses.⁸ She is buried, as if in support of Parrington's argument, in the Cimitière des Gonards in Versailles, a mere mile from the gates of Louis XIV's opulent palace. The upper-class world in which she lived is also the one she recreates in many of her best-known fictions, including *The House of Mirth* (1905), *The Custom of the Country* (1913), and *The Age of Innocence* (1920). Yet the prevailing view of Wharton as an East Coast, Europe-bound aristocrat limits what readers perceive in her writing.

The perception of Willa Cather as a chronicler of prairie life functions in much the same way. While this perception is rooted in facts, thinking of Cather solely as an author who writes in a straightforward way about ordinary people in the Midwest and West elides the complexity and variety of her life and her writings. As with Wharton, much of our view of her has been shaped by influential early critics. Indeed, while Wharton was beginning to be challenged in the 1920s because she depicted New York "aristocracy," Cather was celebrated because she depicted "ordinary" people, characters who were perceived as very American (despite their clearly portrayed attachment, in many cases, to their European countries of origin). The prominent critic H. L. Mencken gave Cather a huge boost in his review of *My Ántonia* (1918), referring to it as "one of the best [novels] that any American has ever done, East or West, early or late."[9] In his review of *Alexander's Bridge*, he had noted Wharton's influence favorably, but in his remarks on *Ántonia*, he praised her for breaking away from Wharton and finding her own voice and place.[10] Another important critic, Randolph Bourne, reinforced the idea of Cather as quintessentially American in his review of *My Ántonia*: "Here at last is an American novel, redolent of the Western prairie."[11] To be "American," for these reviewers, was to depict working- or middle-class individuals beyond the cities of the eastern seaboard— preferably out "West," a designation that was used broadly and flexibly.[12] (Ironically, in the 1930s Cather would, like Wharton, be charged with being out of touch with the "real" America.) Cather certainly encouraged the perception of her as a western and therefore an American writer, emphasizing her experiences in Nebraska and the Southwest in interviews and writing her own promotional materials.[13] The novels that made her famous, *O Pioneers!* (1913) and *My Ántonia*, are both set in Nebraska, and part of their success was the fact that in them she depicted a kind of life that was perceived as uniquely American—and as the opposite of Wharton's project in *The Age of Innocence*.

Yet for Cather, as for Wharton, the reality of her life and her literary range is far more complex. Parrington, who dismissed Wharton as insufficiently American because her "windows ... open[ed] only ... to London, Paris, Rome," might have been surprised by a 1908 letter Cather wrote in which she declared that "Rome, London, and Paris, were serious matters" when she was in school: "They were the three principal cities in Nebraska, so to speak."[14] While academic critics have, for the last three decades or more, steadily revealed aspects of this much more complicated Cather, the popular image of her has, like that of Wharton, remained static. Both authors and their works have been neatly pigeonholed along lines that are simultaneously geographic and social: Wharton as a chronicler of an East Coast Europeanized elite, Cather of the daily lives of western and midwestern immigrants and farmers.

Once we look into family background, we realize that even in terms of class associations, the portrayals of Wharton as aristocratic and Cather as middle class are limited at best. Certainly there *are* class differences between the two. If property ownership is an indication of class, it has to be acknowledged that at the time of Wharton's death, she owned two villas in France, while the only home Cather actually owned was a small cottage on Grand Manan Island off the coast of New Brunswick.[15] Certainly as children, Edith Jones and Willa Cather were in different places on the socioeconomic scale. The Jones family belonged to the leisure class; Edith's father did not need to work in order to support the family. This does not mean that the family had the wealth associated with the millionaires of the Gilded Age, on whose vast expenditures Wharton would look with skepticism. But it does mean that in order to economize, the family traveled in Europe for several years so that her father could rent their homes in New York City and Newport at a profit.[16] Cather's background was quite different. Born in Virginia, she was the eldest child of seven in a family that was decidedly middle class. Cather's father, who had some legal training, was a sheep farmer in Virginia; when the family moved to Nebraska, he farmed for eighteen months and then, relocating to Red Cloud, sold real estate and insurance and made farm loans. He seems to have had something of a challenge in providing for his growing family.[17]

When we look at their family backgrounds more carefully, however, the picture becomes more complex. In her memoir, *A Backward Glance*, Wharton noted that her mother "always said that old New York was composed of Dutch and British middle-class families, and that only four or five could show a pedigree leading back to the aristocracy of their ancestral country"; she confirmed that "my own ancestry, as far as I know, was purely middle-class."[18] Yet Wharton traced her ancestry back to General Ebenezer Stevens, an officer in the Revolutionary War, and to the Dutch colonial settlers of New Amsterdam.[19] In an American context, tracing one's ancestry to important precedents before the Revolutionary War constitutes its own form of aristocracy, as Wharton well knew; even the protest that her family was not *truly* aristocratic conveys a note of aristocratic authority. But Cather could make similar claims. Cather's parents were "fourth-generation Virginians," with her paternal grandmother tracing her roots to Jeremiah Smith, who had arrived in Virginia in 1730 and been "deeded land on Back Creek in 1762 by Lord Fairfax."[20] (The Fairfax family is mentioned in Wharton's memoir as well; unlike her own middle-class family, she notes, the Fairfaxes had "a pedigree leading back to the aristocracy of their ancestral country.")[21] Wharton's great-grandfather was a general in the Revolutionary War; Cather's ancestor Jasper Cather also fought in that war.[22] One fact suggests that the common understanding of the social class of these two authors should be, if anything, the reverse. As an adult, Cather learned that an early ancestor from Wales "had fought for Charles I"; in recognition of his services, Charles II had given land in Ireland to his descendants.[23] She also learned that British heraldry includes a Cather coat of arms.[24] Strictly speaking—using the standards of Wharton's mother, that aristocracy was a matter of heredity—it turns out that it is not Wharton but Cather who is "our literary aristocrat."

Nevertheless, broad cultural references continue to reiterate the perception of Wharton as sophisticated eastern aristocrat and Cather as western democrat. A travel writer's 2017 article strikes a note often heard, praising Cather's 1902 sketches of England and France for the *Nebraska State Journal* partly by denigrating Wharton: "She was not blue-blooded Edith Wharton, who had grown up in the first-class section of European trains, with servants unpacking her trunks. Willa Cather was of the American prairie."[25] A 2015 Edward Sorel cartoon in *Vanity Fair*, accompanying a review of Harold Bloom's book *The Daemon Knows: Literary Greatness and the American Sublime* (from which Wharton and

Cather are both excluded), offers a brilliant visual equivalent (fig. 1). Wharton is depicted as bejeweled and elegantly dressed in decidedly nineteenth-century style, peering up indignantly through her lorgnette at a God-sized Bloom, while Cather, a head shorter, hovers behind Wharton in the middy blouse she wore in the well-known Edward Steichen portrait. Sorel's portrayals are successful precisely because they reiterate the usual views of both authors, with Wharton looking very much the aristocrat and Cather decidedly middle class; the cartoon also suggests their overall status in American culture, with Cather somewhat obscured behind the larger, more prominent Wharton.

Other references reiterate these associations of class and place, including the authors' surviving homes and even their graves. The Mount, the estate built by Wharton and her husband Teddy in Lenox, Massachusetts, and the place most visibly associated with Wharton and her work, was called "a delicate French chateau mirrored in a Massachusetts pond" by Henry James.[26] In 2012 it was used for a *Vogue* magazine photo shoot featuring fashions based on clothing Wharton wore and described in her work; it received additional publicity when it was visited by Julian Fellowes, the creator of the BBC's popular *Downton Abbey*, who credits Wharton as an inspiration.[27] While The Mount is associated with high fashion and high incomes, the house most associated with Cather, known as the Cather Childhood Home, is determinedly midwestern and middle class. A modest structure of a story and a half (its upper level unfinished, as it was in Cather's day), the Childhood Home is located in Red Cloud, Nebraska, commonly thought of as Cather's hometown. (Red Cloud is also the home of the Willa Cather Foundation and the National Willa Cather Center, further solidifying its connection with Cather.) The emblem of "Catherland," as the area around Red Cloud has been nicknamed, is the plough, a reference not only to local agriculture but also to a famous passage in *My Ántonia* in which the central characters see a plough on the horizon magnified by the rays of the setting sun. Wharton is buried in a cemetery in Versailles, France; Willa Cather is buried in Jaffrey Center, New Hampshire, in a quiet, wooded cemetery from which Mount Monadnock can be seen. Even in the marketplace "Wharton" connotes upscale,

1. Wharton and Cather among other authors outraged not to be included in Harold Bloom's *The Daemon Knows: Literary Greatness and the American Sublime*. *Vanity Fair*, April 24, 2015. Illustration by Edward Sorel. Used with the permission of the artist.

European-inflected products, "Cather" the middle-class and American. For its seventy-fifth anniversary in 2010, French cosmetics manufacturer Lancôme named a particular shade of "peachy pink" lipstick "Rose Edith" in Wharton's honor;[28] Cather's fiction has inspired an American beer, Dogfish Head's "My Antonia" pilsner.

This general sense of the difference between Wharton and Cather often extends to a sense of the difference between their fictions; they are often perceived as very different kinds of authors whose plots and worldviews appeal to different readers. Wharton is often thought of as satirical and pessimistic, even fatalistic, while Cather is usually thought of as sincere and optimistic. The worlds depicted in their fiction are often seen as so different that it can be hard to remember that the two authors were writing in and of the same historical and geographic world—to remember, for instance, that Wharton's Lily Bart, heroine of *The House of Mirth*, and Cather's Thea Kronborg, of *The Song of the Lark*, inhabit the same New York or even the same America; Lily's prospects are limited by her relative poverty, despite her social accomplishments and her beauty, while Thea's seem nearly unlimited, despite her modest beginnings. Even the social and sexual mores of their worlds seem to be mirror opposites. The mere rumor of an affair precipitates Lily's disinheritance and eventually her death, while Thea's affair with Fred Ottenburg brings her no disapprobation. The contrast between Lily and Thea seems to epitomize what many would see as the difference between Wharton's fictional world and Cather's; Wharton's characters seem never to get what they want, while Cather's are thought of as getting where they are going. Wharton's characters fail (or at least do not succeed) for a variety of reasons— because they are incapable of adapting to a changed world or because they are too moral, kind, and sensitive. Characters like Ethan Frome in Wharton's eponymous novel, Ralph Marvell in *The Custom of the Country*, and Newland Archer in *The Age of Innocence* lead frustrated, even blighted lives. Ethan is severely crippled in an attempted suicide, while Ralph's life ends in suicide; Newland Archer is far more fortunate, but never fortunate enough to attain what he thinks of as "the flower of life."[29]

In contrast, Cather's Alexandra Bergson becomes a successful farmer in *O Pioneers!* and Thea Kronborg a famous opera singer in *The Song of the Lark*. In *Death Comes for the Archbishop*, despite its gloomy title, Father Latour lives a long life full of accomplishments, solidifying his diocese in the Southwest and building the beautiful cathedral of which he has dreamt—for him, the "flower of life." Many readers of both authors have an innate sense that if Cather characters were to find themselves embroiled in a Wharton plot, they would somehow find a way out. Critics have specifically contrasted Cather's characters with Wharton's; Alexandra, for instance, is not a "doomed heroine like ... Wharton's Lily Bart."[30] Indeed it is easy to imagine that if Alexandra Bergson were to find herself in Lily Bart's situation (penniless and unwilling to marry the not entirely unpleasant man who would set her up for life) she would toughen up, marry him, and make a success of it, or find another way out of the impasse altogether, perhaps by attending secretarial school and making a modest living or by going west to make a new beginning—something Ethan Frome contemplates but never does.

Critical studies have often contributed to the sense of difference between Wharton and Cather, not only contrasting the two authors but sometimes pitting them against each other long after their deaths. Such has not always been the case, of course. The two authors are sufficiently prominent that both appear in a number of studies, particularly in those of American women writers. One such study is Margaret Lawrence's 1935 *The School of Femininity*. Lawrence never directly compares Wharton and Cather, but she sees them in very different terms, establishing some of the parameters that still govern our perception of these authors. She groups Wharton with those she calls "Helpmeets," authors who portray women who are "helpless" when faced with "economic struggles," women who want to lean on a man.[31] Noting that Wharton is sympathetic to the man's perspective in her fiction, Lawrence singles out *The Age of Innocence* as Wharton's "key" novel.[32] Wharton is focused on the "sex-relation" and the issue of marriage, Lawrence remarks, while in Cather's work, "women are not creatures to be studied as new creatures just emerging from subjection. They are ordinary human beings linked with men through the need of men and women for each other in the making of a [human] race."[33] She groups Cather with Virginia Woolf and Katherine Mansfield as "artistes," a category it is hard to imagine Cather objecting to. Further, she calls Cather "the great artist American women writers have produced" and remarks that Cather's work captures "the shine of life."[34] There is no indication that Wharton was aware of *The School of Femininity*, published two years before her death. But we do know that Cather greatly liked Lawrence's discussion of her work, writing her friend Carrie Sherwood that "If there is any real merit in my books, [Lawrence] puts her finger on the root of it.... She seems to understand that I can write successfully only when I write about people or places which I very greatly admire; which, indeed, I actually love."[35]

In 1961 Louis Auchincloss's *Pioneers and Caretakers* included both authors. Working in broad strokes, Auchincloss groups them together with other women fiction writers as being simultaneously "pioneers" and "caretakers of [American] culture [who] have struck a more affirmative note than the men."[36] Predictably he associates Wharton with "Europe and the American East Coast" and Cather with pioneers, although his summary of Cather's fiction recognizes the wide range of her settings.[37] The rise of feminist literary criticism in the 1970s brought increased attention to women writers *qua* women writers, leading to landmark works like Ellen Moers's 1976 *Literary Women*, a wide-ranging study of British and American female writers. Such works did not necessarily include treatments of both authors; Moers, for instance, includes several discussions of Cather but mentions Wharton only in an appendix. Yet the new scholarly climate meant that critical work on both authors took off. Such work was facilitated, even catalyzed, by the publication of major new biographies of both, including R. W. B. Lewis's Pulitzer Prize–winning biography, *Edith Wharton*, in 1975; Cynthia Griffin Wolff's *A Feast of Words: The Triumph of Edith Wharton*, in 1977; and, a decade later, James Woodress's *Willa Cather: A Literary Life* and Sharon O'Brien's *Willa Cather: The Emerging Voice*, both in 1987, followed by Hermione Lee's *Willa Cather: Double Lives* in 1989.

Yet discussions of Wharton and Cather from this period often reveal tensions generated by a sense of class and regional differences and are haunted by the idea that Wharton, the eastern aristocrat, was at the top of the literary pyramid, while Cather, the scrappy western underdog, was working hard to claim her own rightful place near, if not next to or above, Wharton. This is certainly the case with Cather's American biographers of the 1980s. Woodress notes that while Cather was present at the gala dinner in honor of Mark Twain's seventieth birthday in 1905, "No one had thought E[dward] A[rlington] Robinson, Edith Wharton, or Theodore Dreiser worth inviting."[38] O'Brien sometimes treats Wharton as a foil for Cather, understating Wharton's childhood experiences with reading in order to bolster Cather's early literary adventures. This dynamic is also in play when she remarks that "at the same age when Edith Wharton was preparing for her debut, Cather was planning her entrance into Red Cloud society as William Cather"—a much bolder move, she hints, than anything Wharton was capable of.[39] East-West and class tensions are decided in the preface to *Cather's Kitchens*, in which the authors write, "It may seem strange to be offering a book about that mundane, inelegant peasant pursuit of cooking in terms of Willa Cather, that literary star who hobnobbed with the Menuhins and was the toast of Europe and all that. Well ... Willa Cather was a woman, a peasant at heart, a Nebraskan, a plainswoman—and a cook."[40] Binary contrasts dominate: one is either famous or "a peasant"; Europe and implicitly New York are pitted against Nebraska and the plains.

In contrast, British biographer Hermione Lee's references to Wharton in *Willa Cather: Double Lives* are neutral or positive, as are her references to Cather in her 2007 biography of Wharton. This contrast suggests that the perceived rivalry between Wharton and Cather, the often unspoken tensions related to class and place, may be an American phenomenon. Certainly the perception of Wharton as someone who writes about social aristocrats and Cather as an author who portrays ordinary people has kept them apart in many people's minds, as have Wharton's associations with the East and Europe and Cather's with the West. These associations reflect continuing tensions not only between social classes but also between regions. In a nation and a social climate in which, as Guy Reynolds has written, the center of the country is no longer seen as central,[41] and in which everything west of Philadelphia and east of Los Angeles is all too often referred to as "the flyover states," what we might call "prestige of place" in the United States remains powerful and hugely influential, yet underacknowledged in many realms, from politics to literary criticism.

One exception to the sense of rivalry between Wharton and Cather in the 1980s was Judith Fryer's 1986 *Felicitous Space: The Imaginative Structures of Edith Wharton and Willa Cather*. While making foundational comparisons between the authors and serving, until now, as the only extended study exclusively of the two, it generally separates them, grouping the Wharton-related material in one part of the study and the Cather material in another. (Fryer's work focuses primarily on women's domestic spaces as sources of creativity; my work, which focuses on public, cultural, and geographic places, might be seen as complementing hers.) More recent studies have escaped the tendency to pit Wharton and Cather against each other, instead comparing the authors' stances on a number of topics, from depictions of war to domesticity and public health, and alongside a range of authors, from Howells and James to Ellen Glasgow, Zona Gale, Fannie Hurst, Nella Larson, Louisa May Alcott, and others.[42]

Recent criticism has, in general, developed far more complex views of both authors. No longer dismissed as the society novelist of Old New York, Wharton is being taken seriously as a writer who expressed philosophical, scientific, and social views in her work. Similarly, recent work on Cather has allowed her to emerge as a writer whose life and work expressed not only social but also environmental concerns, and as someone who, far from being bound by Nebraska or by the West, led a "cosmopolitan life."[43] Yet discussions of Wharton and Cather as peers often compare their work in very focused ways, rarely acknowledging the deep underlying similarities between them. To some extent the authors continue to be haunted by an aura of unbridgeable difference based on geography and social class. Even a work as authoritative as Elaine Showalter's 2009 *A Jury of Her Peers: American Women Writers from Anne Bradstreet to Annie Proulx*, which perceptively pairs the authors as critics of "the tradition of American women's literature," reiterates what is so often seen as the difference between them: "Wharton was the daughter of New York high society, Cather the prairie dweller."[44] Whether in literary studies or marketing, Wharton has been seen as an elite East Coast author, Cather as a democratic western one, and only rarely have the twain met on common ground.

SHARING THE STAGE

Despite the common sense of difference between Wharton and Cather, the two authors lived, worked, and published in the same world—in what the historian Nancy Green calls "a common time-space capsule."[45] Beginning with Wharton's best-selling *The House of Mirth*, which launched her to fame in 1905, and Cather's success with *O Pioneers!*, which gave her national prominence in 1913, the two authors shared the national stage for decades, with both of them publishing in the country's most important magazines, including *Century*, *Scribner's*, *Harper's*, the *Saturday Evening Post*, and the *Atlantic Monthly*. Perhaps most remarkably, both published in the pages of *McClure's Magazine*. The magazine has strong associations with Cather, who was on its staff from 1906 until 1912, serving as its managing editor for the last four years of her tenure.[46] With the encouragement of the editor-in-chief, S. S. McClure, Cather published several of her own poems and stories in the magazine, including "The Sculptor's Funeral" and "Paul's Case" in 1905 and "The Bohemian Girl" in 1912, the year in which Cather left the magazine to devote herself full time to writing.[47] Five years later Wharton serialized her novel *Summer* in *McClure's* after withdrawing from an agreement with *Cosmopolitan* because she objected to the wartime politics of *Cosmopolitan*'s owner, William Randolph Hearst. *McClure's* was happy to publish Wharton's new novel, paying her the handsome sum of $7,000.[48] Also in 1917, Sara Teasdale's anthology *The Answering Voice: One Hundred Love Lyrics by Women* included works by both authors, Wharton's sonnet "Yet for One Rounded Moment" and Cather's poems "The Hawthorn Tree" and "Grandmither, Think Not I Forget."

In the popular press Wharton and Cather sometimes shared the spotlight. A 1921 *Vanity Fair* feature, "American Authors Who Have Set Art Above Popularity," was comprised of photographs of six American authors, with Wharton described as "the greatest living American novelist" and Cather shown with a reference to Mencken's judgment of *My Ántonia* as "the best novel ever written by an American woman" (fig. 2). The article illustrates a certain rivalry for preeminence. Visually Wharton dominates, having not only the largest photograph but also being at the center of the group, while Cather is in the upper right corner; Wharton is called the best American novelist overall, but Mencken's remark suggests that among women novelists Cather's work is superior to Wharton's—an inconsistency the editors either missed or decided, probably wisely, not to address. Yet the article's title and subtitle—"A Group of Authors Who Have Consistently Stood Out Against Philistia"—emphasize their similarity and the principles they shared. Paradoxically, standing "above popularity" was a popular stance, and standing "against Philistia," the culture of the masses, seems to have pleased the masses—or at least the readers of *Vanity Fair*. Six years later *Vanity Fair* would feature Cather as "An American Pioneer" and call her "the heir apparent to Edith Wharton's lonely eminence among America's women novelists."[49]

Both authors were also featured in a 1921 series of articles on "Contemporary American Novelists" by Carl Van Doren in *The Nation*. The very first article in the series discussed Wharton, mildly faulting some of her society novels for creating characters too easily stymied by "decorum," but comparing her favorably to Henry James and Jane Austen and praising her for creating "universal figures of aspiration or disappointment" in works like *Summer* and *Ethan Frome*.[50] Cather was seventh in the series of twelve articles. At the time she had published only four novels, but on the basis of these Van Doren praised her for combining the "delicacy" of Sarah Orne Jewett with the "strength" of Walt Whitman and for understanding "almost alone among her peers in this decade . . . that human character for its own sake has a claim upon human interest."[51] Overall the works of both authors were reviewed in more than forty of the same magazines and newspapers, including the *Atlantic Monthly*, the *Boston Evening Transcript*, *The Nation*, the *New Republic*, the *New York Times* and *New York Times Book Review*, *Scribner's Magazine*, and the *Yale Review*. Opinion makers like Henry Seidel Canby, John Farrar, and William Lyon Phelps reviewed works by both authors, as did a number of significant novelists, among them the English writers L. P. Hartley, J. B. Priestley, and Rebecca West.[52]

2. "American Novelists Who Have Set Art Above Popularity." *Vanity Fair*, January 1921. © Condé Nast. Used with the permission of Condé Nast.

Wharton and Cather were also recipients of several of the same honors. Both received honorary Doctor of Letters degrees from Yale University. Wharton was the first woman to be so honored, in 1923; a mere six years later Cather was the third woman to receive the degree (figs. 3 and 4). Cather was awarded an honorary doctorate by Columbia University in 1928;[53] Columbia offered the same honor to Wharton in 1930 and 1931. Although Wharton had planned to accept the honor, she had to decline it because of poor health, and her trip to receive the Yale doctorate in 1923 would prove to be her last visit to the United States.[54] In 1921 Wharton won the Pulitzer Prize for the Novel for *The Age of Innocence* and found it a mixed blessing; two years later Cather won the Pulitzer Prize for *One of Ours* and had a similar experience. (The 1921 Pulitzer Prize for drama points up another connection between the two: it was given to their mutual friend Zona Gale for her dramatization of her own best-selling novel, *Miss Lulu Bett*, a work that both Wharton and Cather admired.) Both authors were decorated by the American Academy of Arts and Letters: Wharton received "the gold medal... for 'special distinction in literature'" in 1929, and Cather was awarded the Howells Medal for *Death Comes for the Archbishop* in 1930.[55] And both were honored by the National Institute of Arts and Letters. In 1925 Wharton became "the first woman to be awarded the gold medal... for 'distinguished achievement in Fiction'"; in 1944 Cather received the same prestigious award.[56]

Other literary intersections abound; in today's jargon, the degree of personal separation between the two authors was very slight. Figures associated with one author frequently surface in the life of the other or hover just in the wings. The decades-long literary friendship between Edith Wharton and Henry James is well known; less well known is the fact that the young Willa Cather, who, like Wharton, intensely admired James's work, on one occasion met him—almost. Cather was a guest at the Manchester, New Hampshire, home of the famous literary hostess Annie Fields when James was expected to visit, but as Cather recounts, the "intense heat" of the summer led him to cancel his visit. Cather was disappointed, but Fields reassured her that perhaps it was all for the best, as "Mr. James is always greatly put about by the heat."[57] James's

A PART OF THE COMMENCEMENT PROCESSION

In the foreground, reading from left to right, are: Dr. Jacques Loeb, who received an honorary Sc.D.; Rev. Charles E. Jefferson and Clarence H. Kelsey of the Corporation; Edith Wharton, who received an honorary Litt.D.; Henry W. Farnam, '74, who received an honorary LL.D.; and at the extreme right, Harry Emerson Fosdick, who received an honorary D.D.

3. (*above*) Wharton in procession of honorees at Yale University, 1923. *Yale Alumni Weekly*, July 6, 1923. Edith Wharton Collection, Yale Collection of American Literature, Beinecke Rare Book and Manuscript Library.

4. (*left*) Detail of Cather portrait by Nicholas Murray, featured in "The Conferring of Honorary Degrees." *Yale Alumni Weekly*, July 5, 1929. Item 17370, Nebraska State Historical Society.

discomfort in hot weather was something his close friend Wharton knew from firsthand experience. Her admiration for him did not prevent her from providing a humorous picture of "the Master" in her memoir, depicting him trying to get through a heat wave with "the electric fan clutched in his hand, and a pile of sucked oranges at his elbow."[58]

Sarah Orne Jewett also links Wharton and Cather. Certainly Cather's name is far more associated with Jewett's than Wharton's is; Annie Fields introduced Cather to Jewett, who played a pivotal role in Cather's career, urging her to find her own subject and to make the break with her editorial work at *McClure's* in order to pursue her own work as a fiction writer. In a letter to the younger writer on December 13, 1908, Jewett urged Cather to "keep and guard and mature your force, and above all, have time and quiet to perfect your work" and to "write to the human heart, the great consciousness that all humanity goes to make up."[59] Cather replied on December 19, admitting the "perfectly deadening" effect of office work on her and confiding that "when it comes to writing I'm a new-born baby every time—always come into it naked and shivery and without any bones."[60] Jewett's advice and encouragement bolstered Cather's decision to devote herself full time to writing fiction.

When Wharton is associated with Jewett in literary criticism, it is frequently in the context of her negative remark in her memoir, written in the 1930s, that when she wrote *Ethan Frome*, she "wanted to draw life as it really was in the derelict mountain villages of New England, a life . . . utterly unlike that seen through the rose-coloured spectacles of my predecessors, Mary Wilkins [Freeman] and Sarah Orne Jewett."[61] In spite of this negative association, the critic E. K. Brown compared Wharton's *Ethan Frome* to Jewett's work in positive terms, commenting that "in *Ethan Frome* she accomplished something as bleak and simple as a sketch of Sarah Orne Jewett."[62] Indeed in the early years of the century Wharton was eager to meet Jewett, with whom she shared a number of friends and acquaintances, including her friend and correspondent Sara ("Sally") Norton.[63] In the summer of 1902 she accepted an invitation from Fields to meet Fields's good friend Miss Jewett; writing Fields before the meeting, Wharton expressed her anticipation of "the pleasure of seeing you & Miss Jewett."[64] It may have been

Wharton's own growing success that led her to distance herself from Jewett, who, as the twentieth century progressed, was being relegated to the status of a minor writer. Cather too would come to hold Jewett at arm's length when Jewett's reputation waned. In the early years of her career Cather portrayed Jewett in "almost universally laudatory" terms, linking her with James and Twain as great American authors.[65] But in her 1936 preface to Jewett's work, as Deborah Carlin has shown, Cather spoke of Jewett as a relatively minor author, thereby emphasizing her own centrality in twentieth-century American literature, just as Wharton had done.[66]

Far from existing in separate literary worlds, then, Wharton and Cather shared a wide range of literary friends and acquaintances. Wharton's and Cather's similar literary tastes are epitomized in their acquaintance with A. E. Housman, a poet whose work both admired greatly. One well-known, unhappy episode in Cather's biography is her meeting with Housman. While in London with her friends Isabelle McClung and Dorothy Canfield on her first trip to Europe in 1902, she called on the poet in his flat.[67] Thinking them some Canadian cousins he had been expecting, he welcomed them, only to find they were strangers. The meeting became increasingly awkward, with Cather—who, in her role as a journalist, had met and interviewed many famous authors—increasingly embarrassed as she found herself unable to engage Housman in a discussion of his work. Finally Canfield was able to save the day by mentioning her research on Corneille and Racine, a scholarly topic on which she and Housman could converse.[68] The experience was profoundly unsettling, even humiliating, for Cather. Combined with events later in the same trip—events that made her feel provincial compared to her more sophisticated friend Dorothy—it drove a wedge into her friendship with Canfield, a relationship that was not mended until decades later.[69] Yet Cather's admiration of Housman's poetry remained central "to her own sense of what she was striving for in her art, to her own sense of what literature is for and what it should do," as Robert Thacker has written.[70]

Wharton also admired Housman's poetry deeply, finding in it "that great gift of experience, the only one we can count on between the cradle and the grave (and that only if we're capable of receiving it)."[71] But her relationship to Housman was quite different from Cather's: she was not the young admirer seeking him out in his lodgings but a social equal. Housman's publisher, Grant Richards, had been the first husband of her close friend Elisina Tyler.[72] Wharton's good friend Gaillard Lapsley, an expatriate who had become a fellow of medieval history at Trinity College, Cambridge University, was also a friend of Housman and was probably responsible for Wharton's meeting with Housman during her 1921 visit to Cambridge; Wharton may have socialized with Housman on other visits to England as well.[73] Certainly she knew him well enough that she sometimes included messages to him in her letters to Lapsley. In December 1929, for instance, she wrote, "Tell Mr. Housman we've had two evenings of reading him aloud, & 'Last Poems' are still supreme to me, well after the cherry-bloom of the Shropshire Lad."[74] In May 1936 she wrote, "If you have the chance to say to Housman what those two little books of his have been to me, please do. I have them in my bones."[75] Housman would die in December of that year.

Cyril Clemens, a distant cousin of Mark Twain, provides an additional, if strange, link between Wharton, Cather, and Housman. In August 1936 Wharton received a letter from Clemens on the stationery of the International Mark Twain Society, of which he was president.[76] Informing Wharton that he was writing a biography of Housman, he told her that he was planning a chapter on Housman's friends, including "a paragraph or two" on Wharton. Asking for some additional facts about her friendship with Housman, he wrote (apparently unaware that Wharton knew Housman fairly well) that she would be happy to know that Housman had "five or six" of her books near his desk at Cambridge. Wharton immediately forwarded the letter to Lapsley. "This horror has just come, & ... I beg you to cast an eye over it, & write just a word on a p.c. [post card] to tell me what to do," she wrote. In a marginal comment she added (apparently thinking Clemens was Twain's son), "Clemens has been hounding me for years to join the Paternal Glorification Society."[77]

Wharton makes no remark on the fact that on the letterhead of the International Mark Twain Society "H. E. Benito Mussolini" is listed as

5. Letter to Edith Wharton from Cyril Clemens, August 8, 1936, requesting information about A. E. Housman. Letterhead lists Willa Cather as a vice president of the International Mark Twain Society (along with H. G. Wells, T. S. Eliot, Robert Frost, Thomas Mann, John J. Pershing, and many eminent others). Benito Mussolini is listed as honorary president. Edith Wharton Collection, Yale Collection of American Literature, Beinecke Rare Book and Manuscript Library.

the "Honorary President of the Society" or that, along with T. S. Eliot, James Barrie, Thomas Mann, and John Pershing, Willa Cather is listed as a vice president of the society (fig. 5). Cather had received an award from the society in 1934 and appears to have accepted Clemens's offer of a vice presidency in August 1936.[78] But when Clemens wrote her a few months after he had written Wharton, also asking for information for his Housman biography, she was as put off as Wharton had been. Refusing to understand his question about a "pilgrimage" to see

Housman, she replied that she did not know what he was referring to and considered his request rude. A month later she rebuffed a second round of inquiries from Clemens.[79]

More than merely coincidental, these incidents remind us that both authors had a decided sense of their own privacy and a dislike of what they considered prying requests. Further, Wharton's and Cather's love of Housman's lyrical poetry suggests the deep similarity of their literary tastes and values. They also shared an admiration for a very different poet, Walt Whitman, to the extent that each used a Whitman phrase as a title: Cather's *O Pioneers!* takes its title from Whitman's poem of that name, and Wharton's memoir, *A Backward Glance*, alludes to Whitman's *A Backward Glance o'er Travel'd Roads*.[80] Both women wrote poetry throughout their lives, finding it a vehicle for non-narrative, lyrical expression that allowed them to express emotions more directly than fiction. A number of other authors were part of the network connecting Wharton and Cather. F. Scott Fitzgerald sent them both—along with Gertrude Stein and T. S. Eliot—copies of *The Great Gatsby*.[81] Wharton sent him a letter of thanks and invited him to tea, although the meeting went badly, with Wharton "at her most grande dameish" and Fitzgerald "inebriated or terrified, or both."[82] It appears to be the only time they met in person.[83] Fitzgerald also corresponded with Cather, apologizing to her for having "plagiarized" (his own word) from *A Lost Lady* in his description of Daisy in *Gatsby*.[84] Like Wharton, Cather wrote a complimentary letter in reply, although she and Fitzgerald apparently never met. Cather was good friends with the author and playwright Zoë Akins, with whom she met and corresponded regularly; among Akins's successful theatrical endeavors was her 1935 adaptation of Wharton's *The Old Maid*, which won her a Pulitzer Prize for drama.[85] Wharton and Akins never met but exchanged letters that were "warm but formal, befitting women of their class, education, and background."[86]

Sinclair Lewis also played a significant role in the lives and careers of Wharton and Cather, corresponding with both.[87] His correspondence with Wharton began when he wrote her to congratulate her on the Pulitzer Prize she received in 1921 for *The Age of Innocence*; when she found out that the selection committee's first choice for the novel had been Lewis's *Main Street*, she wrote him a letter explaining her dismay about the situation and expressing her liking for his novel.[88] The two became friends, with Lewis asking Wharton if she would allow him to dedicate *Babbitt* to her; she responded,

> I am a little dizzy!
> No one has ever wanted to dedicate a book to me before—& I'm so particularly glad that, now it's happened, the suggestion comes from the author of Main Street.
> Yes—of course![89]

As a writer who by 1921 was firmly established, Wharton particularly appreciated the praise from a younger writer: "What you say is so kind, so generous & so unexpected, that I don't know where to begin to answer. It is the first sign I have ever had—literally—that 'les jeunes' [younger people] at home had ever read a word of me.... So you can imagine what a pleasure it is to know that you have read me, & cared, & understood."[90]

Lewis praised the work of both novelists, writing in 1922 that "Miss Cather ranks with Mrs. Wharton, Mr. Tarkington, Mr. Hergesheimer, and a few others as one of the American talents which are not merely agreeable but worth the most exact study."[91] He praised Wharton and Cather as "American masters" of the short story, included them both in a list of great writers in "a half-century [1885–1935] crowded with genius!" and as late as 1948—after the deaths of both—included them in a list of authors whom aspiring writers should read.[92] Such praise is the more remarkable as—although Wharton and Lewis met twice, agreeably—each "became less enthusiastic about the other";[93] in some later reviews Lewis compared Wharton's work unfavorably to Cather's. Yet Lewis was well situated to appreciate the work of both Wharton and Cather, as he often wrote about the same material as Cather—life in midwestern towns—but from the satirical vantage point Wharton often assumed when she used western and midwestern settings in her fiction. Younger than both women (born in 1885, he was twenty-three years younger than Wharton and twelve younger than Cather), he elicited similar responses from both. After Lewis praised Cather's fiction during a speech in Omaha, Cather wrote him a letter of thanks in which she, like Wharton, addressed him as a much younger writer: "I would rather have the respect of a few (about three) strong, straight-hitting young writers like yourself than anything else that can come out of the writing business."[94] Cather, like Wharton, met Lewis only twice, but with the exception of *One of Ours*, Lewis continued to praise Cather's work. In 1938 Cather forwarded a column by Lewis to her nieces Margaret and Elizabeth Cather, noting, "I've never met Lewis but twice, yet he's always doing these 'big brother' acts for me. Nice and friendly of him."[95]

As the connections between Lewis, Wharton, and Cather illustrate, what today seems to be a huge literary and geographic distance between Wharton and Cather was, at the time, not so vast. Their parallel friendships with Zona Gale, a Wisconsin writer, illustrate their proximity. Gale had strong ties to both Wharton and Cather; her own work was sometimes compared to Sinclair Lewis's. During the adjudication for the 1921 Pulitzer, midwesterner Hamlin Garland, chair of the selection committee, noted in his diary that of his readings to date, "[Lewis's] *Main Street* and [Gale's] *Miss Lulu Bett* have the most distinction"; he preferred both to *The Age of Innocence*, although he also thought *Age* "good."[96] Wharton herself paired Lewis and Gale, writing Gale that "'Miss Lulu Bette'[*sic*] & 'Main Street' seem to me the two significant books in recent American fiction."[97] Cather and Gale not only corresponded but met several times when Gale was in New York.[98] Wharton and Gale, although they never met, exchanged admiring, affectionate, and thoughtful letters over an eleven-year period.[99] Their correspondence hints at the underlying similarities in Wharton's and Cather's understanding of literature. Cather's best-known statement on literary aesthetics is her essay "The Novel Démeublé" (on which more in chapter 2). Within this essay the single most-quoted passage is Cather's statement that "Whatever is felt upon the page without being specifically named there—that ... is created. It is the inexplicable presence of the thing not named, of the over-tone divined by the ear but not heard by it ... that gives high quality to the novel or the drama."[100] There are distinct echoes of Cather's "thing not named," her "over-tone" of emotion, in one of Wharton's letters to Gale. Unlike so much of "the hollow & tinny fiction of today," Wharton said, Gale's choice of language creates a "deep undertone of emotion."[101]

Wharton and Cather have also attracted the same biographers. In 1989 Hermione Lee published *Willa Cather: Double Lives*; in 2007 she published *Edith Wharton*, the most thorough biography of the author to date, with Knopf, Cather's long-time publisher. Lee was not the first to chronicle the lives of both. E. K. Brown, Cather's first biographer, had also done a study of Wharton's works, *Edith Wharton: Étude Critique*. When Brown, who had corresponded with Cather but never met her, died suddenly before finishing his biography, his work was taken over by a friend from the Sorbonne, the Canadian scholar Leon Edel—who met Edith Wharton while he was beginning his work on Henry James's theatrical experiments, an endeavor that led to his multi-volume biography of James. He became friendly enough with Wharton that she invited him to lunch on several occasions.[102]

In a nearly dizzying circle of relationships, Edel also knew and was at least once the guest of Dorothy Canfield Fisher, an important writer in her own right, and one of Cather's most significant personal and literary friends.[103] Fisher herself, who lived in Paris for a period during World War I and was involved in war relief work, may have met Wharton. Both were involved with the American Ambulance: Wharton was on an executive committee, and Fisher's husband worked there for several months. During the summer of 1917 Dorothy joined her husband at a training camp for American ambulance drivers, "getting and preparing food for the camp."[104] Fisher and Wharton were equally frustrated with American neutrality,[105] but in spite of this common opinion, Fisher had a strong negative impression of Wharton. In sketching out a novel, *The Brimming Cup*, she described the mother of a main character as "a very interesting type to me, the sort of last-generation American woman, like Mrs. Wharton, who (so it seems to me) takes Europeans with a funny, prayerful certainty of their innate superiority. This American woman would consider that it was the opportunity of her life to become 'cultured' and would do her pathetic, silly best to be like what she considers European women to be."[106] The character of Mrs. Putnam in Fisher's story "A Little Kansas Leaven," a wealthy, oblivious lady who supervises war charities in France during World War I, may also reflect her view of Wharton. Far from being distinct, the worlds of Wharton and Cather are thoroughly interconnected.

ANXIETIES OF AUTHORSHIP: "MRS. WHARTON" AND "THE LADY WITH THE BLURRY NAME"

Given their activity in a shared literary world, it was inevitable that the two women should be aware of each other's work. As the junior of the two, Cather was more aware of Wharton's work than Wharton seems to have been of Cather's. In 1912, when Cather published her first novel, *Alexander's Bridge*, Wharton published her fifth novel, *The Reef*. In all, Wharton already had eighteen books to her credit: not only the five novels, including *The House of Mirth* and *Ethan Frome*, but also five collections of short stories, three novellas, three travelogues, and a number of other works. Cather seems to have been quite aware of Wharton's status, her accomplishment perhaps both inspiring and rather intimidating.

In her often-quoted essay "My First Novels (There Were Two)," Cather remarked that when she wrote *Alexander's Bridge*, she was too much under the influence of the work of Henry James and Edith Wharton. At the time "the drawing-room was considered the proper setting for a novel, and the only characters worth reading about were smart people or clever people.... Henry James and Mrs. Wharton were our most interesting novelists, and most of the younger writers followed their manner, without having their qualifications."[107] Reviewers of *Alexander's Bridge* also remarked on this influence, though their remarks on the connection were not always positive. The reviewer for the *Independent*, apparently not a fan of psychological realism, wrote that "we sometimes doubt whether it is a compliment after all to be likened in literary style to Mrs. Wharton. What it means is that ... there is a deal of introspection and little outward action."[108] Mencken, however, praised Cather for her choice of influences. "*Alexander's Bridge* ... has the influence of Edith Wharton written all over it," he wrote, adding that this "is not to be taken as a sneer but as hearty praise, for the novelizing novice who chooses Mrs. Wharton as her model is at least one who knows a hawk from a handsaw, an artist from an artisan."[109] Other critics have commented on Wharton's influence as well but have rarely delved into exactly what this influence means within the novel.

Despite the importance of maintaining a skeptical attitude toward Cather's remarks on her own fiction, it seems to me that her assessment of the influence of Wharton and James on *Alexander's Bridge* is fair. Cather's calling it a "studio piece" suggests a set piece for an apprentice, a work that is relatively formulaic. In this novel that formula is very much derived from the fictions of Wharton and James: works about "smart"—that is, fashionable—people, generally in sophisticated urban settings. The novel is also about a love triangle, one of the oldest of plots, and not the sort of plot central to Cather's succeeding novels.

Particularly in its opening, *Alexander's Bridge* shows the influence of Wharton's best-selling *The House of Mirth*. That novel opens with Lawrence Selden observing the beautiful Lily Bart from a distance in a public setting, his eyes "refreshed by the sight" of her, admiring and evaluating her beauty and aware of her before she is aware of him.[110] *Alexander's Bridge* opens similarly, with Professor Wilson observing Winifred Bartley, Alexander's wife, in a Boston street: "He had already fixed his sharp eye upon the house which he reasoned should be his objective point, when he noticed a woman approaching rapidly from the opposite direction. Always an interested observer of women, Wilson would have slackened his pace anywhere to follow this one with his impersonal, appreciative glance. She was a person of distinction he saw at once, and, moreover, very handsome. She was tall, carried her beautiful head proudly, and moved with ease and certainty."[111] There are Jamesian overtones here as well. Cather's portrayal of Wilson, with his analysis of Winifred's beauty, is reminiscent of James's "Daisy Miller," in which Winterbourne has "a great relish for feminine beauty" and, connoisseur-like, prides himself on being able to distinguish the features that make Daisy especially pretty.[112]

The scene in *Alexander's Bridge* continues in a distinctly Whartonian way. Economics are a central issue in *The House of Mirth*, manifested both in Lily's awareness of her decreasing income and in Selden's awareness of Lily as the product of wealth: "He had a confused sense that she must have cost a great deal to make."[113] *Alexander's Bridge* echoes this concept: "One immediately took for granted the costly privileges and fine spaces that must lie in the background from which such a figure [i.e., Winifred] could emerge with this rapid and elegant gait."[114] Lily acknowledges frankly that she is "very expensive";[115] so too is Winifred, who has studied in Vienna, wears the luxurious furs Wilson admires her in, and fills the house with flowers in winter. Cather's own voice emerges distinctly in the course of the novel, and yet it never quite shakes off the influence of her predecessors. It would take *O Pioneers!* to do that.

Also important to Cather was Wharton's *Ethan Frome*, which would serve as a touchstone for her; in the judgment of one critic, "Cather's Wharton was ... the Wharton who wrote *Ethan Frome*."[116] This may be because it was published just as Cather was writing *Alexander's Bridge* and beginning to test her own powers as a novelist, and perhaps also because, as one of Wharton's two rural novels (*Summer* is the other), *Ethan Frome* has more in common with much of Cather's material than most of Wharton's other works. *Ethan Frome* was a subject of some interest to Cather and her friends. The novel was a topic of conversation between Cather and Elizabeth Shepley Sergeant, who noted that the two discussed it over dinner one night in the fall of 1911, not long after its publication. As Sergeant recounts the discussion, Wharton's "story of stark frustration ... challenged Sarah Orne Jewett's New England, her spirit of mercy and compassion. We recalled 'Poor Joanna' in *The Country of the Pointed Firs*—the woman who had a misadventure in love and to expiate went to live alone on an island. ... Mrs. Wharton could never have written 'Poor Joanna,' nor Miss Jewett *Ethan Frome*."[117] Sergeant continues, dismissing Wharton's work through an argument built on the stock image of her: "The brilliant outsider, a New York summer visitor for a mere six years, had levelled her cold lorgnette relentlessly and with a kind of bang, snapped up New England curtains that William Dean Howells had been nervous about raising, even as much as an inch."[118] In a further comment on *Ethan Frome* that she omitted from the final version of her book, Sergeant added, "How did Mrs. Wharton know that the fatal sled-ride of the lovers was suicidal in intent? Miss Jewett might have seen it as a last moment of desperate bliss, ending in tragedy for two who were trying to be scrupulous in love and sex."[119] Paradoxically, Sergeant's last phrase seems to describe Ethan and Mattie's last sled ride perfectly. It is *both* "suicidal in intent" *and* "a last moment of desperate bliss" for two people "trying to be scrupulous in love and sex"; perhaps Wharton was not that far from Jewett after all.

It is difficult to know the extent to which Sergeant's account reflects Cather's view of *Ethan Frome*, but there is no doubt that Cather also found it a chilly novel. In 1926 Fisher had just published a new novel, *Her Son's Wife*. After reading it, Cather wrote her with characteristic forthrightness, "It's too grim, this. I can admire it, but I can't honestly like it, anymore than I can Ethan Frome.... It affects me very powerfully, but I protest. I say 'All right, cut out everything but moral beauty; but why does moral beauty usually have to happen in a sordid atmosphere? I think that's a convention—it doesn't!'"[120] In 1937, when Scribner was preparing to issue a new edition of *Ethan Frome*, editor Maxwell Perkins invited Cather to write an introduction for it, noting that "I thought it not unlikely that this particular book was one you had a high regard for" and stating that "the main consideration would be your own feeling about Mrs. Wharton as a writer, and this book in particular."[121] Cather declined on the grounds that she was about to leave on "a rough trip" to rural Canada (although no record indicates that she took such a trip). She added with tantalizing vagueness, "I have not the mood, or the time, or even the tools for writing. If I wrote anything about Mrs. Wharton at all, I would want to give it time and pains."[122] One can only wonder what she would have said had she taken "time and pains"—and whether her dislike of the novel was the real reason for her decision.

Yet for those interested in literary influence, it is hard not to wonder whether *Ethan Frome* shaped some of Cather's own work. Cather herself wrote that she often was not fully aware of the ways in which she incorporated events from her own life into her fiction; "I remember unconsciously," she explained.[123] The same may well hold true of her literary influences and the ways in which they shaped her writing. Wharton's use of an external narrator to introduce Ethan's tale may well have influenced Cather's technique in *My Ántonia*, which uses an outside narrator to introduce Jim Burden, who himself recounts Ántonia's story. (This narrative choice has, not coincidentally, occasioned a great deal of literary criticism challenging the validity of the central tale in both works.) *Ethan Frome* may well have influenced Cather's work in other significant ways. As Richard Harris has pointed out, the squash vine that Claude Wheeler grows over the trellis on the porch of the home he has built for himself and Enid in *One of Ours* echoes the dead vine fluttering in the breeze on the porch of the house Ethan shares with Zeena;[124] once Claude leaves his house behind, the flourishing vine will probably end up as withered as the one over the entrance to the Fromes' blighted household.

The novels resonate in deeper ways as well. One of the many common threads in Wharton's and Cather's work is their valuing of sensitivity to other human beings and to beauty, and Ethan's perceptions are very much like Claude's. Both Ethan and Claude feel isolated with, and by, their sensitivity. Wharton writes that Ethan "had always been more sensitive than the people about him to the appeal of natural beauty.... But hitherto the emotion had remained in him as a silent ache, veiling with sadness the beauty that evoked it. He did not even know whether any one else in the world felt as he did, or whether he was the sole victim of this mournful privilege. Then he learned that one other spirit had trembled with the same touch of wonder."[125] Claude, who is also "more sensitive than the people about him" in a number of ways, hardly allows himself to acknowledge this "mournful privilege"; he concludes that overall "it was better not to think about such things, and when he could he avoided thinking."[126] Ethan senses a soul mate in Mattie Silver, someone who understands him in a way his wife Zeena never will; Claude senses that Gladys Farmer and, later, Mlle Olive understand him far better than his wife, Enid. Sensitive, fundamentally inarticulate men who have married sterile, unimaginative women and who search desperately for an honorable way out of their situation, Ethan and Claude are remarkably similar.

Cather's reading of *Ethan Frome* may have subtly influenced other aspects of her work as well. Although she protested the harsh ending of the novel, Wharton's description of the deep and fundamentally healthy attraction of two people, Ethan and Mattie, who cannot legitimately be together, may well have shaped the attraction between Emil and Marie in *O Pioneers!* Certainly the suffering of Ethan and Mattie after the sled crash is echoed in Cather's description of the deaths of Emil and Marie in *O Pioneers!* Only semiconscious after the crash, Ethan senses a "stillness ... so profound that he heard a little animal twittering somewhere near by under the snow. It made a small frightened *cheep* like a field mouse, and he wondered languidly if it were hurt. Then he understood that it must be in pain"; he gradually realizes that "the soft thing he had touched was Mattie's hair and that his hand was on her face" and "drag[s] himself" closer to her.[127] The characters suffer "excruciating" pain,[128] and the scene is painful for readers as well—too painful, according to some reviewers.

Yet Cather echoes it in the deaths of Marie and Emil. The scene is first narrated from the perspective of Frank, Marie's husband, who shoots the pair in a drunken rage, hardly knowing what he is doing. Once he has stopped firing, "The cries followed him. They grew fainter and thicker, as if she [Marie] were choking. He dropped on his knees beside the hedge and crouched like a rabbit, listening; fainter, fainter; a sound like a whine; again—a moan—another—silence."[129] The scene is later depicted by Ivar, the elderly man Alexandra has taken in, who sees the "trail of blood" Marie has left as she "dragged herself back to Emil's body. Once there, she seemed not to have struggled any more. She had lifted her head to her lover's breast, taken his hand in both her own, and bled quietly to death."[130] The animal-like cries, the wounded lover dragging him or herself closer to the beloved: Cather may have perceived *Ethan Frome* as "too grim," but the double death in *O Pioneers!* is strongly reminiscent of the attempted double suicide in *Ethan Frome*.

Over two decades after the publication of *Ethan Frome*, Wharton's imagery in that novel may still have been resonating in Cather, whose depiction of the reddish rays of the winter sun slanting across the snowy landscape in *Lucy Gayheart* (1935) may have its origin not only in her observations of winter in Nebraska but also in similar passages in *Ethan Frome*—just as the lively Lucy's "long crimson scarf" evokes Mattie's "cherry-coloured scarf."[131] Nor was the influence entirely in one direction: on some occasions, as we will see, Wharton may well have been echoing Cather.

Cather was aware of Wharton's work and reputation throughout her career. Following the publication of *The Song of the Lark*, Cather wrote to Ferris Greenslet, her publisher at Houghton Mifflin, asking, "Have you seen the article 'Nordica in Fiction' in the *Musical Courier* of Sept. 29. [*sic*] Why am I said to write like Mrs. Wharton? It is an honor that I dream not of."[132] Cather's tone here seems oddly mixed. The emphasized "why" suggests frustration; the following remark initially seems almost over-awed. Yet "an honor I dream not of" is an allusion to Shakespeare's *Romeo and Juliet*—Juliet's response to her mother when she is told that she is to marry Paris, which she has no interest in doing. Cather's line, then, may imply a polite demurral; yet it may simply be a phrase that sprang to her mind, as she knew Shakespeare thoroughly. Greenslet's response suggests that he took Cather's words at their face value and that it was indeed an honor to be compared to Wharton: "I suppose the reason why you are said to write like Mrs. Wharton is that you both write like the real thing and 'things equal to the same thing.'"[133] Similarly, when Cather was apparently fretting that *A Lost Lady* was not long enough to be published on its own, her publisher Alfred Knopf wrote her that the novella "belongs alone, exactly as 'Ethan Frome' belongs, alone"—presumably a reassuring response to Cather.[134]

Cather was usually pleased to have her name paired with Wharton's and sometimes used Wharton's status to explain her own actions or convey the importance of an honor. A few days after the publication of Van Doren's article about her in *The Nation*, she wrote to him, referring to Wharton to anchor her comments on literary form: "The new novel which I am just bringing toward the close [*One of Ours*] is better than the others for several reasons, but I wonder whether you will find much improvement in form. As Mrs. Wharton once said; even among good things one must choose, and one must renounce. I chose what I cared for most, and I had to renounce 'form'—in any very sound and gratifying sense. Probably ... I shall always be weak on that side."[135]

(Although she could not have known it, she was echoing concerns about balancing form and detail that Wharton had expressed in 1907: "I am beginning to see exactly where my weakest point is.... I sacrifice, to my desire for construction & breadth, the small incidental effects.")[136] When, in 1929, Cather was invited to receive an honorary doctorate from Yale, she wrote to Carrie Miner Sherwood, noting that "Yale has given a degree to only one woman writer before this, Mrs. Wharton."[137] Similarly she wrote to her brother Roscoe explaining that she would soon "receive a doctorate degree from Yale—the second they have ever given a woman writer. The first was given to Mrs. Wharton.... She came over from Paris and stayed in New York one week to take it."[138] Cather's comparison of herself to Wharton emphasizes her point: this was a major accomplishment.

Yet in some contexts Cather tried to distance herself from Wharton. In a 1922 letter to Mencken she specified James and Wharton as American authors from whom she had learned something. Earlier in her career, she noted, she had been very influenced by Tolstoy, to the extent that "I could not see the American scene as it looked to other Americans—as it, presumably, really was. I tried to get over all that by a long apprenticeship to Henry James and Mrs. Wharton, and to make an entrance in good society... with [']Alexander's Bridge.'"[139] Only after publishing *Alexander's Bridge* did she realize that the "drawing-room" pattern of Wharton and James was not the pattern that would suit her own work—or that she must adapt it to her own purposes.

Cather's relationship to Wharton was complex. The age gap between the two of them—almost twelve years—means that, as Williams has written, Wharton was "both a predecessor and a contemporary" for Cather.[140] On one hand, Cather's statements about Wharton seem to lend themselves to Harold Bloom's famous concept of the anxiety of influence. Like James, Wharton was a model for the young Cather to follow; she was an influence powerful enough that Cather may have needed to "swerve" from her model through "misreading or misprision" in order to establish her own voice.[141] On the other hand, Wharton's example may also have been an inspiration—an example of Sandra Gilbert and Susan Gubar's theory of the "anxiety of authorship" so common to women writers, particularly in the nineteenth and early twentieth centuries. Could women, in fact, become writers who would be taken seriously as artists? "Frequently," Gilbert and Gubar write, women aspiring to be writers "can begin such a struggle only by actively seeking a *female* precursor."[142] Sharon O'Brien's *Willa Cather: The Emerging Voice* pursues this topic through Cather's connections with Jewett and other women in her life; Cather's comments about Wharton suggest that this may also have been a role Wharton played for her. Both women took themselves seriously as professionals and as artists, a stance that meant rejecting the role of the "typical" female author. For Cather, Wharton may well have been both the predecessor to be vanquished *and* the model to be emulated.

MAKING WHARTON HER OWN

In the works that followed *Alexander's Bridge*, Cather's relationship to Wharton's work is "less a matter of influence" as we usually think of it and more a matter of resonance, to adopt the terms in which Thacker has written of Cather's debt to Housman.[143] Writers inevitably borrow from authors they admire. William Faulkner, for instance, commented that "A writer is completely rapacious. . . . He will steal from any source. He's so busy stealing and using it that he himself probably never knows where he gets what he uses."[144] In more moderate tones British novelist A. S. Byatt, who has written introductions to most of Cather's novels, has similarly remarked that authors absorb the words of others whose work they admire, often echoing them unconsciously in their own work.[145]

After *Alexander's Bridge* Cather made any Whartonian material thoroughly her own. Cather's reading of *The House of Mirth* may subtly have shaped her own later work, not so much in style as in the way in which it may have sensitized the independent and financially self-sufficient Cather to the drama of the lives of women dependent on the income of men. Lily Bart's financial dependence on men and her consequent need to cater to their whims is echoed in a number of later Cather characters, including Lillian St. Peter in *The Professor's House* (whose name echoes Lily's), Marian Forrester in *A Lost Lady,* and Myra Henshawe in *My Mortal Enemy.* Like Wharton's Lily, Cather's Lillian "couldn't pinch and be shabby and do housework.... Under such conditions she became another person, and a bitter one";[146] Marian and Myra are the same. All three characters are women whose lives are shaped by the money that they may or may not inherit, by their marriages, and by their husbands' incomes. Lily Bart's father fails to leave her an inheritance; as Lily refuses to marry for money alone, her life spirals downward. Lillian St. Peter is luckier than Lily: she is spared the indignities of "pinch[ing] and be[ing] shabby" only because her father has left her money. Myra is disinherited by her wealthy uncle when she insists on marrying for love; far from her being rewarded for this romantic behavior, her later life is shabby indeed. Marian, in her need to be sparkling, entertaining, and beautiful in order to please a series of men who will support her, is most like what Lily would have been had she acceded to the patriarchal demands of the world in which she lived.

Cather may have adopted the economic language in which men sometimes evaluate women from *The House of Mirth*. In scenes we will return to, Lily learns the men around her have not only gossiped about her but calculated her "worth" in a very precise way. After her stunning success in an evening of *tableaux vivants*, Rosedale is reported to have said that "if I could get [the artist] Paul Morpeth to paint her like that, the picture'd appreciate a hundred per cent in ten years."[147] During Trenor's near assault on Lily, he assumes that Lily has gotten money from other men and then refused to sleep with them. To him she has an almost monetary value that drops with each encounter: "I don't doubt you've accepted as much before—and chucked the other chaps as you'd like to chuck me. I don't care how you settled your score with them—if you fooled 'em *I'm that much to the good*."[148] Near the novel's end, when Lily attempts to maneuver Rosedale into marrying her, he tells her forthrightly that he will not do so; he loves her, but "if I married you now I'd queer myself [socially] for good."[149] The same kind of calculations are made in some of Cather's fiction, especially in *Lucy Gayheart*. Like Rosedale, the successful businessman Harry Gordon assumes that he can choose whom to marry: Lucy for love or Harriet Arkwright for social position; like Trenor, he thinks in financial terms as he calculates Miss Arkwright's value: "her stock was going down" as she reaches her late twenties—Lily's age when *The House of Mirth* opens.[150] Like Wharton and sometimes in the same terms, Cather portrays the economic realities of many women's lives.

Wharton's importance to Cather resonates particularly in two of her last stories, "Before Breakfast" and "The Old Beauty," both published in the posthumous collection *The Old Beauty and Others* (1948). In "Before Breakfast," a hard-working young westerner, Henry Grenfell, marries into a wealthy New York family who could easily be related to many of Wharton's upper-class New Yorkers. Like May Welland, Newland Archer's wife in *The Age of Innocence*, Henry's wife, Margaret Grenfell, is sophisticated, refined, and never acknowledges that her husband might be less than completely happy at home. Even when Grenfell picks a fight with his wife and their eldest son over dinner, she seamlessly smooths it over: "Margaret, by being faultlessly polite, often saved the situation."[151] Yet Grenfell chafes under such faultless manners. As Newland Archer and Ellen Olenska discover in *Age*, a society in which one is never allowed to acknowledge anything "unpleasant" can prove very restrictive. Luckily Grenfell has an island to which he can escape—something Archer might well have envied.

"The Old Beauty" initially seems a deeply Whartonian story. It is told from the perspective of a man, Henry Seabury, through whom we learn the story of Gabrielle Longstreet de Couçy, and has other elements typically associated with Wharton: it is a transatlantic tale of the upper classes, set mostly in Aix-les-Bains, France, but also in London, Paris, and New York, while Martinique and China also figure. Further, it is, in part, a story of entrapment and disillusionment, elements often associated with Wharton. The story's proliferation of subplots might also strike some readers as Whartonian or even Jamesian: Cather creates a thoughtful but slightly cumbersome subplot about another family whom Seabury befriends and through whom he recognizes in Mme de Couçy a woman whom he used to know. Further, Cather reprises three elements central to *The House of Mirth* in "The Old Beauty." At the same time, this story is deeply Cather's own, in which Cather employs some of her own most powerful themes: youth and age, the passing of time, the central role of friendship, and place and natural beauty.

The first of the three elements that might be seen as Whartonian is relatively simple: the story's fascination with a beautiful woman and what it might mean to be that beautiful woman. One of the driving factors in Lily Bart's story is her physical beauty, which Lily's mother exhorts her to deploy in order to win a handsome husband and assure her own future financial security and social dominance. Yet while emphasizing, even in the story's title, the beauty of Gabrielle Longstreet, Cather gives us a different kind of beauty and a different kind of personality. Unlike Lily, Gabrielle is never fully conscious of her beauty or of the ways in which she can use it to her advantage. She isn't even conventionally beautiful: "There was no glitter about her, no sparkle. She never dressed in the mode.... Into drawing-rooms full of ladies enriched by marvels of hairdressing..., she came with her brown hair parted in the middle and coiled in a small knot at the back of her head."[152] While treating one of the central issues of *The House of Mirth*, Cather creates a beauty who is both like and utterly unlike Lily Bart, suggesting that Gabrielle's lack of conventional beauty contributes to the sense that "she was beautiful, that was all"; similarly her lack of social mannerisms contributes to the fact that people, men in particular, find her house "attractive."[153]

Cather treats the topic of beauty in another way as well, allowing Gabrielle to grow old, something Lily never has a chance to do. When Seabury sees her for the first time in the story (watching her from a distance, much like Professor Wilson with Mrs. Bartley or Selden with Lily), he sees her as "a stern, gaunt-cheeked old woman with a yellowing complexion."[154] "Plain women," Seabury reflects, "when they grow old are—simply plain women. Often they improve. But a beautiful woman may become a ruin. The more delicate her beauty... the more completely it is destroyed."[155] Cather tempers this harsh remark through Seabury's wondering whether "the few very beautiful women he remembered in the past had been illusions, had benefited by a romantic tradition which played upon them like a kindly light... and by an attitude in men which no longer existed."[156] Cather thus treats the topic of beauty differently from Wharton, who never wrote anything quite as absolute as Cather's lines about the complete ruin of a beautiful woman's beauty. Yet in Seabury's final reflection here, there is much of Wharton's own sense of a kinder past that was irretrievably lost after World War I.

The second of the Whartonian elements in the story is plot-related. In a scene distinctly reminiscent of the one in which Gus Trenor traps Lily Bart in his New York townhouse and comes very close to raping her, Cather depicts Gabrielle Longstreet, then in her prime, struggling alone with a man who is attempting to rape her in her own drawing room in a New York hotel. In Wharton's 1905 novel there is no actual physical attack, but Wharton conveys the threat clearly when Trenor, looming over Lily, blocks her exit from the room. By the time Cather was writing her story four decades later, it was possible to be more explicit. The situation is similar: Gabrielle Longstreet is alone in her drawing room with a man she thinks she can trust, only to find that she cannot. The man, who (like Trenor with Lily) has invested money for her, takes advantage of the situation in a scene that is explicit: "His left arm . . . pinioned her against the flowered silk upholstery. His right hand was thrust deep into the low-cut bodice of her dinner gown."[157] The threat inherent in the scene in *The House of Mirth* is realized in "The Old Beauty." Gabrielle is saved not, as Lily is, by her attacker's returning sense of what is proper but by the arrival of Henry Seabury. But like Lily, Gabrielle is left exhausted and helpless. Lily is ministered to by her friend Gerty Farish, Gabrielle by her young admirer. Both women must adjust their view of the kindliness of the world and of men in whom they had put their trust.

Yet "The Old Beauty" is deeply Cather's own. This is clear in the depth and detail of the story's setting: Cather beautifully evokes both the resort town of Aix-les-Bains and the nearby mountains. Further, it is a story that is profoundly about friendship, the relationship between Gabrielle de Couçy and Chetty Beamish, who befriended Gabrielle in her time of need and has remained staunchly with her in her declining years, keeping the older woman company and saving her from her own worst tendencies. It is further about the relationship between youth and age, often so central in Cather, and about two ways of growing old, with Gabrielle (and Seabury) resenting the present and hanging onto their past as hard as they can, and with Chetty finding good in new ways. Yet even in the tension between looking backward and living in the present, the story echoes the resolution of Wharton's *The Age of Innocence*, in which Newland Archer thinks that "there was good in the old ways.... There was good in the new order too."[158] The relationship between Wharton's and Cather's work is complex indeed.

An October 1946 letter from Cather to E. K. Brown, her first biographer, clarifies one of the distinctions that the mature Cather drew between her own work and Wharton's. Not long after the publication of *O Pioneers!*, she had a chance meeting with Louis Brandeis, an acquaintance from her time in Boston in 1907 and 1908 and later a Supreme Court justice.[159] She recounted, "We had a long talk.... What he had to say was that whatever faults the book had, there was real feeling in it <u>for some places and some people</u>, and the thing that he, personally, did not find in contemporary writers was just that thing. He named three, I remember. Mrs. Wharton was one of them. (She being no longer living, I can use her name.)"[160] Any tacit rivalry between the two authors had, on Cather's side, resolved itself by this point in her career; yet she was undeniably pleased by this distinction between her own work and Wharton's, made so clearly to her advantage. It confirmed what she had so long been after—and that she had done it well.

There is far less documentation of Wharton's thoughts about Cather. It is difficult to know the extent to which she was aware of the younger author, although it is hard to imagine that she would not have been aware of the prominent publications including them both, like the *Vanity Fair* pictorial and Van Doren's series in *The Nation*. Wharton's name occurs quite frequently in reviews of Cather's work—it is natural for reviewers to compare newer authors to more established ones—yet Cather's name appears only twice in reviews of Wharton's work, both times in reviews of Wharton's World War I–related novel, *A Son at the Front*.[161] In one case a negative comment about Wharton is applied more or less equally to Cather: H. W. Boynton argued that *Son* was "chiefly of cathartic value for its author. Every creative writer who felt deeply those war years has sooner or later to get them out of his system. Miss Cather has just done it—thoroughly, we may hope. I believe Mrs. Wharton has done it once for all in *A Son at the Front*."[162] In the second case the comparison was to Wharton's disadvantage. In the *New York Tribune*, Burton Rascoe accused Wharton of belated publication: "One wonders, after reading *A Son at the Front*, where in the world Mrs. Wharton has been all this time.... It must be conceded at once that Mrs. Wharton has been wholly oblivious of the war inspired fiction of the Messrs. Wells,... Barbusse,... Dos Passos, Cummings and Boyd, to say nothing of the work of the Misses Sinclair, West,... and Cather," he wrote,[163] referring to such landmark works as Henri Barbusse's *Le Feu* (*Under Fire*, 1916), John Dos Passos's *Three Soldiers* (1921), E. E. Cummings's *The Enormous Room* (1922), Rebecca West's *The Return of the Soldier* (1918), and of course Cather's *One of Ours*. As with the charge that she was a mere "literary aristocrat," Wharton was being called out of touch.

The charge may well have touched a nerve. In her later years Wharton feared being seen as a hopelessly outmoded Victorian, "the Mrs. Humphry Ward of the Western Hemisphere" as she wrote to Sinclair Lewis.[164] If there is an anxiety of influence in which younger authors half-deliberately misunderstand and discard their predecessors, metaphorically murdering them so as to dispense with their over-awing presence, perhaps there is an equivalent on the other side of that equation: the elder writer's fear of being seen as outdated, unappreciated, and in effect killed off—while still alive and publishing—by the hungry generations of up-and-coming writers. It would have been hard for Wharton not to bristle at a 1922 review in which Rascoe compared her work unfavorably to Cather's, remarking that "the high place Mrs. Wharton's achievement occupies... is, I think, something of an accident" and arguing that "the difference between Mrs. Wharton and Miss Cather is largely a difference between fine workmanship and genius, talent and passion, good taste and ecstasy. It is, essentially, that Miss Cather is a poet in her intensity and Mrs. Wharton is not."[165]

The one written comment we have from Wharton regarding Cather's work is indeed a bit bristly. In a 1928 letter to Gaillard Lapsley, Wharton indicates that she was not impressed with Cather's 1923 novel, *A Lost Lady*: "The Lost Lady, with your note enclosed, came the day before yesterday, & I agree with you in thinking the book much better than any other by the lady with the blurry name. But I find all her books blurry—like the name! She had a splendid *donnée* this time, but, oh, how much more she might have made of it! Nothing has any edge—."¹⁶⁶ Clearly Wharton had read more than this single novel of Cather's but found them all, as she herself rather impressionistically remarks, too "blurry."¹⁶⁷

Ironically Wharton's remark that the younger writer "had a splendid *donnée* this time" and the hint that she herself might have "made more" of it reiterate a dynamic she had protested repeatedly as a writer: "There could be no greater critical ineptitude than to judge a novel according to *what it ought to have been about*," she wrote in her memoir, adding, "There are but two essential rules: one, that the novelist should deal only with what is within his reach . . . , and the other that the value of a subject depends almost wholly on what the author sees in it, and how deeply he is able to see *into* it."¹⁶⁸ Wharton herself had chafed at such criticism. She had found some of Henry James's remarks frustrating, including his comment regarding *The Custom of the Country*: "I wished Undine's experience of la Vieille France . . . needn't perforce to be so sommaire!"¹⁶⁹ For James, master of the international theme, the most intriguing part of Undine's epic was her experience with the aristocracy of old France, a topic he felt Wharton had treated too briefly. Yet for Wharton to have focused more extensively on this part of Undine's experience would have been counter to the episodic nature of her novel. Despite such protests, Wharton's response to *A Lost Lady* is similar, as she implies that she could have "seen into" Cather's subject more deeply than Cather herself could.

After the 1905 publication of Cather's first volume of stories, *The Troll Garden*, an associate of Cather's at *McClure's Magazine* sent a copy to Henry James, urging him to read it; James responded by expressing his lack of interest in works by young American novelists.¹⁷⁰ Similarly, Wharton in her later career seems to have had diminished interest in works by younger writers unless she was able to see a clear link to her own perspective or literary tradition. She admired Proust not for his innovation but because she saw him as belonging to "the great line of classic tradition."¹⁷¹ She admired works of Lewis and Fitzgerald partly because she saw them as taking up her own satirical attitude toward an uncultivated and frivolous America. By the same token, she liked Anita Loos's satirical *Gentlemen Prefer Blondes* (1925)—a work with plenty of "edge." To a friend she declared, tongue in cheek, that "the literary committee of Ste. Claire . . . unhesitatingly pronounce [it] the greatest novel since *Manon Lescaut*," Antoine-François Prévost's eighteenth-century novel, which Wharton had adapted for the stage in 1901.[172] Some of Wharton's enthusiasm came from her perception of Loos's Lorelei Lee as "vindicat[ing]" her own Undine Spragg.[173] She was, in fact, so enthusiastic about *Gentlemen Prefer Blondes* that, very uncharacteristically, she "allowed herself to be quoted as calling it '*the* great American novel'" in advertising, an endorsement that continues to appear on paperback editions of the novel.[174] Such enthusiasm over a clever but shallow fiction seems misplaced in an author who was unable to appreciate Cather's work—although, of course, no literary law dictates that one great writer appreciate the work of another. Yet a close reading of Wharton's later fiction in particular may show familiarity with the work of "the lady with the blurry name," as we will see.

In *French Ways and Their Meaning*, her 1919 discussion of French culture, Wharton wrote, "Unfortunately surface differences—as the word implies—are the ones that strike the eye first. If beauty is only skin deep, so too are some of the greatest obstacles between peoples who were made to understand each other. . . . We must dig down to the deep faiths and principles from which every race draws its enduring life to find how like in fundamental things are the two people[s] whose destinies have been so widely different."[175] Wharton was writing in the context of World War I; the "races" and "peoples" she refers to are the French and the American, two peoples separated not only by language and culture but also by a great deal of geographic space. But the principle is strikingly applicable to Wharton and Cather, and to the fictional worlds they created. Perhaps geography, while formative, is not quite as "fatal" as Cather feared, for beneath the "surface differences" that have separated Wharton and Cather are many of the same "deep faiths and principles," as we will see in greater depth in the next chapter.

Perhaps both the proximity and distance between Wharton and Cather are epitomized by the fact that both sailed on the Cunard Liner *Berengaria* three months apart, Wharton in July 1923, when she returned to France after receiving her honorary doctorate from Yale, and Cather in October of the same year, returning to the United States from one of her European trips.[176] Though Wharton and Cather may seem to be the proverbial ships passing in the night, this coincidence figures the link between them much more concisely. They were two women deeply attached to both American and European culture, sailing on the same ship just a few months apart, each returning to her adopted home—Wharton to France, Cather to New York City. That they sailed on this particular ship, named for Queen Berengaria of England, the well-traveled wife of Richard the Lion Hearted, is strikingly appropriate.[177] Wharton and Cather never met, but as we will see in succeeding chapters, their lives and works intersect in profound and meaningful ways.

2

THE LAND OF LETTERS, THE KINGDOM OF ART

I must return to "The Greater Inclination," and to my discovery of that soul of mine which the publication of my first volume called to life. At last I had groped my way through to my vocation, and thereafter I never questioned that story-telling was my job.... I felt like some homeless waif who, after trying for years to take out naturalization papers, and being rejected by every country, has finally acquired a nationality. The Land of Letters was henceforth to be my country, and I gloried in my new citizenship.
  EDITH WHARTON, *A Backward Glance*

In the kingdom of art there is no God, but one God, and his service is so exacting that there are few men born of women who are strong enough to take the vows.
  WILLA CATHER (quoted in Slote, *The Kingdom of Art*)

THE ART OF FICTION

For Wharton and Cather literature itself existed almost literally as a location in itself—a quasi-mystical place to which one might finally find one's way or to which one might, through strenuous effort, be admitted. Wharton wrote in her memoir that she never felt wholly at home in any of the places she had lived until the publication of her first book of short stories, in 1899, "called" her "soul . . . to life" and helped her find her "vocation." This in turn led to her sense that she had finally "acquired a nationality."[1] For Cather too the Land of Letters was very close to a geographic place, one that, as with Wharton, elicited a religious vocabulary. Wharton speaks of her "soul" and of a "vocation";

6. (*top*) In the "Land of Letters": Edith Wharton at her desk, Pavillon Colombe, 1931. Edith Wharton Collection, Yale Collection of American Literature, Beinecke Rare Book and Manuscript Library.

7. (*bottom*) Entering the "Kingdom of Art": Willa Cather at the desk of her friend George Seibel in Pittsburgh, ca. 1900. PHO-4-085, Willa Cather Foundation Special Collections and Archives, National Willa Cather Center, Red Cloud, Nebraska.

Cather chooses the trope of a feudal kingdom where Art is a demanding deity whom few are "strong enough" to serve.[2] When Cather left Nebraska for Pittsburgh in 1896, the Kingdom of Art may have been "clearer far [to her] than the land she was leaving," as Bernice Slote has remarked.[3] Both Wharton and Cather felt fortunate to have found this new place; both felt that the relationship was permanent and irreversible. Cather wrote, "If art does not often claim a man, when she does, she claims him irrevocably, for life and death"; Wharton described her writing as an "inexorable calling" (figs. 6 and 7).[4]

If Wharton and Cather shared the idea of art as a civilizing force and the Land of Letters as a place, they also found that the world of art could be absorbing, even dangerously seductive. In "Life and I," Wharton wrote that as a little girl, she felt that words had "visible, almost tangible presences, with faces as distinct as these of the persons among whom I lived. And, like the Erlkönig's daughters, they sang to me so bewitchingly that they almost lured me from the wholesome noonday air of childhood into some strange supernatural region . . . where the normal pleasures of my age seemed as insipid as the fruits of the earth to Persephone after she had eaten of the pomegranate seed."[5] Wharton draws on Goethe's *Die Erlkönig* and Greek mythology to convey her sense of art's potentially dangerous power; Cather references Victorian writers to express the same sense that art could become a dark temptation. One of the two epigraphs to Cather's first collection of stories, *The Troll Garden*, is from Christina Rosetti's poem "Goblin Market"; the other is from Charles Kingsley's fable from *The Roman and the Teuton*. Both tell of the temptations of art, as Susan Rosowski has observed,[6] the potential of art to draw one away "from the wholesome noonday air . . . into some strange supernatural region," to use Wharton's phrase. Kingsley's fable conveys this clearly. The healthy "forest children" lead lives that are not simply fortunate but exciting, playing with "forest beasts" and even "conquer[ing] them in their play; but the forest is too dull and too poor for them; and they wander to the walls of the Troll-garden and wonder what is inside."[7] Once the children wander over the walls into that enticing garden, they are "bewitched," and few ever escape. They are as changed by their experience as Wharton's Persephone is by tasting the pomegranate seeds; "normal pleasures" seem "insipid" in comparison. That Wharton and Cather spoke of art in virtually identical terms points to their similar experience of art, and of writing in particular, and to their need to escape from a quotidian world. Yet these passages also make it clear that both authors had a sense that there was a danger of losing one's self too completely in the world of art.

The strong resemblance between these passages is only one example of the many ways in which Wharton and Cather shared the same literary tastes and were shaped by the same literary heritage. Goethe was one of Wharton's favorite authors throughout her life; a line from his *Wilhelm Meister*, "'*Kein Genuss ist vorübergehend*'—'No pleasure is transitory,'" was a favorite of hers, and one of the epigrams she chose for *A Backward Glance*.[8] Cather also admired Goethe, whose work she mentions in *The Song of the Lark* and "Old Mrs. Harris," in which college-bound Vickie Templeton browses through a copy of Goethe's *Faust*, hoping that someday she will be able to read it in the original German.[9] Even more central to both was the work of the French naturalists, the great English novelists, and the work of Leo Tolstoy. Both were, especially in their early careers, devotees of the work of Henry James, as we will see in more detail. Both wrote perceptively of the role of the reader in completing the meaning of any written text and complained of the lack of acuity of literary critics. Both employed theatrical metaphors in their expression of a literary aesthetic and emphasized the importance not of comprehensiveness but of selection in the creation of literary art. Despite their fascination with modernist art (particularly Cather) and interest in modernist music (especially Wharton), both expressed an uneasy relationship to literary modernism; their love of Housman's work suggests their loyalty to many of the literary values of the nineteenth century, even as both evolved styles that responded to the twentieth.

Within the Land of Letters Wharton and Cather were rooted in the same literary territory, that of nineteenth-century realism, which began in France and Russia and extended to England and America. Among the favorite authors of both were Balzac and Flaubert;[10] the work of the French naturalists appealed to both because of the naturalists' inherent, sometimes even grim, honesty about life—what Wharton would call the intellectual honesty of the French[11]—and for their nonmoralistic approach to fiction. Wharton and Cather also admired the naturalists' ability to create characters whom readers experienced as if they were real people. Indeed for both Wharton and Cather this was the hallmark of great fiction. "The test of the novel is that its people should be *alive*," Wharton states.[12] Cather illustrates this principle by noting that in Paris, "one sees [Balzac's] people everywhere"; she praises the best work of Sarah Orne Jewett as being "not stories at all, but life itself."[13]

Partly because of his ability to create such characters, Tolstoy was a touchstone for both. Cather was deeply absorbed in his novels (as well as Balzac's) in her late teens, drawn by the authors' "vitality,"[14] and listed Tolstoy (with Turgenev) as one of "the two greatest writers of fiction in modern times" in a 1924 letter.[15] When asked in 1941 which work of literature she would like to have authored, she named *War and Peace*: "Simply for the grand game of making it.... I would like to have had that torrent of life and things pour through me."[16] Wharton also admired Tolstoy's novels profoundly. In a 1929 essay she coined the term "visibility"—the sense that a character is so real that he or she exists almost as a "visible" person outside the novel—as the hallmark of great writers, and she stated that "Tolstoi is equalled only (and never surpassed) by Jane Austen, Balzac, Thackeray—and at times by Stendhal, Flaubert, and Trollope."[17] Citing Tolstoy's "intense power of seeing his characters in their habit as they lived, and ... his ability to reproduce the color of his vision in words," she calls him one of the "greatest of life-givers," those authors who, when they "touched the dead bones[,] they arose and walked."[18] Using strikingly parallel terms, Cather wrote that the novelist's project was "not to dissect the dead men of old, but to vivify them"; writers must "make men and women and breathe into them until they become living souls."[19]

It is no wonder, then, that both should also have been admirers of Henry James, who was also influenced by the French and Russian novelists. The links between James and Wharton, and James and Cather, have been much discussed. Wharton was early described as a "disciple" of James, although this was not always a compliment; James's work was not uniformly admired at the time, as Shari Benstock has pointed out, and some critics preferred Wharton's writing to James's. Yet soon "literary history reversed these claims: James was the master.... Edith Wharton's writing was a pale shadow."[20] The master-disciple description was in place as early as 1933, four years before Wharton's death, when E. K. Brown declared that "Mrs. Wharton's debt [to James] [was] almost incomputably great."[21] Yet Wharton herself had protested being seen as James's disciple as early as 1904, when she wrote to her editor, William Crary Brownell, that "the continued cry that I am an echo of Mr. James ... makes me feel rather hopeless."[22] She was decidedly not enamored of the style of James's later novels. A few months before this letter to Brownell, she had written to him that James "talks, thank heaven, more lucidly than he writes"; in 1902 she had told Brownell, "Don't ask me what I think of the Wings of the Dove."[23] A good deal of critical effort has been expended since the mid-1970s in drawing Wharton out from under James's shadow; as if to deny the influence, Lewis's 1975 biography and Benstock's 1994 biography acknowledge little influence at all. Hermione Lee's 2007 study of Wharton's life explores in more complex ways the manner in which Wharton and James interact, examining not only the differences between their works but also the creative ways in which Wharton often responded to James's work.[24]

The influence of James on Cather has long been acknowledged. Cather herself mentioned it more than once, and biographers and critics have noted it as well, citing early stories like "Flavia and Her Artists" and "The Marriage of Phaedra" as her most Jamesian.[25] In his biography E. K. Brown remarks that some of Cather's pre-1908 stories were "obtrusively Jamesian both in substance and in form" and that a story like the stiff "Eleanor's House" (1907) is "a Jamesian experiment, almost ... a pastiche."[26] If Cather was, at this point, overly imitative, she nevertheless learned a great deal about technique from James. Lee has commented on James's positive influence on Cather's narrative technique and especially on *Alexander's Bridge*, including Cather's "dramatic presentation" of the plot, the use of a minor character as an observer, and "the use of a controlling symbol."[27]

Recently critics have explored the James-Cather relationship in more detail. Elsa Nettels has remarked on a number of themes Cather adapted from James, including a sense of lost youth (with strong echoes of *The Ambassadors* in *The Song of the Lark*, for instance).[28] She also points out principles and techniques Cather learned from James, including "unity, economy, and selection."[29] But "the most important lesson that Cather learned from James [is] how to unify a novel by centering the narrative in the mind of a single character."[30] John J. Murphy points to further strong resemblances between Cather and James, including their use of "visual art as a paradigm" for verbal art; their parallel, visual compositions in their work; and their concern with the "corrupting power of American wealth."[31] Wharton and Cather resemble each other yet again in the distance both put between themselves and James's elaborate later style. In her memoir Wharton said straightforwardly that in these works, James "sacrifice[d] [the] spontaneity which is the life of fiction" to his theory of fiction.[32] While James moved "toward amplification of characters' consciousness" in his later novels, "Cather [moved] toward simplification," as Nettels points out.[33]

Despite their disagreements with James, Wharton and Cather learned a great deal from the principles underlying his work, principles that were not only realized in his work but often articulated by him more clearly than by any preceding author. James himself was profoundly influenced by the Russian novelists, particularly Turgenev, and by the French naturalists, many of whom he knew in his early career.[34] As Lyall Powers demonstrated, the work of these authors moved James away from both the moralizing novel and the romanticized novel, which, by idealizing life and human character, misleads its readers; like Zola, James came to believe that "to be engaged in the discovery of truth, in the overcoming of ignorance, is to be moral enough," as Powers states.[35] These principles powerfully shaped James's own conception of art: "Serious art, James would maintain, has no concern with the conventionally moral: it is irresponsible—or responsible only to its own integrity as a faithful representation of actual life. The only duty of a novel, he felt, was to be well written."[36] Wharton and Cather agreed. Wharton referred to the nineteenth-century novel of social reform, including the work of Harriet Beecher Stowe, as "that unhappy hybrid, the novel with the purpose."[37] Cather concurred, arguing, "If the novel is a form of imaginative art, it cannot be at the same time a vivid and brilliant form of journalism."[38] A good novelist, she added, must focus on story and character rather than on social issues; if it is the latter that really interest the author, "he ought to be working in a laboratory or a bureau."[39]

James's most famous statement of his principles is his essay "The Art of Fiction," in which he promulgates these and other principles: the futility of attempting to distinguish between the novel of incident and the novel of character, for "What is character but the determination of incident? What is incident but the illustration of character?"; the refusal to limit the idea of "incident" to large actions ("It is an incident for a woman to stand up with her hand resting on a table and look out at you in a certain way; or if it be not an incident I think it will be hard to say what it is"); his insistence that mental, emotional, or psychological events, as well as physical "adventures," constitute valid material for fiction; the need for the novelist to be "one of the people on whom nothing is lost"; the author's free choice of subject; the ability of accomplished fiction to "catch the very note and trick, the strange irregular rhythm of life."[40] All of these principles permeate Wharton's and Cather's statements about fiction as well as their work itself, as well as much current literary fiction.

James also emphasized that fiction should not attempt to portray everything; instead, art was "essentially selection."[41] This was another principle he had learned from the French naturalists, and specifically from Flaubert and Maupassant, whose works modeled "the careful selection of significant detail, rather than the abundance of Balzac and Zola."[42] Wharton and Cather would reiterate this concept in their own statements about fiction. In her 1920 essay "On the Art of Fiction," Cather objected to fictions that included "sharp photographic detail" but that were "really nothing more than lively pieces of reporting."[43] In contrast, writing that aspires to the stature of art "should simplify. That, indeed, is very nearly the whole of the higher artistic process."[44] In "The Novel Démeublé" she both echoes James and cites the French naturalists, arguing that while "power of observation" and "power of description" matter, "they form but a low part of [the writer's] equipment."[45] The essential ability is the ability to select: "Mérimée said in his remarkable essay on Gogol: 'L'art de chosir parmi les innombrables traits que nous offre la nature est, après tout, bien plus difficile que celui de les observer avec attention et de les rendre avec exactitude'" (the art of choosing among the innumerable traits that nature offers us is, after all, much more difficult than that of observing them with attention and rendering them precisely).[46] Wharton's statements in *The Writing of Fiction*, published three years after Cather's "Novel Démeublé," are notably parallel. The foundation on which her idea of fiction is built is "the need of selection": "No matter how restricted an incident one is trying to give an account of, it cannot but be fringed with details more and more remotely relevant. . . . To choose between all this material is the first step toward coherent expression."[47] This principle is so central to Wharton's beliefs that she soon reemphasizes it, arguing that "the art of rendering life in fiction can never . . . be anything, or need to be anything, but the disengaging of crucial moments from the welter of existence."[48]

Ultimately the goal of writing was, for both Wharton and Cather, to create something beyond the page itself. Although they objected to the novel's being "overpopulated," to use Cather's word, they admired the details of Tolstoy's work because "the clothes, the dishes, the haunting interiors of those old Moscow houses, are always so much a part of the emotions of the people that they are perfectly synthesized; they seem to exist, not so much in the author's mind, as in the emotional penumbra of the characters themselves."[49] In *The Writing of Fiction* Wharton also stated the importance of the author's power of suggestion. "The real achievement" of a fine short story, she wrote, "is to suggest illimitable air within a narrow space."[50] Similarly she wrote that one of the most difficult things for the novelist to convey is a sense of time passing. Yet the great novelists can do so: "How mysteriously yet unmistakably, as [a novel's characters] reappear after each interval, the sense is conveyed that there *has* been an interval, not in moral experience only but in the actual lapse of the seasons! The producing of this impression is indeed the central mystery of the art."[51] Cather best summarized this "central mystery"—the great writer's ability to create, through words, something that is not actually stated in the words themselves—in her often-quoted statement in "The Novel Démeublé": "Whatever is felt upon the page without being specifically named there—that, one might say, is created. It is in the inexplicable presence of the thing not named, of the overtone divined by the ear but not heard by it, the verbal mood, the emotional aura of the fact or the thing or the deed, that gives high quality to the novel or the drama, as well as to poetry itself."[52]

Both authors captured this sense by using the theater as an analogue for fiction. In "The Novel Démeublé" Cather compares artistic writing to the stripped-down stage of a Greek theater, which "leave[s] the scene bare for the play of emotions, great and little."[53] Over twenty years earlier she had cited the French theater to articulate the same principle: "Once, when the elder Dumas was asked what were the materials he required to make a play, he replied: 'A stage, four walls, two characters and one passion.'"[54] In *The Writing of Fiction* Wharton makes the same point in the same way: "The traditions of the Théâtre Français used to require that the number of objects on the stage—chairs, tables, even to a glass of water on a table—should be limited to the actual requirements of the drama." As a "guide in the labyrinth of composition," she states, this is an excellent principle.[55]

Given the deep continuity of their underlying beliefs about fiction, it is less surprising that Wharton and Cather shared so many other literary opinions. Both drew a distinct line between fiction that was written for the mass market and fiction that achieved the stature of art. Cather distinguished between "the novel as a form of amusement" and the novel "as a form of art," stating that "the novel manufactured to entertain great multitudes of people must be considered exactly like a cheap soap or a cheap perfume, or cheap furniture."[56] Wharton echoes Cather, speaking disparagingly of mass-market "railway novels" and dismissing "the machine-made 'magazine story' to which one or the other of half a dozen 'standardized' endings is automatically adjusted at the four-thousand-five-hundredth word of whatsoever has been narrated."[57] The comments of both convey their distrust of an age of mass production, of the "manufactured" and the "machine-made," while also conveying the idea that their own work is painstakingly handmade—something that not everyone will appreciate but that has the status of art.

If the handmade work is slower coming to completion, this was, they concurred, a necessary part of the artistic process. Quoting a letter from Jewett in which the elder writer stated that "The thing that teases the mind over and over for years, and at last gets itself put down rightly on paper—whether little or great, it belongs to Literature," Cather wrote that "the shapes and scenes that have 'teased' the mind for years . . . make a very much higher order of writing, and a much more costly, than the most vivid and vigorous transfer of immediate impressions."[58] Wharton argued the writer who is "drawn to a subject" should "let it grow slowly in his mind instead of hunting about for arbitrary combinations of circumstance."[59] The writer should allow ideas to incubate at their own rate: "The creative imagination can make a little [experience] go a long way, provided it remains long enough in the mind and is sufficiently brooded upon."[60] It is no wonder, then, that neither of them trusted "the short-cut in everything which is the ideal of the new generation, with the universal thirst to surpass the speed-record in every department of human activity," including writing.[61] Wharton resisted the tendency of publishers and critics to lionize writers publishing their first work but commented wryly, "Luckily the story-telling gift is a tough plant, and will survive the indiscriminate praise of the present day."[62] In virtually identical terms Cather stated, "The most talented youth won't get on very well if he tries to eat all the dinners people give him and drink all the cocktails that he doesn't have to pay for."[63] She also disliked the idea of instruction in creative writing: "Without doubt the schools develop good mechanical writers."[64] But, she added, echoing Wharton's remark about storytelling as "a tough plant," "If a born artist happens to take the [writing] course it won't do him any harm. . . . You can't kill an artist any more than you can make one."[65]

For Wharton and Cather the sense that great writing could not be hurried was strongly related to their sense of the language itself and to the history of the language. To Zona Gale, Wharton wrote that her language in one work was too simple; she had "needlessly limited [her] field of expression."[66] She urged Gale to draw on the full resources of the language: "There is that mighty inheritance of English speech . . . , that great river of innumerable tributaries, with words of every conceivable weight and colour, rhythms of every conceivable speed or slowness, inflections, modulations, twists, turns."[67] Cather expressed the same enthusiasm for English in a letter to E. K. Brown, telling him, "Good Heavens, we have language enough behind us! No other people has such a glorious heritage of language. We have the King James translation of the Bible and Shakespeare, and Chaucer."[68]

Given the similarity of their views, it is not surprising that Wharton and Cather resisted high literary modernism, seeing it as lacking "selection" and looking down on what they saw as its overemphasis on physical sensation. Wharton focused on these two elements in a 1923 letter to Bernard Berenson in which she critiqued James Joyce's *Ulysses*: "It's a turgid welter of pornography (the rudest schoolboy kind) & unformed & unimportant drivel; & until the raw ingredients of a pudding *make* a pudding, I shall never believe that the raw material of sensation & thought can make a work of art without the cook's intervening."[69] (In published essays she was more circumspect, regretting that "laborious monuments of schoolboy pornography are now mistaken for works of genius" without naming Joyce.)[70] It was not that Wharton was prudish; in fact, she argued that the nineteenth-century English novel after Austen was overly restrained by Victorian prudery.[71] But she objected to "the 'now-that-it-can-be-told school'" of the early twentieth century, seeing it as "rush[ing] to the opposite excess of dirt-for-dirt's sake, from which no real work of art has ever sprung."[72] Cather too continued to stress the principle of selection, objecting to mere "enumeration," and protested that there was more to the novel than the listing of physiological processes.[73] Wharton used Joyce as an example of writing she did not like; Cather used D. H. Lawrence, criticizing his work in terms much like Wharton's: "A novel crowded with physical sensation is no less a catalogue than one crowded with furniture. A book like *The Rainbow* ... sharply reminds one how vast a distance lies between emotion and mere sensory reactions. Characters can be almost dehumanized by a laboratory study of the behaviour of their bodily organs under sensory stimuli—can be reduced, indeed, to mere animal pulp. Can one imagine anything more terrible than the story of *Romeo and Juliet* rewritten in prose by D. H. Lawrence?"[74]

Both authors also disliked high modernism's extended depiction of mental processes and the influence of Freud, though both acknowledged the existence of what he would call the unconscious. Wharton remarked that the great novelists had long been "aware of the intensity with which . . . irrelevant trifles impinge upon the brain," but she argued against modernists' recording "every half-aware stirring of thought and sensation."[75] (Eventually, she hoped, "the new novelists will learn that it is even more necessary to see life steadily than to recount it whole.")[76] In a 1922 letter to Berenson regarding a young friend, Wharton requested that his wife, Mary, not "befuddle her with Freudianism & all its jargon. She'd take to it like a duck to—sewerage. And what she wants is to develop the *conscious*, & not grub after the sub-conscious."[77] In the same year Cather wrote to Fisher, recalling the period "before Freud had escaped into the English tongue," when "there was no sub-conscious—except that which everybody always knew there was—from personal experience";[78] she "assumed the presence and agency of the human unconscious in daily life," even as she objected to "Freudian terminology."[79] A year later she confirmed her liking for "the modern novelist," although she objected to his "chopping up his character on the Freudian psycho-analytical plan." Echoing her comment about Lawrence, she added, "Imagine what Hamlet would have been if Shakespeare had applied Freudian principles to his work."[80]

During the rise of high modernism Wharton and Cather maintained their firm footing on the *terra cognita* of realism, even if this meant writing quiet work in a splashy age. Cather experimented with toning down the central events in her 1927 novel *Death Comes for the Archbishop*: following the visual cues of Puvis de Chavannes's murals in the Pantheon depicting St. Geneviève's life, she said, she "wanted to do something in the style of legend, which is absolutely the reverse of the dramatic treatment. . . . The essence of such writing is not to hold the note, not to use an incident for all there is in it—but to touch and pass on."[81] Although Wharton once accused Cather of lacking "edge," she too spoke in praise of the quiet novel. In some contexts, she wrote, it was important for writers "to go slowly, to keep down the tone of the narrative, to be as colourless and quiet as life often is."[82]

At the same time, their work responded to the currents of their own day. In some works—as in Wharton's *Twilight Sleep* and *The Children* and Cather's *The Professor's House*—they did so directly, depicting cultural destabilization and social excesses. In others, their apparent retreat into the past—Wharton's in *The Age of Innocence* and *Old New York*, Cather's in *Death Comes for the Archbishop* and *Shadows on the Rock*—could not help but reflect light on the moment. In subtle ways as well, their approaches to fiction responded to the modern. Sharon Kim has argued persuasively that while Wharton's use of the epiphany deliberately deviated from the modernist epiphany of writers like James Joyce, she "develop[ed] this new epiphany, one that is modern without being strictly modernist," a phrase that encapsulates her postwar work.[83] Similarly Richard Millington has argued that although Cather's work may not appear to be "modernist" in its techniques, it is profoundly modernist in its response to a moment in which cultural meanings were deeply destabilized; her work is itself about the making of meaning.[84]

As critics, Wharton and Cather not only articulated many of the same fundamental principles but often spoke in the same tone. One perceived difference between the two is that Wharton writes an elaborate, sometimes acerbic prose, while Cather is simple, sincere, and straightforward. While this may be said of some of their work, it is often not the case. It may be fairly easy to guess which of the two voiced the thought that "I used to say that I had been taught only two things in my childhood: the modern languages and good manners. Now that I have lived to see both these branches of culture dispensed with, I perceive that there are worse systems of education." But it may be harder to identify which of them remarked, "We take it for granted whoever can observe, and can write the English language, can write a novel. Often the latter qualification is considered unnecessary," or which of them denounced modern poetry by writing, "So far, the effort to make a new kind of poetry, 'pure poetry,' which eschews (or renounces) the old themes as shop-worn, and confines itself to regarding the grey of a wet oyster shell against the sand of a wet beach through a drizzle of rain, has not produced anything very memorable: not even when the workmanship was good and when a beat in the measure was unexpectedly dropped here and there with what one of the poet's admirers calls a 'heart-breaking effect.' Certainly the last thing such poetry should attempt is to do any heart-breaking." The acerbic, half-humorous tone, the antimodernist attitude, and the witty turn of phrase in the second two passages are far more associated with Wharton but are, in this case, Cather's.[85] As critics, both knew the value of a pithy remark, and Cather could be just as epigrammatic, just as dismissive and critical, as Edith Wharton at her most *grande dame*. Wharton was caricatured (even in her lifetime) as a supercilious lady with a lorgnette.[86] But the girl from the prairies, later famous for her pellucid prose, began her career as a theater critic who gained a reputation as the "meat-ax young girl."[87] When it came to literary value and particularly to literature they did not care for, the lady with the lorgnette and the meat-ax young girl stood side by side on common ground.

Both faced additional challenges because of their gender; neither wanted to be limited by the conventional expectations for women's writing. As Elaine Showalter has written, Wharton and Cather "openly criticized the tradition of American women's literature, disliked the 'feminine' sensibility, and wrote often from the viewpoint of men."[88] In 1895, several years before she committed herself to a career as a novelist, Cather stated unequivocally her dislike of what was often thought of as "women's writing." In a commentary on the novels of "Ouida" (Marie Louise de la Ramée), she wrote the following:

> Sometimes I wonder why God ever trusts talent in the hands of women, they usually make such an infernal mess of it. . . . I have not much faith in women in fiction. They have a sort of sex consciousness that is abominable. They are so limited to one string and they lie so about that. They are so few, the ones who really did anything worth while; there were the great Georges, George Eliot and George Sand, and they were anything but women . . . and there was Jane Austen who certainly had more common sense than any of them and was in some respects the greatest of them all. Women are so horribly subjective and they have such scorn for the healthy commonplace. When

a woman writes a story of adventure, a stout sea tale, a manly battle yarn, anything without wine, women and love, then I will begin to hope for something great from them, not before.[89]

Such a passage begs for analysis. To begin, Cather's choice of pronoun is telling. Women are "they," not "we"; "they" are "so limited," "so horribly subjective," and they "lie." The "great Georges" are "anything but women," she says, without any attempt to elucidate what, beyond their choice of male pseudonyms, she means by this. Her admiration for Austen is hardly unusual—a very safe choice. And it is certainly worth noting that the subgenres of fiction that Cather values here ("adventure," "sea tale[s]," and "battle yarn[s]") are not gender-neutral topics, having long been the province of male authors, who had far greater opportunities to experience adventure or life at sea, not to mention war.

Similarly, although Wharton accorded the highest respect to Austen and "the great Georges," she distanced herself from women writers in general, including Ouida, Louisa May Alcott, and others. She concludes that her mother's general prohibition on her reading novels was, in the end, a good thing: it kept her from "wasting my time over ephemeral rubbish."[90] (Cather faulted Ouida for "technical errors": "Adjectives and sentimentality ran away with her, as they do with most women's pens.")[91] The restrictions on her reading, Wharton later wrote, "threw me back on the great classics, and thereby helped to give my mind a temper which my too-easy studies could not have produced."[92] Indeed the collection of books available to her in her father's library was impressive; she lists everything from the "diaries and letters" of John Evelyn, Samuel Pepys, and Madame de Sévigné through the great Victorian writers of prose and poetry, classics of French literature, and volumes of art history and philosophy.[93] Both Wharton and Cather would have agreed with George Eliot's remark in *Silly Novels by Lady Novelists*: a novel by a woman should be more than a tale in which an impossibly perfect heroine spends her life being admired by men, who "see her at a ball, and are dazzled; at a flower-show, and they are fascinated; on a riding excursion, and they are witched by her noble horsemanship; at church, and they are awed by the sweet solemnity of her demeanor."[94]

Such a heroine may "pass through many *mauvais moments*, but we have the satisfaction of knowing that her sorrows are wept into embroidered pocket-handkerchiefs, . . . and that whatever vicissitudes she may undergo, . . . she comes out of them all with a complexion more blooming and locks more redundant than ever."[95] Such novels (which a work like Wharton's *House of Mirth* inherently challenges, almost point by point) accomplish little, and far from earning women respect as writers, they make it more difficult for women writers to be taken seriously. Given this literary environment, it is unsurprising that both authors followed the grammatical norm for the day, invariably using the pronoun "he" with the noun "author" throughout their works of literary criticism.

Indeed in the nineteenth century, "masculine" or "manly" writing, as Nettels observes, was associated with "strength and vigour combined with moral qualities such as courage, candour and self-restraint."[96] Influential figures such as William Dean Howells "liked a 'candid and manly style' [and] praised the poetry of Robert Frost for its 'manly power.'"[97] A "feminine" style also included positive elements—"grace, delicacy, fastidiousness and ideality," yet "the connotations of *masculine* were rarely negative, whereas *effeminacy* was always bad and *feminine* was at best graceful and delicate, at worst perfervid and shrill."[98] To be manly (one thinks of Cather's wish that a woman might write "a manly battle yarn") was clearly superior, and the prevailing view of gender differences as rooted in biological fact was so "deeply ingrained" that reviewers "attributed qualities of one sex to the other rather than dispense with the categories."[99] Refusing to be pigeonholed as "women writers" allowed Wharton and Cather to stake their claim as serious artists, as Deborah Williams has said: "They were working against what they saw as a tradition of women's writing that itself made no claim to be 'art' and that was taken less seriously than men's writing."[100] In Showalter's terms, they had a "commitment to an art beyond the limitation of gender. For any literary subculture . . . aesthetic maturity requires a rejection of special categories, and an insistence on access to any subject, any character, and any style. Paradoxically, American women's writing could not fully mature until there were women writing against it."[101] When Wharton found her place in the Land of Letters and when Cather staked her claim in the Kingdom of Art, they insisted on access to every bit of territory that interested them.

"DRAMATIC EARLY DISLOCATIONS"

As Hermione Lee has written, "Dramatic early dislocations often make a writer,"[102] and Wharton's and Cather's deep sensitivity to place may owe a great deal to the fact that both moved at an impressionable age from a place they found comfortable, home-like, and beautiful to a place that was none of these things. For Wharton the move was from Europe back to New York City, where she had been born; for Cather it was from Virginia to Nebraska.

Although Wharton's earliest childhood memories, as she recalls them in her memoir, were in New York City, she lived in Europe—Rome, Paris, and Germany—from ages four until ten, years that gave her, she wrote, a "background of beauty and old-established order."[103] Later she would recall her childhood impressions of Rome, including "the steps of the Piazza di Spagna thronged with Thackerayan artists' models, and heaped with early violets, daffodils and tulips" and "long sunlit wanderings on the springy turf of great Roman villas."[104] Most vivid of all were hours "spent with my nurse on the Monte Pincio," where she played with childhood friends and sometimes admired the "procession of stately barouches and glossy saddle-horses which, on every fine afternoon of winter, carried the flower of Roman beauty and nobility" around the park.[105] Her time in Rome was followed by an exciting trip to Spain and then by a prolonged stay in Paris, where—budding author that she was—she began to make up stories.

The return to New York was a shock:

> I did not know how deeply I had felt the nobility and harmony of the great European cities till our steamer was docked at New York.
>
> I remember once asking an old New Yorker why he never went abroad, and his answering: "Because I can't bear to cross Murray Street." It was indeed an unsavoury experience, and the shameless squalor of the purlieus of the New York docks in the 'seventies dis-

mayed my childish eyes, stored with the glories of Rome and the architectural majesty of Paris.[106]

She put the matter more bluntly in "Life and I": "I shall never forget the bitter disappointment produced by the first impressions of my native country. I was only ten years old, but I had been fed on beauty since my babyhood, & my first thought was: 'How ugly it is!' I have never since thought otherwise."[107]

Cather's move from Virginia to Nebraska made a strikingly similar impression on her, as she recounted on more than one occasion. In a 1905 letter she echoed Wharton's terms, explaining that her first experience of Nebraska was one of "discovering ugliness.... You simply can't imagine anything so bleak and desolate as a Nebraska ranch of eighteen or nineteen years ago."[108] She elaborated further on the shock of the contrast between her old home in Virginia and her new home in Nebraska in a 1913 interview: "As we drove further and further out into the country" after leaving the train at Red Cloud, she said, "I felt a good deal as if we had come to the end of everything—it was a kind of erasure of personality.... I would not know how much of a child's life is bound up in the woods and hills and meadows around it, if I had not been jerked away from all these and thrown out into a country as bare as a piece of sheet iron."[109] Despite Cather's glowing descriptions of Nebraska in many of her works, her reaction to moving there was, if anything, more absolute and negative than Wharton's to returning to New York. For both, the transition from an older, beloved, and beautiful place to a new place experienced as a personal and aesthetic shock was an event that shaped their perception of the profound differences between places and their sensitivity to place in their work.

For both authors it was important to live in a particular kind of place—preferably a place that was itself beautiful (using the subjective but essential standard articulated by Nehamas: a place *they* found beautiful)—and one that also allowed them to live among people who acknowledged the importance of beauty and culture. Wharton's account of her return to New York moves immediately from the ugliness of New York to the fact that the family very quickly left the city: "It was summer; we were soon at Newport," where the ten-year-old Edith relished freedom, activity, and natural beauty, including "lawns and trees, a meadow full of clover and daisies, . . . a sheltered cove to bathe in," and other delights.[110] Although the family remained in the United States for several years—years that she enjoyed—she was excited to return to Europe: "So we were going back to Europe at last! During our seven years at home, through all my other interests & emotions, the longing to return had persisted; & now all the delights of society . . . were as nothing to the joy of knowing that my wish was to be fulfilled. . . . I was going to see pictures & beautiful things again, & . . . I went without a backward glance!"[111] A return to Europe meant a return to beauty.

Although she had come to appreciate, even love, many aspects of her life in Nebraska, Cather in her early twenties was equally eager to move from Nebraska to a place with a richer cultural life. While she was living in Red Cloud and in Lincoln, however, she made the best of her situation, eagerly taking in every theatrical performance, musical performance, and art exhibition she could; her reviews of these for the *Nebraska State Journal* and the Lincoln *Courier*, collected in the two-volume *The World and the Parish*, demonstrate not only the extent of her attendance but her emotional and intellectual involvement with the cultural scene. When she moved back to Red Cloud following her graduation from the university in 1895, she was nearly desperate to move to someplace bigger. Sometimes dated "Siberia" and "Province," many of her letters from this period are humorous, but they also contain a darker strain. "One of the charms of the Province," she wrote in an 1896 letter to friends from college, "is that one gets indifferent toward everything, even suicide."[112] The letter, with its amused and amusing sketch of a local dance, makes it clear that Cather now felt like an outsider, one who had a higher standard: "The men fell down every now and then and you had to help them up. Yet this was a dance of the elite and bon ton of Red Cloud."[113] In a letter written four months later, she mentions suicide again, half-wondering whether she should "just quietly take a dose of Prussic acid to rid myself of my own company."[114] The letter is both rambling and desperate, expressing not only her frustration with herself for "liking somebody or other too well" but also the sense that Red Cloud was limited, limiting, and no longer felt like home: "In the years I have been away I have kind of grown away from my family and their way of looking at things.... People have joshed them about my 'ability' until they sort of expect something unusual of me.... How can I 'do anything' here? I have'nt [*sic*] seen enough of the world or anything else."[115] Near the end she states that she is now "get[ting] the happiest letters" from one of her former professors at the university; "he is so gay now that he is in a hill county where people care about [the pianist] Paderewski and [the poet Algernon] Swinburne. I think he has come into his kingdom."[116]

Cather too was waiting to "come into [the] kingdom" of the arts, a place where people cared about such things, and when she was offered a job in Pittsburgh, she jumped at it; she was thrilled to be leaving "Province" at last. Although Pittsburgh did not offer her the kind of beauty that France and Italy provided for Wharton—Cather was brutally honest about the dirt of the city, home of many steel mills long before air pollution controls came into being—she was nevertheless in a city that, thanks to the wealth generated by those steel mills, offered a relatively rich cultural life. Pittsburgh boasted not only a Carnegie Library, art museum, and music hall but also a symphony orchestra, theaters, and plays; Cather soon became the arts critic for the *Pittsburgh Leader*.[117]

The confluence of place, beauty, and survival itself emerges in some of the earliest works of both authors. "Mrs. Manstey's View" (1891), Wharton's first published story, tells the tale of a widow who has fallen on hard economic times. Living alone in a boarding house in New York, her main pleasure in life is the view from her window. Wharton describes a view that others might not find appealing: the yards onto which she looks are "stony wastes, with grass in the cracks of the pavement," and many are "in a state of chronic untidiness," but Mrs. Manstey manages to focus on its pleasanter aspects.[118] These include the trees and other plants that flourish outside her window: "In the very next enclosure did not a magnolia open its hard white flowers against the watery blue of April? And was there not ... a fence foamed over every May by lilac waves of wisteria?"[119] In the evenings she admires "the distant brownstone spire ... in the fluid yellow of the west," which allows her "to lose herself in vague memories of a trip to Europe, made years ago."[120] The view becomes so central to her life that when Mrs. Black, the owner of a neighboring boarding house, begins to build an addition that will block her view, Mrs. Manstey makes several attempts to prevent its construction. She complains to her landlady, and when nothing comes of that, she overcomes years of reclusiveness to confront Mrs. Black. (Wharton comments on the difference in human sensibilities when Mrs. Black fails to comprehend Mrs. Manstey's concerns about beauty, assuming that Mrs. Manstey must be mentally unstable.) When this effort proves unsuccessful, the meek Mrs. Manstey ventures out after midnight and attempts to burn the addition down. Despite the small scale of the fire, she believes she has succeeded. But in the process of attempting to save her view—to protect her access to the beautiful— she has contracted a fatal case of pneumonia. She dies looking out her window, smiling as the morning light illuminates the church spire and the magnolia: "The view at least was there."[121] The story's final sentence, however, tells otherwise: "That day the building of the extension was resumed."[122] Economic expansion triumphs over one woman's need for the beautiful, without which she cannot live.

Wharton's concern with the importance of beauty, and her sense of the lack of it in the United States, is clear in other early writings as well. While "Mrs. Manstey's View" addresses the topic obliquely, her story "Friends" (1900) approaches the topic of civic aesthetics more directly, opening with the sentence, "Sailport is an ugly town."[123] Published in the magazine *Youth's Companion*, the story encourages younger readers to consider the topic. Wharton concedes that one "favored quarter" of the town makes "certain concessions to the eye" and that "the inhabitants of Sailport would doubtless be surprised to hear their 'city'" called ugly.[124] But she states unequivocally that the town epitomizes "the harsh progressiveness of a New England town."[125] In Sailport "aesthetics" are governed by profitability: most in the town "are probably of the opinion that handsome is as handsome does; and according to the national interpretation of this adage, Sailport is doing very handsomely, increasing in public and civic wealth, and multiplying with astonishing rapidity its telephone poles and electric wires, its car tracks and factory chimneys."[126]

The issue of aesthetics was important enough to Wharton that in spite of her dislike for moralizing and for public speaking, she sometimes addressed the matter directly. In an 1897 speech in Newport, Wharton emphasized the need for people to inhabit beautiful spaces. As the co-author of the recently published *The Decoration of Houses*, Wharton drew on some of the principles she articulated in that work to emphasize the importance of decoration in Newport's schoolrooms.[127] She stressed that "put[ting] some beauty into the bare rooms of Newport is not only a good thing but a necessary thing, and necessary not only on artistic grounds but on moral grounds as well. Our object ... is not to turn all the school children into painters and sculptors or to teach them history, but to surround them with such representations of beauty as in older civilizations the streets, the monuments and galleries of almost every city provide."[128] Since a newer country like the United States lacks these things, "we must teach our children to care for beauty before great monuments and noble buildings arise."[129] Far from being gratuitous, beauty had moral and practical value; children should be taught "to love and reverence" beauty; "thrift, order, refinement, ambition and the countless daily pleasures of the observant eye" are also "kept alive by the miraculous influence of beauty."[130]

Cather's early stories also portray a deep human need for beauty and the difficulty of surviving in a world that neither provides beauty nor honors it as a legitimate concern. Well-known stories like "A Wagner Matinée" and "The Sculptor's Funeral" portray life on the prairies not in the glorious terms that would make her famous in *O Pioneers!* and *My Ántonia* but with a grimness that recalls Nebraska as nine-year-old Willa first perceived it. "A Wagner Matinée" tells the story of a New England woman with great musical talent who has spent most of her adult life farming in Nebraska with her husband. When she finally returns east to Boston on a short visit, her nephew takes her to a Wagner concert. When it concludes, leaving the stage as "empty as a winter cornfield," Aunt Georgiana "burst into tears and sobbed pleadingly. 'I don't want to go, Clark, I don't want to go!' ... I understood. For her, just outside the concert hall, lay the black pond with the cattle-tracked bluffs; the tall, unpainted house, with weather-curled boards, naked as a tower;

the crook-backed ash seedlings where the dishcloths hung to dry; the gaunt, moulting turkeys picking up refuse about the kitchen door."[131] The painfully ugly, culturally starved farm is a place Aunt Georgiana can hardly bear to return to.

"The Sculptor's Funeral" portrays a scene that is, if possible, even grimmer. In this 1905 story, Cather portrays the return of the body of Harvey Merrick, a sculptor of international renown, to his hometown in Sand City, Kansas. The house of Merrick's family, to which the coffin is brought, bears a strong resemblance to Aunt Georgiana's: "a naked, weather-beaten frame house.... The front yard was an icy swamp, and a couple of warped planks, extending from the sidewalk to the door, made a sort of rickety footbridge. The gate hung on one hinge."[132] There are no "moulting turkeys" by the kitchen door, but the scene is no less grim, and the human scene is even bleaker than that portrayed in "A Wagner Matinée," in which Aunt Georgiana somehow kept a strand of her musical life alive. Instead, Merrick's family and the townspeople are wholly lacking in any appreciation of what Merrick has accomplished. Even as they sit up with the coffin, they express no comprehension of what he has done; rather, they mock him for his impracticality on the farm, telling stories about how he was once duped into buying eighteen-year-old mules as if they were only eight or how he allowed a cow to die (or so it is claimed) because he was distracted by a beautiful sunset. Phelps, the banker, expresses the common opinion in stating, "Where the old man made his mistake was in sending the boy East to school."[133] Steavens, the young eastern artist who has accompanied Merrick's coffin back from Boston, feels he must have come to the wrong place: surely the artist he admired could not have come from a place so inimical to the arts; he eventually realizes that not only did Merrick, "whose mind was... an exhaustless gallery of beautiful impressions," come from "this raw, biting ugliness," but that part of his achievement was overcoming that ugliness.[134] It is also clear that Merrick could never have become a sculptor had he stayed in Sand City.

One of the stories Cather published while still in college is even blunter about the costs of cultural deprivation. "Peter" tells the story of an immigrant who finds his life in Nebraska so harsh, and who misses the cultural life of his native Prague so badly, that he breaks his beloved violin rather than allowing his son to sell it and then shoots himself—a story based on the suicide of Cather's Bohemian neighbor Francis Sadilek, who would also serve as the model for Mr. Shimerda in *My Ántonia*.[135] When Cather wrote that "geography is a terribly fatal thing sometimes," she meant it quite literally. Like Wharton, she fled eastward, traveling from a place that she found culturally starved to one that offered sustenance.

FINDING THEIR PLACE IN LITERATURE

Wharton's and Cather's sensitivity to place may have had its roots in their early experiences. Both were saturated not only in the nineteenth-century novel but also in travel writing, a genre many prominent fiction writers also took up. James wrote *Italian Hours* and *A Little Tour in France*; Howells set his novel *Indian Summer* in Italy, writing the travel books *Venetian Life* and *Italian Journeys*. The success of novels like James's *The Portrait of a Lady* and Howells's *Indian Summer* may have rested partly on the authors' ability to write their characters into realistic landscapes. If *The Portrait of a Lady* portrays Isabel Archer, it also portrays the places she visits and lives, including England, Rome, and Florence; *Indian Summer* describes its Florentine setting, allowing readers to recognize places they had traveled. In an age before the inexpensive reproduction of artwork and photographs and long before the plethora of online images, the ability to write evocative descriptions of people, places, landscapes, and cityscapes was both admired and marketable. Cather helped to pay for her first trip to Europe in 1902 with the travel columns she wrote for the *Nebraska State Journal*;[136] Wharton's travel books include *Italian Villas and Their Gardens* (1904), *Italian Backgrounds* (1905), *A Motor-Flight through France* (1909), and *In Morocco* (1920).

Wharton's and Cather's love of place occasionally spilled over into their letters, sometimes to the point of making them feel self-conscious about their eloquence. Near the end of a long, beautifully descriptive letter to her former governess, Anna Bahlmann, the young Mrs. Wharton wrote semi-apologetically from Italy, "I hope you won't think that this letter is too much of a 'describe'—I know you like to see pretty places, with your mind's eye if no other way is practicable—& so I hope you may enjoy this glimpse of it with me."[137] Her self-consciousness here leads directly to a statement of one of the central reasons behind writing the picturesque: "to see pretty places" in one's "mind's eye." Cather also wrote in enthusiastic detail about place in some letters. During a long stay in 1933 in Jaffrey, New Hampshire, one of the places to which she routinely escaped in order to write, she wrote a letter to Alfred and Blanche Knopf. After addressing business matters, she turned to a description of the landscape: "The weather is glorious. . . . Wild clouds and very low ones, as in France; the mountain dark purple all day yesterday, the top of it powdered with snow, and the sky rolling masses of silver and purple and black from morning until night."[138] Like Wharton apologizing for her "'describe,'" Cather self-consciously adds, "(This sounds as if I were trying to work off some 'writing' on you.)" But like Wharton, she immediately adds a justification: "(but since you know the mountain, there's some point in mentioning it's [sic] present complexion.)"[139] Cather's rationale is the opposite of Wharton's: to evoke a place the Knopfs are familiar with, rather than to create an image of one they had not seen. But in both cases, it is clear that accurate and beautiful descriptions of specific places matter to these authors; and in both, it is hard to imagine the recipients being anything other than happy to receive these evocative letters.

For Wharton and Cather, literary experience was an integral part of the experience of place. What Irene Goldman-Price has said of Wharton could equally be said of Cather: "Reading and study educated her perceptions; writing about her journeys exercised her precision and pleasure in language."[140] In a letter the eighteen-year-old Edith wrote to Bahlmann, she bubbles over with excitement about an upcoming trip to Italy. Her anticipation is deeply literary, as she ponders which books to take "and how hard it will be to leave the rest—Milton, Shelley, and Browning must certainly go—and Wordsworth of course."[141] For her, imagining a place also means imagining works set there: "Think of reading Shelley's 'Evening' at Pisa where it was written—think of seeing the Campo Santo, and the pine woods where Byron rode near Ravenna."[142] Literary experiences would remain at the heart of many of her travels. Recalling a cruise she had taken years earlier, Wharton wrote that the *Odyssey* "was our constant companion in our wanderings through the Aegean."[143] In a 1925 letter she describes a trip to Spain's Val d'Aran, "which, in its singular spring purity, all narcissus & gentian & golden poplars & flowering fruit-trees & cold rushing rivulets, was so like Keats's Eve of St. Mark that my heart trembled."[144]

Cather also experienced Europe through the lens of her reading. This phenomenon was most intense during her 1902 visit to Shropshire, where she matched Edith Jones's excitement about "reading Shelley's 'Evening' at Pisa where it was written." From England she wrote Dorothy Canfield about the continuity between Housman's poems in *A Shropshire Lad* and the place itself, quoting his poems ecstatically and explaining how accurately the poetry depicts what she was finding: "We sat for two sunsets on the very spot where he must have."[145] The fact that the geographic reality corresponded to Housman's poetry gave it additional validity and intensity: "Somehow it makes it all the greater to have it all true."[146] She expressed the same concept during her 1908 trip to Italy, writing that Naples was "the place to read" Tacitus and Suetonius, "for details cannot mean much unless you are in the place where it [i.e., Roman history] has a physical and concrete reality."[147] Her experience of literature continued to shape her vision of place. In 1930 she sent her nieces a postcard showing the gargoyles of Notre Dame Cathedral; in her message, she alludes to Victor Hugo's *Notre-Dame de Paris*: "I am sure all the figures were Quasimodo's playfellows, and that he had special friends among them."[148] For both authors the experiences of literature and place were profoundly complementary, even recursive: their reading made their experience of place more meaningful, and their experience of place deepened their sense of their reading.

This dynamic weaves itself into their novels. Lily Bart, on board the yacht *Sabrina* in *The House of Mirth*, "had listened to Ned Silverton reading Theocritus by moonlight, as the yacht rounded the Sicilian promontories, with a thrill."[149] In *The Professor's House* Tom Outland reads Virgil's *Aeneid* on the Blue Mesa. "When I look into the *Aeneid* now," he tells Professor St. Peter, "I can always see two pictures: the one on the page, and another behind that: blue and purple rocks and yellow-green piñons with flat tops."[150] In some cases Wharton and Cather transposed specific experiences of place into their fiction. Wharton's travels in France near the front with Germany during World War I, captured in letters she wrote, wove themselves into her war-related story "Coming Home"; Cather's description of a moonlit Nebraska landscape viewed from a windmill, recounted in an 1893 letter, reappears in Claude Wheeler's experience in *One of Ours*.[151] For both, place was so significant that it sometimes functioned as a character. While working on *O Pioneers!*, Cather wrote Zoë Akins: "In this new one the country itself is frankly the hero—or the heroine."[152] Wharton had used identical language in a letter after the publication of her first novel, *The Valley of Decision*. The novel is set in Italy, and Wharton expressed her pleasure with one reviewer's remark "that Italy is my hero—or heroine, if you prefer."[153]

The integral importance of place to both authors is also demonstrated by their first great successes as novelists, which were not their first novels but their second—the novel that each set in a place she knew intimately. In "My First Novels (There Were Two)," Cather acknowledged that her first novel had been a "studio piece," shaped by an abstract sense that a novel should be a drawing-room fiction set in a major city.[154] Wharton could have written an essay with the same title, as her first novel could also be called a studio piece. *The Valley of Decision*, set in eighteenth-century Italy, was informed by the budding novelist's admiration of the historical novel and was accordingly shaped by a host of historical works.[155] Like *Alexander's Bridge*, it is a good novel that garnered some positive reviews, but it was hardly the success that *The House of Mirth* would be. Only in their second novels did they "hit the home pasture," in Cather's phrase.[156] Wharton's *The House of Mirth* and Cather's *O Pioneers!* owe much of their vivid reality to the fact that their authors finally took the leap of choosing a setting that was profoundly familiar to them, creating works in which character, plot, and place are integrally intertwined. And for both, the choice of a place that was less conventional but more congenial was influenced by older writers. In 1902 James had urged Wharton to seize upon "the American Subject ... the immediate, the real, ... the yours, the novelist's that it waits for," famously telling her to "Do New York!"[157] Six years later Jewett urged Cather to "be surer of your backgrounds,—you have your Nebraska life" to draw on.[158] In their second novels both found the "American Subject" that had been "wait[ing] for" them, tethering themselves to places they knew from "the ten thousand unconscious experiences which come from living" there: turn-of-the-century New York for Wharton's *House of Mirth* and the Nebraska of her adolescence for Cather's *O Pioneers!*[159]

THE "INDIVIDUAL MAP"

In *Lucy Gayheart* Cather's title character escapes from the small Nebraska town of Haverford to explore a musical career in Chicago. As she lives in the city, she comes to have a very distinct sense not so much of the city as a whole but of *her* Chicago: "Lucy carried in her mind a very individual map of Chicago: a blur of smoke and wind and noise, with flashes of blue water, and certain clear outlines rising from the confusion; a high building on Michigan Avenue where Sebastian had his studio—the stretch of park where he sometimes walked in the afternoon—the Cathedral door out of which she had seen him come one morning—the concert hall where she first heard him sing. The city of feeling rose out of the city of fact like a definite composition."[160] Lucy's map of Chicago is indeed very individual; it is not the average tourist's map, or the resident's map, or even the map that might be drawn by Thea Kronborg, Cather's other musical heroine who spends time in the city. Instead it is a map of the city in which Lucy has come to love Clement Sebastian; everything on her mental map is associated with him. For Lucy the city is so imbued with his presence that she "often came upon spots which gave her a sudden lift of the heart, made her feel glad before she knew why."[161]

Wharton also conveys the idea of the individual map in many works but perhaps most memorably near the end of *The Age of Innocence*, a work that resonates with *Lucy Gayheart*. For Newland Archer, the city of Paris is as imbued with the presence of Ellen Olenska, the woman he has loved, as Lucy's Chicago is with Clement Sebastian. His individual map of the city emerges as he strolls one afternoon: "Archer knew that Madame Olenska lived in a square near one of the avenues radiating from the Invalides; and he had pictured the quarter as quiet and almost obscure, forgetting the central splendor that lit it up. Now, by some queer process of association, that golden light became for him the pervading illumination in which she lived. For nearly thirty years, her life . . . had been spent in this rich atmosphere."[162] Through his semi-conscious (therefore "queer") "process of association," so like the "sudden lift of the heart" that Lucy experiences "without even knowing why," Newland associates Paris, and particularly this part of Paris, with Ellen Olenska; the entire quarter—centered as it is on the gilded Dôme des Invalides—becomes "filled with golden light" for him. His individual map of Paris is created by her presence there. The strong parallel between these two passages points to even stronger parallels between *Lucy Gayheart* and *The Age of Innocence* and, again, to the underlying sensibility the authors shared. Both novels are chronicles about deeply romantic, unfulfilled love: Newland Archer's for Ellen Olenska, Lucy Gayheart's for Clement Sebastian—and Harry Gordon's for Lucy Gayheart herself. The end of Cather's novel suggests another individual map: years after Lucy's death Harry feels her presence in the town of Haverford, in her room in the Gayheart house, and in the mere impression she had made, as a girl, in the just-poured concrete sidewalk outside her house.

Despite the common perception that small towns and big cities are very different, Cather's description of the emotional dynamics of the small town of Haverford captures the essence of Archer's old New York, where, as Wharton explains, not only does "everyone" know everyone else, but on any given evening, they know exactly where everyone else is.[163] In Haverford, Cather writes, "lives roll along so close to one another; loves and hates beat about, their wings almost touching. On the sidewalks along which everybody comes and goes, you must . . . at some time pass within a few inches of the man who cheated and betrayed you, or the woman you desire more than anything else in the world. Her skirt brushes against you. You say good-morning, and go on. It is a close shave."[164] If New York City is larger geographically than Haverford, the circle in which Newland Archer moves is small.

In the farewell dinner for Ellen, Archer suddenly realizes that "all the harmless-looking people" gathered around the dinner table are "a band of dumb conspirators" and "that to all of them he and Madame Olenska were lovers."[165] Knowing that Ellen is leaving for Europe and that he may not see her again for years, he attempts to say farewell to her privately but is prevented from having a single moment alone with her by the subtle but conscious efforts of others. Like Harry, he experiences simultaneous tantalizing proximity and agonizing distance from "the woman [he] desire[s] more than anything in the world." It is a "close shave" for Lucy and Harry; it is one for Newland Archer and Ellen Olenska as well.

In other ways as well Cather's small towns and Wharton's cities often resemble each other. The fact that both authors moved at an impressionable age also contributed to their awareness of different social structures and social hierarchies; while it is Wharton who is usually thought of as the chronicler of social hierarchies, Cather's work is equally sensitive to such matters. Both illustrated the social conflict that occurred when westerners moved east and, in some cases, when those from the eastern seaboard moved west; both had a certain sympathy for a social aristocracy that felt lost or undervalued in a newer, brisker society. If Wharton's Lily Bart and Ralph Marvell feel swept aside by crassly moneyed invaders from the West, so too, in Cather's "Old Mrs. Harris," the southerner Victoria Templeton never quite adjusts to living in a "snappy little Western democracy" where her social accomplishments are unappreciated.[166] The same struggle is portrayed in the margins of *A Lost Lady*, in which Niel Herbert's mother, and Niel himself, never feel sufficiently recognized in a new western town. If there are individual maps, there are social maps as well. Not only New York and Paris but every town and village has its social hierarchy and its struggle for dominance.

Throughout their works and in settings far too numerous to consider in a single study, Wharton and Cather created individual maps of a range of places; place itself matters, as Warf and Arias state, "not for the simplistic and overly used reason that everything happens in space, but because *where* things happen is critical to knowing *how* and *why* they happen."[167] Wharton and Cather write so beautifully of a range of places that they evoke a sense of those places—whether of Paris, Chicago, New York, or Cather's many fictional variants of Red Cloud—for those who have been there, while their carefully crafted descriptions also create a sense of these places for those who have not. Central to this accomplishment is their ability to create a strong sense of a particular individual's personal relationship to a place, helping us understand the integral relationship between character and location. Yet, as we will see, their use of place extends beyond geographic location or individual identity, invoking complex, and frequently competing, cultural ideals as well.

PART 2

The Place of Culture

3

NEW YORK CITY

Beauty, Business, and Hothouse Flowers

> Paul took a carriage and drove up Fifth Avenue toward the Park. . . . Here and there on the corners whole flower gardens [were] blooming behind glass windows, against which the snow flakes stuck and melted; violets, roses, carnations, lilies of the valley—somehow vastly more lovely and alluring that they blossomed thus unnaturally in the snow. The Park itself was a wonderful stage winter-piece.
>
> WILLA CATHER, "Paul's Case"

> They turned into Madison Avenue and began to stroll northward. . . . "Oh, dear, I'm so hot and thirsty—and what a hideous place New York is!" [Lily] looked despairingly up and down the dreary thoroughfare. "Other cities put on their best clothes in summer, but New York seems to sit in its shirt-sleeves."
>
> EDITH WHARTON, *The House of Mirth*

MAPPING WHARTON AND CATHER IN NEW YORK CITY

Wharton is associated with New York for familiar reasons: Edith Newbold Jones was born there, at 14 West Twenty-Third Street, in January 1862, and lived there until age four and again from age ten until she was eighteen; following her father's death in 1882, she lived with her mother first at 7 Washington Square North and then at 28 West Twenty-Fifth Street.[1] She was married in Trinity Chapel in 1885 to Edward (Teddy) Wharton, and the two of them lived at 882–884 Park Avenue from 1896 to about 1905.[2] The city serves as the most common setting in her fiction, not only in her best-known works, including *The House of Mirth*, *The Custom of the Country*, and *The Age of Innocence*, but throughout her career, from her earliest stories, including "Mrs. Manstey's View" and "Bunner Sisters," to her last novel: although the main setting of her unfinished work, *The Buccaneers*, is England, it also includes crucial scenes in the New York of her youth.

While Cather is less often thought of as a New York author, a list of her residences in the city and her use of New York in her fiction emphasize the proximity of her world to Wharton's (see fig. 8). During a 1906 visit she stayed at the Hotel Griffou, not far from Washington Square; her first apartment in the city was on Washington Square South. From 1908 until 1912 she lived at 82 Washington Place West and then moved to 5 Bank Street in Greenwich Village, where she remained until 1927. Between 1927 and 1932 she lived in the Grosvenor Hotel on Fifth Avenue, near Washington Square; when, in 1932, she finally relocated to an apartment, she moved east and north, living until her death in 1947 at 570 Park Avenue, only sixteen blocks from Wharton's former residence at 882–884 Park Ave. The authors shared other New York places, including memberships in the New York Society Library. Wharton's great-grandfather, Peter Schermerhorn, had been a trustee of the library in the early 1800s,[3] and her father was a shareholder; in all likelihood Wharton read books from the Society Library as a child.[4] Wharton's beloved sister-in-law Mary ("Minnie") Cadwalader Jones and niece Beatrix Ferrand were also members of the library—as was Cather, who joined the library shortly after her move to the Grosvenor Hotel in 1927, when the library was located nearby at 109 University Place, and later at her Park Avenue address, when the library had relocated uptown.[5] In one of the startling illustrations of the proximity of Wharton's and Cather's lives, Minnie or Beatrix purchased a copy of the 1932 edition of Cather's *April Twilights* and read it carefully, as marginalia attest; when Minnie died, Beatrix left the copy to the Society Library. New York City was central to Cather, arguably "the place *most* central to the life Cather chose for herself," its ferment essential to her growth as an artist.[6] As John J. Murphy has written, "the energy and inventiveness of New York breathes through most of her work."[7] The city appears

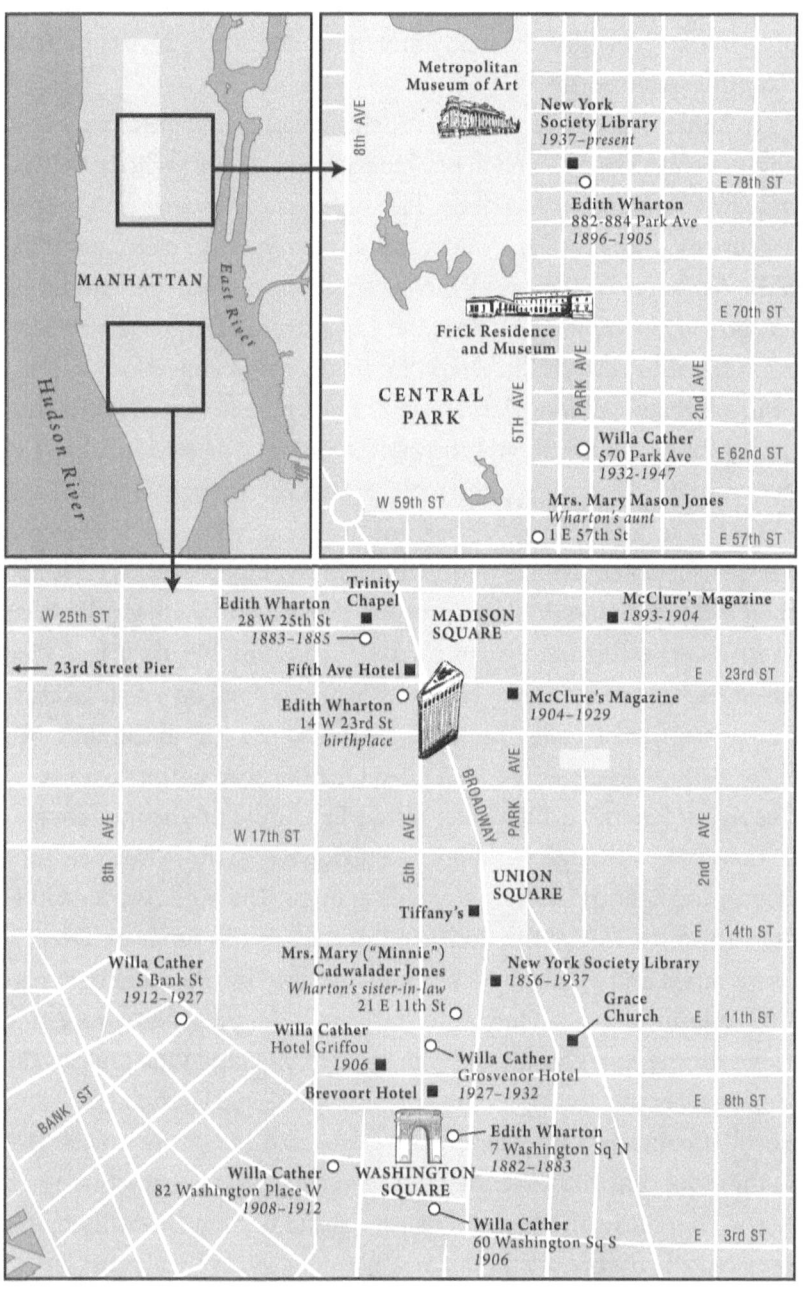

8. New York City in the lives of Edith Wharton and Willa Cather.

in a wide range of her fiction, including *My Mortal Enemy*, *The Song of the Lark*, "Neighbor Rosicky," and, most notably, "Paul's Case" and "Coming, Aphrodite!"

To some degree Manhattan is such a small geographic space that comparisons could be drawn between any two authors who have lived in New York or set works there. Part of the city's fascination for literary history is exactly this quality, as many works make clear, including E. B. White's 1949 essay *Here Is New York*, Susan Edmiston and Linda Cirino's 1976 *Literary New York*, the pages devoted to the city in Malcolm Bradbury's 1996 *The Atlas of Literature*, and collections such as Philip Lopate's *Writing New York: A Literary Anthology* (1998), and Cyrus Patell and Bryan Waterman's *Cambridge Companion to the Literature of New York City* (2010). Nevertheless, placing Wharton's and Cather's lives and fictions on the same map emphasizes the deeper connections between them. Twenty-Third Street runs like an axis through their lives and works. Wharton, as previously mentioned, was born on West Twenty-Third Street; in Cather's 1905 story "Paul's Case," Paul disembarks from the New Jersey ferry at the dock on West Twenty-Third Street, as do Nellie Birdseye and her Aunt Lydia in Cather's 1926 novella *My Mortal Enemy*—and Ellen Olenska in Wharton's 1920 novel *The Age of Innocence*. Ellen later settles in a house on the western end of the street, although her family persuade her to move because they do not consider the area fashionable enough. The Fifth Avenue Hotel appears in works by both authors. Located at the corner of Twenty-Third Street and Madison Square and managed by the father of Wharton's one-time fiancé Harry Stevens, the hotel provided interesting views for the Jones family as Edith was growing up.[8] One tableau she glimpsed became the basis of her plot in *New Year's Day*, one of the four novellas comprising her 1924 work *Old New York*. In the novella, set in the 1870s, the Fifth Avenue Hotel is the location of a tryst between Lizzie Hazeldean and Henry Prest—a scandalous relationship that is revealed when a fire breaks out and everyone in the hotel must scurry out. At the time, the narrator tells us, the hotel was "no longer fashionable. . . . It was frequented by 'politicians' and 'Westerners.'"[9] The hotel is indeed used by the westerners Nellie Birdseye and Aunt Myra in Cather's *My Mortal Enemy*—although in this work it appears more as the gateway to a lovely city than as a place for assignations. At 44–60 East Twenty-Third Street stood the offices of *McClure's Magazine*, which brought Cather to New York in 1906, when she assumed an editorship under S. S. McClure, one of the leading journalists of the day.

Washington Square also demonstrates the depth of Wharton-Cather intersections in New York. As noted, Wharton lived at 7 Washington Square North from the winter of 1882 through at least the end of 1883, while Cather's first apartment in New York, in 1906, was at 60 Washington Square South.[10] As Woodress writes, "On the north side of Washington Square the long row of mellow brick houses gave the area an aristocratic look."[11] These classical townhouses, built in the 1830s as homes for affluent New Yorkers, were among the most fashionable residences of their time.[12] From the perspective of Edith Wharton's youth on West Twenty-Third Street, "aristocracy" was "to the south"[13]—around Washington Square. This is, of course, the setting of Henry James's novella *Washington Square*, and the townhouses on the square figure repeatedly in Wharton's fiction as the habitations of Old New Yorkers. In *The Age of Innocence*, set in the 1870s, the Dagonets, one of the families acknowledged even by Old New Yorkers as truly aristocratic—descended from European aristocracy—are thought of as "the Dagonets of Washington Square"; other "venerable" habitations hovered nearby "in University Place and lower Fifth Avenue."[14]

The Dagonets also appear in *The Custom of the Country*, Wharton's 1913 chronicle of the social climber Undine Spragg. In that novel the Dagonets and their Marvell relatives remain ensconced in a Washington Square townhouse. But in the new century—Wharton's notes establish that the main action begins in 1900—their location, while continuing to convey the family's aristocracy, also suggests their increasing obsolescence.[15] Cather's story "Coming, Aphrodite!" takes Washington Square in the same period for its setting. Although Washington Square had long had a population "more diverse than its early image as a bastion of wealth and propriety might suggest,"[16] juxtaposing Cather's story with Wharton's novel indicates that by the early 1900s the era of Washington Square as the enclave of the social elite was over: Cather's impecunious artist Don Hedger rents an apartment on Washington Square South, just across the square from Wharton's Dagonets. If one stands in Washington Square Park today, it is relatively easy to imagine the shades of Wharton, Cather, and their characters coming and going.

Paired with *The House of Mirth*, "Coming, Aphrodite!" also provides an excellent example of the complementarity of Wharton's and Cather's works in the context of New York City. As "a foundling [who] had grown up in a school for homeless boys," Hedger is a deeply asocial adult: "He belonged to no clubs, visited no houses, had no studio friends, and he ate his dinner alone . . . even on Christmas and New Year's."[17] The narrator relates that Don "got on well enough with janitresses and wash-women. . . . He had friends among the silk-skirt factory girls."[18] But he is suspicious of women of higher social classes:

> He felt an unreasoning antipathy toward the well-dressed women he saw coming out of big shops, or driving in the Park. If, on his way to the Art Museum, he noticed a pretty girl standing on the steps of one of the houses on upper Fifth Avenue, he frowned at her and went by with his shoulders hunched up as if he were cold. He had never known such girls . . . ; but he believed them all to be artificial and, in an aesthetic sense, perverted. He saw them enslaved by desire of merchandise and manufactured articles, effective only in making life complicated and insincere and in embroidering it with ugly and meaningless trivialities.[19]

Don Hedger is looking askance at someone very much like Wharton's Lily Bart. Don and Lily inhabit not only the same place but the same time frame: Cather's story is set in the very early 1900s, like *The House of Mirth*. Moreover, the two works exist on the same continuum of thought. Although Wharton's Lily is more sympathetic (and Don's perspective is exaggeratedly critical), Lily could easily be seen in the terms Don Hedger uses. She herself confesses to something very like being "enslaved by desire of merchandise and manufactured articles" when she confesses to Lawrence Selden that she is "horribly poor—and very expensive. I must have a great deal of money" or when she admits that she can "always understand how people can spend much more money—never how they can spend any less!"[20] In certain moods she might agree with Don's charge that the upper-class life to which she aspires is made up of "complicated and insincere" behaviors and "meaningless trivialities"; in one scene she looks down a dinner table lined by those she calls her friends and thinks, "What a long stretch of vacuity! How dreary and trivial these people were!"[21]

If Wharton's Lily stands on the edges of Cather's "Coming, Aphrodite!," in *The House of Mirth* Lily has at least one moment in which she seems to find herself in Cather's New York—a city not of shopping and leisurely lunches but of women who are professionals or serious amateurs pursuing their own goals. Near the novel's end Lily finds herself in a restaurant: "The room was full of women and girls, all too much engaged in the rapid absorption of tea and pie to remark her entrance. . . . The sallow preoccupied women, with their bags and note-books and rolls of music, were all engrossed in their own affairs, and even those who sat by themselves were busy running over proof-sheets or devouring magazines between their hurried gulps of tea. Lily alone was stranded in a great waste of disoccupation."[22] The women may be "sallow" (at least by Lily's high standard of beauty), but they are all remarkably "engrossed in their own affairs." The woman studying music might be Cather's Thea Kronborg; the one reading page-proofs could be Cather herself, who would arrive in New York to take up her editing position at *McClure's* only a year after *The House of Mirth* was published. In a city intent on getting things done, only Lily is "stranded in a great waste of disoccupation."

Other well-known features of New York appear in works by both authors. Central Park is the place where Lily Bart meets Gus Trenor in Wharton's *The House of Mirth*; in *The Custom of the Country* it is there that Undine Spragg engages herself to a spurious Austrian count and later, deeply veiled to avoid recognition, meets Elmer Moffatt to implore him not to reveal the fact that they were once married. In Cather's "Paul's Case" the title character sees Central Park in January as "a wonderful stage winter-piece"; Edith Beers flirts with Fred Ottenburg there in *The Song of the Lark*, and Nellie Birdseye enjoys "a long, delightful afternoon" there in *My Mortal Enemy*.[23] Nellie also attends a

Christmas service at Grace Church, where the infant Edith Jones was baptized and where the adult Edith Wharton set the scene of the wedding of Newland Archer and May Welland in *The Age of Innocence*.[24] Of course Fifth Avenue with, in that era, the mansions of the *nouveaux riches* appears in works by both. In *The House of Mirth* one character remarks that the mansions "awe the Western sight-seer"; in *My Mortal Enemy*, Myra Henshawe's drive down Fifth Avenue, "sniffing the purple air," reveals her "insane" material aspirations to Nellie Birdseye.[25]

As with their sailing only a few months apart on the *Berengaria*, Wharton and Cather just missed each other in New York. Cather moved to New York City in April or May 1906—a year during which Wharton moved constantly, leaving New York for England and France in March and then passing most of the rest of the year at The Mount.[26] The following year, 1907, was the year in which Wharton left not only New York but also, in effect, the United States.[27] She began spending at least half the year abroad, renting the apartment of George Vanderbilt at 58 rue de Varenne in Paris in 1907; in 1910 she took a long lease on an apartment a few doors away, at 53 rue de Varenne. Although Cather, like Wharton, traveled frequently and for extended periods, New York remained her home address from 1906 until her death in 1947. Wharton made only brief returns to New York after 1906; both geographically and spiritually France became her permanent home.

This chapter's epigraphs suggest the nearly diametrically opposed views of the city of Cather's Paul and Wharton's Lily: Paul finds it "lovely and alluring," while Lily finds it "dreary." Like their characters, the authors did not always see New York in the same terms. For Wharton it was the setting of some of her earliest memories; she happily recounted walks she used to take with her father and in particular being kissed under the veil of a favorite bonnet during one of those walks.[28] But much of the time, as we previously saw, she found the city terribly ugly, a place she was happy to leave behind in order to return to the beauty and the richer cultural life of Europe. To her New York epitomized not the acme but the poverty of American culture. The highest praise she could bestow on one New York City art exhibit, in 1893, was that it was so well done that it was "more like Paris than N.Y. in [its] dignity & elegance of arrangement, & the collection was far finer than any I ever saw in this country."[29] At least temporarily it gave her hope for her native country: "When one is ready to 'despair of the republic' such a sight is a consolation."[30]

But this relatively optimistic view of New York culture was the exception to the rule. Visiting the city in 1914, Wharton described it as possessing "a newly developed self-consciousness"—not a positive development, as "the one distinction of ugly, patchy, scrappy New York was that it didn't get off from itself & measure and generalize: it had that in common with Paris & London. But now it hasn't any longer."[31] When she had visited New York four years earlier, she had written of the "infernal heat" of the city and described herself "looking over the brick & iron landscape of this appalling city" from her window, "from which it looks exactly like a Mercator's projection of hell—with the river of pitch, & the iron bridges, & the 'elevated' marking off the bolgie, & Blackwell's Island opposite for the City of Dis!"[32] Seeing New York as hell was extreme even for Wharton, yet her view of New York as not only "ugly, patchy, [and] scrappy" but also deprived of a cultural life summarized her view of American cultural life in general. In 1895 Bahlmann gave her a book on European architecture; in her letter of thanks Wharton wrote that "I have been all through the delicious pages once already, & feel in consequence an irrepressible longing to pack up & be off at once to lands where such things grow. Sometimes I feel that, like Nature, I abhor a vacuum. Life is too starved here, really!"[33]—a feeling that would remain with her all her life.

Cather, especially during her earlier visits to New York, saw it from the opposite perspective; for her it was the most important cultural center in the United States. Her first impressions of the city were positive; "she was thrilled to be a part of the metropolis."[34] Her evocative portraits of parts of the city—of Washington Square in "Coming, Aphrodite!" and Madison Square Park in *My Mortal Enemy*—suggest that, unlike Wharton, she found much of the city beautiful. Although she would, as early as January 1907, complain that the city "is as big and raw and relentless as ever,"[35] she found in New York exactly what Wharton missed: a rich home for the arts. Even when her finances were tight, she attended operas and other musical events. Edith Lewis, Cather's partner, reports, for instance, that when she and Cather were so poor that they had to debate whether to replace a coffee pot, they nevertheless went to the opera, "sitting high up, in the cheap seats."[36]

To some extent Wharton's and Cather's differing views of the city have to do with their early experience: Wharton's formative years were in the great cities of Europe, Cather's in Nebraska. But they also had to do with chronology. Places exist in time as well as in space, and the New York City of one era is, in many ways, not the city of another. Cather came to the city at the time Wharton was leaving it, which was also a period in which the city's arts scene was beginning to flourish. The history of the Metropolitan Museum serves as a useful touchstone. In 1870, speaking at the founding of the museum, the poet William Cullen Bryant referred to New York as the "third great city of the civilized world," but noted that it had had no art museum.[37] Wharton would have concurred with one of the founders' major motivations to build a museum: the idea that the United States was culturally inferior to the great European cities, and therefore less civilized, and needed to catch up.[38] Edith Jones—eight years old when the Metropolitan Museum was founded and eighteen in 1880, when it moved to Central Park—was one of many cultivated Americans who "still looked to Europe for guidance in the fine arts."[39] In broader terms New York City in 1872—the year in which Edith Jones returned with her family from her six years abroad and found the city "ugly"—was, in comparison to Paris or Rome of the same period, certainly rough, even raw, as Wharton's friend William Crary Brownell described in his 1888 work *French Traits*: instead of "Parisian regularity, order, decorum, and beauty," one was welcomed into New York by "the gaping black holes of broken pavements, the unspeakable filth, the line of red brick buildings prematurely decrepit, [and] the sagging multitude of telegraph wires."[40]

Cather found a very different city when she moved there in 1906. The Metropolitan Museum was well established, having received its current Beaux Arts façade in 1902.[41] In Wharton's childhood, the mansion her aunt Mary Mason Jones had built at Fifty-Seventh Street, two blocks south of Central Park, was "almost in the countryside";[42] by the time Cather arrived, the city stretched beyond Central Park. If the city was—compared to today—a quiet place, it was bustling compared to the place in which Wharton had been a child. As we have seen, Cather took in as many musical and arts events as she could—and the number of events, like her capacity for absorbing them, was high. The city itself was more finished than the city of Wharton's youth. In 1891, for instance, Augustus Saint-Gaudens's Diana statue, which Cather describes in *My Mortal Enemy*, was installed atop Madison Square Garden; Nellie Birdseye sees Madison Square as "so neat, after the raggedness of our Western cities; . . . like an open-air drawing room."[43] It is no wonder that the provincial visitors in Cather's fiction, like Cather herself, fell in love with the city.

Regardless of their differing views, both authors drew not only on the geography and history of the city but on its near-mythic status in American culture. What Paris is to French literature and London to English literature, New York has long been in much of American literature: the home of aristocrats, bohemians, immigrants, and everyone in between; a testing ground for character, for success and failure; for money grubbing and for money transmuted into art and architecture. Perhaps more than any other city of its day, New York represented two different and often conflicting strains in American culture: one that emphasized the importance of business and money making and another, less powerful, that valued beauty and those who appreciated and even needed beauty.

BEAUTY AND ECONOMICS: *THE HOUSE OF MIRTH* AND "PAUL'S CASE"

The extent to which Wharton's and Cather's works and thought intersect in New York is illustrated powerfully by two of their best-known works, Wharton's novel *The House of Mirth* and Cather's story "Paul's Case"; both were published in 1905, tell fundamentally similar stories, and set major portions of the action in New York. Wharton's Lily Bart and Cather's Paul are deeply attracted to a world of beauty, even opulence, but that world is an expensive one that neither can afford. Nor can they find someone to underwrite their longings for this world; both turn away from the "jobs" for which others think them suited—Lily as the wife of a wealthy man, Paul in an entry-level business position. Ultimately both die; Paul's death is a suicide, while Lily's is in a profoundly ambiguous gray area between suicide and an accidental medication overdose. Their deaths are largely caused, I will argue, by the characters' inability to face life in a world without beauty.

Lily and Paul also share the fact that both have elicited mixed reactions: although they have received a certain amount of sympathy, they have also been the objects of a great deal of criticism. Since the publication of *The House of Mirth*, Lily has elicited sympathy as a victim of circumstances. A review in *Outlook* noted, "From the first chapter, trifling indiscretions, careless compromises, minor infidelities, begin to close round Lily Bart and bind her hand and foot until she becomes the victim of a series of circumstances" that "forge an iron chain of fate"; *Harper's* called the society in which Lily lives a "pitiless, self-indulgent world" with "an utter lack of ideals," making Lily's plight more pitiable and perhaps more noble as well.[44] Criticism since the 1975 publication of R. W. B. Lewis's biography of Wharton has been largely sympathetic to Lily, seeing her in feminist terms as a woman who, because she has been educated primarily to be ornamental, is fated to fail in the world she inhabits. Elizabeth Ammons notes that the "problem" in the novel is that Lily does not want to give in to the socioeconomic system; she "does not want to barter herself in marriage" or "to spend her life owned and ruled by a man any more than she wants to spend it dependent on the charity of her old-fashioned aunt."[45] Lillian Robinson's analysis takes Ammons's argument further, demonstrating that Lily is only a cog in a larger economic machine. Lily may also be the victim of history, existing, as J. Michael Duvall has written, at the time when disposable products were coming into use; she herself is treated, in the end, as disposable.[46]

But Lily has also been criticized. An early English review faulted her for being "void of virtue, of passion, and of intellect"; the *Atlantic Monthly* called Lily a "siren of a girl."[47] *The Nation*'s reviewer was so offended by Lily's momentary contemplation of blackmail that he or she proclaimed, with Mrs. Peniston-like firmness, that "a decent girl . . .

would have sent Mrs. Dorset's compromising letters back to her as soon as they fell into her hands."[48] More recently Lily has been criticized for snobbism—for not really understanding the "working classes," although she says she has "become one of them."[49] She has also been faulted for impracticality and passivity, with some readers echoing the character Carrie Fisher, who observes that Lily "works like a slave preparing the ground and sowing her seed; but the day she ought to be reaping the harvest she oversleeps herself or goes off on a picnic."[50] Even sympathy for Lily can shade into fault-finding. Louis Auchincloss refers to Lily condescendingly as one of the "poor beings who are weak enough to care for the luxury, but too squeamish to play the game as roughly as it must be played."[51]

Auchincloss's phrase could be applied equally to Paul, who, like Lily, has received a mixture of criticism and sympathy. Criticism of Paul came early; one reviewer wrote him off as "the young degenerate with a sort of inarticulate longing for beauty," while another combines sympathy and criticism in calling the story "a sympathetic study of one form of sin to which 'temperament' is liable" (neither the "sin" nor the problematic "temperament" is specified).[52] When the story reappeared in 1920 in Cather's second story collection, *Youth and the Bright Medusa*, critics were more generous. Focusing on Paul's relation to beauty, some saw him as representative rather than as an individual "case." The New York *Bookman* wrote admiringly of "the tragedy of Paul and his sacrifice to beauty," while a Nebraska reviewer argued that Paul was typical of "the hatred of the young and undisciplined dreamer for the sordid and unbeautiful surroundings in which he is misplaced."[53] More broadly, Paul was described as representative of Americans. *The Nation* referred to Paul's flight into "the life of art" as "the one imaginable escape for an American from ugliness to beauty, from bondage to freedom"; a British reviewer claimed that Paul "is a whole section of America, the largest section, perhaps," and suggested that in his pursuit of beauty "Paul stands for [American] men, and for [American] women stands Aunt Georgiana" of "A Wagner Matinée."[54] This reviewer also defends Paul's week in the Waldorf, describing it as "one delicious week of luxurious, not depraved, life in a great New York hotel."[55]

More recently many critics have returned to harsher judgments. Like Lily, Paul has been faulted for his impracticality, for the fact that his love of art and beauty do not translate into career aspirations, and for admiring and desiring the wrong thing—material beauty. Critics have written that Paul lacks both imagination and analytical ability, faulting this high-school age boy for his "failure to analyze his society and to perceive possibilities of accommodation within it"; they argue that he has a "pretentiously fraudulent temperament," is "essentially a philistine," and that, because Paul does not appreciate all the art in the gallery equally, he does not have "an artist's 'genuine' feeling for art."[56] "Paul's Case" has been summarized as a story in which "an appetite for the trappings of glamour ... lapses into an orgy of effete consumption"; one critic writes that Paul "ends up destroying himself by his deluded pursuit of the glittering accoutrements of success and glamour."[57] He has been charged with laziness: he is "too idle to climb the social ladder rung by rung."[58] Even those generally sympathetic to Paul's plight may end by condemning him. Sharon O'Brien, for instance, does a splendid job analyzing the complex gender dynamics of Paul's situation in Pittsburgh yet concludes that he is a "parasite-vampire greedily drawing life from an external source."[59]

The variation and extremity of these reactions indicate the extent to which Wharton and Cather hit a nerve in creating Lily and Paul and point to some of the larger questions these works raise. It is no accident that both are set in New York City, which has long encapsulated the tension between money making and art in a small geographic space; the southern tip of Manhattan is home to Wall Street, while further north the Metropolitan Museum of Art might stand as a representative of the city's outstanding arts institutions, visible testimony to the value the city has placed on beauty. In between them, laid out in a semi-mythological way, are some of the world's most famous theaters and expensive stores, the places where business and beauty, cash and art, intersect. Wharton and Cather use the background of New York City to reinforce a central tension in their works: the tension between capitalism and art, between energetic industry and the beauty it makes possible and yet at some level disdains. In their New York works, Wharton and Cather take on the complex relationship between these two poles, including the still widespread view that beauty, though a very good and nice thing, is not really essential—a view both challenge.

As we have seen, the early works of both authors revolve around the need for the beautiful and the American disregard of it. Mrs. Manstey, in Wharton's first published story, and Peter, the eponymous main figure in the first story Cather published in college, die of a lack of beauty. While it would be a mistake to reduce either work to allegory, in both works one character's love of beauty is sacrificed to a lesser character's obliviousness to anything but profit. Ammons's *Edith Wharton's Argument with America*, a classic critical text, describes Wharton's frustration with "the tragedy of... the waste, the crippling, the curtailment" of women's lives.[60] Wharton had another argument with America, as did Cather: its refusal to value beauty or, at best, to treat it as an afterthought.

Wharton addressed the aesthetic issue publicly, as we saw in chapter 2, speaking in favor of the purchase of art for Newport schoolrooms. She clearly linked art and money, urging her audience to support their belief in beauty with their dollars—"We must prove our readiness to be taxed for beautiful as well as for useful things"—while also challenging the common distinction between the "beautiful" and the "useful" by arguing that the beautiful was itself useful.[61] In *The Decoration of Houses* she had argued that parents should invest in making children's rooms beautiful: "The aesthetic sensibilities wake early in some children," who may have "suffer[ed]" by their parents' ill-advised "habit of sending to school-room and nurseries whatever furniture is too ugly or threadbare to be used in any other part of the house."[62] (Paul would have been a happier child if Wharton had had a say in decorating his room.) She asked readers to take beauty seriously: "If art is really a factor in civilization, it seems obvious that the feeling for beauty needs as careful cultivation as the other civic virtues"; art should be integral to life rather than "a thing apart from life."[63]

In other contexts Wharton despaired of her efforts to convince a broader American public that beauty mattered. Writing in 1903 to Sally Norton, who was then in London, she complained of the ugliness of the United States and expressed her sense of being a "useless" hothouse flower:

> Your letter ... made me feel more acutely than ever the contrast between the old & the new, between the stored beauty & tradition & amenity over there, & the crassness here. My first few weeks in America are always miserable, because the tastes I am cursed with are all of a kind that cannot be gratified here, & I am not enough in sympathy with the "gros public" [general public] to make up for the lack on the aesthetic side. One's friends are delightful; but <u>we</u> are none of us Americans. . . . We are the wretched exotics produced in a European glass-house, the most déplacé and useless class on earth![64]

Wharton's cry that she was "déplacé and useless" is surely not an authentic self-evaluation but a cry for a culture that would value beauty, giving it a use of its own.

Deep under much of Wharton's work are the values of both the English Romantics and the American Transcendentalists, particularly Ralph Waldo Emerson,[65] whose poem "The Rhodora" uses a wild rhododendron to illustrate the inherent value of beauty:

> Rhodora! if the sages ask thee why
> This charm is wasted on the earth and sky,
> Tell them, dear, that, if eyes were made for seeing,
> Then beauty is its own excuse for Being.[66]

Although Emerson is among the most American of philosophers, his claim in this poem that "beauty is its own excuse for Being" was not, in Wharton's view—or Cather's—one that was appreciated in the Gilded Age.

Cather was equally invested in the beautiful and equally troubled by the disregard for it; her early life is often summarized as "the starvation of a girl avid for a richer environment."[67] Although many of the works that made Cather famous included beautiful, even idyllic, portraits of prairie life, her earliest stories about the prairie presented it as a place both nightmarishly ugly and culturally starved, as we have seen. Contradicting Frederick Jackson Turner's belief, articulated in his influential "The Significance of the Frontier," that it was the challenge of life on the frontier that made Americans American, Cather suggests in these stories that for many, the major effect of the frontier was not to strengthen settlers but to exhaust them, draining them of what made them fully human. In "A Wagner Matinée," for instance, Georgiana's hands—once the hands of a pianist—have "been stretched and twisted into mere tentacles to hold and lift and knead with."[68]

Although Cather found a richer cultural scene when she moved east to Pittsburgh, she found much of the same attitude toward the arts that she had encountered in Nebraska: that art was not integral to life but rather an afterthought or an ornament. Cather explored this most clearly in "A Gold Slipper," in which a Pittsburgh businessman is first forced by his wife to attend a musical performance and then forced by circumstances to talk with the performer, a singer named Kitty Ayrshire, when he finds they are traveling on the same train from Pittsburgh to New York. For him concerts are "nonsense," possibly suitable for the young but which adult men stop attending when they become "person[s] of substance."[69] He is practical through and through; even his religion is "not very spiritual" but rather "made up of good, hard convictions and opinions."[70] When Kitty asks him to explain his objections to art, he cannot do so coherently; she observes that his love for the "golden mean" of behavior is really a fear of anything taken very far and that he actually hates the beautiful: "When righteousness becomes alive and burning, you hate it as much as you do beauty."[71] When, as Rosowski has written, "Cather... took up the romantic challenge to vindicate imaginative thought in a world threatened by materialism," it wasn't just about Nebraska or Pittsburgh but about a larger cultural issue.[72] Sinclair Lewis would also cite this problem with America, stating in his 1930 Nobel Prize address, "I have for myself no conceivable complaint to make, and yet for American literature in general, and its standing in a country where industrialism and finance and science flourish and the only arts that are vital and respected are architecture and the film [sic], I have a considerable complaint."[73]

It would be a mistake, however, to think that Wharton and Cather were naïve about the relationship between wealth and art. Along with their audiences, they were very aware that the fortunes of Gilded Age millionaires were behind the creation of the museums, libraries, and auditoriums that were springing up not only in New York City but across the country, funded by the huge fortunes of Andrew Carnegie, Henry Clay Frick, J. P. Morgan, and others. (Wharton's family made their money through Manhattan real estate investments; she was also related to the founder of New York's Chemical Bank.)[74] There is no dewy-eyed naiveté in these texts, or in their authors, about the fact that the "big money-makers from the West" and "lords of Pittsburgh," who in turn became the lords of New York, were the ones who financed these institutions, which made art available to a wide public and which, directly and indirectly, supported the careers of many artists.[75] Later works by both authors included more nuanced or sympathetic portraits of wealthy entrepreneurs. Wharton's Elmer Moffatt, despite his manipulative nature, develops a sense of the beautiful in *The Custom of the Country*;[76] in Cather's *Song of the Lark* Fred Ottenburg (whose family has become wealthy in the brewing business) is not only a fine musician himself but also, like Dr. Archie (whose wealth comes from mining), supports the arts very literally, providing emotional and economic support for the aspiring singer Thea Kronborg. Wharton and Cather themselves dealt carefully with their money and were on the alert for fair financial treatment from their publishers. When the artistry of their writing generated income, they were happy to transmute that income into other materials. Wharton wrote that "the most satisfactory thing" about the success of *The Age of Innocence* "is that it enables me to build [garden] walls and plant orange-orchards!"; Cather wrote happily that "Professor St. Peter," the protagonist of *The Professor's House*—a work that challenges American materialism—"has just gone and bought me a grand mink coat!"[77] Far from imagining that beauty emerges unaided from the artist's mind, like Venus rising from the sea, both acknowledged the complex relationship between the arts and money.

Yet for both authors the love of beauty was a counterbalance to American materialism and consumerism. In 1913 Wharton's *The Custom of the Country* would "gesture toward the bleak fate awaiting a society that sets material wealth over cultural riches," as Jenny Glennon has written;[78] in 1905 Wharton was alerting readers to that "bleak fate" in *The House of Mirth*, as was Cather in "Paul's Case." For them as for many in the post-Darwinian world, beauty and art were to some extent a replacement for religion. As Carol Singley has written, "Something akin to a 'religion of culture' flourished among the upper and middle classes in both England and the United States.... Art, with its principles of order, balance, and beauty, offered an alternative to traditional faith... provid[ing] abstract values for a materialistic age."[79] For Wharton's friend Bernard Berenson, an influential art connoisseur, "religion could become art"; moreover, "art might substitute for religion."[80] Art as a religion was a creed for Cather as well, as we have seen; she repeatedly "joined art and religion" and adapted religious language to the arts, sometimes conflating ideas of the muse with references to the Virgin in phrases like "Our Lady of Art" and "Our Lady of Beauty."[81] Paul's attraction to art and beauty has an element of religious devotion: an actor Paul knows "recognized in Paul something akin to what churchmen term 'vocation.'"[82]

Further, both authors commented on the tension between the world of the newly wealthy and an older, more cultured tradition. Wharton wrote that one aspect of *The House of Mirth* was its portrayal of a class to whom "the sudden possession of money has come without inherited obligations."[83] Her friendship with Charles Eliot Norton, Harvard's first professor of art history, rested partly on their similar views: Norton "embodied the tradition of 'genteel' American culture which felt alienated from modern America's 'aggressive materialism.'"[84] Wharton herself sometimes assumed that the men who prospered in business would inevitably be uncultivated; in the New York exhibition of paintings she had admired in 1893, she reported with surprise that "Most of the finest early English landscapes belong to Fuller, the wall-paper man in 42nd St.!!"[85] Cather also saw a tension between the wealthy and the pursuit of beauty, perhaps epitomized in *My Mortal Enemy*, in which Myra Henshawe has two distinct sets of friends in New York, the "artistic" and the "moneyed."[86] She socializes with the latter for the sake of her husband's business, but she is "irritated" by their "solemnity";[87] her true friends are writers, actors, and musicians, with whom she is at her best. Yet although Myra dislikes the rich, she envies them their wealth, conveying the very complexity of the issue. Cather's overall opinion of the tension between money and beauty was encapsulated in her remark that "Religion and art spring from the same root and are close kin. Economics and art are strangers."[88] Historically even the wealthy thought of business and culture as very different. When the trustees of the Metropolitan Museum decided to locate the museum in Central Park, they agreed that it should be "removed from the noise and shadows of this great city, the commercial center of the Western Hemisphere"; one speaker described the museum as an "oasis" in the surrounding "temples of Mammon."[89]

As we have seen, Wharton's and Cather's views of the profound importance of beauty were shaped by the work of Walter Pater, who reminded his readers that life is short, and that "to burn always with this hard, gem-like flame ... is success in life."[90] Surely the Paterian spirit burns in both Paul and Lily, and yet the relationship between beauty and money in "Paul's Case" and *The House of Mirth* has been overlooked; critics have sometimes referred to analyses of Cather's story that focus on art and the artistic as "superficial."[91] Yet Nehamas reminds us that the very lack of "universal agreement" about what constitutes beauty "creates smaller societies" of those who find a particular thing beautiful and echoes Pater in remarking that beautiful things "quicken the sense of life" and that the worth of beauty "is its own reward."[92] These are surely statements with which Lily, Paul, and Emerson would immediately agree. Struggling with the issue of beauty in "Paul's Case" and *The House of Mirth* is essential to understanding these works as well as the larger cultural issues they raise.

The transition from the admiration of beautiful things to the philosophical and moral suspicion of them occurred in the period in which Wharton and Cather were writing, as we saw; further, it is reflected in skepticism about Paul and Lily. Matthew Arnold delineated the difference between two strains of culture; he dubbed one "Hebraism" ("Puritan morality and energetic devotion to work") and the other "Hellenism" ("cultivation of the aesthetic and intellectual understanding of life").[93] "The Puritan's great danger," Arnold wrote, "is that he imagines himself in possession of a rule telling him the *unum necessarium*, or one thing needful, and then he remains satisfied with a very crude conception of what this rule is and what it tells him."[94] Translated to the United States, the *unum necessarium* was the much-vaunted American work ethic, which carried with it a disregard for the senses and thus for beauty. This narrowed perspective was the mind-set Cather encountered in Pittsburgh, where she renamed Hebraism "Presbyterianism." Although the city had a prosperous economy and a comparatively bustling arts scene, much of what she experienced was "an alliance between business and an unpleasant religious formalism"; the Presbyterianism to which she was exposed "offered little encouragement to any sort of artistic activity.... Duty was the law of life. Aesthetic impulse too often led to a dangerous laxity."[95] With a "bourgeois ethos [that] enjoyed perpetual work, compulsive saving, civic responsibility, and a rigid morality of self-denial," Pittsburgh not only epitomized much of American culture in the period but was suspicious of any activity that did not adhere to its code.[96] Cather early intuited the tension between business and art: Pittsburgh had a thriving art scene precisely because wealthy businessmen supported the arts, and yet they were mistrustful of what the arts represented.

Through Lily and Paul, Wharton and Cather reflected their sense of the importance of beauty, while suggesting that American culture's valuing of hard work and material wealth decreased the real value placed upon beauty. Whether because of education and temperament (Wharton's implied argument about Lily) or temperament alone (Cather's implication about Paul), both of these characters are profoundly sensitive to the world about them. Lily sighs over the ugliness in New York City in summer, declaring it "hideous" and observing that "Other cities put on their best clothes in summer, but New York seems to sit in its shirt-sleeves."[97] Paul rebels against the "ugliness and commonness" of his neighborhood; he echoes Lily's comment about New York "in its shirt-sleeves" in his dislike of his neighbors' custom of sitting on their stoops, the men "all in their shirt-sleeves, their vests unbuttoned ... [and] their stomachs comfortably protruding."[98]

Lily and Paul are helpless to change public ugliness; one might think that their own private rooms, which typically are under one's own control and can therefore reflect one's own taste, would be more to their satisfaction. But this is not the case, for their rooms are not really their own. Lily lives with her aunt, Mrs. Peniston, and takes the room she is given. She sleeps in the black walnut bedstead that was moved from her uncle's room after his death; this room, with its "magenta 'flock' wall-paper" and "large steel engravings of an anecdotic character," is clearly not an environment Lily would have chosen for herself. She attempts to mitigate its ugliness with "a lace-decked toilet table and a little painted desk surmounted by photographs."[99] Yet given her artistic sensibility, Lily sometimes finds her room at Mrs. Peniston's oppressive: "The haunting sense of physical ugliness was intensified by her mental depression, so that each piece of the offending furniture seemed to thrust forth its most aggressive angle."[100] The novel is book-ended by descriptions of Lily's rooms. The boarding-house room she occupies at the novel's end, although at the opposite end of the economic spectrum, is not that different from her room at her aunt's; here too she adds "a lace cover" to the dresser on which she has set out "a few gold-topped boxes and bottles" and other items that make the room less spartan.[101] These physical objects, Wharton notes, are on a continuum with Lily's abstract values, representing her "clinging to the minute observance of personal seemliness."[102] But Lily, who is increasingly honest with herself, realizes that she can hardly bear life in a boarding house.[103]

Paul, similarly, lives in a room that is not his own. Cather calls it a "sleeping-chamber," suggesting that that is all it is good for;[104] Wharton might have used the same term for Lily's. Like Lily, Paul finds his room depressingly bleak and dreads its "horrible yellow wall-paper, the creaking bureau, with the greasy plush collar-box, and ... the pictures of George Washington and John Calvin, and the framed motto, 'Feed my Lambs,' which had been worked in red worsted by his mother, whom Paul could not remember."[105] Paul dreads both his room and his father (with "his hairy legs sticking out from his nightshirt")[106] so much that arriving home very late, he spends the night in the cellar despite his fear of rats; he prefers it to facing the visual and emotional ugliness upstairs. Just as Lily attempts to mitigate the ugliness of her room, Paul keeps a bottle of "violet water ... hidden in his drawer" to counteract the "greasy odour of the dish-water."[107]

Like Lily's efforts, Paul's protest may be small and ineffectual, but it is a protest nonetheless.

Lily and Paul are literary cousins, and Wharton and Cather use the same imagery—hothouse flowers—to convey their characters' love of beauty and the idea that they are complex organisms, people with both special sensibilities and special requirements. Critics have long noted Cather's effective use of flowers in "Paul's Case." The red carnations Paul wears to meet his teachers at the beginning of the story are balanced by those he buys and then buries in the snow just before he jumps in front of a train at the story's end; in New York he admires the blooms in the many florist shops, sending out for some to fill his room at the Waldorf. In a nicely constructed sentence, Cather subtly suggests the parallel between Paul and his flowers: "When the flowers came, he put them hastily into water, and then tumbled into a hot bath." Both are refreshed by their immersion in water: when Paul emerges, he is "resplendent... and playing with the tassels of his red robe"; he has donned the color of the carnations.[108] Cather implies Paul's similarity to a flower; Wharton explicitly states that Lily "was like some rare flower grown for exhibition, a flower from which every bud had been nipped except the crowning blossom of her beauty."[109] Lily is, of course, a lily, a delicate flower often evoked in Art Nouveau that typified purity and elegance; lilies also suggest (perhaps ironically) a concept of effortless beauty through their evocation of the much-quoted biblical phrase, "Behold the lilies of the field: they toil not, neither do they spin."[110] Lily is also a rose, another flower that needs careful nurturing. One working title for the novel was "The Year of the Rose," and the fading beauty of the American Beauty roses Lily objects to early in the novel rehearses her eventual decline.[111]

Wharton and Cather acknowledge the tenuousness of a hothouse existence: shortly before his death, Paul realizes "that all the flowers he had seen in the show windows that first night must also have gone the same way" as the carnations drooping in his coat, and Lily is aware that a "dreary limbo of dinginess lay all around... that little illuminated circle in which life reached its finest efflorescence, as the mud and sleet of a winter night enclose a hot-house filled with tropical flowers."[112]

Within this specialized environment, however, Paul and Lily flourish. As Paul drives up Fifth Avenue in a carriage, he notes, "Here and there on the corners whole flower gardens [were] blooming behind glass windows, against which the snow flakes stuck and melted,"[113] an image reiterated in Cather's description of Paul in his hotel room: "The snow was whirling so fiercely outside his windows that he could scarcely see across the street; but within, the air was deliciously soft and fragrant."[114] When he is arrayed in newly purchased, well-made clothing, the nervous tension that has plagued him for years ceases; he has "a curious sense of relief."[115] In his hotel room he feels, for the first time, at home: "His dearest pleasures were the grey winter twilights in his sitting-room; his quiet enjoyment of his flowers, his clothes, his wide divan."[116] Paul blooms; at last he is "exactly the kind of boy he had always wanted to be."[117] Lily also thrives in a specific environment. Her room at the Trenors' mansion is softly lighted, warm, and scented; in the glow of "its softly-shaded lights," with "her little embroidered slippers before the fire [and] a vase of carnations filling the air with perfume," she reflects that "she was not made for mean and shabby surroundings.... Her whole being dilated in an atmosphere of luxury; it was ... the only climate she could breathe in."[118] Lily needs this special climate, just as Paul needs the "soft" air of his room.

Within this environment, Paul and Lily are artists. For Paul "the call of beauty" is "the call to the soul's life."[119] At the Waldorf he demonstrates his aesthetic imagination, ordering beautiful flowers for his beautiful rooms because they will complete the "one detail in his mental picture that the place did not realize."[120] Leon Edel observed that "the artist as performer interested" Cather greatly,[121] and Paul is a flawless performance artist; in New York he knows what he is doing because he has "written the script" and "successfully combines the roles of playwright, actor, and audience."[122] He almost persuades himself that he had "always been thus"; his one-man play is so convincing that he seems to persuade everyone around him: "Nobody questioned the purple."[123] One could say that it is all an act, yet it is a role he plays superbly and inhabits fully. Like Cather's Lucy Gayheart, who "becom[es] more and more herself" during her time in Chicago,[124] Paul seems to be coming into his own, even if, paradoxically, he is most himself when he is most artificial. Art, after all, is artifice.

Lily too becomes most herself when she is at her most artificial, her most artistic. Like Paul assuming the role of a wealthy young man in New York, Lily projects herself into the role she wishes to inhabit in the *tableaux vivants* scene; in portraying Joshua Reynolds's "Mrs. Lloyd," Lily becomes, however briefly, the loving and presumably loved wife of a wealthy, important man. This enactment also allows Lily to be an artist. Under Paul Morpeth's guidance, her "vivid plastic sense . . . found eager expression. . . . The gorgeous reproduction of historic dress stirred an imagination which only visual impressions could reach."[125] In performing the tableau, she supersedes the artwork; the audience responds with a "unanimous 'Oh!' . . . not to the brush-work of Reynolds's 'Mrs. Lloyd' but to the flesh-and-blood loveliness of Lily Bart."[126] She is not "killed into art" but brings art to life, "banishing the phantom of [Reynolds's] dead beauty by the beams of her living grace."[127] Lily is both artist and artwork, and her success allows her to bask in the environment she requires: "In a warm atmosphere of praise . . . her beauty expanded like a flower in sunlight."[128]

Beauty is valued in the New York in which Paul and Lily move; Paul fits into the world at the Waldorf, and Lily's beauty is much admired. Yet Lily's and Paul's lives are about to take a downturn, largely because neither of them is willing to accede to American practicality, which admires but does not necessarily want to pay for beauty. Neither Paul nor Lily is naïve; both know that beauty of the sort that attracts them is expensive. For both, the money-making options are obvious: Paul needs to submit himself to the dull routine of a business job, and Lily needs to parlay her beauty and social skills into a job as the wife of a millionaire. Yet both seem to believe in a deep, unarticulated way that doing so would require them to make compromises that would cost them too much personally. A younger Lily had imagined herself wavering between an English duke and an Italian prince; a more mature and realistic Lily sees that her actual choice is between Percy Gryce, who will, if she plays her cards right, "do her the honour of boring her for life," and Rosedale, who has his good moments but whom she finds physically and morally repugnant.[129] Through these men Wharton suggests the gap between wealth and appreciation; though Rosedale and Gryce have the money that could provide the environment Lily needs, neither fully values Lily herself. Gryce is frightened by her vitality; Rosedale proves too ambitious to marry her. She has lost her social capital, and Rosedale knows he can "do better."[130] If beauty is not socially valuable, he will not invest in it.

Paul also challenges the parameters of the society in which he lives, specifically the *unum necessarium*, the belief that hard work will lead to financial success. The dismissal of Paul as impractical—of failing because he refuses to subordinate his love of beauty to the work ethic— relies on the assumption that if Paul works hard enough, he will be able to obtain the things he wants. At a fundamental level Paul apparently intuits that this may not be the case; realistically the best he is likely to do is to end up like the men on Cordelia Street, struggling to maintain a middle-class existence. The world Wharton depicts in *The House of Mirth* confirms this scenario: Gryce's fortune is managed by "a batch of pale men on small salaries" who have "grown grey" in his service.[131] If Paul works very hard, he might "succeed" by becoming one of these pale, aging, underpaid men. Both Paul and Lily know that the beauty they crave is supported by wealth, but they are deeply mistrustful of what wealth demands and suspicious that compliance with social rules would require a denial of what, for them, makes life worth living.

Through Lily and Paul, then, Wharton and Cather query the dynamics of success in the Gilded Age. As one character says in *The Custom of the Country*, the "emotional centre of gravity" in American life was business: "In America the real *crime passionnel* [crime of passion] is a 'big steal.'"[132] The newly rich "lords of Pittsburgh," as Wharton called them[133]—people like steel magnate Carnegie and coal king Frick, the sort of tycoons for whom Paul's neighbors on Cordelia Street were working—fascinated many; it is their "epic effrontery" that generates the "legends of the iron kings" that are bandied about Paul's neighborhood.[134] Yet these tales suggest a strange loophole in the ideology of the work ethic. When Paul's neighbors talk about their bosses, they are not discussing hard work and thrift but are talking admiringly, even enviously, about their extravagance, recounting "stories of palaces in Venice, yachts on the Mediterranean, and high play in Monte Carlo."[135] Paul's father, who lets Paul usher at the theater because "he thought a boy ought to be earning a little,"[136] probably hopes that the success stories of men like Carnegie will motivate Paul to work harder. But what attracts Paul is the "epic effrontery" of these men: they have somehow escaped the work ethic into a life of extravagant beauty.

In their depiction of the tense relationship between business and beauty, Wharton and Cather follow a long line of American thinkers who have argued that the labor necessary to generate great wealth may limit the ability to appreciate beauty. Thoreau observes that "Most men ... are so occupied with the factitious cares and superfluously coarse labors of life that its finer fruits cannot be plucked by them. Their fingers, from excessive toil, are too clumsy and tremble too much for that."[137] Men's association with business in a time in which women were systematically excluded from it led to a distinct gender divide between business and culture.[138] Hawthorne's "The Artist of the Beautiful" dramatizes the masculine, physical power of financial success and its crushing disregard for art and the feminized artist, while in *The American Scene* James contrasts "the overwhelming preponderance ... of the unmitigated business-man's face" with the "concomitantly striking ... fact that the women ... appear to be of a markedly finer texture than the men."[139] This divergence of gender roles leads, James argues, to an "apparent privation, for the man, of his right kind of woman, and ... for the woman, of her right kind of man."[140] Wharton illustrated such mismatches in the attraction of the "red and massive" businessman Gus Trenor to the "dryad-like" Lily Bart,[141] Cather in banker Harry Gordon's attraction to the light-footed Lucy Gayheart.

American culture, then, leaves little room for men who are cultivated, of whom Paul may simply be the most obvious example. In the works of both authors many successful businessmen are portrayed as physically and temperamentally coarse. Trenor and Rosedale both fit this mold in *The House of Mirth*; in "Paul's Case" the type is represented both by Paul's father and the "young man of a ruddy complexion, with a compressed, red mouth, and faded, near-sighted eyes" who is constantly held up to Paul as a model.[142] Conversely men who are less financially successful or even view themselves as failures are more attuned to the "finer fruits." In *O Pioneers!* Alexandra is drawn to Carl Linstrum, an artist who considers himself a financial failure; in *One of Ours* Gladys Farmer, although engaged to the prosperous Bayliss Wheeler, is far more interested in his brother Claude, who also believes himself a failure. Carl and Claude, like Paul, possess an alert sensitivity that eludes the financially successful men in their communities. So too Lily Bart is put off her pursuit of the wealthy but obtuse Gryce by "a rapid comparison between" him and Lawrence Selden.[143] She finds Selden "more agreeable than most men, and . . . vaguely wished that he possessed the other qualities needful to fix her attention."[144] Selden has often been faulted for his judgmental approach to Lily;[145] but what Lily does not quite see is that these two qualities—Selden's "agreeable" nature and his lack of ostentatious wealth—are both manifestations of his finer nature and of his own resistance to American business culture.

In *Only a Promise of Happiness* Nehamas states, "Both in art and in the rest of life, beauty may take a long time to emerge, but, once it does, it will absorb you completely and make the rest of the world recede, if only for a moment."[146] The utterly absorbing quality of beauty is exactly what Paul experiences when he listens to music or loses himself in front of paintings; it is what Lily feels when she admires her well-dressed friends in the beautiful setting of Bellomont or inhales the scent of her violets in the morning. "The rest of the world recede[s]"; the moment is paramount. While beauty allows us to live in the moment, Nehamas writes, it is also "forward-looking"; it "points to the future, and we pursue it" even though we are unsure "what it will yield."[147] Even if it is "*only* a promise of happiness," it gives us something to live for.[148]

In Lily and Paul, Wharton and Cather portray characters whose lives no longer have that promise. Although both characters flourish within a very specific environment, once they are removed from it, they perish. Lily's demise is slow but inexorable. Near the end of the novel, living west of Sixth Avenue in a boarding house near the Garment District,[149] she knows that without any additional source of income, all she has to look forward to is a "shabby, anxious middle-age, leading by dreary degrees of economy and self-denial to gradual absorption in the dingy communal existence of the boarding-house."[150] Although Lily is steeling herself to be more practical and more frugal, the process of resigning herself to a future of poverty is quite literally killing her. Wasting away under her beautiful clothes and suffering from chronic insomnia, she adds another drop to her sleeping medication one night and fails to wake up in the morning. Although she has made her room in the boarding house as beautiful as she can, as Selden will see the next morning, she herself is overwhelmed by fatigue, solitude, and the certainty that dreariness is all she has to look forward to.

The circumstances leading to Paul's death are strikingly similar: Lily's fear of a dreary future is paralleled by Paul's dread of the future awaiting him in Pittsburgh. His beautiful week in New York ends abruptly when he reads in the newspaper that his theft has been discovered and that his father is coming east to find him. Equally bad, the newspaper reports that his minister and Sunday school teacher vow that they will "reclaim the motherless lad"; they will insist on his return to the cultural homilies he had finally escaped. He is overcome with weakness: "It was to be worse than jail, even; the tepid waters of Cordelia Street were to close over him finally and forever. The grey monotony stretched before him in hopeless, unrelieved years."[151] In leaving New York, he leaves beauty behind; everything he sees becomes "part of the ugliness of the world."[152] The nervousness that typified him in Pittsburgh returns; he has a "frightened smile" and "glance[s] nervously sidewise, as though he were being watched"—his old fear—just before he jumps in front of the train.[153] With tragic literalness, he would rather die than return to that world of physical and moral dreariness. His last thought, ironically, confirms Nehamas's sense that the pursuit of beauty gives us something to live for. In the instant after he has thrown himself in front of the train, Paul thinks of "the blue of Adriatic waters, the yellow of Algerian sands."[154] He realizes, too late, that he has given up all chance of ever seeing that beauty.

There is no doubt that Lily and Paul are both extreme examples. Wharton acknowledges Lily's "craving for the external finish of life";[155] Paul feels truly alive only when he is stimulated by beauty. Surely if they had been more reasonable, they would have found ways out of their predicaments. Let us say, for instance, that Lily succeeds in marrying Rosedale. After her initial euphoria at having "smarter gowns than Judy Trenor, and far, far more jewels than Bertha Dorset,"[156] she accepts her compromise, leading a very wealthy and reasonably contented life, perhaps finding some meaning in motherhood or in charitable work (both have some appeal for her) or finding that the possession of untold wealth really does bring happiness. Yet Lily as a happily married Mrs. Rosedale seems deeply implausible; such an alternative ending would undermine one of the novel's central tenets. In this altered vision of the novel it seems far more likely that an unhappy Mrs. Rosedale would be haunted by Selden's words: "I am not divine Providence, to guarantee your enjoying the things you are trying to get!"[157] Even Lily as Mrs. Selden seems an unsatisfactory solution; she would always be haunted by the life of beauty that she had missed. It is all too easy to imagine her and Selden, after a happy year or two, arguing about their lack of money, perhaps with Lily pushing Selden to work harder, making her all too much like her own mother or like Undine Spragg Marvell, who pushes Ralph to exhaustion in her wish for ever-greater wealth in *The Custom of the Country*.

Similarly let us imagine that Paul does the reasonable thing: he waits for his father to arrive, then returns to Pittsburgh and gets a job. Barring any implausible change in his character, he would do his job just well enough to keep it but not well enough to excel; he would spend most of the rest of his life in Pittsburgh, perhaps saving enough money for an occasional week in New York (at a hotel less expensive than the Waldorf). Or if he works very hard and is exceedingly thrifty, he might—*might*—manage a trip to Europe. But it is hard to imagine him developing "a mind for the cash-boy stage" of work or adhering to the *unum necessarium* of Presbyterian Pittsburgh and of much of America— hard work for its own sake—with (despite the inherent contradiction) the belief that that hard work will someday pay off in luxury. Paul will never be one of the lords of Pittsburgh.

While such outcomes would be preferable if Lily and Paul were actual people, it is obvious they would undermine the deeper issues in *The House of Mirth* and "Paul's Case," particularly their implied plea that a culture that sets the highest value on money making needs to acknowledge the importance of beauty and the value of people who can perceive and appreciate beauty. Both Wharton and Cather defended the "temperament" to which beauty was a necessity. Far from being a weakness, Wharton wrote in a letter, such sensitivity is a gift, despite its cost: "To have as few numb traits in one's consciousness as possible—that seems to me . . . the most desirable thing in life, even though the Furies do dance in hob-nailed shoes on the sensitive tracts at a rate that sometimes makes one wish for any form of anaesthesia."[158] Her comments echo Pater, who argued the importance of "a certain kind of temperament, the power of being deeply moved by beautiful objects."[159] Similarly Cather wrote in response to a letter, "You speak of a 'universal longing for a world beautiful.' In the first place, this longing is by no means universal. It is rather exceptional. . . . A desire for beauty—a strong desire—is the important thing, is the real gift. . . . If one has that desire, no circumstances can keep him from the treasure house of the world. All the great literature and the great music and the great art are his."[160] Far from being a weakness, Paul and Lily's sensitivity to beauty is a strength.

Wharton famously commented that when she wrote *The House of Mirth*, her challenge was to confer significance on "a society of irresponsible pleasure-seekers. . . . The answer was that a frivolous society can acquire dramatic significance only through what its frivolity destroys. Its tragic implication lies in its power of debasing people and ideals. The answer, in short, was my heroine, Lily Bart."[161] Lily's own ideals are debased by her experiences; her heroism is that she does not descend to the level of the people around her. Her ideal of a beautiful life encompasses both the moral and the visible, a concept that aligns with Plato's belief that the "contemplation of beauty is not a haphazard gazing into the blue but a whole mode of life that combines creative thought and considered action and transforms the desire to possess beautiful things into the urge to create . . . beauty of one's own."[162] When Lily says, early in the novel, "If I could only do over my aunt's drawing-room I know I should be a better woman," it is partly in jest.[163] But this statement also conveys something significant. Lily's desire to create a beautiful life is not trivial, and it reminds us that Wharton's first book was *The Decoration of Houses*. Great novelist as she was, Wharton was no bohemian artist starving in a garret; in addition to being a writer, she was a creator of beautiful places. If Lily Bart's last name evokes "barter," it also plays on the word "art."[164] "The answer was my heroine, Lily Bart" suggests more than it says, also conveying, "Yes, sacrifice Lily Bart, but see what you lose when you do"; you also sacrifice art and the love of art.

In "Paul's Case" the issue is not a "frivolous society" but a society at the opposite end of the spectrum: the overly earnest, overly strict society of Cordelia Street, smugly pleased with its own platitudes. Yet Wharton's question about dramatic significance fits Cather's story as well. How could Cather create such significance when she was writing about people wholly devoted to practicality and hard work? The answer was Paul. "Paul's Case" is not just a depiction of a life gone awry but a reflection on the cultural environment that fails to acknowledge his gifts, on "the opposition between aesthetic aspirations and individualism, and the crushing unimaginative orthodoxy of the bourgeois business world."[165] Sacrifice Paul, but see what you lose when you do: someone who is imaginative, intelligent, resourceful, and possesses a rare receptivity to a wide range of art forms. His death is a loss not just to himself but to society.

As previously mentioned, some readers and critics have criticized Paul and Lily harshly. Surely some dismissals stem from the fact that *The House of Mirth* and "Paul's Case" implicitly challenge fundamental American beliefs. What Martha Banta has written about *The House of Mirth* applies equally to "Paul's Case": the work "defies the principles that give force to the two most famous narrative traditions that secure other American classics: the twin faiths in the ability to control one's rise to riches and social success (Benjamin Franklin's contribution), and to attain self-sufficiency (the legacy of Ralph Waldo Emerson)."[166] Lily rebels against her aunt's "copy-book axioms" and refuses to become a trophy wife who will be "bored for life"; Paul rebels against "the homilies by which the world is run" and refuses to work a mortally dull job.¹⁶⁷ Lily and Paul, like Melville's Bartleby, "prefer not to adapt to a deadening normalcy" and challenge American beliefs that life is constituted of self-sufficiency, self-reliance, and a rise to riches.¹⁶⁸

Perhaps even more alarmingly, *The House of Mirth* and "Paul's Case" suggest that a life could be self-sufficient, self-reliant, and affluent and yet be impoverished by a dearth of beauty. Wharton and Cather believed that "culture is not an ornament... but a crying need" and wrote vigorously of the need for beauty.¹⁶⁹ Writing to Berenson about a study of Italian art he had just published, Wharton remarked, "Oh, bless you again & again: especially for [writing] 'What is true of life is true of art: its ultimate aim is ecstasy.'... It coincided so thrillingly with the 'aesthetic' of my own métier that I've so long yearned to write that I could hug you—& myself!"¹⁷⁰ When Paul experiences in the concert hall "the delicious excitement which was the only thing that could be called living at all," he is experiencing just such ecstasy.¹⁷¹ He is also speaking partly for Cather, whose devotion to the performing arts suggests her own search for ecstasy. Paul's feeling for New York City, she wrote, was "the feeling I myself had about New York City... when I first left college and was teaching latin [*sic*] in the Pittsburgh High school."¹⁷² The "desire for beauty" was "the real gift";¹⁷³ it is a gift both Paul and Lily have but which America made hard to gratify.

ARTISTS' WIVES

The tension between beauty and economics, between art and money, reappears repeatedly in works by Wharton and Cather, including two of their narratives about artists, Cather's story "Coming, Aphrodite!" and Wharton's novel *A Son at the Front*. In both the authors contrast a male artist's insistence on following the bent of his own genius with his female partner's urging a more practical, and profitable, course of action. Although Banta sees the "twin faiths" of Franklin and Emerson as parallel, in some ways American culture has polarized them: Ben Franklin's pragmatic voice as "Poor Richard" urges hard work and (arguably) conformity in order to achieve financial success ("Early to bed, early to rise, makes a man healthy, wealthy and wise"), while Emerson's voice leads not to making money in the workplace but to

Thoreau living alone on Walden Pond, minimizing his material needs in order to maximize his freedom to lead a life according to his own principles, a life simultaneously ascetic and aesthetic. The latter sort of life, of course, is much more in accord with the Romantic idea of the artist. While James and others may have aligned men with business and women with culture, Cather and Wharton also depicted the durable opposite of that pairing, with men claiming the high ground as true artists and women serving as the voices of down-to-earth Franklinian pragmatism. Cather's "Coming, Aphrodite!" and Wharton's *A Son at the Front* depict these roles in startlingly similar terms.

In terms of overall plot "Coming, Aphrodite!" and *A Son at the Front* are very different works. Set in New York, Cather's story describes the experiences of a disheveled, unworldly artist named Don Hedger who unexpectedly falls for his summer neighbor, Eden Bower, a beautiful, self-possessed opera singer on her way up. Wharton's novel initially seems the opposite: set in Paris, it is the story of a bitterly divorced American expatriate couple, the painter John Campton and his ex-wife Julia Brant. Cather's tale is, in its own way, a summer idyll, while Wharton's novel opens when World War I erupts; Campton and Julia suddenly have a common cause when their adult son, an American born in France, is required to report for service in the French military. Yet the opening chapters of Wharton's novel, which depict Campton's early years, are strongly reminiscent of Cather's story. In both works the male artist falls in love, believing that *this* woman, of all women, understands his dreams and his vision. Once the couple is substantially involved, the woman in question secures an invitation from a well-known and wealthy painter to meet "her" artist and give him a chance at fame and fortune. But in both cases the artist laughs this idea to scorn, mocks the older artist, realizes that the woman in his life does not understand him after all, breaks with her, and goes on to achieve success, at least by his own standards.

The tension between Franklinian pragmatism and Emersonian idealism is particularly clear in parallel scenes in these works, in which both the direction of the conversation and the dialogue are strikingly similar. In "Coming, Aphrodite!" Eden asks Don, "What's the use of being a great painter if nobody knows about you? ... Why don't you paint the kind of pictures people can understand, and then, after you're successful, do whatever you like?"[174] Julia tells Campton, "It's a great mistake to try to be original till people have got used to you.... If you'd only been civil to Beausite he would have ended by taking you up, and then you could have painted as queerly as you liked."[175] Although the wording is different, these sentences not only pursue the same idea—the younger, lesser-known painter should butter up the older, more popular one—but also follow the same logical order and use similar phrases: Cather's "What's the use of being a great painter ... ?" is paralleled by Wharton's "It's a great mistake to try to be original," as are the succeeding phrases, including the argument-inducing conclusion, Eden's "after you're successful, [you could] do whatever you like" and Julia's "then you could have painted as queerly as you liked."

The men's reactions to these proposals are also parallel. Hedger "thr[ows] down his brushes" and mocks Ives as "almost the worst painter in the world; the stupidest, I mean," when Eden tells him that she has visited Ives; when she asks, "What would you do if I brought Mr. Ives down here to see your things?," he replies, "Well, for God's sake, don't! Before he left I'd probably tell him what I thought of him."[176] When Julia triumphantly brings a dinner invitation from Beausite to Campton, it plays out similarly:

> Campton, with a laugh, threw the card into the stove.
> "If you'd only understand that that's not the way," he said.
> "What is, then?"
> "Why, letting all that lot see what unutterable rubbish one thinks them!"[177]

The similarities in plot, gesture, and language seem more than coincidental and more than an indication of attitudes shared by Wharton and Cather. We normally think of influence as proceeding from an older writer to a younger one, and in fact Eden's and Don's conversation about success in "Coming, Aphrodite!" may owe something to Lily's and Selden's discussion of the same topic in chapter 6 of Wharton's *House of Mirth*. Lily hesitatingly defines success as "get[ting] as much as one can out of life," and Eden defines it as the objects and opportunities money can buy; Selden asserts that success is "personal freedom," freedom "from everything—from money, from poverty... from all the material accidents. To keep a kind of republic of the spirit."[178] Hedger, with his free pursuit of his artistic vision, embodies Selden's ideals better than Selden himself does.

But if Cather echoed *The House of Mirth* in "Coming, Aphrodite!," Wharton may have borrowed back in *A Son at the Front*, so striking are the parallels in the dialogue between the arguing couples. The first draft of Wharton's manuscript of *A Son at the Front* (which she began in 1918) does not contain the scene in which Campton and Julia argue, while the completed novel, published in 1923, does; between the two versions she may have read Cather's story, published in 1920. As we saw previously, Wharton faulted Cather's writing for lacking "edge." The dialogue in *A Son at the Front*, though so like Cather's, is turned up a notch, decidedly "edgier": Hedger's "I'd probably tell him what I thought of him" becomes Campton's "what unutterable rubbish one thinks them!"; Eden's "do whatever you like" becomes Julia's "paint as queerly as you like."

Regardless of the question of influence, the crux of the matter in both is the idea of success—which, for Eden and Julia, Franklinian pragmatists, means material wealth. Eden sees Ives as successful because "He has a Japanese servant and a wine cellar, and keeps a riding horse."[179] These, along with the "gorgeous" studio where he entertains Eden and some of her friends, attest to his wealth—his success; by the same token, Beausite has a "sumptuous" mansion in a fashionable district of Paris.[180] For Eden and Julia the equation between expensive possessions and success is automatic and beyond debate; and if Ives and Beausite are successful, then Hedger and Campton—with their messy studios and lack of conspicuous material wealth—are, well, not quite failures but not successes either. Don may defend himself to Eden by equating success with freedom, declaring that "I have the most expensive luxury in the world, and I am much more extravagant than Burton Ives, for I work to please nobody but myself."[181] But Eden fails to grasp this Thoreauvian concept of success and replies—apparently with great surprise—"You mean you could make money and don't? That you don't try to get a public?"[182] When Don suddenly intuits that Eden sees him as a "scrub painter," he is no doubt correct.[183] It is more difficult to determine Julia's attitude toward Campton, but she certainly plays the role of manager to him, rather than that of lover, muse, or mentor, and is "bitterly offended" by Campton's rejection of her suggestion that portraits might be more marketable than the other projects he is engaged in.[184]

In spite of Campton's resentment of Julia's interference, he (unlike Hedger) sees that her suggestion that he paint portraits is "shrewd" and eventually follows it.[185] As the novel opens on the eve of an unforeseen World War I, Campton has replaced Beausite in popularity, and although doing portraits bores him, he has exercised some financial shrewdness of his own: "For two years he had let it be as difficult and as expensive as possible to be 'done by Campton.'"[186] Through this strategy he has, in his mid-fifties, begun to command high prices. Yet it is clear that profitable portrait painting is rarely the work Campton would choose. John Campton and Don Hedger are both drawn squarely in the tradition of the Romantic artist, which embraces the pursuit of one's own vision; the sacrifice of material well-being for the sake of art, including living in scruffy, underlit, messy quarters in the tradition of *La Bohème*; a near absolute scorn of money (or at least of creating art specifically to make money); and the suspicion that if one is making money, one must have sold out. When Eden encourages Don to let her introduce him to Ives, she does not know that Don has "twice been on the verge of becoming a marketable product" and has twice turned away from that prospect; it would have meant doing "simply the old thing over again."[187] He does not want to repeat himself nor to commodify himself. (Cather's language is specific: it's not his paintings but he himself who would become the "marketable product.") Don chooses against this rapidly, almost instinctively, apparently not even weighing the fact that he will lose income by choosing to do something different.

Part of the Romantic attitude is the assumption that the artist is male and that women, who cannot comprehend the artistic nature, are generally (when not models or maids) distractions for the great artist. In addition to the French authors mentioned in chapter 2, Wharton and Cather also shared an admiration for the fiction writer Alphonse Daudet (1840–97), who depicted just such artist-husband, business-wife scenarios in *Artists' Wives*.[188] This story collection opens with a prologue in which a happily married artist warns a younger colleague not to marry. "For all of us, painters, poets, sculptors, musicians, who live outside of life," he says, marriage is rarely a good idea, for "to that nervous, exacting, impressionable being, that child-man that we call an artist, a special type of woman, almost impossible to find, is needful, and the safest thing to do is not to look for her."[189] A wife is more likely to distract the artist with uncongenial social and material demands than truly to support his career; worse, she will not even understand what she is doing. "Ah! how many of these ill-matched couples have I known," the artist states, "where the wife was sometimes executioner, sometimes victim, but more often executioner, and nearly always unwittingly so!"[190]

The story in *Artists' Wives* that best portrays this relationship, prefiguring Julia Campton's and Eden Bower's attitudes, is "A Misunderstanding," a clever work in two side-by-side parts, with the left page conveying the attitude of the wife of an artist and the right page depicting the artist's perspective. The wife is practical and worldly, and she wants her husband to succeed financially; she manipulates their social connections to obtain a government post for him—a move that disgusts him as much as Eden's and Julia's maneuverings disgust Hedger and Campton. Like the fish in the aquarium that Don Hedger is painting, which he pretends is "only an experiment in unusual lighting" but which is really an attempt to portray "the incommunicability of one stratum of animal life with another,"[191] "incommunicability" governs these relationships. Compared to the men, the women are another "stratum of . . . life," completely failing to understand the deepest thing about them: their dedication to art.

In Daudet's story the conflict could be summarized as the cultural gap between the bourgeois wife and the bohemian husband; in the hands of Wharton and Cather it is a conflict between American pragmatism and the arts. The argument between Don and Eden takes place in New York and the one between Campton and Julia in France, but Julia, in spite of her European upbringing, has the same attitude toward success as Eden Bower: if it doesn't make money, it's not a success. Campton's life changes when the inheritance he expects to receive from his father, a manufacturer who invented a laundry device named the "Magic Mangle," falls through; instead he inherits "only a series of law-suits."[192] He is abruptly demoted from the status of aspiring painter to being "merely the unsuccessful son of a ruined manufacturer," and "painting became a luxury he could no longer afford" instead of a calling others respect.[193] Because, by American standards, business responsibilities trump artistic aspirations, Campton's mother and sisters expect him and his wife to return to Utica and take over the family business. The Mangle would indeed mangle his aspirations. Both Campton and Julia "face the fact desolately"; they are too enamored of France, and dread the cultural starvation of Utica too thoroughly, to want to return to the United States.[194] Julia points out that Campton knows little about business: "Since you've taken up painting you'd better try to make a success of that," she reasons.[195] All too eager to find a rationale to stay in France, Campton agrees, but he fails to take seriously enough Julia's point that painting is now his business; "mak[ing] a success" of painting means making money at it.

This was an attitude Wharton knew well from her youth in New York. One of her many criticisms of American culture in her ironically titled *The Age of Innocence* is that New York—the nation's leading metropolis—was so little a city of the arts. When Newland visits Ellen Olenska in her house "far down West Twenty-Third Street," he notes that it is "a strange quarter" for someone of her social importance to have chosen. "Small dress-makers, bird-stuffers and 'people who wrote' were her nearest neighbors"; Archer wonders, "with a little shiver, if the humanities were so meanly housed in other capitals."[196] In the culturally starved New York of the 1870s Archer is understandably intrigued by Mme Olenska; her unconventionality extends to an interest in the art of her own day, which is reflected in the books and paintings in her drawing room—paintings so new that they "bewilder" Archer even as they intrigue him.[197] Later, when a Frenchman mentions to Newland that he is considering moving to New York to pursue a literary career,

Newland finds himself "wondering how to tell him that his very superiorities and advantages would be the surest hindrance to success."[198] The same grim view is portrayed in Wharton's novella *False Dawn*, the first of the four novellas comprising *Old New York*. In this tale, set in the 1840s, a young New Yorker acquires valuable paintings abroad after an influential chance meeting with Ruskin. But when he returns to New York, he and his collection are mocked. His collection is appreciated a generation later; even then, however, it is only because family members discover that his "peculiar" paintings—by artists such as Giotto and Piero della Francesca—can be turned into "pearls and Rolls-Royces," not to mention a "new house in Fifth Avenue."[199]

In Cather's novel *One of Ours* the protagonist, Claude Wheeler, leaves his home in Nebraska to fight in France in World War I. His experience of France sheds new light on his past, and he is finally able to say what has bothered him at home: "I never knew there was anything worth living for, till this war came on. Before that, the world seemed like a business proposition."[200] This is the essence of Wharton's and Cather's argument with America. To Eden Bower and Julia Brant, the financially profitable "business proposition" is the only sign of success. But for Don Hedger, John Campton, Claude Wheeler, and others like them—including Lily and Paul, Wharton and Cather—any life worth living must include more than that: it must include beauty and others who appreciate beauty.

4

THE WEST

Provinciality, Vitality, and the "Real" America

Looking back at that little world [of my childhood], and remembering the "hoard of petty maxims" with which its elders preached down every sort of initiative, I have often wondered at such lassitude in the descendants of the men who first cleared a place for themselves in a new world.... What had become of the spirit of the pioneers and the revolutionaries?

EDITH WHARTON, *A Backward Glance*

In Nebraska, as in so many other States, we must face the fact that the splendid story of the pioneers is finished, and that no new story worthy to take its place has yet begun. The generation that subdued the wild land and broke up the virgin prairie is passing.... [That generation] came into a wilderness and had to make everything, had to be as ingenious as shipwrecked sailors. The generation now in the driver's seat hates to make anything, wants to live and die in an automobile, scudding past those acres where the old men used to follow the long corn-rows up and down.

WILLA CATHER, "Nebraska: The End of the First Cycle"

WHARTON, CATHER, AND THE WEST

While charting Wharton and Cather onto the grid of New York illustrates the proximity of their lives and works, there is little point in plotting their lives, at least, onto a map of the West. While highlighting the wealth of sites important to Cather's life—including locations in

Nebraska, Colorado, Wyoming, Arizona, New Mexico, and California and cities as wide-ranging as Chicago, Lincoln, and San Francisco—such a map would show Wharton as glaringly absent from the West. In the United States her life revolved around New York City, Lenox, and Newport—of which New York is the westernmost. The furthest west she ever traveled was Detroit, a quick trip to see the premier of the dramatic version of *The House of Mirth* in September 1906.[1] As R. W. B. Lewis writes, "It was her first and last journey any real distance west of the Hudson River."[2] The play did well in Detroit—Wharton called the portrayal of Lily Bart "simply perfect"—a sharp contrast to its failure in New York, where she remarked that the play was "badly acted."[3] But Wharton was neither "converted to the American midlands" nor impressed by Detroit,[4] and certainly not by her hotel, which she described in her diary as "vile hole opposite station."[5] Wharton's negative and extremely limited exposure to the United States west of the Hudson seems to have shaped her lifelong perspective; her "West" is more emblematic than geographic and rarely positive. As Gary Totten has observed, her stories often "mine ... western stereotypes," and "the lurid and the sensational [are] western forces" in stories such as "Bunner Sisters."[6] Nor is her West geographically specific. Many of Wharton's characters come from "the West," yet that broad designation is often as specific as she gets. Wharton's individual map of the West seems little more detailed than old maps marked "here be monsters."

In fact Wharton is at her satirical best—or her elitist worst—in depicting westerners, who often come across as monsters in her work. Hinda Warlick, a minor character in her 1918 novella *The Marne*, is representative. Determined to go to France to "help" in the war effort, Hinda "appeared to think that Joan of Arc was a Revolutionary hero, who had been guillotined with Marie Antoinette for blowing up the Bastille; and her notions of French history did not extend beyond this striking episode."[7] Many other characters from the West and Midwest, most infamously *The Custom of the Country*'s Undine Spragg, are equally brash, ignorant, and uncultivated. A single sentence from *The Custom of the Country*, which describes Undine as having a "mind as destitute of beauty and mystery as the prairie schoolhouse in which she had been educated,"[8] suggests the chasm between Wharton's usual view of the West and Cather's; one has only to glance at Cather's story "The Best Years," the tale of a young Nebraska teacher, to see that in Cather's West the prairie schoolhouse has its own dramas and tragedies, its own beauty and mystery.

Wharton is also geographically vague, giving no details about exactly where these characters are from. Hinda is simply "from the Middle West";[9] Undine is from Apex City, which Wharton does not assign to a specific state. Critics have suggested states as various as Indiana, Illinois, Ohio, Kansas, and Arizona, but within the parameters of the novel, its actual location hardly seems to matter.[10] "Apex City" functions as an allegorical representation of a range of equally undistinguished locations in a vast, undifferentiated West.[11] Like "American City" in James's *The Golden Bowl*, the cultural desert to which the cultivated Charlotte Stant is sentenced to return at the conclusion of that novel, its very name is parodic, mocking the large ambitions of some western cities; "Apex City" is neither the apex of anything nor a substantial city. Until late in her career, Wharton seems to have been uninterested in drawing a complex character from the Midwest; an Alexandra Bergson or a Thea Kronborg was not within her scope. Similarly her descriptions of western settings in novels such as *The Custom of the Country* and *Hudson River Bracketed* are thin at best, betraying her lack of knowledge of the places of which she wrote. Sinclair Lewis, as we saw earlier, remarked that authors could adequately describe only the places they knew from experience; in contrast, "'get[ting] up' a scene by reading about it" is "a handicap."[12] Lewis uses Wharton as an illustration, stating that "the Edith Wharton of *Ethan Frome* is greater than the Edith Wharton of *The Valley of Decision*."[13] Wharton knew western Massachusetts better than Italy, at least at the time she wrote *The Valley of Decision*; similarly, she knew New York and Paris, but not the West.

Like Lewis, Cather stressed that if artists were going to depict specific places, they should know them well. When a young Marguerite Yourcenar (later to be the first woman elected to the Académie Française) began to translate *Death Comes for the Archbishop* into French, Cather objected that Yourcenar "has never been in the Southwest at all, and seems to have no conception of how very different that country is from any other part of the United States."[14] Responding to Yourcenar's plan to paraphrase her landscape descriptions, Cather asked, "How can one paraphrase descriptions of a landscape which one has never seen, or even informed oneself about?"[15] The same principle applied to illustrators. At one point Cather considered writing a nonfiction book about the Southwest but stipulated that any illustrator would need to know the region firsthand. To her editor, she wrote that although Scribner's had employed the celebrated illustrator Ernest Peixotto to illustrate a book on the Southwest, she was not impressed with the results: "He stayed <u>one day</u> at the richest places and merely rode through the others in a motor.... He knows nothing at all about the country."[16] In contrast, she admired Harold von Schmidt's illustrations for *Death Comes for the Archbishop*; von Schmidt knew the West well, having grown up there.[17] Her own ability to recreate an authentic West was grounded in her experience, as the *Chicago Daily News* noted; Cather's West in *My Ántonia* is the real West, the reviewer stated, not the "pasteboard west" of many earlier writers, which "can be done perfectly by a man who was never outside New York."[18]

The vagueness, the relative flatness, and the harshness of most of Wharton's western characters and landscapes throw into relief the specificity and nuance of Cather's western characters and the three dimensionality of the western towns, cities, and landscapes in many of her best-known works, including *My Ántonia, O Pioneers!, The Song of the Lark,* and *Death Comes for the Archbishop*. Further, Cather was aware of differences within "the West" to which Wharton was apparently oblivious. For instance, in choosing to set *O Pioneers!* in Nebraska rather than some other western states, Cather knew that she had taken a risk: "As everyone knows, Nebraska is distinctly déclassé as a literary background.... Kansas is almost as unpromising. Colorado, on the contrary, is considered quite possible. Wyoming really has some class... like well-cut riding breeches."[19] She concludes by acknowledging the power of the East in determining publications from and about the West and by reconfirming the riskiness of setting her work in Nebraska: "A New York critic voiced a very general opinion when he said: 'I simply don't care a damn what happens in Nebraska, no matter who writes about it.'"[20]

Yet just as the East appears frequently in Cather's work, so the West appears often in Wharton's. In fact, as Jean Griffith has observed, "westerners are everywhere in Wharton's fiction,"[21] even if they sometimes seem to share no historical reality with Cather's or seem the opposite of hers. The two authors' midwestern millionaires, Wharton's Elmer Moffatt (*The Custom of the Country*) and Cather's Fred Ottenburg (*The Song of the Lark*), provide a good example. Moffatt is grasping, crude, manipulative; Ottenburg is charming, musical, sophisticated, a westerner who would never appear in a Wharton novel. Yet as soon as we draw such a comparison, we see its limitations. Wharton's "bad" Moffatt is more complex than he first seems; he also has a good heart (at least at moments) and gradually develops a deep appreciation of the beautiful; the "good" Ottenburg marries a close friend's fiancée and, when the marriage proves disastrous, proposes a bigamous marriage to Thea without so much as informing her of the situation. There is also a middle ground in Wharton's and Cather's portrayals of westerners. Ottenburg's wife, Edith Beers, is a character either author could have invented. A scheming and manipulative western heiress, she seems more likely to have sprung from Wharton's parodic eastern pen than from Cather's more sympathetic western one. Yet both authors disliked the vampish, proto-flapper type of woman she represents.

In fact, once we mentally chart Wharton's fictional references to the West onto our hypothetical map, she makes a much stronger showing. The West may hover at the edges of Wharton's fiction, but it does so persistently and meaningfully, frequently filling the position it so often has in American literature and culture: as "the fresh start, the safety valve for illiterates and misfits, the last gasp of the American Dream."[22] Yet Wharton's work also suggests that the fresh start does not always work out and that "the West" can be a difficult place for easterners to reach. As we saw in "Mrs. Manstey's View," the title character's only child, living at the opposite end of the country in California, is unreachable. In another early work, "Bunner Sisters," Wharton again reminds readers of the vastness of the country and questions the West as a fresh start.[23]

In this novella two middle-aged sisters in New York fall in love with the same man; he marries the younger, Evelina, and carries her off to a new life in St. Louis. But neither the marriage nor the new location works out well. In a letter to her sister, Evelina describes St. Louis as "not near as large or handsome as New York"; Wharton emphasizes the distance between East and West, with Evelina referring to St. Louis painfully as "this great City so far from home."[24] When Eliza Ann, the older sister, fears for Evelina's welfare, she is unable to track her or to raise the money to travel to St. Louis to look for her.

The West also figures as a possible escape valve in *Ethan Frome*. Trapped in an unhappy marriage and powerfully attracted to another woman, Ethan ponders running away to the West: "He knew a case of a man over the mountain . . . who had escaped from just such a life of misery by going West with the girl he cared for. His wife had divorced him, and he had married the girl and prospered"; the happy couple now have "a little girl with fair curls, who wore a gold locket and was dressed like a princess."[25] As the golden-haired "princess" hints, it is nearly a fairytale outcome, for even the abandoned first wife has done well, starting her own business and "bloom[ing] into activity and importance."[26] The West hovers as the chance of new beginnings, yet Ethan, like Eliza Ann in "Bunner Sisters," realizes he is too poor to make the trip.

At the other end of the economic spectrum, the affluent world Wharton portrays in *The House of Mirth* occasionally reminds readers of the linkages between New York and the West. After all, westerners came east, and New Yorkers went west. The mansions of the *nouveaux riches* are described as impressing western visitors; the consummate easterner, Lily Bart, at one point accepts the offer of an extended train trip to Alaska from her *nouveau riche* friends the Gormers, a trip that succeeds in "removing her from the fiery centre of criticism and discussion" for a time.[27] Of the trip itself, much less Alaska, nothing is said. Within the novel "Alaska" is less a geographic place than a function, a place far removed from the social complications of New York, which remains the center of Lily's existence. East and West interact again when Lily accepts a job as social secretary for Mrs. Norma Hatch, who is vaguely defined as "coming 'from the West,' with the not unusual extenuation of having brought a great deal of money with her. She was ... rich, helpless, unplaced: the very subject for Lily's hand."[28] Yet Lily's association with Mrs. Hatch further damages her reputation. Although the West exists as the possibility of new beginnings, it fails to fulfill that promise in Wharton's work.

As we have seen, Wharton and Cather were united in their concerns about American cultural starvation, particularly beyond the eastern seaboard. Yet Cather's West is still far more cultivated than Wharton's. In *The Song of the Lark* Thea has valuable musical experiences growing up in Moonstone. While her piano teacher, Wunsch, has a drinking problem and her friend Spanish Johnny is subject to wanderlust, both are genuine musical talents from whom Thea learns a great deal. Similarly Cather's depiction of Chicago emphasizes its artistic culture. In terms of literary portraits of Chicago in this period, the city is perhaps best known as "Hog Butcher for the World," a place that was "alive and coarse and strong and cunning," thanks to Carl Sandburg's 1914 poem, or as the grim city to which Carrie Meeber moves in Theodore Dreiser's *Sister Carrie*. Although Cather depicts the city's grittiness, she also highlights its musical and artistic life, incorporating the historical figure Theodore Thomas, founding director of the Chicago Symphony, into her story.[29] Cather dramatizes crucial moments in Thea's artistic education at a performance of Dvorak's "New World Symphony" and in the Art Institute, as Thea views paintings and sculptures.[30] Thea's musical instruction in Chicago under Anders Harsanyi is excellent; one of Thea's first professional appearances as a singer is in the home of the Nathanmeyers, wealthy patrons of the arts who are based on the historical figures Bertha and Palmer Potter.[31]

Cather's portrayal of the Nathanmeyers is a reminder of the cultural life of the city at the turn of the twentieth century. A story in a 1954 volume of the *Art Institute of Chicago Quarterly* relates that Chauncey McCormick, a president of the Art Institute and a friend of "leading citizens who wanted Chicago known for its culture as well as for its stockyards," relished telling "distinguished guests ... how our great collections of nineteenth century art had been purchased years ago by daring Chicagoans when Renoir and Monet and Degas were little known and valued even in France. Once he was showing our Renoir room to a somewhat top-lofty visitor. 'My, my,' exclaimed the guest, 'all these Renoirs must have cost you a great deal of money.' 'Oh, no,' replied Mr. McCormick. 'In Chicago we don't *buy* Renoirs. We inherit them from our grandmothers.'"[32] There was, in short, a far richer cultural scene west of the Hudson than Wharton had any idea of.[33]

Yet Cather herself wrote in "polarized terms" about the West; many of her early stories, "characterized . . . by stark grimness and an almost cynical tone,"[34] would have confirmed Wharton's view of a culturally barren West. Even as an adult, Cather occasionally found the West frightening. In a 1912 letter from Winslow, Arizona, to Elsie Sergeant, Cather explained that sometimes her negative response to the West manifested itself physically: "The West always paralyzes me a little. When I am away from it I remember only the tang on the tongue. But when I come back [I] always feel a little of the fright I felt when I was a child. . . . It's real enough to make a tightness in my chest even now. . . . I used always to be sure that I'd never get out, that I would die in a cornfield."[35] Wharton's awareness of the challenging vastness of the United States emerges in Cather's voice as she tells Sergeant, "I would run over to see you if we had not the misfortune to be born in such a big country."[36]

Not until Cather had been away from the West for well over a decade—she left Nebraska in 1896 and published *O Pioneers!*, the first of her prairie novels, in 1913—would the prairie become a beautiful place in her writing. Even then she would never be uniformly positive about the West, and the barrenness Wharton portrayed in the Midwest is much like the scene Cather witnessed in some places in the far West. Although Cather liked San Francisco, she called Long Beach "the most hideous and vulgar place in the whole world";[37] her portrayal of "a sprawling overgrown West-coast city . . . in the throes of rapid development" in *My Mortal Enemy* is Whartonian both in its vague identification of place and in its negativity about the West.[38] For both, the East meant culture, and the West meant a lack of it. Yet the West also increasingly meant energy, vitality, and determination.

The East-West gap was widening in the late nineteenth century.[39] Even as the country moved westward and the completion of the first transcontinental railroad in 1869 was expected to help unify the nation after the divisive Civil War, deep cultural questions arose about what America was and who the "real" Americans were. Such questions were not made any simpler by the fact that the "West" itself has never been a stable category. James Fenimore Cooper is often seen as the first writer of the American western, although the Leatherstocking series begins not in the West but in the geographic center of New York state, near Lake Otsego and Cooperstown (which was founded by and named for James Fenimore Cooper's father). In 1859 the artist George Catlin asked "where" the West was, and "conclude[d] that 'phantom like it flies before us as we travel.'"[40] Historically and culturally the West kept moving west, and "one frontier ... succeeded another: the Allegheny Mountains, the trans-Mississippi Valley, the Great Plains, [and] the Far West."[41] Even now there is no common national understanding or standard definition about what constitutes "the West" or "the Midwest."

The East-West divide has also been a divide between "civilization"—a word that has its roots in the Latin *cīvis*, "citizen," a city dweller—and the frontier, an area that is by definition outside, or at best on the fringes of, civilization. The contrast between East and West itself generated a central question about American identity: whether urban power and sophistication, encapsulated in the cities of the eastern seaboard, or the rough, tough, innovative frontier, were "more" American; which, indeed, was the "real" America? Frederick Jackson Turner propounded his famous thesis in 1893, proclaiming that the frontier—the West— was closed. He also defined the frontier as the place in which the true American came into being: "The frontier is the line of most rapid and effective Americanization. The wilderness masters the colonist. It finds him a European in dress, industries, tools, modes of travel, and thought. It takes him from the railroad car and puts him in the birch canoe. It strips off the garments of civilization and arrays him in the hunting shirt and the moccasin. . . . Little by little he transforms the wilderness, but the outcome is not the old Europe. . . . The fact is, that here is a new product that is American."[42] If the "new product" that emerged from the encounter between the frontier and the settler was a true American rather than merely a transplanted emigrant, so too the land itself was defined as truly American: "Moving westward, the frontier became more and more American.... The advance of the frontier has meant a steady movement away from the influence of Europe, a steady growth of independence on American lines."[43]

Turner's thesis, despite its many limitations (including his deeply troubling equation of native peoples with "savagery"), was tremendously influential in the period in which Wharton and Cather were writing. Both within the United States and beyond, the frontier—or a romanticized idea of the frontier—was (and often still is) seen as inherently American, reflected in that most American genre in fiction and film, the type of story simply called "the western." The elevation of the frontier in American culture inevitably meant the decline in importance, at least in terms of the national imaginary, of the cities of the eastern seaboard, which had long assumed that they were the very origins and definition of the United States: Virginia with its tidewater aristocracy, Boston with its ties to the Pilgrims, and New York City with its Dutch settlers and traders. Even now tension exists between East and West, and between urban and rural: which is more American, the Metropolitan Museum of Art or a rodeo? An urban skyline, a red barn in a lush green countryside, or towering mountain peaks? Tellingly the images in current U.S. passports, certainly chosen to emphasize "American" scenes, emphasize the West: of twelve double-page illustrations, nine show images most would call western, from a Twainian riverboat on the Mississippi to images of Mount Rushmore, the Rocky Mountains, saguaro cacti, and grazing bison. Now as then, debates rage over who and what constitute the "real" America and "real" Americans.

Such broad cultural struggles are rarely carried on in a coherent fashion or in a single form or forum, and the struggle over defining "the real America" inevitably entered the literary field as every other, enacted as the struggle between two literary subgenres: realism, associated with the East, and naturalism, associated with the Midwest and West. An entire set of attitudes, usually hinted at rather than stated, went along with this debate, which burgeoned in the decade 1910–19 and throughout the 1920s and 1930s. In this period realism was sometimes conflated with "the genteel tradition," the post–Civil War movement in American literature to idealize American culture, "to abolish the evils and vulgarities and sometimes the simple changes in American society by never talking about them"; the goal was to protect the "purity" of a hypothetical American middle-class girl by "ignoring or denying the brutalities of business life" and of life in general.[44] Wharton's work is sometimes associated with the genteel tradition, despite the fact that her work rebelled against such factitious purity from its beginning. Nevertheless, she was one of the authors pushed aside by younger writers who, if anything, went to the opposite extreme in their depictions of American life. The rebellion against the "genteel" relied (as all such arguments do) on polarized camps; invoking the terms of place and class often used to separate Wharton and Cather, one critic called it a "conflict between the Eastern seaboard and the Middle West" and "between the old rich families and the lower middle class."[45]

The division between the two camps was perhaps most clearly delineated in a 1957 essay by Philip Rahv. The essay suffers from an unfortunate title, "Paleface and Redskin," and would better have been called "Realists and Naturalists," or even "East and West," since, with only minor changes, the cultural division between the eastern United States and the West is what the essay articulates. "At one pole" of American literature, Rahv argues, is work depicting "the lowlife world of the frontier and of the big cities; at the other the thin, solemn, semi-clerical culture of Boston and Concord.... For the process of polarization has produced a dichotomy between experience and consciousness—a dissociation between energy and sensibility, between conduct and theories of conduct, between life conceived as an opportunity and life conceived as a discipline"; Rahv's exemplars are Walt Whitman and Henry James.[46] More than half a century after the publication of this essay, Rahv's lines of polarization still delineate the perceived gap between Wharton and Cather. Wharton, the easterner, is associated with "consciousness," "sensibility," "theories of conduct," "life as a discipline," and other qualities Rahv names, including a "patrician" perspective and an "exquisite moral atmosphere"; those who dislike her work may see it as depicting a "refined estrangement from reality" and see Wharton herself as "genteel, snobbish, pedantic."[47] Cather, the westerner, is associated with "experience," "energy," and "life as an opportunity," as well as with a "plebeian," or at least a middle-class, perspective and is often seen as "giving expression to the vitality and to the aspirations of the people." (Cather seems exempt from the potential faults Rahv lists for this class of writer—for instance, "vulgar anti-intellectual[ism].")[48] Even today the East-West division remains an entrenched part of American culture.

The eastern realist/western naturalist split also includes elements of gender, as scholars like Marjorie Pryse, Judith Fetterley, and June Howard have argued.[49] Donna Campbell summarizes the situation nicely. In 1887, she points out, William Dean Howells had praised the writing of women, particularly in short stories, as being "faithfuler and more realistic than those of the men.... Their tendency is more distinctly in that direction, and there is a solidity, an honest report of observation, in the work of such women as Mrs. Cooke, Miss Murfree, Miss Jewett, and Miss Woolson."[50] Only fourteen years later, in 1901, Frank Norris opined that women were too fragile to "grind on steadily for an almost indefinite period," which prevented them from writing great fiction; in Campbell's summary of his argument, "The crucial issue . . . is that although women may study 'real life' through literature, they are barred from direct experience of 'life itself, the crude, the raw, the vulgar' by their natural reluctance to force themselves 'into the midst of that great, grim complication of men's doings that we call life.'"[51] Real writers, Norris wrote, "are recruited from the razor-using contingent."[52] Much of the decline of the realists (and ascendency of the naturalists) might be attributed to a pithy statement by Norris, which, in one fell swoop, wrote off Howells, the realists, women writers (especially the New England local colorists), and, by extension, the literary values associated with the East: "Realism is minute, it is the drama of a broken teacup, the tragedy of a walk down the block, the excitement of an afternoon call, the adventure of an invitation to dinner. . . . Realism . . . says to me, . . . 'That is life.' And I say that it is not."[53] In contrast, Norris implies, real life and real literature—literature worth reading—were expansive, western, and male.

Inevitably this underlying cultural dynamic contributed significantly to the reception of Wharton's and Cather's fiction. Some of Wharton's work could, by a dismissive critic, be called "the tragedy of a broken teacup"; Norris might have summarized *Ethan Frome* as the tragedy of a broken pickle dish, while her story "The Other Two" ends, quite literally, as a comedy, rather than a tragedy, of teacups. But Wharton distanced herself from the ebbing tide of local color and its association with "genteel" themes and assumed a naturalistic outlook in much of her fiction, as Donald Pizer and Donna Campbell have persuasively argued.[54] Cather's characters and plots were at a safe distance from the teacup tragedies Norris scorned; the identification of her work with the West through *O Pioneers!*, *The Song of the Lark*, and *My Ántonia*, although it stemmed from her strong personal identification with the region, may also have been influenced by the good business sense to align herself with the rising tide in western literature. Yet she steered her own course: her novels eschew the grand, even melodramatic, endings of many naturalistic novels.

The strength of the identification of Wharton with the East and Cather with the West, examined briefly in the introduction, now becomes more explicable: they and their works participate in the larger cultural struggle to determine whether American identity was "eastern" or "western." When reviewers pitted Wharton and Cather against each other, asking which of the two was the greater novelist (even when they limited the field, as they often did, to "women novelists"), they were also asking a question about culture, place, and class in American identity. As we saw earlier, Vernon Parrington admired the skill of Wharton's *Age of Innocence* but also declared the novel irrelevant, preferring "the honest crudities of the younger naturalists," associated strongly with the West, to the "little clan of first families" in New York whose windows "open only to the east."[55] Meanwhile, Cather's star had risen not only because of her skill as a writer but because her choice of western settings and subjects was increasingly identified as "American." The *Nation*'s review of *O Pioneers!* describes the westward shift in literature as a *fait accompli*: the novel of the West is "the newer Americanism which has displaced the New Englandism of our nineteenth-century fiction."[56] Contrasting "the big spaces and big emotions of Western life" with "the smug theory and languid practices of society in the smaller sense of the word,"[57] the reviewer writes off fiction like Jewett's, James's, and Wharton's. In celebrating *My Ántonia* as "one of the best [novels] that any American has ever done, East or West," Mencken not only articulated the East-West conflict but praised Cather for having moved away from the eastern setting, and the influence of Wharton, which had affected *Alexander's Bridge*.[58] As with *O Pioneers!*, reviewers praised *My Ántonia* specifically for its western setting, equating it with an American setting, and for its American quality and American language. *The Nation* contrasted Cather's style with another novel in the "post-Jacobite [i.e., Jamesian] manner that appears to attract so many of the current women story-tellers, Mrs. Wharton among them," a style that "touches snobbishness" and is "too niggling ... for much real usefulness on this side of the water."[59] In contrast, Cather's style is praised as that "of an artist whose imagination is at home in her own land, among her own people, which happens to be a democratic land and a plain people."[60] Randolph Bourne's remark—"Here at last is an American novel, redolent of the Western prairie"[61]—equated the novel's Americanness with its westernness, as did the reviewer who declared, when *My Ántonia* was republished in 1926, "The language is redolent of the soil, clean-cut American writing, and yet dignified. It pulsates with the life of the people it describes."[62]

The sense of the West as the real America prevailed in England as well. A reviewer for London's *Times Literary Supplement* noted in 1921, only half-jokingly, that any traveler to the United States should be "warned" that New York and New England "are not the real America at all; if he wants to find that, ... he must go inland" to the "'Middle West.'"[63] By the same token, he argues, readers interested in American literature should read Dreiser—and Cather's *My Ántonia*. Four years later another English reviewer, in this case Virginia Woolf, made much the same point. In an essay titled "American Fiction," she stated firmly that the category did not include anything by James or Wharton; while one could not "dismiss" them as writers, "they are not Americans; they do not give us anything that we have not got already."[64] While admitting that her attitude is a "tourist's" attitude, Woolf nevertheless maintains that in order to "see" America, she wants to read literature that depicts what

England does not have. In his remarks on Hawthorne, James had commented on the paucity of culture about which an American author could write.⁶⁵ That very paucity, however, was exactly what interested Woolf, who wanted the view of "a vast continent, scattered here and there with brand new villages which nature has not absorbed into herself... as in England, but [which] man has built recently, hastily, economically."⁶⁶ She briefly acknowledges authors whose works describe such settings, including Cather, but focuses on works by Sherwood Anderson and Sinclair Lewis. This does not mean she lavishes praise upon them; "both suffer as novelists from being American," she says, arguing that American writers are hampered by their cultural self-consciousness.⁶⁷ But she does credit them with being truly American writers.

Unsurprisingly Woolf's article did not find favor with Wharton, who wrote to Gaillard Lapsley that "Mrs. Virginia Woolf... writes a long article to say that no interesting American fiction is, or should be, written in English; and that Henry Hergesheimer [sic] & I are negligible because we have nothing new to give—not even a language! Well—such discipline is salutary."⁶⁸ She formalized her complaints about expectations like Woolf's in a 1927 article in the *Yale Review*. In "The Great American Novel" Wharton argued against the demand that to be considered "American," a "novelist's scene must be laid in the United States, and his story deal exclusively with citizens of those States; furthermore, if his work is really to deserve the epithet 'American,' it must tell of persons so limited in education and opportunity that they live cut off from all the varied sources of culture which used to be considered the common heritage of English-speaking people. The great American novel must always be about Main Street, geographically, socially, and intellectually."⁶⁹ In a 1934 essay, "Tendencies in Modern Fiction," she stated the same concerns, protesting reviewers' equation of "the 'real America'" with its most rural and least privileged classes.⁷⁰ She also protested the overuse "of dialect and slang" in many American novels.⁷¹ Wharton's frustration, linked to both geographic and class issues, is palpable in these essays. If at some moments she comes across as deeply elitist, in others she displays great critical acumen. At one point, for instance, she argues against expectations like Woolf's that all "American" literature must be set in the United States; no one would say that Stendhal's *The Charterhouse of Parma* is not a French novel because it is set in Italy, she notes.[72] If "American literature," by definition, meant a setting in the United States and a depiction of individuals "cut off" from culture, nearly all of Wharton's work, except *Ethan Frome*, *Summer*, and a few stories, would be excluded. But far from worrying simply that her own work was being discredited, she objected to such a limiting definition of "American literature" and what it implied about the United States and American character. Cather was also concerned about the direction American literature was taking. Asked in 1942 about works of American literature she would recommend for an anthology for soldiers, she remarked, "I could tell you a lot about what to keep out of your anthology!" If many of the "American classics" were, she felt, "too mild" for soldiers of eighteen or nineteen, she also felt that "many of the new books are too 'strong' and are passionately devoted to the ugliness and baseness of American life."[73]

Wharton and Cather were inevitably aware of the East-West shift in cultural balance and what it meant for them as authors. As early as 1904, the year before her major success with *The House of Mirth*, Wharton complained to her editor at Scribner's that she felt hemmed in as a writer by expectations that were too rigid and formulaic. While she was frustrated by "the continued cry that I am an echo of Mr. James," she was also irritated by "the assumption that the people I write about are not 'real' because they are not navvies & char-women.... I write about what I see, what I happen to be nearest to, which is surely better than doing cowboys de chic."[74] The critics, it seemed, wanted her to be either James or one of the naturalists—or perhaps Owen Wister, whose novel *The Virginian* had achieved phenomenal success two years earlier, quickly becoming "*the* transitional text" in the creation of the western as a genre in fiction and film.[75]

As we saw in chapter 1, Wharton admired fiction that confirmed her view of the Midwest and West as culturally barren. In the 1920s her letters to fellow expatriate Gaillard Lapsley often included clippings and advertisements that confirmed her sense of the primitive state of American culture. She also forwarded items to him, including a letter she had received from "The People's Popular Monthly" of Des Moines that seemed almost calculated to confirm her sense of American callowness. The letter, addressed to "Miss Wharton," asked for a "serial story of from sixty to seventy thousand words," for which the editor was "willing to pay ten thousand dollars." The editor added, "We want the story to be worth the price" and stipulated that "the story must be clean, wholesome and happy and must have a great deal of human interest. It must be a story that will appeal to real home folks and the love theme should be quite prominent."[76] With the redundancy of the magazine's title, the editor's addressing Wharton incorrectly, his offering her a sum of money but insulting her professionalism by implying that she might send them shoddy work, and his prescribing exactly the sort of story that Wharton objected to in the kind of language she objected to ("real home folks"), the letter is nearly a parody of the offer made to a novice author, Ivy Spang, in Wharton's 1919 story, "Writing a War Story." In that tale an editor had asked for "a good rousing story . . . a dash of sentiment of course, but nothing to depress or discourage . . . a good stirring trench story, with a Coming-Home scene to close with . . . a Christmas scene, if you can manage it." The only thing Wharton might have appreciated in the letter was the editor's specifying that the story *not* be a western, "as we have had many of them."[77]

Wharton's skepticism about the West remained with her. In 1934 she was offered an honorary doctorate by Columbia University; her editor, Rutger Jewett, apparently hoped that this distinction would boost sales of her just-published memoir, *A Backward Glance*. Wharton was unable to accept the degree because of poor health, but she doubted that the honor would have had any effect on sales: "The Western morons to whom [Jewett] wishes to sell the book wd [would] not be much affected by my Academic distinction," she wrote to Minnie Jones.[78] This was her stance despite the fact that she felt that her audience was shrinking: "The rest of the public—the small rest!—will, I think, be interested in the 'costume' side, the pictures, the Old New York stories, & so on. And about 100 will want to read about H. James."[79] Thirty years after her protest against "cowboys de chic," she retained a low opinion of western booksellers and western readers.

While Wharton "lost" status in terms of American literature's increasing orientation toward the middle and lower middle classes and the West, Cather gained status. Surely Cather was aware of this when, in 1931, she distanced herself from the "drawing-room" fiction of Wharton and James and associated her own work with the West in "My First Novels."[80] But like Wharton, she experienced a sense of creative confinement when she found that readers expected her to write of the West. "Poor Knopf, anyhow!" she wrote to Fisher in 1924. "Just when he has got his booksellers where they can sell most any old book I do about the West, I refuse to have anything to do with the West."[81] Yet she embellishes the situation with a humorous, western-flavored word picture: "My familiar spirit is like an old wild turkey that forsakes a feeding ground as soon as it sees tracks of people—especially if the people are readers, book-buyers. It's a crafty bird and it wants to go where there aint [sic] no readers."[82] Like Huck Finn lighting out for the territories, Cather imagines a place—no doubt in the mythically unsettled West—where "there aint no readers"; even while objecting that she doesn't want to be limited to writing about the West, she invokes it.

Despite her deep familiarity with her western settings, Cather also faced a certain disadvantage in writing novels set in the West. As Ida Rae Egli has written, the gap between eastern and western literature was particularly disadvantageous to women, who "found the gap much harder to bridge than did their male counterparts."[83] By the early 1900s the American public had also been saturated with paintings by artists like Frederic Remington and Thomas Moran, paintings that helped to establish the idea of the West as a rugged, almost exclusively masculine place, as Janis Stout has shown.[84] Like Wharton, Cather suffered as a woman writer from expectations that the West, and therefore literature about the West, would be masculine in a very narrow sense. This dynamic explains her happiness with a positive review of *O Pioneers!* that appeared in *The Nation*. Sending a copy to her sister Elsie, she wrote, "I am very proud of it. I used to meet [novelist David Graham] Phillips about the Waldorf and talk to him and I used to think 'you big stuffed-shirt-and-checked-pants, I know more about the real west than you do, but I could never make anybody believe it, because I wear skirts and don't shave.' But you see people do believe it, after all, and I call that very jolly."[85] Besides challenging Phillips's portrait of the West, Cather's remark that she "wear[s] skirts and d[oesn't] shave" nicely challenges Norris's remark that real writers were "recruited from the razor-using contingent."

Unlike Wharton, Cather frequently wrote the West; while Wharton had reservations about what others saw as "American," Cather had concerns about how others saw "the West" and insisted on writing the West in a way that seemed true to her. In a 1919 letter to her brother Roscoe she commented, "Long before I began to write anything worth while, I hated [William Allen] White and Grahame [sic] Phillips for the way they wrote about the West. I knew that there was a common way of presenting common life, which is worthless, and a finer way of presenting it which would be much more true. Of course Antonia's story could be told in exactly the same jocular, familiar, grapenutsy way that Mr. White thinks is so American. He thinks he is presenting things as they are, but what he really presents is his own essentially vulgar personality."[86] In an interview she explained that she did not care to write like another popular western writer: "I could have written ['Tom Outland's Story'] like a Zane Grey novel, but I would have died of boredom doing it."[87] Both Wharton and Cather protested not only narrow definitions of the "American," but also the language in which other writers presented American subjects. Wharton objected to excessive use of slang; Cather protested White's "vulgar" tone and Grey's uninventive style. In 1915 Cather wrote to Henry Boynton, the critic who had penned the encouraging review of *O Pioneers!*, to thank him for his sense that "the cow-puncher's experience of the West was not the only experience possible there" and that a writer might be able to "give some truthful account of life in a new country without pretending to a jovial brutality which . . . cannot be successfully affected—at least, not by women."[88] Gender was an issue in writing the West—for Cather, the westerner, as for Wharton, the easterner.

"THE SPIRIT OF THE PIONEERS": THEA AND UNDINE

The complex dynamics of Wharton's and Cather's relationship to the West and the intersection of some aspects of their vision of America are made particularly clear in their creation of remarkably similar western heroines, Undine Spragg, protagonist of Wharton's 1913 *The Custom of the Country*, and Thea Kronborg, heroine of Cather's 1915 *The Song of the Lark*. While quite different in some ways, the novels tell fundamentally similar stories: both are tales of girls from the western provinces who work hard to be successful in a wider, more sophisticated world. Wharton's Undine Spragg is a westerner who forces her parents to move east so that she can climb the social ladder and enter society's top ranks, an ambition in which she is, mostly, successful, building pragmatically on men's susceptibility to her beauty. Cather's Thea Kronborg is a girl from Colorado who always feels herself different from nearly everyone in her town; a talented musician, she goes to Chicago for training, discovers that her true talent is not as a pianist but as an opera singer, and gradually makes her way to the stages of Europe and the Metropolitan Opera. She too is a success.

Yet Thea and Undine have usually been seen in very different terms. Undine has been reviled since her first appearance in print, with the *New York Times Review of Books* calling her "the most repellent heroine we have encountered in many a long day," *The Nation* referring to her as "a mere monster of vulgarity," and England's *Saturday Review* stating that she is "cold, greedy, heartless, and wayward, without a soul."[89] Edmund Wilson labeled Undine for a generation in 1941, calling her "the prototype in fiction of the 'gold-digger,' of the international cocktail bitch."[90] In 1975 R. W. B. Lewis described Undine, slightly more sympathetically, as what Wharton might have been if "all her best and most loveable and redeeming features had been suddenly cut away."[91] Within the novel, a minor character, Charles Bowen, comments that Undine is the "monstrously perfect result of the [American] system" of valuing business over all else, including love; within this system, women are condescended to, excluded, and bought off with "money and motors and cars," and they come to "pretend to themselves ... that *that's* what really constitutes life!"[92] Following this clue, feminist critics have portrayed Undine not so much victimizer as victim. If Undine is "monstrous," critics such as Cynthia Griffin Wolff have argued, it is because she has had her energies and abilities "grotesquely perverted ... by reasons of sex."[93] As a woman, she is excluded from achieving her ambition—reaching the pinnacle of social and financial prominence—through any means except marriage. Even such arguments are, of course, apologies for Undine—a character readers love to hate. In contrast, readers love to love Cather's Thea, the young woman who "makes [her]self born" as an artist.[94] The *Boston Evening Transcript* called Thea Kronborg "a genius"; in *The Nation* Boynton declared, "Thea Kronborg we believe in. . . . She becomes a great singer not only because she is born with the gift, but because she has the strength to develop it."[95] A further comment by the *Transcript*— "Sorry indeed must be the condition of one in whom Thea Kronborg's struggle would not stir some answering pulse"—captures the tone critics often assume when they discuss Thea.[96]

And in many ways the two characters are very different, even opposites. Undine is Wharton's nightmare version of the American girl, the exact type she objected to in "The Great American Novel": someone from "Main Street, geographically, socially, and intellectually . . . so limited in education and opportunity that [she] live[s] cut off from all the varied sources of culture."[97] In contrast, Cather's Thea is heroic, someone who emerges from a Main Street culture (albeit one not quite as culturally starved as Lewis's or Undine's) and who works doggedly, even valiantly, to connect herself to "all the varied sources of culture" in order to achieve meaningful success as an opera singer. Yet this very difference also suggests their fundamental similarity: both are girls who, recognizing the limited horizons of their hometowns, leave them behind in order to lead their lives in a larger world. Pairing Thea and Undine allows us to see how similar the much-loved Thea and the much-hated Undine really are. Both embody the characteristics increasingly associated with the West and, in turn, with America: energy and determination, sometimes to the point of ruthlessness.

As we saw in chapter 2, Wharton and Cather saw the "aliveness," the vitality, of literary characters as a touchstone of literary greatness. "The test of the novel is that its people should be *alive*," Wharton stated;[98] Cather admired Jewett's work as being "not stories at all, but life itself."[99] As the epigraphs to this chapter suggest, this literary principle was an extension of their personal belief in the importance of vitality and their admiration of energy. Both bemoaned the passing of a more energetic past, with Wharton wondering in her 1934 memoir about the conformity and the "lassitude" of the world into which she had been born and asking, "What had become of the spirit of the pioneers and the revolutionaries?"[100] Cather had sounded the same note in a 1923 essay: "the splendid story of the pioneers is finished, and... no new story worthy to take its place has yet begun."[101] Yet far from being purely elegiac, Cather also expressed hope, stating that the population of Nebraska is as "full of vigor as the soil."[102] Similarly Wharton had at least a grudging admiration for the "big money-makers of the West" and the "lords of Pittsburgh"[103] who swept into Old New York and gradually dominated it; she was fascinated by the energy these newcomers displayed.[104] Seeing her own social class as "creat[ing] the grounds for their own destruction" through their "disengagement from social issues and customary lethargy," she saw in the *nouveaux riches* an impressive, if sometimes alarming, display of "energy... power, assertion, drive, [and] ambition," as Benstock has argued.[105] Wharton's and Cather's admiration for those who "first cleared a place for themselves in a new world," who "had to be as ingenious as shipwrecked sailors,"[106] is hinted at through their shared love as children for *The Swiss Family Robinson*, Johann Wyss's tale of a shipwrecked family who must fend for themselves. In her memoir Wharton recalled the story as "fresh and leafy and adventurous"; Cather remarked that any child who had not read it had "missed a part of his or her childhood."[107] Its importance to her is reflected in the fact that Alexandra reads the story aloud in *O Pioneers!*, as does the Burden family circle, ingenious pioneers themselves, in *My Ántonia*.

Like the pioneers they admired, Wharton and Cather were themselves highly energetic. This is easy to remember with Cather, who fostered the image of herself as a child who "ran wild playing with the little herd girls" in Nebraska or "spen[t] most of her time in the open on horseback";[108] she was once photographed working a handcar on the railroad tracks, and many photos of her show her hiking or on horseback (fig. 9). The best-known images of Wharton are far less dynamic, often showing her standing or sitting in furs or laces. But a photograph

9. (*top*) Cather on horseback in the Southwest. Robert and Doris Kurth Collection, Archives and Special Collections, University of Nebraska–Lincoln Libraries.

10. (*bottom*) Wharton (on right) on donkey in Santorini, Greece, 1926. Courtesy Lilly Library, Indiana University, Bloomington, Indiana.

of her riding a donkey in Santorini, Greece, attests to her physical activity even in her later years (fig. 10). She was active throughout her life. In her memoir she describes her little-girl self riding her pony, swimming, and hiking on the rugged rocks that form the Atlantic shore of Newport;[109] letters from her adolescence and early married life show an athletic young woman playing tennis, ice skating, and bicycling as much as twenty miles a day around Newport and in Italy.[110]

Energy was much on the minds of Americans in this period, when Henri Bergson, John Dewey, and William James were all exploring ideas of energy and its relationship to "potential, ... will, and the creative life."[111] At the same time Henry Adams was observing that the dynamo had become the new focus of worship in the modern world, "the most expressive [of] the thousand symbols of ultimate energy."[112] The West was increasingly associated with energy and the East with a loss of vitality. As Lee Mitchell points out, the title character in *The Virginian*, America's first literary cowboy, leaves the East because "they was talking about the same old things" and will never have "any new subjects."[113] As Mitchell summarizes, "Eastern conversation is as exhausted as its soil and ... drained of significance."[114] In Rahv's "dissociation between energy and sensibility, between conduct and theories of conduct, between life ... as an opportunity and life ... as a discipline,"[115] it is the West that is aligned with energy, conduct, and opportunity; the East is left with mere "sensibility," overly cerebral "theories of conduct," and life as a potentially harsh, even Puritanical, "discipline." Energy was the West, and the West was increasingly the American.

The works of Wharton and Cather participate in this cultural shift. Their western heroines are embodiments of western energy, as exhibited in their "talent, ambition, hard-headedness, egocentricity, and a certain ruthlessness"—a description that fits Undine Spragg perfectly, although it was written by Susan Rosowski as a summary of the characteristics of Cather's Thea Kronborg.[116] Indeed, although "ambition," even blind or driving ambition, is frequently associated with Undine, many descriptions of Thea establish that she is equally ambitious—as well as egocentric, hard-headed, and ruthless. In fact many phrases used by or about one character apply equally to the other, and even readers who know both novels well might have a hard time knowing whether Thea or Undine is the character described in the following lines. One of the young women, asked what she "expects" from life, replies, "Why, *everything*!"; the other says, "I only want impossible things." One character reflects that many "young people . . . meant to have things. But the difference was that *she was going to get them*!" Of both it could be said that they "will always get on better with men"; they are, in fact, reassured about their prospects by influential men. When one girl says, "I can't wait to be off . . . I want to get at it!" her wealthy male companion "look[s] her up and down and laugh[s]," replying, "Don't worry, you'll get at it"; the other is told by a socially prominent older man (after she states that she wants "*everything*!"), "My child, if you look like that you'll get it." Ambition makes both self-centered: a minor character notes of one, "She is very much interested in herself"; another character tells her that she always has "an ulterior motive." Both Undine and Thea want "everything" and are willing to do almost anything to "get it."[117]

Both girls are aware of using their appearance to get "everything," going beyond superficial beauty and exercising a power that derives from their vitality and their sexuality. Henry Adams saw that such power had been written out of American culture: "The Woman had once been supreme; in France she still seemed potent, not merely as a sentiment but as a force; why was she unknown in America? For evidently America was ashamed of her, and she was ashamed of herself. . . . The monthly-magazine-made American female had not a feature that would have been recognised by Adam. . . . Anyone brought up among Puritans knew that sex was sin. In any previous age, sex was strength."[118] In Undine and Thea, Wharton and Cather reintroduced the forceful, beautiful, and alluring goddess-like woman to American fiction. Men from Ralph Marvell to Peter Van Degen, Raymond de Chelles, and Elmer Moffatt find Undine irresistibly beautiful—something Undine takes so much for granted that she is baffled when men are able to resist her charms, as all three men eventually do. Thea is less conventionally beautiful, but others see in her the promise for "quite a regal beauty"—a promise that Thea fulfills as the successful singer Kronborg, who has the face of her younger self but "much brightened and beautified."[119] In older societies, Adams wrote, women—rather, Woman in the abstract—had the potential to be "Goddess because of her force," to be "the animated dynamo.... All this was to American thought as though it had never existed."[120] In puritanical American culture, the goddess-like beauty and power of Thea and Undine are exactly what makes it difficult for American men to know how to respond to them. Like Cather's Eden Bower in "Coming, Aphrodite!," Thea and Undine have the power to exert "a fascination which was to be disastrous to a few men and pleasantly stimulating to many thousands."[121]

Wharton and Cather indicate that energy and ambition may also lead to ruthlessness, as Rosowski suggests. This is abundantly clear for Undine, who leaves a trail of bodies behind her. She exhausts her parents and their finances; she ruins the life of Ralph Marvell and is partly responsible for his suicide; her irresponsible attitude toward her son suggests that he too will lead a blighted life; she shocks and appalls the French aristocrat she marries, disrupting his entire family and quite literally cheating them of their heritage, embodied in a prized tapestry. Thea does not leave such a trail of ruin behind her; instead Dr. Archie and Ray Kennedy provide Thea with money, and Fred Ottenburg "supplies Thea with experience in culture and sex, preparing her to take her place in the world."[122] Yet Thea too is hard-hearted in the pursuit of her goal and indirectly destructive. The accidental death of Ray Kennedy, the Colorado brakeman who is devoted to Thea, frees her from his expectation that they will marry; his life insurance policy gives her the financial freedom to pursue her dream. Thea's mother dies without seeing her beloved daughter one last time because Thea, training in Germany, refuses her mother's wish that she come home. As a successful artist, Thea becomes a diva in the derogatory sense, rude to old friends like Dr. Archie and to new friends like Fred Landry, and subjecting others (including hotel staff) to her bad humor when she is tired or stressed.[123] Frequently associated with minerals, mining, and gems that are beautiful but hard, she becomes "a moonstone of the self, beautiful, cold, prized, unearthly."[124] She is ruthless even to herself, remarking that she has to "work hard to do my worst, let alone my best," and admitting that her professional life has consumed her personal life: "It takes you up, and uses you, and spins you out; and that is your life."[125] In "Coming, Aphrodite!," Cather observes that "a 'big' career takes its toll."[126] This is as true of Thea Kronborg as of Eden Bower. If the ambition to succeed requires ruthlessness, success itself may be ruthless.

Both Thea and Undine are also fiercely competitive. From an early age Undine Spragg judges her own beauty—which is, she knows, the main factor in her social success—against the appearance of other girls. On the summer trips that Undine requires her parents to organize, she "discover[s] that she could more than hold her own against the youth and beauty of the other visitors."[127] She is aware that in "any competition on ordinary lines," she is likely to triumph over all the other women present.[128] But when she finds that the "ordinary lines" are not always the only lines on which women are judged, she is confused and angered. Her first experience of this is when she observes that she is "much handsomer" than plain Nettie Wincher of Washington DC but realizes "that she did not know how to use her beauty as the other used her plainness."[129] She is further frustrated when, years later, she finds that the Madame de Trézac whose name appears so often in the society columns of Paris newspapers is, in fact, her old rival Nettie.[130]

The only factor other than physical beauty that Undine allows as a component in social success is social standing, or (as James's Daisy Miller might put it) how "exclusive" a woman is. From her adolescence Undine is locked in competition with her neighbor Indiana Frusk; when Undine persuades her parents to take her to "the comparative gentility of summer vacations at the Mealey House," she perceives that its relative opulence has "the immense advantage of lifting the Spraggs high above the Frusks."[131] In Potash Springs, Virginia, she is "enraged" when she hears Nettie Wincher and her parents describing the resort at which they are all staying as a "dreadful hole" in which they have "nearly served their term" and realizes that the Winchers have "classed her with the 'hotel crew.'"[132] Early in James's story Daisy remarks that "we don't speak to every one—or they don't speak to us. I suppose it's about the same thing."[133] Undine wants to exclude others, not to be excluded; unlike Daisy, she perceives the difference.

Thea is just as competitive as Undine. Moreover, her sense of competition is much like Undine's; she cannot comprehend, and is enraged by, women who have succeeded without having what she defines as the requisite abilities. Thea's wrath, however, is triggered not by physical beauty or social success but by girls and women who have attained a level of success beyond her own, though they do not sing as well as she does. Her Indiana Frusk is Lily Fisher, who steals the spotlight by winning some of the best roles available in Moonstone. Because Lily "sang all songs and played all parts alike,"[134] Thea cannot comprehend Lily's popularity. Thea's competitiveness with Lily reaches such a pitch that she reassures herself bitterly that she, Thea, "would rather be hated than be stupid, any day."[135] Cather suggests that this rivalry has infiltrated Thea's unconscious; when, in a dream, a seashell is held to her ear, she hears "distant voices calling, 'Lily Fisher! Lily Fisher!'"[136] In her Chicago years, although she has begun to mature and to find herself as an artist, Thea expresses an equally bitter hatred for some other singers. Of a popular soprano, Thea remarks, "I hate her for the sake of what I used to think a singer might be."[137] Her judgments stem not merely from jealousy of another's success but from high standards of artistry (she defends another singer as "a great artist, whether she's in voice or not").[138] Yet she harbors strong, sometimes bitter emotions about her competitors. Even as a famous opera singer in the novel's final section, she is not beyond hating rivals who have succeeded beyond what she sees as their deserts, remarking that one soprano sings her role "big enough, and vulgar enough."[139]

Further similarities between the "monstrous" Undine and the much-admired Thea run deep. Both are repulsed by pictures of conventional domestic happiness, perhaps intuitively aware of the extent to which conventional female domesticity would impair their ascent to the pinnacles of their ambition. When Undine finds out she is pregnant, far from being happy that she and Ralph are starting a family, she bursts into tears and complains that pregnancy "*takes* a year—a whole year out of life!"[140] When Ralph attempts to reassure her that her feelings will change for the better, she refuses to believe it; he is struck by "the chill of her tone."[141] Thea is equally uninterested in domesticity. When the millionaire Fred Ottenburg tests her interest in marriage by describing conventional wedded bliss—"a comfortable flat . . . , a summer camp up in the woods, musical evenings, and a family to bring up"—Thea tells him she finds such a prospect "Perfectly hideous!"[142]

Thea's and Undine's ambition makes them similar in another way: it requires them to move from a smaller, more provincial world to a larger, more cosmopolitan one, revealing the literary roots of *The Song of the Lark* and *The Custom of the Country* in the English and European novel, specifically in a subgenre of the nineteenth-century novel that Lionel Trilling identified as the novel about "the Young Man from the Provinces."[143] According to Trilling, this subgenre—which includes, among others, James's *The Princess Casamassima*, Balzac's *Père Goriot*, and Flaubert's *Sentimental Education*—tells the story of the young man who goes off to "seek his fortune" in the enticing but bewildering world of the great city.[144] The young man, usually "equipped with poverty, pride, and intelligence," "move[s] from an obscure position into one of considerable eminence in Paris or London or St. Petersburg."[145] Although he meets obstacles, "it is not his part merely to be puzzled and hurt. . . . He is concerned to know how the political and social world are run and enjoyed; he wants a share in power and pleasure and in consequence he takes real risks."[146] Through his experience readers "have learned most of what we know about modern society, about class and its strange rituals, about power and influence and about money, the hard fluent fact in which modern society has its being."[147] Wharton and Cather were both widely read in nineteenth-century English and European novels like those Trilling refers to; Cather provides a clue to this influence when Dr. Archie recommends Balzac's *A Distinguished Provincial in Paris* to Thea.[148]

In order to "move from an obscure position into one of considerable eminence," the provincial must become aware of, and shed, his or her provincial habits. Both Wharton and Cather illustrate the rapid, sometimes confusing education of Undine and Thea, who are, like Trilling's young man, "confronted by situations whose meanings are dark to [them]."[149] Both girls sometimes blame their families and their background for their lack of knowledge about a more sophisticated world.

Frustrated by her limited success in New York, Undine is "ready enough to acknowledge her own mistakes" but "exasperated" by "the blunders of her parents," such as her father's initial refusal to buy box seats at the opera—tickets he really cannot afford.[150] Similarly after Mrs. Spragg mentions that Ralph Marvell has called for Undine in her absence and inexplicably remained to chat, she adds, "But I couldn't make out what he was after." Undine replies cuttingly, "You never *can*."[151] When Thea moves from Moonstone to Chicago, she also encounters challenges beyond her ken. In her lessons with Harsanyi, her new teacher, "Things came too fast for her; she had not had enough preparation. There were times when she came home from her lesson and lay upon her bed hating Wunsch and her family, hating a world that had let her grow up so ignorant."[152]

Both girls must learn a range of skills and indeed a new knowledge set in order to shake off their provinciality. Thea must learn many things: how to sit (not with "her knees far apart, her gloved hands lying stiffly in her lap, like a country girl");[153] how to find a more satisfactory boarding house; how to deal with men who make inappropriate remarks to her on the street; and how to make ends meet on a slim budget. And she must learn other, less easily named skills: how to work with a cynical teacher without being overwhelmed by cynicism herself; how to acknowledge, even to herself, her own deepest artistic aspirations. Undine too must learn many things: not to describe the upper class as "swell" and "stylish"; to use locutions other than "'I don't care if I do' when her host asked her to try some grapes, and 'I wouldn't wonder' when she thought any one was trying to astonish her"; and that the latest thing recommended in the newspaper, like the "new pigeon-blood notepaper with white ink," is not necessarily in better taste than older stand-bys such as, in this case, plain white stationery.[154] Further, she must learn what are, to her, subtle gradations of the expression of social aristocracy in New York, although it is unclear whether she ever quite figures out that gilding and a "lavish diffusion of [electric] light" are not necessarily indications of social aristocracy or that a socially prominent family might *not* live in a mansion on Fifth Avenue.[155] Undine even makes assumptions about social importance based on body type and behavior and is surprised that the "little fellow" with the quiet manners, Ralph Marvell, is more prominent than his flashier friend, the society portraitist Claude Walsingham Popple.[156] Yet after a few initial mistakes, Undine develops her central principle: *"It's better to watch than to ask questions,"* and armed with this concept, she gradually works her way into Old New York society.[157]

After her first year in Chicago, Thea reflects that "language was like clothes; it could be a help to one, or it could give one away."[158] To some extent both girls fear giving themselves away—that their provincialism will be conspicuous just when it is most important to be a city sophisticate, or at least to seem like one. Of the two Undine is the more fearful, refining her gestures as well as her expressions and becoming embarrassed when midwestern friends newly arrived in New York use the vocabulary she has discarded, the broad gestures she has refined, or otherwise reveal their provincial origins. Thea gradually becomes less fearful of giving herself away, and eventually she is able to select the best of both the city she has mastered and the provinces she comes from. The manner in which Thea and Undine teach themselves also suggests what, in the end, separates these two young women: Undine learns the lessons that turn her from a provincial into a cosmopolitan—or at least the facsimile of one—by imitation; Thea learns them by becoming more and more herself. Paradoxically, although Thea has made a life of singing and acting a range of roles, she is always essentially herself, while Undine—who is never called on to play a formal role but who is constantly pretending to be someone she is not—has, aside from her ambition, almost no essential self.

Undine and Thea both retain their westernness, what Glen Love calls their "primal creative energy ... emanating from the land itself."[159] Thea's "memories of light on the sand hills, of masses of prickly-pear blossoms she had found in the desert in early childhood" are an essential "part of herself."[160] Undine's frequently destructive energy is rooted in her natal place; when Undine is angry, she is "terrible. Everything had gone down before her, as towns and villages went down before one of the tornadoes of her native state."[161] Yet their differences may be confirmed most clearly by what they actually do with their "primal creative energy" when they reach the East. The scene that occasions Undine's tornado-like anger takes place in New York, when her father suggests that she might not be able to afford to marry Ralph Marvell; when that marriage does not work out as she expects, she is on to the next thing, the next husband, the next social circle. In *A Backward Glance* Wharton wrote that the *nouveaux riches* were less alarming to Old New York than those who followed; the "dearest ambition of the newcomers was to assimilate existing traditions."[162] Real change, she asserted, came only "with the successive upheavals which culminated in the catastrophe of 1914."[163] Yet Undine, whose story is firmly set in the pre-1914 world, is a harbinger of the destruction to come. While she appears "to assimilate existing traditions," she does so only superficially. Despite her many experiences in the world, Undine learns very little. She acquires "turns of speech, tricks of attitude" that suggest she has assimilated to a more sophisticated world, but these are, indeed, merely turns and tricks.[164] She can tell Moffatt a few things about the paintings of Ingres, for instance, but she has no real understanding of art; she has only picked up "as much of the jargon as a pretty woman needs to produce the impression of being well-informed."[165] In his one outburst against Undine, Raymond de Chelles lambastes her merely apparent sophistication, telling her, "You lay hands on things that are sacred to us.... You come among us speaking our language and not knowing what we mean; wanting the things we want, and not knowing why we want them."[166] Surely Ralph could have said the same. Undine never appreciates anything; she merely wants to possess it and then, bored, discard it for the next thing.

In contrast, both Thea's energy and her attitude toward the East are positive. She goes east—to Chicago, to Germany, and finally to New York—not to despoil richer cultures but to embrace a wider cultural tradition. As a musician who performs on the stage of the Metropolitan Opera, Thea becomes part of the cultural tradition Wharton hoped to see preserved. (In the intersection of Wharton's and Cather's fictive worlds, it is conceivable that Wharton's Ralph Marvell could have seen Cather's Thea Kronborg on stage, one of the many hundreds who admire her performance and see it as an integral part of the city's cultural landscape.) As Love has written, "To go east for Cather is to acknowledge one's place in the larger world, to find and accept a role in the social order and to attempt to achieve one's fullest human potentiality."[167] Undine brings tornados east to devastate Old New York; Thea uses her energy to successfully combine eastern culture with "the essential, or western, self."[168]

Some passages of *The Song of the Lark* play with this East-West balance, establishing that Thea's experience in the West has provided her a standard that keeps her safe from some temptations of city life. In a conversation with Dr. Archie near the novel's end, Thea recalls the six hundred dollars she received from Ray Kennedy's insurance: "It was the price of a man's life.... I always measure things by that six hundred dollars, just as I measure high buildings by the Moonstone standpipe. There are standards we can't get away from."[169] When professional bitterness overtakes her and she falls asleep with her "mind ... full of daggers," she is sometimes lucky enough to wake "in the Kohlers' garden, with the pigeons and the white rabbits, so happy! And that saves me."[170] The main products of Undine's western origins are her driving ambition and her furious temper; Thea's western roots give her an ambition that can become ruthless but also a standard "to measure things by" and a restorative sense of sanity and beauty.

Undine's negativity and Thea's contrasting positivity may reveal their authors' very different attitudes toward the West. At this point in her life Wharton seems to have feared western energy as a kind of threat, while Cather saw it as a promise and a contribution to larger American culture. Both novels return to the West near their conclusions, further revealing their authors' underlying attitudes. In *The Custom of the Country*, Wharton uses a flashback to reveal, at last, Undine's origins in Apex City and her early engagement to Elmer Moffatt. As with many of her descriptions of the West, most of the writing in this section seems thin, borrowed from the works of others—"got up," in Sinclair Lewis's phrase. The scene in Apex City is peppered with scare quotes (Elmer "sit[s] on the big 'stage' beside [Undine] on the 'ride' to the grove") and with parodic names like "Luckaback's Dollar Shoe-Store."[171] The episode culminates when a younger Elmer Moffatt, who has appeared from nowhere, is asked to give a Fourth of July speech for the temperance society, "the sons of Jonadab."[172] He wins the town's approval with a "magnificent" speech combining a multitude of stock elements, including "moving references to the Blue and the Grey," "a new version of Washington and the Cherry Tree," "erudite allusions and apt quotations" taken from *Bartlett's Familiar Quotations*, and "a peroration that drew tears from the Grand Army pensioners . . . and caused the minister's wife to say that many a sermon from that platform had been less uplifting."[173] Later the same evening he gives the lie to his entire performance by drinking heavily and encouraging other members of the temperance society to do the same. Moffatt tells the crowd what he really thinks of them, mocking them for their hypocrisy and exposing them as fools for admiring him.[174]

The final portions of this scene have real power, approaching Twain's parody of human gullibility in his creation of the King and the Duke in *Huckleberry Finn* or his indictment of flawed humanity in "The Man That Corrupted Hadleyburg." Yet the scene overall seems not to mock human nature, as Twain does, but to parody a straw-target West. If there is anything good to come out of the West in *The Custom of the Country*, it is not Undine's destructive energy but Elmer's tenacious power, which even Undine perceives: "It was at the moment when Elmer Moffatt's failure was most complete and flagrant that she suddenly felt the extent of his power."[175] It takes an Old New Yorker, Ralph Marvell, to articulate that energy: "There's something epic about him—a kind of epic effrontery."[176] But there is no doubt that Elmer "wins" in this battle of East and West, or that it is a battle. Even if Old New York fails partly through its own inanition, the victory of Elmer Moffatt comes at a high cost: it is what ultimately kills Ralph, the best of Old New York, who, like Lily Bart and, for that matter, Cather's Paul, cannot survive into a harsh new era. Still, even in this parodic novel, Wharton's attitude toward the West is more complex than it seems. Mixing western energy with eastern culture does not "doom . . . the purity" of Old New York families, as has been argued.[177] Instead it revitalizes them; one thoughtful Old New Yorker hopes that Paul Marvell, the offspring of Ralph and Undine, will have "a drop or two of Spragg in him."[178]

The Song of the Lark also returns West in its final pages. In contrast to Wharton's Apex City, Cather's Moonstone is generally positive, a place where life goes on fairly peacefully; Cather depicts not drunken speeches but an ice cream social. Yet Cather's epilogue is far from unreservedly positive about the West; her closing portrait of Moonstone is deeply ambivalent. Contrasted with the intensity of the place that Thea experienced as a child, Moonstone now appears as an ordinary, rather lackluster place much like anywhere else, a place where "the children all look like city children" and where the "fair-haired, dimpled matron who was once Lily Fisher" sits with her too-well-behaved twin sons.[179] This later Moonstone also exhibits the East-West tension of Apex City; like Undine Spragg, the grown-up Lily Fisher "causes envy and discontent among her neighbors" by summering in the East.[180] In the novel's final paragraph the town so central to Thea's life is presented as a rather negligible place, its inhabitants "cut off . . . from the restless currents of the world."[181] Thea's success has a great meaning there, not only to her Aunt Tillie (who revels in Thea's success partly because it connects her to a larger world) but also to "the humbler people of Moonstone."[182] Cather creates a precarious, paradoxical balance between Moonstone and the larger world, between the parish and the world: the town matters only because it is the place from which the great singer "Kronborg" came; Thea's success matters only because it allows those still in Moonstone to dream of escaping Moonstone itself.

Such a paradox is far from a stirring anthem of the importance of the western town, of the West, or of their centrality in American culture; *The Song of the Lark* is not, after all, Cather's 1932 volume of stories titled *Obscure Destinies*, in which she would celebrate the lives of ordinary people in the West. In *The Song of the Lark* she celebrates the celebrated and especially the girl who escaped small-town obscurity to make a name for herself, quite literally. In her 1932 preface to the novel, Cather wrote, "The story set out to tell of an artist's awakening and struggle; *her floundering escape from a smug, domestic, self-satisfied provincial world of utter ignorance.* . . . What I cared about, and still care about, was the girl's escape; the play of blind chance, the way in which commonplace occurrences fell together to liberate her from commonness."[183] This is not a flattering picture of Moonstone. Thea, moreover, is recognized not so much as a "heroine" who triumphs but as someone who benefits from the workings of "blind chance." Yet in the final sentence of the preface Cather sounds a different note: "To persons of her vitality and honesty, fortunate accidents always happen."[184] In the end even "the play of blind chance" favors those with Thea's western energy.

"COUSINS FROM THE WEST"

Given Wharton's mockery of the West in letters and her devastating portrait of Undine Spragg, it is surprising to find, particularly in her work in the 1920s and 1930s, more positive portraits of westerners. In *The Glimpses of the Moon* (1922) she revisits Apex City, Undine's hometown. Although she gives a satirical name to the wealthy family from Apex who are traveling throughout Europe—calling them the Hicks—she also makes them kind, straightforward, and appreciative of European culture. The easterner Nick Lansing, through whom the reader sees them, comes to appreciate "the kind uncomplicated Hickses" and sees their kindness as emanating from their western origins: "A wholesome honesty and simplicity breathed through all their opulence, as if the rich trappings of their present life still exhaled the fragrance of their native prairies."[185] Indeed, although the American prairies are never depicted in this novel, they come off much better here than they do elsewhere in Wharton's work. Further, Wharton makes the Hickses "sympathetic" and "even interesting": they see Venice as more than a place "affording exceptional opportunities for bathing and adultery"; if they are only "confusedly aware" of the city's history, they are also "reverently" appreciative of being "in the presence of something unique and ineffable, and determined to make the utmost of their privilege."[186] Their "muddled ardour for great things" is, in fact, akin to a religion, as Nick realizes.[187]

Coral Hicks, their twentyish daughter, is a "strong minor character" in the novel and a nearly immeasurable improvement on Undine.[188] Coral has "a glance at once confident and critical"; unlike Undine, she is "not pretty," but she is "strong," "assured," and also "well-dressed."[189] Although she is described as "over-educated," we are also told that she can "carry[ ] off even this crowning disadvantage."[190] (It may be Susy

Lansing, the novel's main character, who holds Coral's "over-education" against her, perhaps defensively; the men in the novel seem little troubled by it.) Coral has a number of assets, not only financial but intellectual, including genuine curiosity. Deeply interested in archeology and art, there may even be something of Wharton in her. At an important dinner that the Hicks host, Nick looks at Coral further down the table and sees that "in contrast with the others . . . she looked surprisingly noble. Her large grave features made her appear like an old monument in a street of Palace Hotels; and he marveled at the mysterious law which had brought this archaic face out of Apex City."[191] In her final scene with Nick, with whom Coral has fallen in love, she comes off nobly. Possessing a deep underlying sensitivity, she is also perceptive, seeing through "sham science and sham art and sham everything"; she stoically accepts Nick's failure to reciprocate her love, renouncing him "gallantly," and sets her sights elsewhere.[192] She is ambitious, telling Nick straightforwardly that she wants to be "at the very top" of society; she "want[s] to promote culture, like those Renaissance women you're always talking about."[193] Sounding like Thea, who wants to succeed for Moonstone, she adds, "'I want to do it for Apex City.'"[194] Undine Spragg's ambition makes her selfish and destructive; Coral Hicks's makes her constructive.

In Vance Weston, the protagonist of Wharton's two-novel *Künstlerroman*, *Hudson River Bracketed* (1929) and *The Gods Arrive* (1932), Wharton presents another strong midwestern character. This does not mean, however, that Wharton drops her mocking attitude toward the Midwest; as with her earlier work, she parodies midwestern culture through descriptions, place names, and characters. Vance and his family live in Euphoria, Illinois (at least Wharton situates the town in a specific state in this novel, unlike Apex City). There Vance's father, who is in real estate, has turned the "Pig Lane" side of town into the suburb of Mapledale; neighboring towns include Swedenville *and* Swedenborg.[195] Vance's family lived for a time in "Hallelujah, Mo.," and his grandmother was once a teacher in Pruneville, Nebraska;[196] given Wharton's dismissal of "the lady with the blurry name," one wonders whether this is an oblique reference to the settings that brought Cather to national attention. Other midwestern authors may have shaped these novels; Sinclair Lewis dedicated *Babbitt* to Wharton, and his youth may have been an inspiration for Vance.[197] Certainly there is much of Lewis's self-satisfied Midwest in Wharton's descriptions of Euphoria and perhaps in her decision to make Vance's father, like George Babbitt, a real estate dealer.

The portrayal of Euphoria and the Weston family in the first chapter of *Hudson River Bracketed* is unremittingly harsh—Wharton at her most satirical. And it is a satire aimed specifically at the Weston family's westernness. Vance's grandparents are made ridiculous. His grandmother wants "to reform everything—it didn't particularly matter what."[198] While "Perfection was Grandma's passion—ladies were Grandpa's."[199] As "a magnificent-looking couple, . . . when Old Home Weeks began to be inaugurated throughout the land, Mr. and Mrs. Scrimser were in great demand in tableaux representing The Old Folks at Home. . . . But Grandma liked better figuring as the Pioneer Wife in a log cabin, with Grandpa . . . garbed in a cowpuncher's rig, aiming his shotgun through a crack in the shutters, and the children doing Indian war whoops behind the scenes."[200] Wharton, of course, is often satirical; she also mocked the "Old Home Week" of Dormer, Massachusetts, in *Summer*, and her own social class in a range of works. But the satire in *Hudson River Bracketed* differs in that, unlike Lewis or Cather, Wharton is mocking people, a place, and a culture she neither really knew nor understood. To some extent she was aware that her lack of firsthand knowledge made her portrayals less authoritative, and she may have suffered some misgivings. Her friend Louis Bromfield, an Ohio novelist who lived in France for several years, wrote that she was "a little uneasy" about her portrayal of the Midwest in *The Custom of the Country*; she was pleased by his positive remarks on *The Gods Arrive*, writing him, "What makes me prouder than anything any one can ever say of the book, is your finding the taste of your native air at Euphoria."[201] But to many readers, Wharton's parody in *Hudson River Bracketed* may seem strained; an early reviewer opined that Wharton "writes of the Middle West and its inhabitants as if she had never been west of the Metropolitan Opera House."[202] Nevertheless, Wharton's parody of the well-off Scrimsers depicting pioneers has an interesting point. She is suggesting exactly the problem Cather identifies in "Nebraska: The End of the First Cycle": the pioneer days were over; their descendants were only playing at being pioneers.

In fact Wharton's critique of the Midwest shares a great deal with Cather's, including a critique of commercialism and materialism much like Cather's in *One of Ours*. Vance Weston's family members are thoroughly practical and materialistic, focusing on real estate sales, the latest "electric cleaners," and "the reorganization of school grades,"[203] and the Wheeler family in *One of Ours* would probably get along just fine with them. Claude Wheeler's older brother sells machinery, while his younger brother is obsessed with the latest gadgets; Mr. Wheeler's first reaction to the outbreak of World War I is that wheat prices will rise. Certainly Mr. Wheeler would endorse the dominant note of Euphoria, the belief that "the real business of life was to keep going, to get there—and 'There' was where the money was, always and exclusively."[204] The Weston family and Wheeler family are alike in other ways. As if to balance the materialism of some family members, both families have "spiritual" or religious women and sons who rebel against mere money making. Vance sounds much like Claude when he reflects that "as a diet for the soul," mere efficiency "was deficient in nourishment."[205] In another way as well, Wharton seems to take a page from Cather. Describing the beauty of the "days of the sudden prairie spring, when the lilacs in [Vance's] grandmother's dooryard were bursting, and the maples by the river fringing themselves with rosy keys, when the earth throbbed with renewal," Wharton's writing is reminiscent of Cather's beautiful writing about the prairies.[206]

Certainly Wharton's portrayal of Vance is her most complex portrait of a midwesterner, one that has drawn a range of reactions. Contemporary reviewers ran the gamut from seeing him as "essentially an ironic study" to finding him "a beautifully integrated figure, an unswerving compound of egoism, honesty and passion."[207] More recent views also vary widely. One critic argues the novels "demonstrate Wharton's deep scorn for the model of the artist as male" and that "Wharton's very writing of these two novels undermines, even destroys, the validity of the life Vance Weston leads"; others argue that "Wharton took a considerable risk in presenting . . . such a flawed character as Vance" but that she "offsets his many faults . . . by giving him a capacity for imagination, vision and creativity."[208] Wharton's portrait is indeed complex, written in a range of registers. Vance's full name, Advance Weston, is parodic: he is named after the town, itself ill-named, where he was born. But it is also symbolic: any advance must come from the West. Even more than in *The Custom of the Country*, Wharton draws in *Hudson River Bracketed* a significant contrast between the effete East and the energetic West. In *Custom of the Country* the East may be refined, even over-refined, and lacking in energy, as illustrated by Ralph and his family; but the West, for all its energy, is nearly unremittingly crude and destructive. (Despite his good qualities, Elmer Moffatt is mercilessly manipulative; it is he who suggests to Undine that she should raise money for an annulment of her marriage to Ralph by threatening to take Paul from him; this suggestion leads Ralph to make a huge, risky investment with Elmer himself, the failure of which precipitates Ralph's suicide.)

Wharton's treatment of Vance suggests a different vision of America, one in which western energy and eastern refinement can be productively united. In *Hudson River Bracketed* the East comes off worse than in *The Custom of the Country*, and the West, better. In *Hudson River Bracketed*, a novel full of writers, the best New York City can produce are George Frenside, a critic who is astute but has a "decomposing mind" and rarely sets pen to paper, and Lewis Tarrant, a wealthy, nervous, egotistical would-be editor and novelist who is "brilliantly clever" but lacks "enthusiasm" and eventually proves petty and vindictive.[209] In contrast, the westerner Vance is raw and unrefined, but generous, intelligent, sensitive to literature, history, and ideas, and full of energy. It is he, not Frenside or Tarrant, who becomes a productive writer. Insofar as children are symbolic, the future is also with the westerner Vance. Both Tarrant and Weston have relationships with Halo Spear, whose socially important "old" Hudson Valley family has lost its energy and its fortune; Halo alone exhibits hope and vitality. She marries Tarrant largely because he will make her and her family comfortable, and the two have a child. But the child, who is mentioned only once, dies, and the marriage gradually disintegrates.[210] Only during her later liaison with Vance does Halo conceive a second child, and the conclusion of the second novel in the series depicts Vance's return to the pregnant Halo, apparently to settle down.

Further, Vance, "the cousin from the West," is productive precisely because he comes from the West.[211] When he goes east, he becomes painfully aware of how ill-educated he is, much like Thea in Chicago or Undine in New York. Yet the fact that he comes from a place that has not prepared him for the history he encounters in the East is exactly what enables him to understand, appreciate, and see (both figuratively and literally) the culture he encounters there. His first novel, *Instead*, reimagines the life of Miss Elinor Lorborn, an ancestor of Halo who had become a successful writer and who had lived in The Willows, a house that Halo and her family (Vance's distant cousins) half-heartedly preserve. *Instead* is a success not in spite of Vance's western ignorance but because of it: "He had brought his fresh untouched imagination to the study of the old house and the lives led it in—a subject which to [Halo] had seemed too near to be interesting, but to him was remote and poetic."[212] This passage suggests his underlying similarity to Cather, who remarked that it took a westerner to truly appreciate the atmosphere of Mrs. Fields's house: "I sometimes think that only one who grew up in the rawest part of what she used to call 'our great west' could feel all the complete completeness [sic] of her atmosphere."[213]

Vance's association with The Willows also implies his status as emblematically American. The novel's title, *Hudson River Bracketed*, refers to the architectural style of The Willows, a style unique to the United States, as Wharton's headnote to the novel indicates: "A. J. Downing, the American landscape architect, ... divides the architectural styles into the Grecian, Chinese, Gothic, the Tuscan, ... and the *Hudson River Bracketed*," which is referred to within the novel as "our indigenous style."[214] Vance too is uniquely American in bringing West and East together. Although the novel begins in Illinois, Vance becomes a novelist only after standing in the library of The Willows, surrounded by books and wondering, "Why wasn't I ever told about the Past?"[215] The question has been called "naively ludicrous,"[216] but it recalls Dimock's remark about American indifference to history and suggests the extent to which many Americans are not only oblivious to but deprived of cultural history. Vance's great literary revelation comes when he reads Coleridge's "Rime of the Ancient Mariner" in the library. Further, as a budding writer, Vance also needs his sensibilities stimulated and educated by interactions with literati and critics in New York, Paris, and southern France. While he returns to the Midwest for a Thoreauvian retreat in Lake Belair, Wisconsin, this period is ultimately only a preparation for his return to the East.[217] The novels conclude not with Vance taking Halo out West but with Vance moving east to the Hudson Valley.

In the cross-fertilization of East and West Wharton suggests that the East benefits too. Vance not only gives new life to Miss Lorburn in his novel but also revivifies The Willows; he actually reads books in the library, rather than merely dusting them, as Halo does—or stealing volumes to sell, as her brother Lorrie does. Moreover, he writes there, as Miss Lorburn did, bringing a dusty tradition into the light of the present—quite literally, as Wharton describes long-closed shutters being opened. Wharton described Vance as "an unusually intelligent modern American youth, of average education and situation."[218] He is Wharton's Thea Kronborg; both are portrayed as authentically American artists who succeed by uniting western energy with eastern and European sophistication.

SPEAKING "AMERICAN" IN AMERICAN LITERATURE

As indicted by her remarks in letters and her portrayals of westerners in her fiction, Wharton continued to harbor ambivalent feelings about the United States as a whole and the West in particular, feelings that would only have been confirmed by the experience of Anna Bahlmann, her governess-turned-secretary. Bahlmann had gone to France with Wharton in 1909 and lived with Wharton in her rue de Varenne apartment in Paris.[219] In November 1915 Bahlmann moved back to the United States, and in February 1916 she took the train west to Missouri to stay with her niece's family.[220] In a letter to a former student, she describes the train porter "bring[ing] you every day a new oiled-paper bag to put your hat in & keep it from the dust," and she states, "The food in the dining-cars is uneatable."[221] (No wonder Aunt Georgiana, in Cather's "Wagner Matinée," traveling in the other direction, arrives in Boston exhausted.) Bahlmann's experience of living with her niece was very mixed. She describes her niece's house as "really pretty & practical" but adds that "if there were some doors between the hall, the two parlors & the dining-room, it would be quite charming. But Americans like living on a tea-tray & never feel the want of privacy."[222] While the house is equipped with natural gas ("*not* the human kind," she specifies with Whartonian acerbity), "the gas is unreliable & meals 'might[y] unsartin.'"[223] Such details would have confirmed Wharton's negative vision of the Midwest. Shortly after Anna's death in 1916, Wharton wrote Minnie Jones, "Kansas City could never have seemed as much like home to her as the rue de V[arenne], where she was—I won't say 'comfortable,' for that she resolutely refused to be—but at least used to things, & properly waited on."[224]

In her use of the phrase "'might[y] unsartin,'" enclosed in Whartonian quotation marks, Bahlmann picked up on another aspect of the West that troubled Wharton: its language. As Hermione Lee has noted, *The Custom of the Country* "mounts a vigorous satire on American language," which is equated with western language; Undine's "raw speech is set against the civilised talk of the startled Dagonets and Marvells."[225] Cather does the opposite, embracing western speech in *The Song of the Lark*. In this period, as we have seen, the West was increasingly equated with the "real" America. Did this mean that the language of the American West was also the real American English? One might be tempted to think that the answer would of course be "yes" for Cather and "indeed not" for Wharton. But like so many matters related to these two authors, the answer is far more complex.

Cather very consciously "used a midwestern point of view and spoke with a midwestern narrative voice" in *The Song of the Lark*;[226] this was integral to her very conception of the novel. To Fisher, Cather wrote in 1916, "It's all really done from the Moonstone point of view.... My point is always Moonstone, what she [Thea] got from it, what she gave back to it. It is really written in the speech of Moonstone."[227] The novel was not written in "the purest Ritz-Carlton English"; instead it "is practically in indirect discourse, quotation once removed. I used single quotes and double quotes until I was ashamed and gave it up."[228] Yet Cather, like Wharton, believed that American writers should draw on the entire heritage of English language and literature, on "the King James translation of the Bible and Shakespeare,"[229] as we saw. Her letters emphasize the importance of well-written standard English. In 1931 she remarked that the "awful" portrait of her that had been published in *Good Housekeeping* was "bringing in a flood of letters from the queerest kind of people, splashy ladies on Park Avenue and farmers' wives in Minnesota, all equally unable to write an English sentence."[230] In 1934 she wrote, "I think it is sheer nonsense to attempt to teach 'Creative Writing' in colleges. If the college students were taught to write good, sound English sentences ... and to avoid hackneyed[,] platitudinous, woman's-club expressions ... then creative writing would take care of itself.... I do wish the colleges taught people to write passably clear and correct English."[231] Wharton shared Cather's concerns. In 1918 she wrote to an American soldier who had sent her some poems, offering advice about his reading and recommending that he "study the grammar & etymology of your language."[232] When the journalist Morton Fullerton (also her former lover) sent her a draft of his book, she advised him, "Drop 30 per cent of your Latinisms ... mow down every old cliché, uproot all the dragging circumlocutions, compress, diversify, clarify, vivify."[233]

While the westerner Cather was more insistent on "correct English" than we might expect, the easterner Wharton was sometimes flexible on language. In *A Backward Glance* Wharton wrote of her family's "reverence for the best tradition of spoken English," tracing it "partly ... to the fact that, in the old New York families of my parents' day, the children's teachers were often English," and noting that "my own brothers were educated at home by an extremely cultivated English tutor."[234] As a child, she was not "allowed to read the popular American children's books of my day because, as my mother said, the children spoke bad English *without the author's knowing it.*"[235] But this did not mean that the family was inflexible about language. On the contrary, in wanting their children to speak "better" English, her parents valued not a rigid English but usage that was "easier, more flexible and idiomatic" rather than "priggish" or "pedantic."[236] They even appreciated "any really expressive slang," so long as it was "used as slang, as it were between quotation marks, and not carelessly admitted into our speech," and they "revel[ed] in the humorous and expressive side of American slang," enjoying works by Mark Twain, Bret Harte, and Finlay Peter Dunne's "Mr. Dooley"[237]—all of them, of course, western authors, and a reminder that American slang may have originated with westward expansion.[238] But they objected to sloppiness with language, and Wharton would continue her parents' "abhorre[nce]" of "the habitual slovenliness of those who picked up the slang of the year without having any idea that they were not speaking in the purest tradition."[239] Worst of all was the speech of those who had no sense of "the inflexions and shades of meaning of our rich speech."[240] Some of Wharton's examples make little sense to readers today, for instance, her parents' "ridicule when, excusing [herself] for having forgotten something [she] had been told to do" at about age ten, she replied, "I didn't know that it was *imperative*"; other examples, like her objection to "a phenomena" may still resonate.[241] Some of her objections were class-based: "a new class of the uneducated rich" had moved into her world.[242] Yet her writing about language also makes it clear that she grew up in a family in which language was handled thoughtfully and as if it were a family friend, someone she had "romped with . . . in the nursery."[243]

If Cather wrote *The Song of the Lark* in "the language of Moonstone," Wharton wrote *The Custom of the Country*—and indeed most of her work—in the language of the New York in which she was raised: a well-educated English spiced with American slang, always implicitly, if not actually, inside quotation marks. Despite her long residence in France, Wharton was an American author writing for primarily American audiences and engaging American issues; American language could not have been far from her mind, and the language of "the cousin from the West" inflects, and sometimes troubles, her writing. Insofar as western speech was "slang," Wharton's attitude was particularly complex. She advised Sinclair Lewis to "use slang in dialogue more sparingly";[244]

corresponding with a friend about the speech of the soldiers in her novel *A Son at the Front*, she remarked that "my young Americans don't talk the language as spoken by the Scott Fitzgerald & Sinclair Lewis jeunesse [youth]; but I saw dozens of young Americans from all parts of America during the war, & none of them talked it.... I believe it's a colossal literary convention."[245] Yet far from being a language absolutist, she sometimes used slang very deliberately to emphasize American attributes and concepts. In some cases it is directly connected to the issues of energy that so interested her, echoing Cather's use of it. In *The Song of the Lark* Thea is "a girl with some 'go' in her"; the energetic young Edith Jones, enthusing over the newly popularized sport of lawn tennis, wrote Bahlmann that the game was "difficult" but "delightful": "Pin your skirts up high..., put on a small hat & 'go it!'"[246] In another letter to Bahlmann she writes, "I miss you very much... & am looking forward greatly to all the pow-wows we can have together."[247] "Powwow" is a term borrowed from the Narragansett Indians; it is impossible to use a term more uniquely American.[248]

In some cases Wharton uses western slang in a way that is simultaneously mocking and playful, even patriotic. During World War I she was a strong proponent of the United States' joining the Allies and correspondingly frustrated with President Wilson's policy of neutrality. When the United States finally broke off diplomatic relations with Germany in February 1917, she wrote to Berenson from Paris, "You ought to be here! Not only because you're so wanted, but because I 'kinder feel' that intelligent Americans have a right—since last Sunday—to be in the centre of things."[249] A sentence like this is a study in complexity. In referring to "intelligent Americans," she is implying a strong contrast to those less capable; her use of American slang in "'kinder feel'" is counterweighted by her preference for British spelling in "centre." Her July 1918 letter to Minnie Jones strikes similar notes. After seeing the parade of American soldiers on the Fourth of July, she wrote, "I meant my 'very darndest' to get off a letter last Friday telling you about the greatest 'Fourth' in history."[250] In spite of her mockery, there is a hint of American pride in Wharton's use of the slang at this particular moment in history: if that was how Americans talked, she would talk that way, too.

This chapter opened with parallel quotations from Wharton and Cather, with Wharton asking "what had become of the spirit of the pioneers" and Cather bemoaning a sense that "the splendid story of the pioneers is finished." Yet for neither author is this elegiac note the end of the story. Wharton's question could be seen as rhetorical, but novels like *The Custom of the Country*, *Hudson River Bracketed*, and *The Gods Arrive* suggest that in her mind "the spirit of the pioneers" had not evaporated but had gone West. Similarly Cather turns away from her elegy, expressing her hope that the current "belief that snug success and easy money are the real aims of human life" is only a passing one;[251] her Thea is a pioneer of a different sort, demonstrating the same tenacity and determination in her own "splendid story" as she moves east to a different adventure.

In studies of American literature an emphasis on an author's regionalism, his or her geographic place in American literature, is a two-sided coin. In some instances critics have paid too little attention to an author's regional associations (the case with Wharton), while in other instances, like Cather's, so much attention has been given to region that it is difficult to see the larger picture, the national or international map. An emphasis on specific regions has also meant that critics have expended less energy examining the interchange between regions and the complexity with which regions are portrayed. The tendency is to categorize, as if "East is East, and West is West, and never the twain shall meet," to adapt Kipling's line to an American setting. These perceptions remain so strong a part of our cultural heritage that it is easy to forget that someone like Mark Twain "lived longer in New York City than in Hannibal" and spent much of his adult life in an elaborate house in Hartford, Connecticut, decorated with Tiffany wallpaper and furniture acquired during his European travels.[252] While the West was going east in this period, the East was also going west. Owen Wister's iconic literary cowboy was, as his novel's title emphasizes, a Virginian, like Cather; Wister himself was a member of a prominent Pennsylvania family, a Harvard graduate who was a classmate of Teddy Roosevelt, an acquaintance of Henry James, and a friend Wharton saw in Lenox and London.[253]

Although they differed in the details, Wharton and Cather worked within the same parameters of thought on East and West: the East was equated with culture and refinement, tending to the supercilious and the effete, while the West, while it sometimes tended to the uncouth, even the boorish, also represented strength, vitality, and the future. (Even the consummate easterner Henry Adams remarked that he went "beyond the Missouri river" in 1871 "to spy upon the land of the future.")[254] Yet their works also ask readers to consider a far more complex reality and a deep underlying cultural problem. If, in America, the East was culture and the West was vitality, there might be the beginnings of a fruitful union, a productive balance, in Vance Weston's and Thea Kronborg's going east. Yet such characters do not offer a complete solution to the problem of balancing culture and energy. For that, Wharton and Cather had to cross the Atlantic and venture to France.

5

THE IDEA OF FRANCE

"I don't believe [the war] has killed anything. It has only scattered things." [Claude Wheeler] glanced about hurriedly at the sleeping house, the sleeping garden, the clear, starry sky not very far overhead. "It's men like you that get the worst of it," he broke out. "But as for me, I never knew there was anything worth living for, till this war came on. Before that, the world seemed like a business proposition."

WILLA CATHER, *One of Ours*

I hear a good deal in these days of the phrase: "What America can teach France." My idea is that we'd better leave it to the French to discover that, and apply ourselves to finding out what France can teach us.

EDITH WHARTON, "Talk to American Soldiers"

MAPPING WHARTON AND CATHER IN FRANCE

Although their experiences of France were quite different, the country and its culture played a huge role throughout the lives of Edith Wharton and Willa Cather. Wharton—then Edith Jones—was introduced to Paris as a child, living with her family in an apartment at 61 avenue Joséphine, not far from the Arc de Triomphe, from 1868 until 1870.[1] As she wrote in her memoir, "two episodes" from this period helped to form the future novelist. One was a frequent visitor who told her fascinating tales of the gods and goddesses on Mount Olympus, stories that she found far more interesting than fairy tales. The other was that she herself began to "make up" stories, pacing the floor while she was holding Washington Irving's *Alhambra*, telling her own stories aloud and turning the pages of the book as if she were actually reading.[2] From these years she also recalled seeing "a beautiful lady" traveling with her entourage down the Champs Elysées. Although this woman, the Empress Eugenie,[3] would be swept away by the "crimson hurricane" of the Franco-Prussian War of 1870, Wharton wrote decades later that she could "still see her serene elegance . . . her conscious air of being . . . the centre of the sumptuous spectacle."[4] This memory also became an image of a vanishing world, which would haunt Wharton's later work.

Paris became central to Wharton's life. After her marriage to Teddy Wharton in 1885, the new couple spent time there, where, as Wharton wrote Bahlmann, "[We] have enjoyed every moment," with Edith visiting the Louvre and the Cluny Museum, Edith and Teddy wandering around the city in the morning, and Edith taking afternoon carriage rides with her mother, who was also in the city.[5] Paris remained a constant in her early married life. She was "in and out of Paris" in the 1890s; her mother died there in 1901, and both of her brothers settled there, so that the city became a home base for Wharton in Europe even before she moved there.[6] Wharton had met the French novelist Paul Bourget in 1893 while he was visiting Newport, prefatory to writing *Outre Mer*, his study of American life (a work that Cather would mention in an 1895 column for the *Nebraska Journal*, calling it a "thoroughly creditable book" but remarking that "Mr. Bourget is a novelist, and he should not content himself with being an essayist").[7] In 1905 Bourget returned the favor of Wharton's hospitality, introducing her to the socially exclusive Faubourg St. Germain.[8] She began spending more and more time in the city, renting the apartment of George Vanderbilt at 58 rue de Varenne in 1907 and 1908. In 1909, when the Vanderbilts reclaimed their property, she arranged to rent a spacious apartment just a few steps away, at 53 rue de Varenne; she moved into her new home in January 1910, during "the worst floods Paris had ever known."[9] It remained her home through World War I.

But before the war was over, Wharton purchased an estate, the Pavillon Colombe, a few miles north of Paris in the village of St. Brice-sous-Forêt. As the area was still subject to German invasion, she got it at a reasonable price while also demonstrating her faith in an Allied victory: "C'est mon acte de foi dans la Victoire," she wrote her French attorney.[10] After the war she would give up her Paris apartment and spend her summers at the Pavillon Colombe and her winters in another property in Hyères, a town on the Mediterranean, on which she took a long-term lease; this she would rename Sainte Claire le Château.[11] Far from being focused solely on Paris, Wharton traveled to nearly every region of France. In the winter of 1881–82 she spent significant time in Cannes, making several friends while her father was attempting to regain his health; though he died there in 1882, Edith and her mother returned in spring 1883.[12] Three trips in 1906 and 1907, taken in the then still novel automobile, led to her publication of *A Motor-Flight through France* in 1908, which describes travels to the Loire valley, the Auvergne, the Pyrenees, Provence, and the Champagne region. Other trips taken in peacetime and wartime included Normandy, Alsace, the Vosges, and the towns, countrysides, and coastlines of central and southern France. She died at the Pavillon Colombe on August 11, 1937, and was buried in the Cimitière des Gonards in Versailles.

In comparison, Cather's acquaintance with France was relatively slight; she did not even visit France until 1902, when she was twenty-eight years old. Yet in another way, as Woodress has pointed out, France was central to her life: she "had been a Francophile since early childhood."[13] As a little girl in Virginia, she treasured the stories told her by Mrs. Love, the wife of the doctor who delivered her, about her childhood in France; in Nebraska she admired "the *joie de vivre* of the French Canadian settlement north of Red Cloud" and appreciated the "memories of France" of her cultivated Red Cloud neighbor, Mrs. Wiener.[14] In college and during her decade in Pittsburgh, Cather would "saturat[e] [herself] in French literature."[15] Dorothy Canfield also knew Paris, having lived there as a child; Canfield's mother, "who felt Paris to be a second home, gave [Cather] a yet more intimate sense of what it meant to be French."[16] Canfield spoke French fluently, studied French literature at the Sorbonne, and lived in France for a year during World War I with her husband, John Fisher, and their children.[17] In New York City Cather's friend Elisabeth Shepley Sergeant, a New Englander "fluent in

French and a self-described Francophile," knew France well; Sergeant would also live in France during World War I.[18] Saturated with visions of France, Cather's feeling for the country was such that, approaching it for the first time on shipboard from England, she was struck by the cries "of a little boy who had been born on a foreign soil and who had never been home. He ... kept crying with small convulsions of excitement, 'Is it France? Is it France?'"[19] For Cather too it seems to have been a kind of homecoming,[20] and her descriptions of the country in her 1902 travelogue are almost uniformly positive. France has been described as Cather's "second country"; a French newspaper used the same phrase to describe Wharton when she was made a Chevalier of the Legion of Honor, calling France her *"seconde patrie."*[21]

Wharton's biographer Shari Benstock wrote that Wharton "did not decide on a European life ... but rather found herself already embarked on it. Its aesthetic and psychic structures were laid down in childhood."[22] Although Cather, as a visitor to France rather than a resident, would never equal Wharton's knowledge of the country, the same could be said of her deep-rooted affinity for France. Cather got to know France, and particularly Paris, well, traveling for extended periods in a leisurely way difficult for today's travelers to imagine. Her first European excursion spanned three months: she and Isabelle McClung sailed from Philadelphia on June 14, 1902, returning in late September.[23] They spent five weeks in England, then crossed to France, landing at Dieppe and spending time in Rouen, where Cather admired monuments to Flaubert and Maupassant and first experienced a Gothic cathedral, before proceeding to Paris, where they stayed at a pension at 11 rue de Cluny (today Place Paul Painlevé), exploring the city during most of August.[24] They then ventured south, visiting Arles, Avignon, Marseilles, and other cities before returning home. She would return to France in 1920, 1923, 1930, and 1935, on trips that were sometimes even more leisurely. Of her six trips to Europe, France was her main destination in all but two; while spending time in Paris on each trip, she explored other regions as well. In 1920 she visited areas in northern France devastated by World War I, making a pilgrimage to the grave of her cousin G. P. Cather in Villers Tournelle. In 1930 she visited areas as culturally and geographically distinct as the harbor town of St. Malo in Brittany and the town of Sallanches, within sight of Mont Blanc and the French Alps.[25]

In *A Little Tour in France* Henry James had written that "though France might be Paris, Paris was by no means France."[26] While Wharton and Cather admired Paris, they resonated to many of the same regions outside the capital, although sometimes for different reasons. Wharton visited Arles in 1890 and was particularly impressed by the Church of St. Trophime, with "its exquisite doorway covered with Romanesque sculpture, & the still more beautiful cloister adjoining, a marvel of wonderfully-carved columns & niches."[27] Cather visited the city in 1902, commenting not on St. Trophime but on the city's Roman amphitheater, theater, and art.[28] Avignon struck a chord in both of them. When Wharton was there in 1908, she wrote to Bahlmann, asking her if she remembered how beautiful the city was on "the first day you & I saw Avignon long ago."[29] Cather's first trip to Avignon was equally memorable: after a dusty railway journey, she relished the hotel (in which, she remarked, Henry James had also stayed) and found the Palace of the Popes stunning.[30] Equally important was the sense that "people know how to live in this country."[31] At age twenty-eight Cather was finally having the sort of experience which Wharton had been exposed to as a child, seeing "a life rooted in the centuries—what she later had in mind when she spoke of the things that lie deep behind French history and French art."[32]

The Mediterranean coastline of France with its magnificent views was another shared touchstone. During her 1902 trip, Cather relished the small town of Le Lavandou and the surrounding landscape. She located a small unoccupied villa, "a mere lodge, set on a little table of land between two cliffs," where she could "do nothing for hours together but stare at this great water that seems to trail its delft-blue mantle across the world," an experience that gave her a "sense of immeasurable possession and immeasurable content."[33] Le Lavandou is a mere fourteen miles east of Hyères, where, after the war, Wharton would spend her winters. Wharton's experience of the place reflects a similar sense of possession and contentment; in a 1920 letter she wrote, "The little house is delicious, so friendly & comfortable, & full of sun & air; but what overwhelms us all . . . is the endless beauty of the view. . . . Our quiet-coloured end of evening presents us with a full moon standing over the tower of the great Romanesque church . . . & a sunset silhouetting the 'Îles d'Or' in black on a sea of silver."[34] Le Lavandou made Cather feel an inexplicable happiness: "I do not know why a wretched little fishing village, with nothing but green pines and blue sea and a sky of porcelain, should mean more than a dozen places that I have wanted to see all my life";[35] but it did. Wharton felt the same nearly ineffable contentment at Sainte Claire: "The heavenly beauty & the heavenly quiet enfold me, & I feel that this really is the Cielo della Quieta [*sic*; 'the Heaven of Quiet'] to which the soul aspires after its stormy voyage," she wrote, invoking Dante's *Paradiso* to convey her sense of deep calm.[36]

The landscape of Auvergne, a region in central France, became particularly important to both authors. Wharton found it striking, describing in *A Motor-Flight through France* "its remarkably individual church architecture, and . . . the no less personal character of its landscape," parts of which she defined as "rugged and Alpine in character: the pastures have a Swiss look."[37] Revisiting the area in 1912, she enthused over her "incomparable views over the whole Puy de Dôme region, the Mont Dore, & th[e] Massif du Cantal"; she was pleased when an acquaintance she had introduced to Auvergne's churches "[knew] enough of architecture to be aware of what they 'stand for.'"[38] In her letter she does not delineate exactly what this is, but *French Ways and Their Meaning* suggests that she is referring to the qualities of "reverence" and "continuity," which are valued in French culture. Cather apparently never visited the region, yet it is central to her novel *Death Comes for the Archbishop*, as her Jesuit priests Latour and Vaillant, like their historical models Lamy and Machebeuf, come from towns near what is now the city of Clermont-Ferrand. Cather wrote evocatively of Auvergne's landscape and Romanesque churches in her novel; one wonders whether she drew on Wharton's work in creating her landscapes, as some of Cather's descriptions of Auvergne make it seem steeper, more "rugged and Alpine," than it actually is. (Readers are told, for instance, that Latour "loved the towering peaks of his native mountains," an exaggeration of the geography of the region.)[39] For Cather as for Wharton, the churches of Auvergne "and what they 'stand for'" are central to her vision in *Death Comes for the Archbishop*.

As in New York City, however, the two authors never met in France, despite the fact that in some cases they were tantalizingly close to each other, particularly in Paris (fig. 11). It would have been a pleasant walk of fifteen minutes down the rue du Bac from the Hotel du Quai Voltaire, where Cather stayed in 1920, to Wharton's apartment at 53 rue de Varenne; yet Wharton gave up her lease on that apartment and took up residence in the Pavillon Colombe in May 1920,[40] just as Cather was embarking for her trip to France. Wharton's and Cather's other Paris involvements, and even their non-involvements, demonstrate the consonance of their attitudes, particularly their lack of interest in literary modernism. Both were in close proximity to other American writers whose work defined American expatriate modernism, yet neither pursued any acquaintance with them. Gertrude Stein and Alice Toklas's residence at 27 rue du Fleurus, where they lived from 1903 to 1937, was not far from Wharton's apartment or Cather's hotel.[41] In 1920 a very short walk to 8 rue Dupuytren would have led them to Sylvia Beach's Shakespeare and Company bookstore, which had opened in November 1919.[42] During Cather's 1923 trip to Paris she could have run into a young Ernest Hemingway at the store's new location at 12 rue de l'Odeon, to which it had moved in 1921.[43]

Neither Wharton nor Cather evinced any interest in meeting these writers, whose personal and literary styles were so different from their own. Yet their French literary and artistic circles intersected. The French scholar Albert Feuillerat, who described Cather as "one of the best American novelists" in a 1930 article, was the brother-in-law of Paul Bourget, Wharton's literary friend; another of Wharton's literary friends, Anna de Noailles, was a founder of the Prix Femina Américain, awarded to Cather in 1933 for *Shadows on the Rock*.[44] Wharton and Cather were both attracted by nonliterary modernism in France. In 1910 Wharton attended the Diaghilev production of Stravinsky's *Firebird*, "with its sumptuous costumes and set designs"; the following year she saw the Ballet Russe "in a lavish production of Stravinsky's *Petrushka*."[45] In January 1911 she was looking forward to the premiere of a "Hindu bal-

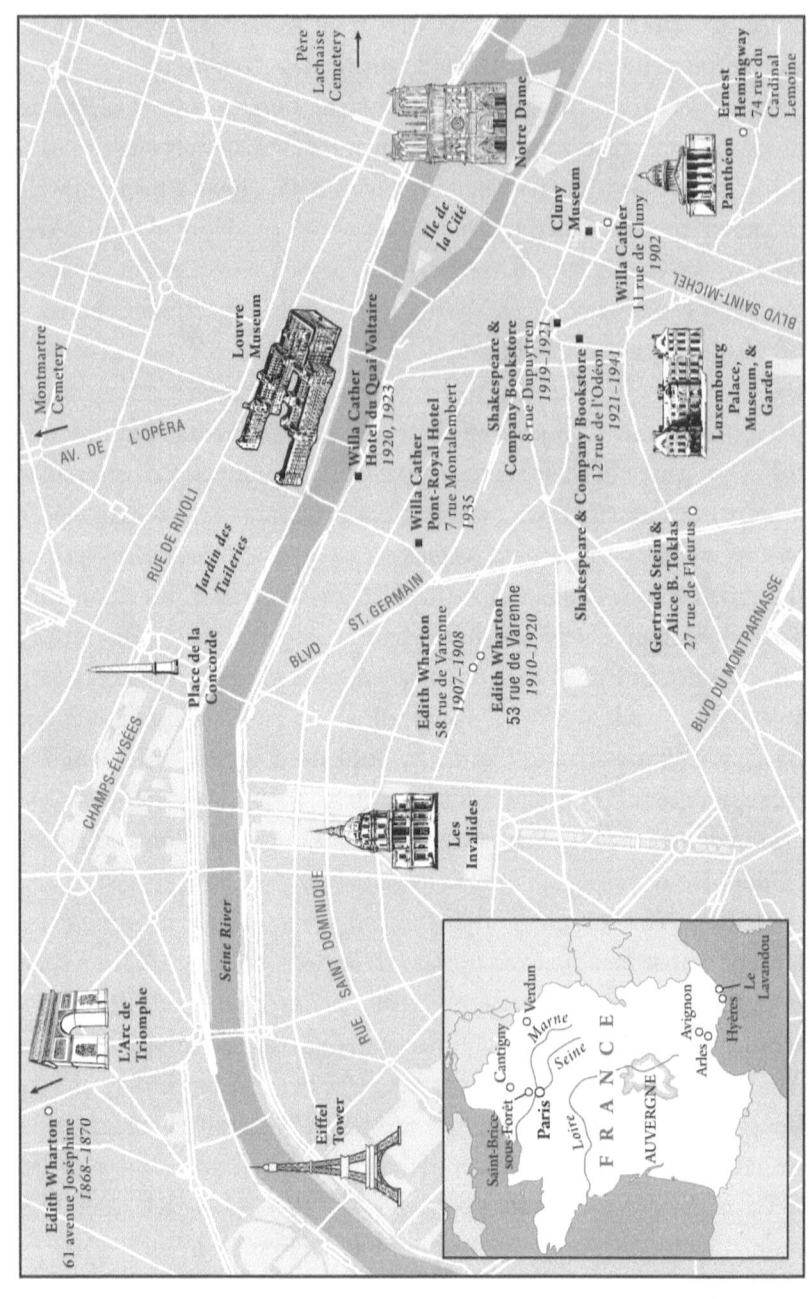

11. Wharton's and Cather's Paris; inset: locations important to both in France.

let" featuring "scenery and costumes by Bakst,"[46] the important artist who, during the war years, would donate two drawings to her edited collection *The Book of the Homeless*.[47] Cather also admired Bakst, who would paint a portrait of her over the course of twenty sittings during her 1923 visit to Paris;[48] the experience also yielded a photographic portrait of Cather looking very at home with Bakst in his studio (fig. 12). Wharton owned a Cézanne, which she loaned to an exhibition of his work at the Grand Palais in 1937; she was sufficiently enthusiastic about Cézanne's work that in 1915, a year after World War I broke out and while she was engulfed in charitable work, she took the time to write a letter to the art historian Royal Cortissoz, telling him that she had asked the art dealer Ambroise Vollard to send him his book about Cézanne, hoping that Cortissoz would give it good press in the United States.[49] Cather was also intrigued by modernist painters, as Sergeant recounted, and referred admiringly to Cézanne's work (as "C——") in "Coming, Aphrodite!"[50] Lee's description of Wharton's attraction to Paris also fits Cather exactly: "Though she was never a part of the bohemian, decadent side of the gay, pre-war city, she had her adventures there, too. Paris meant romance, excitement and beauty to her, as well as order and tradition."[51]

Given the centrality of France to both authors, it is not surprising that France and French culture play a huge role in their *oeuvres*. As with New York City, France appears regularly, almost pervasively, in Wharton's work. It is the focus of three works of nonfiction—*A Motor-Flight through France* (1908), *Fighting France* (1915), and *French Ways and Their Meaning* (1919)—and the main setting of several novels and novellas, including *Madame de Treymes* (1906), *The Reef* (1912), *The Marne* (1918), and *A Son at the Front* (1923). France plays a significant role in many other works, including *The House of Mirth*, *The Custom of the Country*, *The Age of Innocence*, *The Glimpses of the Moon*, and *The Gods Arrive*. (Even Wharton's juvenile novel, *Fast and Loose*, written when she was fourteen, includes scenes in Paris.) France plays a less significant role in her short stories, but "Kerfol" (1916) and "Miss Mary Pask" (1925) are ghost stories set in Brittany, the Celtic region of France, and her war-related stories "Writing a War Story" (1919) and

12. Cather in Leon Bakst's studio in Paris, 1920. Philip L. and Helen Cather Southwick Collection, Archives and Special Collections, University of Nebraska–Lincoln Libraries.

"Coming Home" (1915) are set in France. The country figures in poems written throughout her life, from the 1878 portrait in "Chriemhild of Burgundy" to mature works like "Chartres" (1893) and several poems in her 1926 volume *Twelve Poems*; unpublished manuscript poems include at least two inspired by French places, "Senlis" and "Rambouillet."[52] These poems often combine deep emotion with descriptions of France's natural beauty, sometimes as a solace for the difficulty of life or the fleeting nature of time, attesting to the centrality of France in Wharton's psyche.

For Cather too France figured significantly; it plays a surprisingly large role in her work, including her poetry. An 1899 poem, "Then Back to Ancient France Again," reflects the romanticized France she had read about in Dumas's *Three Musketeers*, and her 1903 volume of poems, *April Twilights*, includes "Mills of Montmartre," "Provençal

Legend," and "Paris"; her unpublished poems include two inspired by France, "Sunday on the Seine" and "Cherbourg."[53] Her first substantial writings about France, however, were the articles she wrote about her 1902 trip through France for the *Nebraska State Journal*. In her articles about Paris she chose, perhaps idiosyncratically, to write about Paris's cemeteries, including a beautifully detailed description of Paul-Albert Bartholomé's Monument aux Morts in Père Lachaise Cemetery; in *Alexandra's Bridge*, her first novel, it is in Paris that Bartley Alexander and Hilda Burgoyne fall in love. The city also plays a crucial role in the life of Godfrey St. Peter in *The Professor's House*, with Cather sketching St. Peter's individual map of Paris as he breakfasts on the rue du Vaugirard, buys a bouquet of pink dahlias on the Place du Pantheon, and, years later, wishes he could have visited the monument to Delacroix in the Luxembourg Gardens with Tom Outland. France plays a major role in *One of Ours* (1922), *Death Comes for the Archbishop* (1927), and *Shadows on the Rock* (1931); medieval Avignon was the setting for the novel on which she was working at the time of her death, "Hard Punishments," of which only fragments remain. In one way France plays a larger role in Cather's fiction than in Wharton's. While Wharton frequently depicts Americans encountering French culture, it is Cather who depicts the importation of French culture into America, as we will see in the final section of this chapter.

"THE LIGHT AND ELASTIC MESH OF THE FRENCH TONGUE"

Wharton's and Cather's admiration of France included their admiration of the French language. Again, what has been written of Cather's relationship to French is equally true of Wharton: "Fluency in French meant more than ... knowing French grammar and having a large vocabulary.... It meant achievement and possession—being at ease and at home in the world of high culture, as if all the riches of European tradition were compacted in the French language."[54] To be sure, their facility with the language differed. Wharton began to speak French as a child, when it is easy to acquire languages; she also read French literature with ease. Yet her reading of the great French literature of the past did not always benefit her facility with modern French. When she moved to France as an adult, she was teased for speaking "the purest Louis Quatorze" and needed to develop a more idiomatic use of the language.[55] Improve it she did, beginning her novella *Ethan Frome* as an exercise in written French for a tutor, writing the story "Les Metteurs en Scène" in French in 1909, and translating her own story "Atrophy" into "very idiomatic French" for publication in the *Revue des Deux Mondes*.[56] After Henry James's death, she wrote a sympathy letter to their mutual friend André Gide in French that was both "impeccable" and graceful, important since Gide himself was "a finicky stylist."[57] During World War I "her charity work ... involved legal, commercial, and political correspondence in French, fields of expertise that required nuances of vocabulary and diction."[58] Knowing French as well as she did, she "thought in French" or, rather, she thought bilingually; as Roger Asselineau observes, the French phrases she uses in her letters are not affectations but reflections of her thought process.[59] Wharton admired French "not only because of its precision, but also because of the way French writers handled it. She admired and tried to emulate the clarity of their style, their sense of form and their restraint."[60] She worked closely with translators of her novels and "preferred to have two translators collaborating on each book, one for 'le gros travail' (the main work) and one for 'la mise au point' (the fine tuning)."[61] The French language ineluctably reflects and shapes French culture, and profoundly influenced Wharton's work as well.

Cather did not have Wharton's facility in spoken French, which sometimes troubled her. On her 1902 trip to France she was relieved to have Dorothy Canfield, who was fluent in French, join her and Isabelle in Paris.[62] Generally speaking, Cather's French appears to have been adequate for less complex situations; Michel Gervaud surmises that "she was able at least to carry on a simple conversation" and that "she had little trouble understanding it when spoken by educated people."[63] Cather's description of herself in "A Chance Meeting," however, suggests that she was not comfortable in more complex contexts. Upon encountering Mme Grout, Flaubert's niece, Cather was reluctant to speak to her in French, explaining in her essay, "I am a poor linguist, and there would be no point in uttering commonplaces to this old lady.... If one spoke to her at all, one must be at ease."[64] She was relieved when Mme Grout opened a conversation with her in English. Yet her admiration of French was deep. In *Death Comes for the Archbishop* an elderly Father Latour wishes he had recorded "old legends and customs" in French so that "he could have arrested their flight by throwing about them the light and elastic mesh of the French tongue."[65] Echoing a central passage in *The Song of the Lark*—Thea's insight that art captures a moment of life "in a flash of arrested motion"[66]—this phrase suggests that for Cather, French is itself a form of art.

Like Wharton, Cather followed French translations of her work closely. Her grasp of the language was imperfect; her objections to Victor Llona's translation of *My Ántonia* were apparently groundless, for instance.[67] But she was concerned that translations capture both her prose and its rootedness in place. As we saw in chapter 4, she protested a French translation of *Death Comes for the Archbishop* that was being prepared by Marguerite Yourcenar, believing that Yourcenar was rewriting rather than translating the novel; Cather was also concerned that Yourcenar, who had never been to the Southwest, would be unable to convey the landscape. Further, she was troubled that Yourcenar refused to use Spanish terms like "arroyo," which were the best, and perhaps the only, way to describe that landscape accurately.[68] Cather specifically linked the linguistic and the geographic in exhorting another translator of the novel: "If you are interested in making a thoroughly good translation, you, like the two priests [Latour and Vaillant], must courageously face the geographical and geological difficulties."[69]

It is particularly appropriate, then, that Cather incorporated French into the works in which she portrayed French immigrants in North America, *Death Comes for the Archbishop* and *Shadows on the Rock*. Françoise Palleau-Papin notes that in *Death Comes for the Archbishop* Cather "plays the crafty game of writing in perfectly correct English that still manages to 'sound' French," as if she had "conformed her expression to its French equivalent, or the structures that both languages share."[70] In that novel Latour comments on the trial in which Mme Olivares has to state her age: "I don't think I ever assisted at anything so cruel." The French verb *assister à* means "to attend," but in English it also subtly reminds readers that Latour "assisted" in the effort to get Olivares to admit her age.[71] In *Shadows on the Rock* Jacques is asked whether he is "very content" (idiomatic French: *très content*) with his new shoes rather than "happy" with them (idiomatic English).[72] Like Wharton's use of French phrases, Cather's use of French and French diction within American English is not a mere flourish, nor merely an homage to France; it "convey[s] a vision of the French culture linguistically."[73] As her French translator Marc Chénetier has written, Cather "may have entirely transferred her passionate relation with the French language into the very fabric of her prose."[74] As with Wharton, who emulated the clarity and restraint of French, Cather's embrace of French is neither merely thematic nor merely a demonstration of her affinity for the language; rather, it enacts her "aspiration to a set of aesthetic and intellectual ideals that French . . . had come to stand for."[75]

LA BELLE FRANCE

Paris in particular, and France in general, offered exactly what Wharton and Cather saw as lacking in the United States: New York City offered a tense mixture of business and beauty, but in the struggle between the two forces it was commerce that nearly always won, with beauty relegated to the role of cultural afterthought. Further, those who most appreciate beauty fall victim to the superior strength of those for whom money and money making were paramount, including the new invaders from the West, who offered vitality but lacked an appreciation of culture. In France, although business, practicality, and energy were valued, beauty and art were integral parts of life—not only in what the United States cordoned off as "the world of art," but in daily life as well.

Wharton and Cather were part of a long line of Americans who have found in Paris something unavailable in the United States. As Adam Gopnik has written, "For two centuries, Paris has been attached for Americans to an idea of happiness, of good things eaten and new clothes bought and a sentimental education achieved. . . . It is the place we go to escape small-town, or even big-town, American life and be happy."[76] Some of what Paris offered could be quantified. Long before

Wharton or Cather arrived in Paris, American artists studied there. The nineteenth-century American artist George Healy explained that "there were no art schools in America, no drawing classes, no collections of fine plaster casts and very few picture exhibitions";[77] as a younger nation, the United States had not had the same opportunities to develop such institutions. But their absence was also a function of the practical American attitude toward business, civic development, and life, and a reflection of a disregard for what cannot always be quantified. In Paris "the glories of the art of architecture, of the arts on all sides, in and out of doors, the conviction of the French that the arts were indispensable to the enjoyment and meaning of life, affected the Americans more than anything else about Paris, and led many to conclude their own country had a long way to go."[78] Thomas Jefferson purchased paintings and books in Paris to "help increase American appreciation of the fine arts and the world of ideas"; painter and inventor Samuel Morse "would bring the good news of time-honored European art home to his own people, for their benefit and for the betterment of his country."[79] Even the socially conscious Harriet Beecher Stowe basked in the glow of Paris in 1853. Far from seeing the beautiful as merely ornamental, she presented America's lack of appreciation of beauty as a social issue, a problem that crushed the human soul. Using terms much like those Wharton and Cather would later employ, Stowe remarked in 1854, "With all New England's earnestness and practical efficiency, there is a long withering of the soul's more ethereal part—a crushing out of the beautiful—which is horrible. Children are born there with a sense of beauty equally delicate with any in the world, in whom it dies a lingering death of smothered desire and pining, weary starvation. I know, because I have felt it."[80] Stowe uses religion to defend her point: "Did not He who made the appetite for food make also that for beauty? And while the former will perish with the body, is not the latter immortal?"[81] As McCullough remarks, "It was a severe indictment of her own upbringing, indeed of American life, and not until she came to Paris had it struck her so emphatically."[82]

A significant reason French culture offered so much was that it was not governed by America's cultural Puritanism, as Wharton knew and

Cather gradually realized. In *French Traits* Wharton's friend William Crary Brownell explained the difference between French enjoyment of life and American restraint as a difference between a Catholic nation and a Protestant one: "Catholicism ... has tended to develop all those sides of man's nature which relate him to the external world, and we have in France, as a result ... a people possessed of the epicurean rather than the ascetic ideal in morals."[83] As we saw earlier, Wharton was pleased, if surprised, to see in 1893 that art was beginning to be displayed as well in New York as in Paris.[84] But art in museums alone was not enough, she argued. Echoing Brownell's contrast between the Catholic, epicurean French and the Puritanical, ascetic Americans, Wharton argued in *French Ways and Their Meaning*, "It was the Puritan races ... who decided that 'Art' ... was something apart from life, as dangerous to it as Plato thought Poets in a Republic, and to be tolerated only when it was so lofty, unapproachable and remote from any appeal to average humanity that it bored people to death, and they locked it up in Museums to get rid of it."[85] In France, Wharton added, art was not locked up; it was visible throughout the cities, towns, and countryside. "*Dieu, que c'est beau* [God, it's beautiful] after six months of eye-starving! ... *Je l'ai dans mon sang*! [I have it in my blood!]," Wharton wrote ecstatically to Sally Norton when she returned to Paris from the United States in 1907.[86] Art, including cuisine, was a part of daily life. In many ways this cultural difference persists today, although attitudes are slowly changing. In twenty-first century America, as sociologist Priscilla Ferguson has written, the new "demand for culinary quality represents a real shift in cultural priorities. ... Benjamin Franklin exhorted his countrymen to abjure the pleasures of the table and set their minds on higher things. ... The pleasures of the palate did not enter into the equation."[87] In contrast, in France, good cooking has long been seen not as self-indulgence but as an essential part of civilization. The cook is "the vital link in the culinary chain that metamorphoses the raw to the cooked and the cooked to the miraculously pleasurable"; cooks "transform eating into dining," and diners themselves "come away from the table transformed."[88]

The broader French understanding of culture was something that Cather began to appreciate on her first trip to France. Writing to Canfield, she related that she had "purchased many foolish underclothing [sic]" and that she had "eat[en] unto discomfort" of her hostess's "delicious fish au gratin."[89] Her wording suggests a combination of enthusiasm and residual Puritanical guilt ("foolish underclothing" and too much fish au gratin are indulgences of which she herself does not wholly approve). Cather then mentions an experience about which she seems to have felt unapologetic, perhaps because it was a more cerebral undertaking: "We went to the Luxemborg [sic], sat in the garden and put in two hours in four rooms" of the Luxembourg Museum.[90]

Yet Cather was already beginning to perceive the cultural unity between clothing, delicious food, and art. While she was writing about food and undergarments to Canfield, she was sharing more abstract thoughts with her father, referring to the city as "the most beautiful that men have ever had the genius to create. I find new pleasure and wonder in it every day."[91] She was paying attention to the daily life of the city around her, seeing a new way of doing things, one devoted both to careful work and to enjoyment: "The people here are the most industrious, neat and painstaking people I have ever seen, and yet they take life comfortably."[92] Cather was starting to see the big picture of French life and culture, to understand that, in Gopnik's phrase, "pleasures of the flesh and instruction of the spirit" can go hand in hand.[93] In Paris "art" meant not only the paintings and sculptures in the Louvre and handsome urban architecture but also the daily things, like fine clothing and fine dining. The seemingly superficial aspects of the city Cather wrote about to Canfield were not so different from the more important aspects she praised to her father but the result of the same cultural impulse. In Paris, Cather discovered, art could be a part of everyday life.

Although Cather came to France much later in her life than Wharton did, she soon learned that France's different way of living allowed a different way of thinking as well: "the weight of Protestant guilt, of thwarted and repressed desire" once left behind, a new perspective was possible.[94] The fact that Cather first experienced France as an adult may have made her more acutely aware of this difference than Wharton, who, having known France since childhood, had early absorbed its values. During her 1920 trip to Paris Cather wrote to the editor Ferris

Greenslet, "I wish you were here. I could tell you a great many things that would sound absurd on either Bank or Park streets!"[95] The beauty she found in Paris suggested ideas far different from those that might have come to mind in busy, business-oriented New York. On the same trip she wrote to Blanche Knopf, the wife of her publisher Alfred Knopf, that her hotel suite included "a writing room in which I do not write one word!"[96] Far from sounding the apologetic note she had used in 1902, she shows no Puritan guilt about her lack of American productivity, explaining that appreciating the beauty of the city itself is more important: "The weather is gold and gray all mixed up—anybody would be a fool to shut themselves up with their own ideas with the city, this rather particular city, swimming in light outside.... The city itself never seemed to me so beautiful.... The streets are lovelier than anything in the art galleries."[97] Wharton "saw that the French reverence for art was in itself a kind of religious faith";[98] Cather, who had equated art with religion since the 1890s, finally found in France a culture that reflected exactly what she had long believed. Like Wharton, she would come to appreciate the beauty not only of many French cities but of French gardens and agriculture, and to understand that in France, unlike Puritan America, the senses were to be enjoyed, not mistrusted.

For both authors France represented other values as well. Wharton's study of French culture, *French Ways and Their Meaning*, written during World War I, delineates these most clearly for her American audience, including American servicemen, who would find the book in the library of navy ships on their trips to France.[99] Originally written as essays published in *Scribner's Magazine*, most of Wharton's chapters are organized around the French values she saw as central, "Reverence," "Taste," "Intellectual Honesty," and "Continuity," or tradition.[100] Of these, as Benstock has written, "The key element is intellectual honesty," which was comprised of "fearless self-regard, maturity achieved through courage, the ability to see and accept things as they are, the will to learn, a commitment to self-discipline and principled conviction, and loyalty to established values."[101] These were fundamental values for Cather too, for whom, as Stéphanie Durrans has written, "France always stands out as a locus of tradition, culture, refinement, and order, as opposed to America's comparative unrootedness and lack of cultural landmarks."[102] Since Cather's days as the "meat-ax young girl" reviewing plays for the *Nebraska State Journal*, she too had valued intellectual honesty and "the ability to see and accept things as they are." In French culture she found "a reassuring sense of the past, a devotion to lasting values."[103] To Sergeant she wrote that the French had "values, aims, a point of view, and have acquired wisdom from the enduring verities. One did not find anything of the sort in the Middle West."[104] French culture was something Sergeant knew well; she published two books related to the war, *French Perspectives* in 1916 and *Shadow-Shapes: The Journal of a Wounded Woman, October 1918–May 1919*, both of which reflect her deep knowledge and love of the country, including France in wartime.[105] In *French Perspectives* Sergeant wrote that France would "liv[e] through these bitter years on the strength of her ancient everyday virtues. Most of all, by force of what has been called her 'professional conscience,' that love of work for work's sake, that passion for technical perfection, that scrupulous patience in carrying things through which ... is ... the deepest source of French national energy."[106] The French "'professional conscience,' ... that passion for technical perfection"; France's "ancient everyday virtues"; and the French ability to enjoy life: together these summarize much of what drew Wharton, Cather, and many others to France. Its national culture balanced perfection and pleasure, energetic work and repose, in a way that was hard to imagine in the United States.

In *French Ways and Their Meaning* Wharton states explicitly her frustration with an American over-valuation of business and the consequent under-valuation of culture. She offers a historically based, measured assessment of the American lack of appreciation of culture: "We are a new people, a pioneer people"; if France offers a great deal more culturally than the United States, it is because France has had "time to acquire" these qualities.[107] Further into her analysis, however, her tone is more critical of American attitudes. Although she faults the French for their reluctance to donate money to causes made crucial by "the most cataclysmic moments of the war,"[108] she explains that this behavior is the result of their habitual prudence and their lack of the American profit motive. "Their thoughts are not occupied with money-making in itself, as an end worth living for, but only with the idea of having money enough to be sure of not losing their situation in life, for themselves or their children.... They want only enough leisure and freedom from material anxiety to enjoy what life and the arts of life offer."[109] She reiterates emphatically: "This absence of financial ambition should never be lost sight of: it is not only the best clue to the French character, but the most useful lesson our own people can learn from contact with France."[110]

It would be several years until 1925, when Calvin Coolidge would assert cheerfully that "the chief business of the American people is business. They are profoundly concerned with producing, buying, selling, investing, and prospering in the world."[111] This attitude was one Wharton had already critiqued in *The Custom of the Country*, and *French Ways and Their Meaning* explains her objections: "Americans are too prone to consider money-making as interesting in itself: they regard the fact that a man has made money as something intrinsically meritorious. But... if a man piles up millions in order to pile them up, having already all he needs to live humanly and decently, his occupation is neither interesting in itself, nor conducive to any sort of real social development in the money-maker or in those about him. No life is more sterile than one into which nothing enters to balance such an output of energy."[112] In decided contrast is the "far more modest ambition" of the French, which "consists simply in the effort to earn one's living and put by enough for sickness, old age, and a good start in life for the children."[113]

Wharton concedes that "This conception of 'business' may seem a tame one to Americans" but points out its advantages: it gives the French, "every day, something the American has not had: Time."[114] The French have time to enjoy life as they live it, rather than merely rushing through their days; this, in turn, matters because although "the great mass of men and women grow up and reach real maturity only through their contact with the material realities of living, [the] growth and the maturing take place *in the intervals between these activities*: and in lives where there are no such intervals there will be no real growth."[115] The result of the American approach, she writes, is that not only the individual but the "collective life" suffers.[116] Her earlier remark, that Americans have not developed a sufficient appreciation for culture because they have not had time, then, suggests a deeper critique: Americans have not developed culture because they do not truly value it. "The very significance—the note of ridicule and slight contempt—which attaches to the world 'culture' in America, would be quite unintelligible to the French of any class," she writes.[117] Only in the United States is it seen as "superfluous," or "even slightly comic, to know a great deal ... to know, in fact, as much as possible."[118] "Theoretically, America holds art and ideas in esteem also; but she does not, as a people, seek or desire them."[119] Her comment that "taste ... is not art—but it is the atmosphere in which art lives, and outside of which it cannot live"[120]—takes us straight back to the deaths of Lily Bart, Paul, and Ralph Marvell in New York, all of them commentary on the American disregard for "the atmosphere in which art lives."

Cather never wrote an extended critique of American culture like the one embedded in Wharton's *French Ways and Their Meaning*, yet she shared many of Wharton's views, including Wharton's underlying critique of the United States. As we have seen, her early stories create a grim picture of the American lack of appreciation of "art and ideas" and of high culture in general. She too used French culture to critique American materialism and the American failure to appreciate the arts. In a 1924 interview Cather both echoed Wharton and cited her work. "France is sensitive," she told her interviewer; "we [Americans] are not."[121] Like Wharton, she attributes some of this insensitivity to "our youth" as a nation; she also sees that the root of the problem is "our prosperity, our judging success in terms of dollars."[122] The rich natural resources of the United States have made this possible; in contrast, she notes, again following Wharton's argument, the French have had to "wrest[] their wages from a miserly master," France itself: "Mrs. Wharton expressed it very well in a recent article when she said that the Frenchman elected to live at home and use his wits to make his condition happy."[123] Cather continues her paraphrase of Wharton's ideas, arguing that "The Frenchman doesn't talk nonsense about art ... ; he is too greatly occupied with building the things that make his home. [In his] house, his garden, his vineyards... he creates something beautiful, something lasting."[124] Given Wharton's extended residence in France, it is unsurprising that her war-related novels, *The Marne* and *A Son at the Front*, praise France for providing what American culture did not. Yet Cather's *One of Ours*, by contrasting Claude Wheeler's life in the United States with the values he finds in France, provides the clearest picture of all of the contrast between American and French values.

Given the centrality of France and French culture to Wharton and Cather, it is hardly surprising that both responded strongly to the Great War. Although it was a world war, for them it was primarily the war in France and a war *on* France, a threat to everything they cherished in French civilization and saw as a valuable alternative to American limitations. Although Wharton lived in Paris and Cather in New York City, their attitude toward the war was fundamentally the same: the United States should do everything it could to save France and thereby civilization.

Nearly as soon as Germany declared war in France, Wharton believed fervently that it was the duty of the United States to come to the aid of the Allies and was deeply frustrated by President Wilson's policy of neutrality.[125] In April 1916 she wrote a friend, "It is indeed hard for some of us to 'accept America as it seems to be today'"; two months later, she wrote to Sally Norton, "France continues to be magnificent, & one envies the people who have a real 'patrie.'"[126] From the time the war began in August 1914, much of her writing was geared first toward encouraging the United States to enter the war, then more broadly toward influencing American opinion and encouraging Americans to appreciate France. She also undertook monumental work relieving the suffering caused by the war, founding homes for Belgian refugees, establishing sanitaria for tubercular French soldiers, and engaging in efforts both exhaustive and personally exhausting to raise the funds to keep these and other crucial charities going.[127] On five separate occasions in 1915, she visited the front to collect information and distribute supplies for the Red Cross, and to provide eyewitness accounts for readers of *Scribner's Magazine*.[128] Wharton was not averse to the notion that some of her writing could be seen as propaganda. On the contrary, she agreed to write a number of articles for *Cosmopolitan* because, as she wrote (using her "American" twang), "it will be good proppergander."[129]

Wharton was jubilant when the United States finally declared war in April 1917, writing Sally Norton a month later, "Let us embrace on the glorious fact that we can now hold up our heads with the civilized nations of the world."[130] She followed American participation in the war closely, as her letters, both published and unpublished, show over and over again. She never wavered in her belief in the Allied cause or in the necessity for France to defend itself. It may be impossible to overstate her relief when the war concluded with an Allied victory. In *A Backward Glance* she describes the church bells that began ringing all over Paris to celebrate the Armistice on November 11, 1918. The sound had begun "softly, questioningly, almost incredulously; then with a gathering rush of sound and speed, precipitately, exultantly, till all their voices met and mingled in a crash of triumph.... We had fared so long on the thin diet of hope deferred that for a moment or two our hearts wavered and doubted. Then, like the bells, they swelled to bursting, and we knew the war was over."[131]

In contrast, Cather watched the conflict from the safe distance of North America. While Wharton diverted much of her authorial energy to writing articles promoting U.S. involvement, Cather maintained her literary focus, publishing *The Song of the Lark* in 1915 and *My Ántonia* in 1918. Yet the war was, as Janis Stout has observed, "a disturbing and engrossing worry, an intrusion on her mental vision that would not go away,"[132] and her letters from this period show that she was tracking the war closely and with great concern. Before the end of September 1914 she wrote Sergeant, "The war broke in on things a good deal.... One can't get away from the pull of it because somehow everything one most cares about seems in danger"; two months later she wrote her Aunt Franc Cather, "We think and talk of little but the war."[133] In March 1916 she wrote to Fisher that "the general misery let loose in the world gets to one," and she questioned human nature: "The pursuit of happiness is not the reality it's supposed to be. The pursuit of pain seems to be just as irradicable a human instinct."[134]

Cather's concerns in New York sometimes dovetailed with Wharton's in France. Germany's invasion of Belgium in August 1914, which led to Wharton to establish one of her first charities, the Foyer Franco-Belge,[135] concerned Cather as well. In November 1914 a Belgian friend had written Cather that her siblings were "starving in Brussels"; their homes had been destroyed, and they were unable even to flee the country.[136] Having heard an eloquent speech by the Belgian minister's wife, Cather decided not to give Christmas presents that year but instead to donate to war relief.[137] Such a decision would have pleased Wharton, who, in newspaper articles like "The Children of Flanders Rescue Committee," encouraged readers to donate to charity. Even in Nebraska, as Cather would later write, women were making underclothing for Belgian refugees, some of whom may have been under the care of Wharton's charities. Moreover, they were setting aside their own modern American ways of doing things to make these garments identical to the old-fashioned ones the Belgians were used to. "Our women simply admired Belgium too much," Cather explained; "they had no suggestions to offer to such a people. Their one wish was that those old men and women should have the kind of clothes they had always lived in, with no feeling of strangeness."[138] Such admiration and cultural sensitivity accorded with the feeling Wharton had expressed in the introduction to *The Book of the Homeless*, a compilation of manuscripts, artwork, and musical scores that she had edited to raise funds for the refugees: "We workers among the refugees are trying, first and foremost, to *help a homesick people*."[139]

Although Cather did not immediately express the idea that the United States should join the Allied cause, she believed that Americans should donate generously to the cause: "We are the only nation not suffering, and I do think History will be ashamed of us if we are niggardly."[140] A month after the American declaration of war she reflected grimly in a letter, "The war has made everything so much more difficult.... One can't feel that writing books is very important."[141] Yet she also emphasized that the United States *had* to enter the war and echoed President

Wilson's argument that democracy itself was at stake: "If America had not gone in, the allies would have been beaten.... We can literally save Democracy—or lose it—for the whole world."[142] Terrible as the war was proving to be, both authors were enthusiastic about American "boys" serving in the war. In September 1917 Cather wrote her Aunt Franc that she wished Jack, her youngest brother, were going to fight in France like their cousin G.P.; a month later Wharton was writing to an American friend, "You must be having thrilling times, with both of the boys in the war already."[143]

As Andrew Jewell has shown, Cather's attitude toward the war varied over time, yet it remained generally enthusiastic.[144] Surely the letter in which she expresses the greatest endorsement of the war is the one she wrote to her Aunt Franc after the death of G. P. Cather, her son, in May 1918, in which she attempts to console her grieving aunt.[145] The news of G.P.'s death as reported in the newspaper, Cather told her aunt, listed his name "under that glorious title 'killed in action' which sets men off from their fellows.... [He] lived to find the work he loved and seemed to be made for, and to give his life to the greatest cause men ever fought for."[146] She did not find G.P.'s death disillusioning; her attitude about the war remained generally positive, even enthusiastic. On July 19, 1918, when she learned that G.P. had been posthumously awarded a Distinguished Service Cross, she wrote to her brother Roscoe, "Isn't the news from France glorious? I was so proud of G. P.'s citation."[147] The headlines for the *New York Times* on July 19 reporting the successful American engagement in the Second Battle of the Marne ("Allies Push Germans Back on 28-Mile Front... Americans Capture 4,000 Prisoners")[148]—the battle Wharton would depict at the end of her novella *The Marne*—probably explain Cather's enthusiastic postscript to her letter: "Aren't the American boys some soldiers!"[149] When the Armistice was declared on November 11, 1918, she wrote to Aunt Franc that "a greater Peace" had been attained and sympathetically told her that, through G.P.'s death, she had "helped to pay the dear price for all that this world has gained."[150] Like Wharton in Paris, Cather recounted the sound of bells joyfully ringing out the Armistice in New York; "for the first time since human society has existed on this planet, the sun rose this morning upon a world in which not one great monarchy or tyranny existed," she added jubilantly.[151] Four years after the end of the war her tone had changed considerably. She wrote, "It seems to me that everything has gone wrong since the Armistice. Why they celebrate that day with anything but fasts and sack-cloth and ashes, I don't know"; yet as early as December 1914 she had remarked with eerie prescience that "I suppose they will patch up a temporary peace and then, in twenty-five years, beat it again with a new crop of men."[152] But during the war, she was committed to it and to American involvement.

The war years not only elicited the same reactions from Wharton and Cather but again illustrate the intersection of their worlds. Wharton, a friend of Theodore Roosevelt, met two of his sons while they were serving in France; a photograph shows her in the company of a number of young American soldiers, including Archie, Roosevelt's fourth child, and Quentin, his fifth and youngest, an aviator who would be shot down and killed in 1918 (fig. 13). G. P. Cather's commanding officer was their eldest brother, Theodore Roosevelt Jr.; both are shown in a photograph from the latter's account of the war, *Average Americans* (fig. 14). John Pershing, commander of the American Expeditionary Force in France, also demonstrates the close proximity of Wharton's and Cather's lives and friendships. A mathematics instructor at the University of Nebraska while Cather was a student there, he had taught Dorothy Canfield.[153] The University of Nebraska presented Pershing and Cather with honorary doctorates in the same year, 1917; Cather accepted hers in person, while Pershing, engaged in the American effort in France, accepted his in absentia.[154] Despite the close connections between Cather and Pershing, there is no indication they ever met, while Wharton and Pershing met at least once, during a reception given for Pershing by the American Embassy in Paris in July 1917.[155] Pershing "express[ed] admiration" for Wharton's war work in a letter he wrote her not long after he arrived in France; while in Paris, he lived near her on the rue de Varenne.[156] The husband of Wharton's close friend Daisy Chanler was an adviser to Pershing; both Wharton's friend Elizabeth Cameron and Cather's friend Fisher were Pershing's dinner guests.[157]

13. Edith Wharton with Quentin Roosevelt (far right), Archie Roosevelt (next to Quentin), James Russell Parsons (seated), and two unidentified soldiers in France, 1918. Used with the permission of Peter Pennoyer.

14. G. P. Cather (#4) with his regiment, commanded by Theodore Roosevelt Jr. (#9). Detail of photograph from Theodore Roosevelt Jr., *Average Americans* (1919).

The American aviator Victor Chapman also played a role in the lives of both. Cather modeled the aviator Victor Morse in *One of Ours* partly on Chapman, who was killed in action in June 1916; she owned a copy of Chapman's *Letters from France*, a collection introduced and edited by his father, John Jay Chapman.[158] Wharton knew and admired John Chapman, who was the brother-in-law of her friend Daisy Chanler, making Victor Chapman Daisy's nephew.[159] Both Chapman's introduction to *Letters from France* and the letters from Victor's fellow members of the Lafayette Escadrille (letters that Chapman included in the volume) strike the heroic note so often sounded during the war. One young man, for instance, wrote that Victor "died the most glorious death, and at the most glorious time of life to die, especially for him with his ideals,"[160] a note Cather in particular would echo in *One of Ours*.

Wharton and Cather also responded with unaccustomed patriotism to Fourth of July parades held for American troops in Paris. Wharton witnessed the 1918 parade, when the recent arrival of American troops was creating a new wave of hope for Allied victory; Cather saw the 1920 parade, after the successful conclusion of the war.[161] Wharton called it "the greatest 'Fourth' in history" and noted that "everything & everybody was beflagged, from buildings to cab-horses"; she admired "our wonderful incredible troops, every man the same height, & marching with a long rhythmical musical stride that filled the French with wonder."[162] While Cather was not in Paris in 1918, her fictional Mlle Olive de Courcy attends the parade in *One of Ours*, sounding as "filled ... with wonder" as Wharton says: "I was in Paris on the fourth day of July, when your Marines, just from Belleau Wood, marched for your national fête, and I said to myself as they came on, '*That is a new man!*'"[163] When Cather was in Paris for the Fourth of July parade two years later, she described a scene much like the one Wharton had witnessed: "20,000 war orphans ... march[ed] down the Champ Èlysèes [*sic*] ... each carrying a little American flag"; the flag was also "flying on all the old palaces of the Kings of France, and on all the public buildings.... The American soldiers are much beloved."[164] In response to this spectacle, both Wharton and Cather overflowed with enthusiasm. Wharton commented that "The historic imagination (mine at least)

15. G. P. Cather, Cather's cousin, in uniform. Item 35801, Nebraska State Historical Society.

fairly burst in the struggle to deal with all the associations & analogies the scene evoked."[165] Cather echoed Wharton's "greatest 'Fourth'" in an enthusiastic postscript: "This Fourth of July in Paris is the most American 'Fourth' I have ever spent—no noise or row, but real feeling about something real, all the ceremonies solemn and beautiful."[166]

Wharton and Cather were also linked by wartime losses. In a major offensive near the town of Cantigny in late May 1918, Cather's cousin G. P. Cather died when a shell exploded while he was "visiting his men in the trenches."[167] Although G.P. and Willa had not been close, she had endorsed his decision to join the American effort in France; his death galvanized her and set *One of Ours* in motion (fig. 15). Despite the difficulties of travel in postwar France, she made a pilgrimage to his grave in Villers Tournelle in 1920, photographing it for G.P.'s parents.[168] In a letter to her father she commented, "I want to do this because I feel it would be some satisfaction to Aunt Franc, and because it is all one can do to show one's appreciation of a kinsman who was a brave soldier." Reflecting her sense of the distance between Nebraska and northern France, she added, "If I were buried in France, I would want my relatives to come and see me if they were in this part of the world."[169]

For Wharton, who had lived in France since 1907 and experienced the devastation of war as only a resident could, the losses were deeper. In 1915 alone she lost her friend Jean du Breuil de Saint-Germain, her friend and translator Robert d'Humières, and her former footman Henri.[170] In May 1918 she had entertained two of Theodore Roosevelt's sons, Archie and Quentin; that summer, as previously noted, Quentin died in an aviation battle.[171] Her cousin Newbold Rhinelander, another young aviator, was shot down over German territory in September of that year and was eventually pronounced dead; in the absence of his parents, Wharton assumed the responsibility of arranging his funeral (fig. 16).[172] Perhaps most personally painful was her loss in August 1918 of a young American friend, Ronald Simmons, who, to his frustration, had been declared unfit for military service. Once the United States entered the war, Simmons worked for the Inter-Allied Intelligence Division; he died, quite suddenly, in Marseilles in the Spanish

16. Newbold Rhinelander, Wharton's cousin, in uniform in France. Edith Wharton Collection, Yale Collection of American Literature, Beinecke Rare Book and Manuscript Library.

flu epidemic.¹⁷³ "This breaks me down to the depths," she wrote Bernard Berenson. "I really loved him dearly—& he had a great sort of younger brotherly affection for me—& we understood each other so completely!"¹⁷⁴

In spite of these losses Wharton continued to believe in the cause of the Allies. In a letter that echoes Cather's reassurances to Aunt Franc about the glorious cause in which G.P. had died, Wharton wrote to Teddy Roosevelt after Quentin's death: "I don't say any word of ordinary sympathy to you or Mrs. Roosevelt, because I know that you both measured in advance what you were giving, & thought nothing & no one too good for the Cause that we older people envy the young the right to die for. And so I know how you feel about Quentin. He flew away into the dawn, & is gathered up to be a part of the great radiance that is breaking over a world redeemed."¹⁷⁵ Like Cather, Wharton made pilgrimages to the graves of her dead, visiting those of Newbold Rhinelander and Ronald Simmons. To Newbold's father she wrote, "I went to see poor Ronald Simmons' pathetic grave, crowded into a narrow corner of a huge cemetery at Marseilles, & was so glad that Newbold is in a country grave-yard where there are birds and flowers."¹⁷⁶

THE IDEA(L) OF FRANCE: CATHER'S *ONE OF OURS* AND WHARTON'S *A SON AT THE FRONT*

Wharton's and Cather's admiration of French culture runs deeply through their World War I novels, Wharton's *The Marne* (1918) and *A Son at the Front* (1923), and Cather's *One of Ours* (1922). The first of these, *The Marne*, was written rapidly. Inspired by successful American fighting in May 1918, it was begun in June and published in book form in December.¹⁷⁷ The novel was greeted enthusiastically, with reviewers applauding the unabashedly pro-French stance Wharton conveyed through her fifteen-year-old American expatriate focalizer, Troy Belknap. "Through it all there breathes a passionate, almost devout love of France," the *Times* remarked;¹⁷⁸ *The Nation* praised Wharton's portraits of Americans "fighting . . . not for France the pitied but for France the adored," and London's *Times Literary Supplement* lauded Wharton's use of the Marne "as a consummating symbol for her conviction of the immortality of the French spirit and the French civilization."[179] But the novel quickly fell from favor; what was seen at the time as the expression of a love of "France the adored" may strike readers today as overwritten and propagandistic. In one passage, for instance, Troy thinks, "War! War! War against his beautiful France! ... War, that seemed suddenly to have escaped out of the history books like a dangerous lunatic escaping from the asylum in which he was supposed to be securely confined!"[180] Although the novel reflects the war in many interesting ways, as I have argued elsewhere,[181] it has been reduced to little more than a footnote to Wharton's career.

In 1918, the same year in which she completed *The Marne*, Wharton began her longer, grimmer, and more enduring war novel, *A Son at the Front*, while Cather began her war novel, *One of Ours*. For both authors, writing the war was an intense experience. Cather described her life while working on *One of Ours* as "a series of assignations, of stolen interviews with Claude," while Wharton described *A Son at the Front* as being "written in a white heat of emotion."[182] In acknowledging the war's horrors, *A Son at the Front* and *One of Ours* are, unlike *The Marne*, clearly postwar novels. John Campton, the irascible middle-aged American expatriate painter Wharton created as her focalizer in *A Son at the Front*, could hardly differ more from Troy Belknap and his adolescent enthusiasm. In *One of Ours* Cather's Claude Wheeler provides a complex consciousness through whom Cather depicts the war. Though less grim than Wharton's novel in some ways, *One of Ours* also depicts the disjointedness and uncanniness of the front-line experience of war in ways that *A Son at the Front* does not. Yet both works reflect, in complex and subtle ways, their authors' admiration of France, while also conveying, to a degree unusual in American fiction, an understanding of the French experience of the grueling war years.

Since their publication both novels have occasioned complex and vexed responses. As with Lily and Paul, Wharton's and Cather's protagonists have come in for a great deal of criticism. Wharton's Campton has been seen as a "modern cannibal, devouring ... others for the sake of his painting" and as a father with "fantasies of incestuous, homoerotic desire" for his sleeping son, George.[183] Cather's Claude has been faulted for his naiveté and described as someone who "is fooled in his entire attitude toward the war";[184] many readers have assumed that, through him, Cather was endorsing the war. Recent criticism of the novel has focused less on discussions of Claude and more on attempts to distinguish between Cather's perspective and Claude's romanticized views.[185] Yet critics' focus on Wharton's and Cather's protagonists as flawed individuals means that their use of Campton and Claude as instruments of cultural criticism has been little examined.

Wharton's and Cather's critique of American culture, the contrast they draw between the American focus on business and the French love of art, continues in these works. Although Wharton's *A Son at the Front* begins on the eve of French mobilization, Wharton quickly fills in Campton's background. Though bitterly divorced from George's mother, Julia, Campton still recalls that what brought them together was his wish to escape from his business-oriented family and his attraction to Julia's apparent existence in a world of art. To "a youth fresh from Utica, ... unwilling to go into the family business, and strangling with violent unexpressed ideas on art and the universe," Julia's life in Venice with a vaguely "Bohemian" uncle seemed to offer Campton a chance both to upset his family and to pursue his own interests: "All the ideas that most terrified and scandalized Campton's family were part of the only air she had breathed."[186] In Campton, Wharton draws a character much like Cather's Thea Kronborg or Lucy Gayheart: he is a provincial with a love of art that goes unappreciated in his thoroughly practical hometown, a place he must escape to develop his own abilities. In Claude Wheeler, Cather creates a character who is more isolated from the arts than any of these characters, a situation that will allow her to emphasize France's value as a culture in which the arts are appreciated. While Campton, Thea, and Lucy are fortunate enough to come from hometowns that provide them an inkling of the importance and power of art, Claude is not so lucky. Although he has intimations of a larger world when he spends time with the Erlichmanns, his friends in Lincoln, he feels cut off from that world, unsure of its very existence and insecure about his own intuitions. In a moving passage, he lies in a tank of water on his Nebraska farm, staring at the full moon and reflecting on the eras and people it has shone down on:

She seemed particularly to have looked down upon the follies and disappointments of men; into the slaves' quarters of old times, into prison windows, and into fortresses where captives languished.

Inside of living people, too, captives languished. Yes, inside of people who walked and worked in the broad sun, there were captives dwelling in darkness.... These children of the moon, with their unappeased longings and futile dreams, were a finer race than the children of the sun. This conception flooded the boy's heart like a second moonrise, flowed through him indefinite and strong, while he lay deathly still for fear of losing it.[187]

But the pragmatism of Claude's life re-engulfs him, and when he wakes in the morning, "he had forgotten, or was ashamed of what had seemed so true and so entirely his own the night before. He agreed, for the most part, that it was better not to think about such things, and when he could he avoided thinking."[188] Living in a place in which his finest insights make him feel "ashamed," he is akin to the Cather who wrote from Paris (while working on this novel), "I could tell you a great many things that would sound absurd on either Bank or Park streets!"[189]

Claude goes to France not to pursue the arts or to seek a world in which such thoughts are possible but to escape the emptiness of his life in Nebraska and his sense of himself as a failure. Yet in France he gradually finds a different set of values and understands for the first time that life can be governed by something other than the demands of American business. This realization does not happen all at once. His first experience of a French town is not positive; shortly after landing, "Claude found himself in a street of little shops, hot and perspiring, utterly confused and turned about. Truck drivers and boys on bell-less bicycles shouted at him indignantly, furiously."[190] He finds the place literally heartless: he has been trying "to get to the heart of the city. It seemed, however, to have no heart; only long, stony arteries."[191] But as Claude and his men move "deeper and deeper into flowery France," Claude begins to feel more at home.[192] Seeing cottonwoods in the countryside, a tree disregarded in Nebraska but clearly treasured in France, he begins to feel "a real bond between him and this people."[193]

In Rouen, Claude visits the church of St. Ouen. His moving experience in the church, which he mistakes for Rouen's cathedral, has sometimes been dismissed as a "blinkered epiphan[y]" reflecting "modernist irony."[194] Yet his reflections in this scene, in which he connects the immediate and personal with the distant and wide-ranging, parallel those he experienced while gazing at the moon at home. Although he begins by attempting to understand the church in purely rational terms, recalling a textbook definition of Gothic architecture, his uninterrupted experience of the church allows him to fall into a deep appreciation of its rose window. As he absorbs the vivid colors of the stained glass, the church's bell begins to strike, and Claude feels as well as hears its "undreamed-of quality of sound"; at the same moment he recalls that "light travels through space for hundreds of years before it reaches the earth and the human eye. The purple and crimson and peacock-green of this window had been shining quite as long as that before it got to him."[195] Claude experiences a moment simultaneously intellectual and intuitive in which he connects nature and culture, past and present, distant suns and the place he is physically standing. It is, as Richard Harris has written, a transcendent experience.[196] Further, it is one that, unlike his earlier reflections on "the children of the moon," Claude does not dismiss. France is allowing him to make up for the cultural deprivations he has suffered, deprivations that are spiritual as well. He is beginning to change, or to become "more and more" himself, as Lucy Gayheart does in Chicago.[197]

Claude's experiences in France sometimes illustrate Wharton's observations in her nonfiction about France. In *French Ways and Their Meaning* she remarks that being in France in wartime occasionally offered unexpected opportunities for Americans to glimpse French domestic life: "The world since 1914 has been like a house on fire. All the lodgers are on the stairs, in dishabille. Their doors are swinging wide, and one gets glimpses of their furniture, revelations of their habits, and whiffs of their cooking, that a life-time of ordinary intercourse would not offer."[198] Wharton illustrates this herself in *A Son at the Front*, in which Campton is suddenly admitted to the inner sanctum of his friend, the doctor Fortin-Lescluze. During an impromptu visit early in the war,

Campton expects to be admitted to "the so-called 'studio'... where Fortin-Lescluze received the celebrities of the hour"; instead he is shown into the family dining room, where the doctor is dining in cozy domesticity with his wife, his mother, and "a plain young man wearing a private's uniform," his son, all of them enjoying a last meal together before Fortin's son goes to the front.[199] Campton has known Fortin professionally and socially for years, but it is the first time he has been admitted into the doctor's private life, and it alters his view of the man: he understands that in spite of Fortin's reputation as a *bon vivant*, he is also, and most essentially, a man devoted to his family.

Claude Wheeler has similar opportunities in wartime. As his company moves deeper into France, Claude moves deeper into French culture, staying first with an older couple, the Jouberts; then having a momentous conversation with Mlle Olive de Courcy, a young Frenchwoman; and finally staying with the Fleury family, whose name, which means "flowered" or "flowering," suggests that Claude has indeed entered the heart of France. Wheeler's journey is not an easy one; his experience of staying within a French household is initially intimidating. As a guest Claude feels awkward "accept[ing] favors"; worse, listening to his fellow officer David Gerhardt converse easily in French with Mme Joubert makes him feel "discouraged" about his ability to speak the language and thereby fit in.[200] It is only when he sees Mme Joubert at a distance that he begins to lose his self-consciousness, allowing him to perceive the sadness of her face.[201] They begin to make a more personal connection when she notices him admiring a rose bush, clips a rose, and puts it in his buttonhole.[202] The next morning he is able to appreciate how beautifully the house is kept and how, despite the fact that M. and Mme Joubert have lost both their sons in the war, they continue living their lives, cooking good food, tending to the garden, and caring for the house. Illustrating the principle of "continuity" that Wharton discusses in *French Ways and Their Meaning*, they are "taking care of the property for their grandchildren."[203]

Claude's experience of France deepens when he meets Mlle Olive de Courcy. Living in an otherwise abandoned Red Cross barracks at the edge of a village that has been almost completely destroyed by the war, she watches over it as a kind of French tutelary spirit, handing out supplies where they are most needed and acting as an unofficial cultural liaison between American soldiers and the French. She has remade the barracks into a homelike space, and Claude appreciates (as he did at the Jouberts') the signs of good housekeeping around him. Yet like the chapel near the front that Wharton described in *Fighting France*, in which "the candelabra on the altar are made of 'Seventy-five' shells [and] the Virgin's halo is composed of radiating bayonets," this civilian space is inflected by war, with flowers in empty shell cases and a war poster on the wall.[204] With its ivory combs and ironed handkerchiefs, on one hand, and its "low iron bed, like a soldier's," on the other, it also combines the feminine and the masculine, the domestic and the military.[205] Further, while decidedly French, the space is inflected by American contributions: Mlle de Courcy's storeroom is stocked with goods "with American trade names [Claude] knew so well."[206]

In this liminal space combining war and peace, military and domestic, masculine and feminine, and French and American, Claude has one of the most important conversations of his life. Earlier in the war, the town had been captured by the Germans; it had been recaptured by the French nearly a year before Claude arrives, and the inhabitants have begun to move back in. Readers are told that "the people brought with them only what they could carry in their arms"; Mlle Olive observes, "They must love their country so much . . . when they endure such poverty to come back to it. . . . Even the old ones do not often complain about their dear things. . . . If they have the ground, and hope, all that they can make again. This war has taught us all how little the made things matter. Only the feeling matters."[207] This registers on Claude immediately: "Exactly so; hadn't he been trying to say this ever since he was born? Hadn't he always known it, and hadn't it made life both bitter and sweet for him?"[208] Only in France does he find someone who can articulate for him what he has intuited since childhood, and what has made life "bitter" for him in Nebraska, even while it has made possible his rare "sweet" moments of insight. Not long afterward, a further insight echoes Wharton's remark that Americans are too preoccupied with money making "to enjoy what life and the arts of life offer": in the

United States, Claude now sees, people are too busy "buying and selling, building and pulling down. He had begun to believe that the Americans were a people of shallow emotions," a case for which there is "no cure."[209]

The culminating stage in Claude's French education is in many ways the most painful. When David and Claude stay with the Fleurys, the family of a young French man, René, whom David knew at the Conservatory and who has been killed in the war, Claude feels so culturally out of place that he nearly leaves. Yet he perseveres and comes to appreciate the family's perseverance in wartime; they speak of the dead son nearly as if he were still alive, keep his memory close, and plan for his younger brother, already a good violinist, to take his place someday in the musical world. As the women of the house talk, Claude can "see that for these women the war was France, the war was life, and everything that went into it. To be alive, to be conscious and have one's faculties, was to be in the war."[210] He also sees that the reverse is true: "to be in the war" is "to be conscious and have one's faculties." Everything around him demonstrates that even in wartime life goes on, and maintaining a civilized daily life is part of the family's heroism.

It is at the Fleury home, where, as David explains, "Music has always been like a religion,"[211] that Claude most clearly understands what such daily heroism requires. David himself must come up to the mark at the Fleurys'. When he is asked to play René's violin, he objects; but René's sister Claire begins playing the Saint-Saëns violin concerto, "the last thing René played . . . the night before he went away, after his last leave," and David too begins to play.[212] This scene is often remarked on for its revelation of Claude's self-awareness: deeply admiring David's musical skill, he feels disgustedly that in comparison he is "a bear cub or a bull calf," someone who "could only paw and upset things, break and destroy."[213] But David is also undergoing a trial here as he finds himself being asked to reenact the family's last memory of René; with a kind of courage different from that required at the front, he rises to the occasion. The family's own emotions and reflections as they hear the concerto can only be imagined. Through the succession of Claude's experiences—the Jouberts have lost two sons; Mlle Olive has lost her brother; the Fleurys have lost their son—Cather conveys both the high rate of mortality for French soldiers and the perseverance of their families. As David says, seeing the Fleurys' well-kept garden, "They have kept it up, in spite of everything."[214] This is a statement not simply about the garden but about French stoicism in a protracted and devastating war.

The French historians Leonard Smith, Stéphane Audoin-Rouzeau, and Annette Becker point out that the French thought about the war, and even defined "victory," in three phases, each succeeding the previous one in a single year, 1915. The first, reflecting early hopes that the war would be brief, was *percée*, the plan to "rupture" the German line and regain French territory, a strategy that resulted in huge losses. The second was *grignotage*, the idea of "nibbling" away at "enemy forces through attrition."[215] Even this modified strategy yielded to a smaller goal, *tenir*, holding out and refusing to give up further territory.[216] For the French the Great War was a total war, "rooted in the suffering day in and day out, endured by an entire society during these four and a half years."[217] *Tenir* became a mentality both within and behind the lines. A drawing by the French artist Jean-Louis Forain, titled simply "Inquiétude" (Worry; fig. 17), shows two soldiers talking in the trenches, with the dialogue: "Pourvu qu'ils tiennent." "Qui?" "Les civils." ("So long as they hold out." "Who?" "The civilians.") The dialogue offers a classic ironic reversal: one would expect that civilians would be saying this of the soldiers at the front; instead soldiers at the front are saying it of those behind the lines. While acknowledging the hard work of civilians on farms, in munitions factories, and elsewhere to provide the food and materials the soldiers needed to fight and simply to live, Forain's drawing also hints at the fragility of the entire situation and at the serious morale problems that existed both at the front and at the rear. Smith, Audoin-Rouzeau, and Becker have argued that "despite the destruction and horrors of the war," France "maintained a remarkable resilience still little understood outside France."[218] Cather's depiction of the moral and emotional tenacity of the French demonstrates this remarkable resilience; "holding out" was itself heroic.

Like *One of Ours*, Wharton's *A Son at the Front* provides complex views of France in wartime. As mentioned earlier, Wharton's Camp-

17. Jean-Louis Forain (1852–1931). No. 8: Inquiétude.—Pourvu qu'ils tiennent! . . .—Qui ça?—Les Civils. 1915. Line block taken from a drawing on ivory wove paper, 260 x 375 mm (image); 380 x 570 (sheet). Gift of Mr. Frank B. Hubachek, 1946.889.8. Metropolitan Museum of Art, New York, New York, USA. Photo credit: Art Institute of Chicago / Art Resource, New York.

ton has come in for a great deal of criticism, much of which seems to overlook the circumstances Wharton creates for him, those of an expatriate artist and father in wartime. Certainly Campton is a flawed human being; he is irritable, self-centered, misogynistic, and generally misanthropic. But he is also a serious artist dedicated to his work, to France, to his son, and to a small circle of friends. In Campton, Wharton describes the liminal existence of the expatriate, who belongs to both his home country and his adopted one but fully to neither. Firmly established in Paris as a successful middle-aged artist, Campton, like most Americans at the time, initially resists the idea that the United States should enter the war and that his son George should have to fight: "After all, we're Americans; this is not our job—," he protests.[219] But within moments of saying this aloud, he questions his own assertion: "*Was* he a foreigner . . . ? And what was the criterion of citizenship, if he, who owed to France everything that had made life worth while, could regard himself as owing her nothing?"[220] Unlike Wharton, he does not immediately believe that the United States should come to France's aid; yet he gradually comes around to believing that America's artists and intellectuals, at least, owe France a debt that can be repaid only by defending her. And he *is* an artist, both by temperament and by profession, making his living through his vision and his hands and finding his life's main meaning in his work. Like other artists, including those who contributed to Wharton's *Book of the Homeless* (Monet, Rodin, Renoir, and Sargent among them), he must reassess what his vocation means in wartime. He is also a father, dedicated, if somewhat erratic, in his attention to his now adult son; surely his reluctance to articulate the word "effigy" as he looks at the form of his sleeping son is not his repression of incestuous homosexual attraction, as has been argued, but a father's instinctive reluctance even to imagine that his son might die—a real possibility now that George has been mobilized.[221]

Campton's status as an American expatriate in France corresponds to Wharton's; like Wharton, he never claims to be French and tells his son George that although both were born in France, "we can never really know what the French feel."[222] Yet the novel has the trajectory of the war written into it: it begins on July 30, 1914, the eve of the war; covers the bloody years of 1914 and 1915 and the stalemate in the trenches; and concludes not with the war's end but in September 1917, when the American military became a strong presence, tipping the balance toward Allied victory.[223] Further, like *One of Ours*, *A Son at the Front* offers readers insight into the French experience of the war.

As someone with French friends, Campton sees their sacrifice. Early in the novel, when Campton asks Fortin-Lescluze whether George might be exempted from military service because of the tuberculosis for which the doctor had treated him, he gets a glimpse of the coming devastation. "Jean is an only son—an only child," Fortin tells Campton. "For his mother and myself it's not a trifle—having our only son in the war."[224] When Jean is wounded, Fortin (who is serving at a front-line hospital) is called upon to amputate both his son's legs, surely a horrific experience; but even this is not enough to save the young man. Fortin is grateful that there was a funeral: "They had that comfort," he says of his wife and mother, alluding to the fact that there was a body that could be buried; this was not the case for many soldiers whose bodies could not be identified or who were "blown to bits by shellfire and the fragments scattered beyond recognition."[225] Campton sees Paul Dastrey, another French friend, brought low by the death of his nephew, Louis, who had been a friend of Campton's son. Although Campton initially holds the war at arm's length, he is increasingly affected by these losses. The death of a young art student, René Davril, whom he had met during a visit to a Paris hospital, also affects him deeply. Even the grudging Campton can see from Davril's sketches that the young man was talented, and his death, so like that of Cather's David Gerhardt, reminds readers that, as a contemporary observer noted, "Men of all classes, from all careers and of all shades of opinion" were soldiers in the war.[226]

As in *One of Ours*, French tenacity across social classes is illustrated in *A Son at the Front*. An aristocratic acquaintance of Campton, the Marquise de Tranlay, has already lost one son in the war, and of her three other sons in the military, another is seriously wounded.[227] Yet she stoically keeps on, appearing at social functions with her marriageable daughter "because in such emergencies a French mother, whose first thought is always for her children," must go on doing her duty, including finding a husband for her daughter even when "the young men were growing so tragically few."[228] With "her mourning veil thrown back from a helmet-like hat," she is another image of heroic stoicism.[229] Fortin-Lescluze and Dastrey, in the upper middle classes, are, as we have seen, also devastated by their losses in the war. It is from the working classes, however, that Wharton draws her most moving portrait of French tenacity: Mme Lebel, Campton's concierge. When the war begins, one of Mme Lebel's two adult sons has already died; her surviving son has a relatively safe job guarding a bridge, but when he finds that his wife and daughter, who have been in the Ardennes, have become victims of the war—his wife has been taken to a German camp, and his little girl, struck to the ground by a German soldier, has cracked her skull and is dying—he leaves his safe position and enlists, wanting only to "run the swine down" or "kill as many of his kind as God lets me."[230] Of Mme Lebel's three grandsons at the front, one is killed early in the war; with the death of the second, Campton finds her bowed over in grief, sure that her third grandson will die as well. Campton sees determination in her face, "the obstinate French gift ... of making one more effort after the last effort."[231] Yet she also expresses profound disillusionment, saying to Campton, "I don't understand any more, do you?"[232] Eventually, with the death of his own son, Campton will share in that sacrifice and in the struggle to understand.

The huge losses suffered by the French led to grief and anger, but paradoxically they also led to a certain idealism: "The more desperate the struggle became, the more important it became to see the war as something that would open the way to a higher civilization, a more just and fraternal world in which right triumphed over force—in short, a new Golden Age. Many soldiers believed in the Great War ... as humanity's final conflict."[233] One of the most striking similarities between *One of Ours* and *A Son at the Front* is the idealism, sometimes grim, of its characters. For Claude Wheeler the booming of guns in the distance is not alarming but reassuring: "The sound of the guns firing had from the first been pleasant to him, had given him a feeling of confidence and safety; tonight he knew why. What they said was, that men could still die for an idea."[234] David Gerhardt may be more alert to the realities of war, pointing out skeptically, "It's a costly way of providing adventure for the young."[235] Yet even David expresses a belief in the war "as something that would open the way to a higher civilization," telling Claude, "I've sometimes wondered whether the young men of our time had to die to bring a new idea into the world."[236] In the end it may be David who is the more idealistic. Claude has realized that "there was nothing picturesque" about a town destroyed by war; "a cyclone or a fire might have done just as good a job."[237] It is David who envisions the millions of deaths "bring[ing] a new idea into the world."

Wharton's John Campton and Paul Dastrey, having suffered losses that Cather's Claude and David have not, are grimmer. Yet they too hang onto the validity of "d[ying] for an idea":

> "If we're giving all we care for so that those little worms can reopen their dance-halls on the ruins, what in God's name *is* left?" Campton questioned.
>
> Dastrey sat looking at the ground, his grey head bent between his hands. "France," he said.
>
> "What's France, with no men left?"
>
> "Well—I suppose, an Idea."
>
> "Yes, I suppose so." Campton stood up heavily.[238]

This insight, however, gives Campton little real comfort; it is not until the United States enters the war that he feels relief. Like Gerhardt, Campton hopes that something new and better may emerge: "At last, random atoms that they were, they seemed all to have been shaken into their places, pressed into the huge mysterious design which was slowly curving a new firmament over a new earth."[239] The deaths of Campton's cheerful young cousin, and especially of his son George, nearly devastate him. Yet like the French, he somehow persists.

Through these characters' tenacious clinging to the ideal of France—to "France's conception of itself, [the] immaterial part"[240] of a culture whose material manifestations Wharton and Cather valued so highly—*One of Ours* and *A Son at the Front* exhibit a French perspective on the war, a quality lacking in other American novels of the era. Better-known works, like John Dos Passos's *Three Soldiers*, stick close to the experience of Americans who never gain a French perspective or grasp that there might be such a thing. Even Dos Passos's John Andrews, a character much like Gerhardt—a composer fluent in French who appreciates the country's culture—rarely considers what the war means to the French themselves. Certainly the same is true of other well-known American works of the war, including Dos Passos's *One Man's Initiation*, E. E. Cummings's *The Enormous Room*, and Hemingway's *A Farewell to Arms*. Ironically Wharton's and Cather's portrayal of French perspectives may have contributed to the neglect of their novels, particularly as Americans returned to a more isolationist mood after the war.

As postwar novels, however, both reflect the gray mood of the years after the war. Although the Allies had been victorious, millions lay dead, and millions more were seriously wounded physically and psychologically. Both novels end with grieving parents, George Campton's father and Claude Wheeler's mother, who have, of course, been concerned for their sons' safety. When George is in a Paris hospital, slowly recovering from a serious wound, Campton reassures himself that George is "safe": "They had him fast now, had him safe."[241] He remembers a clairvoyant's predictions that his son "will come back soon, and will never be sent to the front again"; forgetting the notorious complexities of soothsayers' words, he never imagines that this means George will die.[242] Similarly Claude's mother feels at the end of *One of Ours*, after she has received news of his death, that he is "safe, safe."[243] She does not know that safety was something Claude never cared about. Rather, he has thought that "perfect safety ... kill[ed] all the best qualities in people and develop[ed] the mean ones."[244] "Safest of all," he thinks scathingly, are "those who would never be born ... nothing could happen to them."[245]

Wharton had reassured Theodore Roosevelt, and Cather her aunt, that their sons had died in a glorious cause for a worthy goal. Neither John Campton nor Evangeline Wheeler has that sense of reassurance. Instead the conclusions of *A Son at the Front* and *One of Ours* emphasize their sense of loss. Campton, plunged into grief, finds some consolation in visiting wounded soldiers in hospitals, seeing reminders of George in them; on the novel's last page he begins to sculpt a model for a monument to George. Yet in spite of these consolations and his belief that the victory was worth achieving, he is a hollow and exhausted man. Through Evangeline Wheeler, Cather conveys an even more skeptical view. Her son, she reflects, "died believing his own country better than it is, and France better than any country can ever be."[246] The last phrase is often interpreted as indicating that Cather herself saw Claude's view of France as impossibly idealized. But in this passage Evangeline also criticizes America: "In the dark months that followed" the war, "human nature looked to her uglier than it had ever done before.... She used to think about the passage of the Red Sea ... ; it seemed as if the flood of meanness and greed had been held back just long enough for the boys to go over, and then swept down and engulfed everything that was left at home."[247] The materialism Claude was happy to escape in France has "engulfed" America. Even if Evangeline has failed to truly understand Claude and has no inkling of the richer culture he found in France, she nevertheless grasps and condemns the American materialism he went so far to escape.

BRINGING THE FRENCH MUSE TO A NEW COUNTRY

In the spring of 1918, about a year after the United States declared war, Wharton addressed a group of American soldiers in Paris, giving a talk that would become the introduction to *French Ways and Their Meaning*. Her goal was dual: to introduce American soldiers to French culture in order to help them better understand the country they had come to defend, and to urge them to carry some aspects of French culture back to America after the war.[248] Both played a part in her urging American soldiers not to focus on "what America can teach France" but on "what France can teach us."[249] Placing Wharton's "Talk to American Soldiers" side by side with Cather's *One of Ours* provides an additional illustration of the intersection of Wharton's and Cather's worlds and the extent to which their views coincided; Cather's Claude Wheeler and the men under his command would have been the perfect audience for Wharton's speech.

Although Claude never makes it to Paris, he has seen enough of the rest of France that he surely would have embraced Wharton's remarks in her "Talk" and as she developed them in *French Ways and Their Meaning*. Claude admires the trees and fields of France; he would appreciate Wharton's comments on "the perfection of the vegetable and fruit-culture ... [and] the scientific care of the great forests."[250] As someone who has chafed at the materialism and ugliness of America and who has correspondingly admired the spirituality and beauty he has found in France, Claude would have been particularly impressed by Wharton's closing advice:

> I beg of you ... to spare a little time to look at [Paris]—at the great buildings, the beautiful squares and avenues and parks and fountains and bridges.
>
> We all take a pride in our cities at home—but sometimes we're inclined to think they're beautiful enough because we live there. The French think, on the contrary, that, because they live in Paris it's their duty to keep on making it more and more beautiful....
>
> We all learn in time that we must put something into our lives besides business and hustle; and France learned it a little sooner because she's seven or eight centuries older than we are. But we Americans are all capable of intense pride in our homes.... That is why I ask you to look about you here, and notice the beautiful things, and send home pictures of them, especially of the things we might all have—the splendid solid walls along the rivers, the beautiful bridges, ... the exquisitely kept public parks and gardens.
>
> Send home as many pictures of them as you can, and try to get the people at home to copy these things in the measure in which they can. The more beautiful our towns are the more we shall all love them.[251]

Claude dies in the war and is unable either to realize his daydream of farming in France or to return to the United States.[252] Yet surely there is also a chance that had he returned, he might have carried out something of Wharton's vision either in Frankfort or elsewhere. His glimpse of a culture with different values might have changed his life after the war, allowing him to create his own microcosmic culture within larger American culture. Certainly that is what Cather herself did. Profoundly affected by her encounters with French culture, she incorporated its best aspects into her own life in North America.

In their balance of French and American, Wharton's and Cather's writings and lives mirror each other's. Wharton spent the last thirty years of her life in France, yet never claimed she was French. Although she had French friends and was accepted into French society, her life in France was also bounded by French "formalities and protocols."[253] She was an expatriate and a hybrid, as were many of her closest friends. With a household combining French and American servants and French and American habits, she created her own environment, one that was, for her, the best of both worlds.

Cather balanced France and the United States differently. She treasured her travels in France but never wanted to live there. The poet Louise Bogan, who interviewed Cather for the *New Yorker* in 1931, summarized Cather's views by explaining that "in Paris she misses clear American skies, becomes absorbed in watching the changing soft colors of the Seine, and gets nothing done"; she also missed "the turns and sound of colloquial American speech."[254] In a letter to the violinist Yehudi Menuhin, Cather remarked on the importance of European culture to her: "If we remain always in our own land we miss the companionship of seasoned and disciplined minds."[255] But she also warned Menuhin that "if we adopt Europe altogether, we lose that sense of *belonging* which is so important, and we lose part of our reality. . . . The things his own country makes him feel (the earth, the sky, the slang in the streets) are about the best capital a writer has to draw upon."[256] Clearly Cather's American identity was central to her. Yet within her American life she valued things French. Although she lived in New York, one of the most iconically American cities, it was crucially important to her to maintain a French-inflected life. The key to this was Josephine Bourda, the Frenchwoman who cooked and kept house for her and Edith Lewis for many years.[257] Cather saw her as "an artist in her way; most French people are. She respects my work, and I respect hers."[258] Wharton's household sounded an American note in a French world; Cather's, a French note in an American world.

In their fictions as well Wharton and Cather mirror each other in their balancing of France and America. In works like *The Reef* and *The Custom of the Country*, Wharton often "use[d] the American woman married into a French family as a test case for cultural adaptation."[259] Cather was interested in cultural adaptation in the other direction, and it is the more American Cather, not the more French Wharton, who brings the muse of France into the New World in her fiction. In *Death Comes for the Archbishop* Cather not only shows a Frenchman, the Jesuit priest Father Latour, adjusting to life in the Southwest but also continues the critique of American culture that reaches back to her earliest works—her concern that Americans are so dominated by a focus on profit and practicality that they neglect larger cultural matters. Although Claude fears that there is "no cure" for the "shallow emotions" of Americans, who lack "something that endured... a background that held together,"[260] *Death Comes for the Archbishop* suggests that an infusion of French culture might offer a remedy for the ills of American culture.

Recently *Death Comes for the Archbishop* has been faulted for condoning the colonial project in the United States, specifically in the Southwest. It has been pointed out that Latour, like his historical model, Father Lamy, is sent to the Southwest because the United States had received a vast territory in the southwest in the 1848 Treaty of Guadalupe Hidalgo; part of Latour's mission is to Americanize the inhabitants of the area. As Stout has argued, Latour's "paternalistic assertion that it is 'for the people's good' is the classic claim of the benevolent imperialist."[261] One illustration of Cather's underlying attitude is her derogatory treatment of Padre Martinez. Critics have remarked that Cather vilifies this historical figure for her own purposes, using him as a foil to Latour and Vaillant to portray her French priests as perhaps better than any missionary priests could be. The fact that Cather retains Martinez's name in the novel, while changing those of Latour (historically Lamy) and Vaillant (historically Machebeuf), makes it difficult to defend her treatment of Martinez as a fictionalization. Patricia Smith notes that Cather's portrayal of Martinez "as a proud, lecherous demagogue" has "provoked... resentment in New Mexico ever since [the novel's] 1927 publication."[262] Serious questions have also been raised about the novel's treatment of Mexican and native populations. Smith allows that while "some of her individual Indian and Hispanic characters certainly rise above stereotyping," Cather "tends toward confident generalizing assertions about these infinitely complex colonized cultures";[263] Stout also comments on the novel's stereotyping of Mexicans and Latour's repeated references to Jacinto, his native guide, as a "boy," seeing the term as dismissive.[264]

Indeed it may be almost too easy to write off the novel as a beautifully seductive piece of colonialist propaganda. From our twenty-first century perspective there is no doubt that the shadows of imperialism hang over this era in literature. France's sense of itself as having a "civilizing mission" within its colonies served as a self-justification of its own enrichment. As we have seen, Wharton and Cather both admired French culture profoundly; for Wharton, at least, this admiration extended to her belief in the importance of French colonialism, and her social circle in France "constitute[d] a checklist of statesmen, aristocrats, scholars, and journalists whose work was instrumental in buttressing the implementation of French territorial designs overseas."[265] In her 1920 travelogue *In Morocco* Wharton justified French control of the country, equating "civilization" with European civilization and Moroccan culture with tales like the *Arabian Nights*. Her trip, for instance, is "carefully planned to keep us in unbroken contact with civilization. We were to 'tub' in one European hotel, and to dine in another. . . . But let one little cog slip and the whole plan falls to bits. . . . Civilization vanishes as though it were a magic carpet rolled up by a Djinn."[266] One might wonder, then, whether Cather was equally imperialist; some criticisms of *Death Comes for the Archbishop* almost suggest that it is her version of *In Morocco*, implicitly treating the Southwest as an "uncivilized" place that can be saved by French culture. Such a view, however, overlooks Cather's critique of America in the novel and the parallels it draws between French and Mexican cultures. In importing elements of French culture to the Southwest, Father Latour does less to Americanize its inhabitants than to resist and moderate problematic American influences.

Early in the novel Latour writes to his brother in France, remarking that while he and Vaillant "look like American traders" during the day, he is relieved to "come home at night and put on my old cassock! I feel more like a priest then—for so much of the day I must be a 'business man'!—and . . . more like a Frenchman."[267] While he expresses loyalty to the Americans at the fort, the interpolated comment here is revealing. Latour must dress, think, speak, and act like an American businessman, but he is still, at this point, French. Further, his "I *must* be a 'business man'" (emphasis added) indicates a central tension, as several points in the novel suggest Latour's reservations about American businessmen and Americans in general. While the word "American" is sometimes used in neutral or positive ways (Latour has an American doctor near the end of the novel, presumably an indication of competence), it is often negative. It is an unscrupulous "Yankee trader" who sells Vaillant a horse who proves "a wind-broken wreck";[268] in contrast, the Mexican Manuel Lujon gives Vaillant two splendid mules, who carry him and Latour faithfully for years. When Lujon compares the Mexican Padre Gallegos to an American, it is because Gallegos is an aggressive poker player: "He stops at nothing, plays like an American," an ambivalent portrayal of Americanness at best.[269] Worse, Americans are repeatedly depicted as mistreating Mexicans. Buck Scales, who has murdered passing travelers and even his own infants, and who abuses and terrorizes his Mexican wife, is "an American, of a very unprepossessing type."[270] The Mexican woman Sada is a "slave in an American family" who are hostile to her Catholic faith and force her to sleep in a shed in cold weather; a Mexican named Ramón Armajillo, who murdered another man in a moment of passion, is sentenced to death by an "American judge [who] was a very stupid man, who disliked Mexicans" and who accepts biased and untrue testimony.[271]

The charge of American stupidity extends to American ideas of the conduct of daily life and includes some quiet challenges to the mythologizing of the "Wild West." Early in the novel Latour and Vaillant's peaceful Christmas dinner is interrupted by gunshots; Vaillant explains to Latour that "A band of drunken cowboys, like those who came into the church last night, go out to the pueblo and get the Tesuque Indian boys drunk, and then they ride in to serenade the soldiers at the Fort in this manner."[272] Far from being romanticized figures riding the plains, the cowboys here are drunken, irreverent louts who worsen the situation of the Tesuque Indians and needlessly trouble the men at the fort. The critique is furthered through the experiences of Father Vaillant. When he travels to Colorado to carry Catholicism to gold prospectors, he must endure "stupid, unnecessary discomforts ... that amounted to improprieties. It was part of the Wild West attitude to despise the decencies of life," he concludes.[273] A rough-and-tumble life, Cather hints, was not so much necessitated by conditions as allowed, even encouraged, by an "attitude" that disregarded the "decencies of life." In this context it is clear that far from being negatively portrayed in the novel, the Mexican women of Latour's parish rise to a higher standard of civilization than the Americans; appalled by the discomforts that Father Vaillant has suffered, they quickly send feather beds and table linens.

Such moments presage the attitude expressed so clearly in *Shadows on the Rock*: Cécile Auclair's realization that pots and pans "were tools; and with them one made ... life itself. One made a climate within a climate; one made ... the special happiness of each day."[274] Repeatedly *Death Comes for the Archbishop* suggests parallels between Mexican and French cultures in their valuing of the materials necessary for a civilized life; it is the Mexicans, not the Americans, who offer a civilization like the one Latour and Vaillant have left behind in France: the belief that daily life should have something of beauty in it; the superiority of the handmade article to the manufactured one; and the value of "good eating and good talk, the two forms of aesthetic enjoyment most generally appreciated" in France, as Wharton explains.[275] Early in the novel Vaillant cooks an onion soup that is superb because it has "a thousand years of history" in it; it is the work of an entire culture.[276] On Christmas he and Latour sit down for a very French dinner (the soup is followed by roasted chicken and sautéed potatoes, then a plum compote), during which the thoughtful conversation is just as important as the well-cooked meal. In another instance Don and Doña Olivares provide them the same sort of hospitality "in rooms enriched by old mirrors and engravings and upholstered chairs"; the four enjoy a good dinner while discussing "what was going on in the outside world."[277]

Another theme emerges in Cather's use of "American" within the novel, one that reaches back to "Paul's Case" and her earliest stories: Americans are profit-driven people who have no real appreciation for beauty. Father Vaillant finds the Mexican people generous with money as well as with feather beds, an attitude Cather contrasts with American tight-fistedness. When Vaillant is raising money for churches in Colorado, he finds wealthy American businessmen unwilling to donate: "In his Denver congregation there were men who owned mines and saw-mills and flourishing businesses, but they needed all their money to push these enterprises."[278] The wording is neutral, but the sentence immediately following it offers a strong contrast: "Down among the Mexicans, who owned nothing but a mud house and a burro, he could always raise money. If they had anything at all, they gave."[279]

This critique emerges subtly but repeatedly throughout the novel. Although Latour is in Santa Fe partly to "make these poor Mexicans 'good Americans,'" the words "good Americans" are set within quotation marks, calling the phrase itself into question.[280] Latour resists the aesthetic values he associates with Americans, including cheapness and ugliness. He admires the handmade "figures of the saints" that he finds on the mantel of a rural Mexican home, appreciating their individuality and the fact that they have traveled and endured: "These over Benito's fire-place had come in the ox-carts from Chihuahua nearly sixty years ago. They had been carved by some devout soul, and brightly painted, though the colors had softened with time."[281] Contrasting them with "the factory-made plaster images in his mission churches in Ohio," he finds them much "more like the homely stone carvings on the front of old parish churches in Auvergne."[282] His preference for the handmade and unique over the factory-made and uniform echoes Cather's preferences in literature; it again links the Mexican and the French and prioritizes them over the American. Latour's preference for the handmade is also reflected in his appreciation of the adobe house that, although "much out of repair," is his residence as the bishop. He appreciates its literally handmade beauty: the "thick clay walls" have been "finished . . .

by the deft palms of Indian women, and had that irregular and intimate quality of things made entirely by the human hand."[283] In a statement on the novel Cather expressed the same preference, admiring the individuality of the Southwest's mission churches, including "the utterly unconventional frescoes, the countless fanciful figures of the saints," and regretting that these were being "replac[ed] ... by conventional, factory-made church furnishings from New York."[284]

When Latour envisions building a cathedral, then, he wants nothing to do with the ugliness he associates with American architecture and builders. "I wish to leave nothing ... to the mercy of American builders. I had rather keep the old adobe church we have now than help to build one of those horrible structures they are putting up in the Ohio cities," he says, adding, "It would be a shame ... to make another ugly church on this continent where there are so many already."[285] He will bring an architect from France, he tells Vaillant, to oversee the creation of a cathedral that is in the Midi Romanesque style of Auvergne, a church that is "plain" but "good."[286] This is not an attitude Cather ascribes solely to the fact that Latour is French; it is also individual to Latour. Indeed it is an attitude that Vaillant does not share, sometimes to Latour's sadness. Latour's own sensitivity to beauty is both a blessing—he perceives and appreciates things some others cannot—and a curse, as it also makes him vulnerable. In Ohio "the ugly conditions of life ... had never troubled Joseph," while Latour was "continually depressed" by "the hideous houses and churches, ... [and] the slovenly, sordid aspect of the towns and country-side."[287] Like Paul and Lily Bart, he values beauty and is agitated, even depressed, by ugliness, which Vaillant "seemed scarcely to perceive."[288]

This difference is one of the few sources of conflict between the two friends. Latour recalls Vaillant from Arizona to Santa Fe without telling Vaillant why, eventually taking Vaillant to see an outcropping of golden stone fifteen miles from Santa Fe. For both men the color of this stone calls up memories of the Palace of the Popes in Avignon, bringing them together. But when Latour tells Vaillant that he means to build a cathedral with this stone in the style of the Midi Romanesque, his friend is less than fully supportive, responding incredulously, "'If you once begin thinking about architects and styles, Jean!'" He later adds, "I had no idea you were going in for fine building, when everything about us is so poor—and we ourselves are so poor."[289] As the men turn to ride back to Santa Fe, Latour obliquely asks for Vaillant's approval: "I hope you do not think me very worldly."[290] There is no response from Vaillant, but it is clear that he does not understand Latour's interest in this project; Vaillant "was still wondering why he had been called home from saving souls in Arizona, and wondering why a poor missionary Bishop should care so much about a building.... Whether it was Midi Romanesque or Ohio German in style, seemed to him of little consequence."[291] There is no argument, but there is no meeting of the minds. Vaillant has no real sympathy for the greatest ambition of his dear friend Latour; Vaillant literally cannot see the difference between the utilitarian and the beautiful. Immediately after this episode Vaillant is called away to serve in Colorado, and the two friends are, in effect, separated for the rest of their lives.

The unresolved tension over the cathedral reflects a tension in any organization with limited funds: should a structure be built less expensively, with less concern for aesthetics, freeing up funds for other purposes that may benefit individuals more directly? Or should it be built as a thing of beauty that will endure ("We build for the future," Latour argues)[292] and benefit many, if more indirectly? Cather's sympathetic portrait of both priests suggests her appreciation of both sides of the debate. Yet it is important that Latour's views prevail in this debate with Vaillant. In part, of course, this is because Cather is writing a novel based on historical events that led to the building of the Cathedral of St. Francis in Santa Fe; she cannot ignore the fact of the actual building, even less so because it was partly the statue of Lamy in front of the cathedral that inspired her to write the novel.[293] But more significantly, the building of Latour's cathedral is centrally important to the novel and to Cather's larger concern with American culture. Within the novel the debate over the cathedral in Santa Fe is not between keeping the historic adobe church that preceded it and building a new church; it is between replacing the adobe church with a church that is "a clumsy affair of red brick" and replacing it with one in the Midi Romanesque.[294] The completion of Latour's cathedral does not mean a complete victory of the beautiful over the ugly in Santa Fe. As Latour approaches the cathedral for the last time, he can see that although half the town plaza "was still adobe," the other half "was flimsy wooden buildings with double porches, scrollwork and jackstraw posts and banisters painted white. Father Latour said the wooden houses which had so distressed him in Ohio, had followed him."[295] Still, the cathedral is a triumph over American ugliness.

Father Latour worries that his ambition to build a cathedral may be "worldly"; earlier in the novel he was vexed by the size and difficult construction of the church on Ácoma mesa, seeing it as a building "not altogether innocent of worldly ambition," a church built by earlier priests "for their own satisfaction, perhaps, rather than according to the needs of the Indians."[296] Clearly Latour is cut from different cloth. Although he wants the church to be in the idiom of his native France, he wants it to serve in New Mexico the same purpose it served there: to bring his parishioners closer to God. Neither Vaillant nor Cather directly addresses the question of whether Latour suffers from "worldly ambition." Yet surely the answer is implied in the "December Night" section of the novel, in which Sada finds comfort in the chapel at midnight. Latour himself, who has been suffering from depression, finds hope not in the structure of the cathedral but in Sada's ability to find comfort there.

Cather's and Wharton's deep responses to the churches of France, reflected in moments like Claude's in the Church of St. Ouen and in Wharton's many remarks on French churches, confirm Latour's preference for the beautiful not only in itself but as a resistance to an American practicality that can too easily devolve into ugliness. In Latour, Cather portrays someone doing exactly what Wharton urged American soldiers to do, exemplifying Wharton's remark that "we must put something into our lives besides business and hustle."[297] His concern with the beautiful development of the town reflects Wharton's emphasis on civic development, her hope that the Americans she is addressing will appreciate in France "the things we might all have," like "beautiful bridges" and "exquisitely kept public parks." She neither asked for nor expected a wholesale importation of French architecture into the United States; rather, she asked the American soldiers she was addressing to "try to get the people at home to copy these things *in the measure in which they can*."[298] If Latour introduces French culture to the Southwest, he also adapts it to the new world.

If Latour and Vaillant begin as Frenchmen who are attempting to shape the culture of the Southwest, they end as men who are also deeply shaped by it: the colonizer is colonized, the changer is changed. This may be more conspicuously true of Vaillant. As we saw in the last chapter, one of the elements of "Americanness" Wharton and Cather admired in the West was its energy. Near the novel's beginning Vaillant regrets leaving Ohio and asks not to travel any further; yet he embraces his role as a missionary to Colorado, becoming the very embodiment of nearly endless American energy, a veritable Elmer Moffatt of a priest. His lack of appreciation of beauty and his get-it-done attitude reflect the sometimes single-minded practicality of Wharton's and Cather's westerners. He changes in other ways as well. Near the novel's beginning Vaillant insisted on cooking his mutton in the French style, even when visiting a Mexican household; at the end, although he will never assimilate completely to Mexican ways, he is, as Esther Lopez points out, eating *chili Colorado*.[299] When he travels to Rome, the Pope's secretary finds "something abrupt and lively and naïf about him, a kind of freshness,"[300] qualities frequently associated with Americans. Vaillant's characteristics capture the attention of Pope Gregory, and the two men talk for "three times as long as such interviews were supposed to last."[301] Near the end of their talk Vaillant opens "his big valises like pedlars' packs," which are full of objects to be blessed.[302] The moment recalls the novel's beginning, when Latour described himself and Vaillant as dressing like American traders; yet here Vaillant has transformed the American profit motive into a religious one. As Vaillant leaves, the Pope "call[s] out to the departing missionary . . . '*Coraggio, Americano!*'"[303] From the perspective of a European pope, at least, Vaillant has indeed become an "Americano."

Latour changes also, more subtly but more completely than Vaillant. As Nalini Bhushan has argued, Vaillant, for all his adaptations, remains a missionary priest; Latour becomes a cosmopolitan, a citizen of the world.[304] Cather's technique in this novel—which uses "the reverse of dramatic treatment... *not* to hold the note, *not* to use an incident for all there is in it—but to touch and pass on"[305]—may make it hard to see how dynamic her characters are. Near the novel's beginning Latour was happy at the end of the day to get out of his "American trader" clothes and put on his cassock again, as doing so makes him feel like himself, a priest and a Frenchman; near its end, when he rides into Santa Fe for the last time, he is "wrapped in his Indian blankets."[306] Latour is an example of what Homi Bhabha calls a hybrid and Kwame Anthony Appiah calls a cosmopolitan. Bhabha argues against the insistence on thinking in simple dichotomies (is Latour French or American?) and in favor of "overcom[ing] the grounds of opposition and open[ing] up a space of translation: a place of hybridity" where a different identity can emerge, one that is "new, *neither the one nor the other*."[307] Between the dichotomies is a "Third Space," in which one may conceptualize a truly "*international* culture, based... on the inscription and articulation of culture's *hybridity*.... It is the 'inter'... the *in-between* space—that carries the burden of the meaning of culture."[308] Critics have faulted Latour for his negative views of Mexicans and Indians, yet those are the views of a Latour still new to the Southwest; they are replaced by more thoughtful views as he gains experience. As Bhushan notes, Latour's "earlier assumption of a more hierarchical view of civilization has given way to a more equalized sense of, and indeed respect for, difference."[309] Late in the novel Cather uses the hierarchical, condescending view of a minor character, Zeb Orchard, toward the Pecos ("They've got their own superstitions") to suggest how much Latour has changed; Latour replies thoughtfully that "their veneration for old customs was a quality he liked in the Indians, and that it played a great part in his own religion."[310]

Cather also conveys Latour's respect for the native peoples of the area by contrasting him with Fray Baltazar, the imperialistic priest at Ácoma in an earlier era. Baltazar is described as enslaving the Ácomas, forcing them to create a garden on the top of their mesa by carrying up heavy loads of earth and water from the desert below; similarly, the timbers for the roof of the church Baltazar builds have been transported miles across the desert. When Latour asks Jacinto how this was accomplished, he remarks tersely, "Ácomas carry."[311] The culmination of this imperialistic attitude is the episode in which Fray Baltazar, while hosting a lavish dinner for his fellow priests, kills a young Indian man with a careless blow to the head—an event that prompts the Ácomas to decide that they will put up with no more; they throw him off the mesa to his death.

This episode is memorable not just in itself but as it echoes throughout the novel, suggesting the vital importance of a respectful attitude for anyone bringing an outside culture into a "new" place—that is, into a land and culture that are as venerable as those of the culture being imported. Latour, like Baltazar, builds a garden, a home, and a church, but the manner in which he does so differs significantly: he hybridizes. In finding the home and the garden that he will make his own, he works from what is already there, selecting a site that is naturally well-suited for the type of garden he wants to cultivate. Admiring the beautiful apricot tree on the site, he "concluded that the exposure there must be excellent for fruit. He surmised that the heat of the sun, reflected from the rocky hill-slope up into the tree, gave the fruit an even temperature ... such as brings the wall peaches to perfection in France."[312] He does not force others to work for him or merely pay them; he works alongside his gardener.[313] His cathedral, while designed like those of his native France, uses local stone; it too is a hybrid.

As far as Latour himself goes, it is most telling that he had always expected to retire to France. Yet when the time comes, he finds that his native Auvergne, for all its beauty and culture—"Beautiful surroundings, the society of learned men, the charm of noble women, the graces of art"—cannot "make up to him for the loss of those light-hearted mornings of the desert."[314] At the novel's beginning he described himself and Vaillant as "exiles, happy ones"; now he chooses to "die in exile" for the sake of the air of New Mexico.[315] Yet as he dies well attended in his own room, he is not truly in exile; he is a hybrid who has become, and who has created, his own third space. Cather has been faulted for making Latour someone more sympathetic than Lamy, on whom he was modeled.[316] But in Latour, a twentieth-century fiction created for a twentieth-century audience hotly debating issues of immigration and American identity,[317] Cather offers a model of adaptation and hybridity.

PLACE AND CONSCIOUSNESS

Death Comes for the Archbishop also reinforces the importance of the connection between place and consciousness, demonstrating that our awareness is shaped by our experiences of place and limited by the lack of such experiences. In the prologue, set in Rome, Bishop Ferrand, a missionary to North America, argues to a group of distinguished churchmen the need for a new bishop in the Southwest. The scene is notable for the difference in attitudes of the men gathered for the occasion—men who have never been to the New World—and Bishop Ferrand. Well-educated, intelligent, sophisticated men though they are, these Europeans are still a little bored by Ferrand's insistence on the importance of his task and his attempts to make them imagine the geographic world the new bishop will inhabit. Cardinal Allande, their host, assumes that the new bishop will live in a wigwam, and when Ferrand gently corrects him ("There the Indians do not dwell in wigwams"), the cardinal prefers to stick to his stereotype: "I see your redskins through Fenimore Cooper, and I like them so."[318]

The cardinal's dismissal of reality, the derogatory term, and the very setting of the dinner—a luxurious repast taking place on a terrace set on the side of a steep hill—anticipate the attitude of Fray Baltazar. The cardinal has no sense of the reality of New Mexico and cannot be made to care about that reality. (Father Vaillant later reflects that "at Rome they did not seem to realize that it was no easy matter for two missionaries on horseback to keep up with the march of history"; as a result of a decision made in distant Italy, he and Latour must travel "nearly four thousand miles" to negotiate parish boundaries).[319] The cardinals are sophisticated men, but they are not cosmopolitan as Appiah has defined the term. To be a cosmopolitan in this sense does not mean being heedless and detached but the opposite: to be deeply connected, deeply knowledgeable at any number of levels and to care. In contrast to the cardinals, Latour displays the characteristics Appiah enumerates:

he "take[s] an interest in the practices and beliefs" of various peoples and realizes that "there is much to learn from our differences," seeing not just cultures in the abstract but "particular human lives"; he is able to "see the world from perspectives remote from the outlook in which he had been brought up."[320] By the novel's end Jean-Marie Latour is a far more cosmopolitan person than the cardinal who sent him to the Southwest. He is no longer an Auvergnat, nor simply French; he is a hybrid of all the places he has been and the cultures and individuals he has experienced. It is no accident that he enters Santa Fe "wrapped in his Indian blankets."

One of the things Latour is not is "American," in the sense in which the term has been implicitly defined through the novel; he resists what the novel portrays as the worst strains of American culture. These include not only all the things that have been discussed so far—greed, stinginess, a failure to value art and beauty—but also the American tendency to hurry and bustle, apparently for its own sake. Commenting on the fact that he has been able to travel from Gallup, New Mexico, to Santa Fe by train in a single day—the same route that used to take nearly two weeks on muleback—the Navajo leader Eusabio remarks, "Men travel faster now, but I do not know if they go to better things."[321] In the same 1924 interview in which Cather endorsed Wharton's views on the role of art in French life, she also remarked, "This passion for Americanizing everything and everybody is a deadly disease with us.... Speed, uniformity, dispatch, nothing else matters."[322]

Cather believed that "if a novel is a form of imaginative art, it cannot be at the same time a vivid and brilliant form of journalism"[323] and urged writers with political causes to write journalism, not novels. Yet near the end of *Death Comes for the Archbishop* she gives Latour some very political thoughts about events that still hover over the United States today, events that were much more recent when the novel was published in 1927 and were very recent indeed within the time frame of the novel. Latour tells Bernard, a younger priest, that he is fortunate to "have lived to see two great wrongs righted; I have seen the end of black slavery, and I have seen the Navajos restored to their own country."[324] While some critics have seen Latour's comment as too little and too late in the novel, it stands out in this quiet text. The novel includes little about slavery, although it is acknowledged in the discussion of Sada. (Her putative owners sold their slaves before moving to New Mexico but were unable to sell Sada, as they did not have a deed to her—an incident reported in an understated, matter-of-fact way like many other horrors in this novel.) Given the novel's setting in the Southwest, Cather does much more with native history. In Book Nine she devotes an entire chapter to the mistreatment of the Navajo, describing the U.S. government's disastrous decision in 1863 to drive them three hundred miles from their own country in the Canyon de Chelly in northeastern Arizona to the Bosque Redondo in New Mexico. Latour is also troubled by the long-term conflicts between the Navajo and the Apache. Far from excusing this as an unavoidable historical event or cultural conflict, Latour squarely puts the blame on American greed: "Too many traders and manufacturers made a rich profit out of that warfare; a political machine and immense capital were employed to keep it going."[325] Throughout the novel "profit" and "capital" have been critiqued; in this understated but powerful passage Cather shows the horrific results of these motivations. Perhaps this is why Latour puts quotation marks around the phrase "good Americans" when he writes to his brother early in the novel: he is not quite sure what it means to be a "good American."

Do Wharton and Cather idealize French culture? When Wharton published *French Ways and Their Meaning*, the *New Republic* remarked, "Can it be possible that America will survive this apologist and France this defender?"[326] Some reviewers sounded similar notes, faulting Wharton for her admiration of French civilization—the very quality they had praised only a year previous in reviews of *The Marne*, and perhaps a good indicator of the rapid change of mood between the late-war and postwar periods. Certainly Cather's portraits of the French in *One of Ours* and *Death Comes for the Archbishop* are profoundly positive, as they would be, primarily, in *Shadows on the Rock*, her story of French colonists in Quebec.[327] Gervaud's comment about Cather may apply equally to Wharton: "The France she loved may represent just a myth.

Yet... the myths... stimulate [the human] imagination and heart and, as such, are essential to religion, art, literature."[328]

Such myths offered alternatives to the limitations of American culture. The postwar period in which *One of Ours* and *A Son at the Front* were published was also, of course, the Jazz Age. Fitzgerald's *The Great Gatsby*, both a paean to materialism and an exposé of its limits, was published in 1925, only three years after *One of Ours* and two years after *A Son at the Front*. The year 1925 was also when Cather's Godfrey St. Peter, the protagonist of *The Professor's House*, tells his wife, "Let's omit the verb 'to buy' in all forms for a time" after observing his daughter in "an orgy of acquisition."[329] (*Death Comes for the Archbishop* was published two years later.) Wharton and Cather both found the materialistic indulgences of the 1920s appalling. Wharton "found more of her countrymen had grown incapable of distinguishing between the tasteful and the merely expensive"; her continued use of French settings in the 1920s implies her concerns about "the Jazz Age's easy gratification, and the increasing standardization and commodification of Euro-American culture."[330] Cather too was increasingly troubled by an America "wallow[ing] in prosperity" and increasingly "preoccupied with the corrupting power of money."[331] The arguments made in *One of Ours* and *A Son at the Front* for the thoughtful conduct of life and for values that endure, like Latour's objections to American materialism, are reflections that both emerge from the war years and provide a commentary directed to readers in the 1920s. Wharton's and Cather's admiration of French culture was not only about what America needed but about what it didn't need: heedless materialism and self-indulgence.

It is hard to overstate the importance of French culture to both authors. Yet ultimately their relationship to France and French culture differed. Only two weeks after the mobilization of France on August 1, 1914, Wharton wrote from Paris that although she was proceeding with her plan to go to the English country house she had rented, she wished she were staying in France: "This is the heart of the universe at present, & I'd rather stay here.... The French people are admirable, & have developed unguessed qualities of coolness, courage & patience."[332] Late in her life she voiced not only her distaste for the United States but also her admiration for France, writing Minnie Jones in 1932 that "I am so sickened at the thought of what America has become that I want to stop [up] my ears and close my eyes when it is mentioned! I can't be thankful enough that I am ending my days among civilized people."[333] Cather loved and admired the "civilized people" of France, happily created a French-inflected household in New York, and portrayed the positive influences of French culture in her work. Yet as much as she worried about the direction in which the United States was heading, she felt herself fundamentally American. Writing to her father during her 1920 trip to France, she remarked, "I am beginning to be a little homesick from time to time, and I shall not be sorry to turn away from all this beauty and from this wonderful people and face the West, toward the people and country that are my own."[334] She needed to return to her own country. But in doing so, she also brought along some of the beauty she found in France and some of the qualities of "this wonderful people."

6

QUESTIONS OF TRAVEL AND HOME

I simply have to have a dwelling place and my own books and things about me. Then I can travel in comfort and not feel like a tramp.
WILLA CATHER, *Selected Letters*

[Madame Olenska] remarked that . . . every form of travel had its hardships; to which he abruptly returned that he thought them all of no account compared with the blessedness of getting away.
EDITH WHARTON, *The Age of Innocence*

TRAVEL AND HOME

Chapters 3, 4, and 5 examined the relationship between geographic place and national or regional culture that Wharton and Cather observed in New York City, the West, and France and discussed the ways in which the authors' experiences shaped their thinking about the figurative place of culture in the United States. This final chapter moves from the level of national or regional culture to the smaller scale of the individual life in order to examine the central importance of two ways of experiencing place, each with its own value. The first is travel, the experience of deliberately and repeatedly exchanging one place and culture for another. The second is home, the attachment of the self to a single place over an extended period. If these are antithetical modes of being, they are also complementary. "Mobility implies 'to' and 'from' somewhere, and . . . that 'somewhere' is often 'home,'" despite the fact that "'home' in the context of American travel writing is rarely simple."[1] In short, this chapter is about the value not of specific places but of place itself—the place of place, as it were—within Wharton's and

Cather's lives and works, particularly in a world that both experienced as deeply fractured by the effects of World War I (and, for Cather, who lived a decade longer than Wharton, of World War II) and by the ever-increasing materialism of the 1920s.

One of the many things Wharton and Cather had in common was their love of travel—for both, a natural extension of their nearly inexhaustible energy and their nearly endless curiosity. As we have seen, their pre-adolescent relocation from an older, beautiful, beloved place to one that was shockingly new and perceived as ugly was a decisive factor in the evolution of both into writers, particularly into writers sensitive to place. As adults both found in travel—deliberate, carefully chosen relocation—what many others have: excitement, knowledge, the opportunity to compare one's home culture with that of other places, the opportunity to try on different selves or even to change.[2]

Wharton had travel in her blood. As she related in her memoir, extended European travels were the norm for her social class; dinner table topics in her youth included the "plans of European travel which filled so large a space in the thought of old New Yorkers."[3] The Jones family lived in Europe from the time Edith was four until she was ten, as we have seen, and she happily recalled playing in parks in Rome and walking in the Black Forest.[4] But it was a strenuous jaunt through Spain, she surmises, that confirmed her as a lifelong traveler: "As the offspring of born travellers I was expected, even in infancy, to know how to travel.... From that wild early pilgrimage I brought back an incurable passion for the road."[5] When at age eighteen Edith Jones learned that she was to return to Europe, she was as excited as if it were a trip to an imaginary place. To Bahlmann she wrote, alluding to a poem by Goethe, "We shall be standing together on the deck of the Brittanic a month from today—Doesn't it seem strange? Dahin! Dahin! [There! There!] Can it really be you are going *dahin*?"[6] The excitement, even the euphoria, of travel would remain with her all her life. On a 1913 trip to Sicily she enthusiastically reported that "we lassoed two mettlesome mules & pranced up the sacred heights to the most inspired solitude on earth. What a place!... Just before sunset we climbed to the top of [Mount] Eryx, & pottered about that strange little dream-town of S.

Giuliano."[7] Besides traveling extensively and intensively within Europe, Wharton explored the eastern Mediterranean and North Africa at a time when few Americans were doing so. Wharton was pleased by her reputation as a traveler, recounting in her memoir that Henry James "called me 'the pendulum woman' because I crossed the Atlantic every year!" (fig. 18).[8]

Even a glance at Willa Cather's life makes it clear that she too was a "pendulum woman" who traveled frequently, often for months at a time (fig. 19). Not only did she brave the ten-day Atlantic crossing on seven separate trips to Europe, from 1902 through 1935, but she also crisscrossed North America on her many train trips. She was nearly constantly in motion. In the momentous year of 1902, for instance, when she took her first trip to Europe, she visited at least nine cities in England and fifteen locations in France between late June and late September. The following year, she undertook extensive American travels from her base in Pittsburgh, visiting New York City; Cheyenne, Wyoming; Red Cloud; and Lincoln to catch up with relatives and friends.[9] Like Wharton, she remained an enthusiastic and active traveler all her life. In a 1924 letter to the English novelist Frank Swinnerton, for instance, she outlined her travels for that summer: Ann Arbor, Michigan, in June (to receive an honorary doctorate), followed by a visit to Red Cloud, then to her cottage on Grand Manan Island in early August; she planned to go to Boston and then return home to New York.[10] Far from being an unusually busy summer of travel for Cather, this was fairly typical.

As with Wharton, stories of travel had been an essential part of Cather's childhood. Living in Nebraska, she was fascinated by tales of the West and Southwest;[11] she was equally intrigued by tales of Europe. She wrote that "Rome, London, and Paris . . . were the three principal cities in Nebraska" when she studied geography in school, places that attained a mythic status in her mind.[12] When she was about to go to Rome for the first time in 1908, she realized that the city's presence in her psyche was so powerful that it was hard to grasp that it was a geographic place. "I got my guide book for Rome the other day," she wrote to her brother Roscoe. "Seems queer to be really on the way to Rome; for of course Rome . . . was always the Capital of one's imagination."[13]

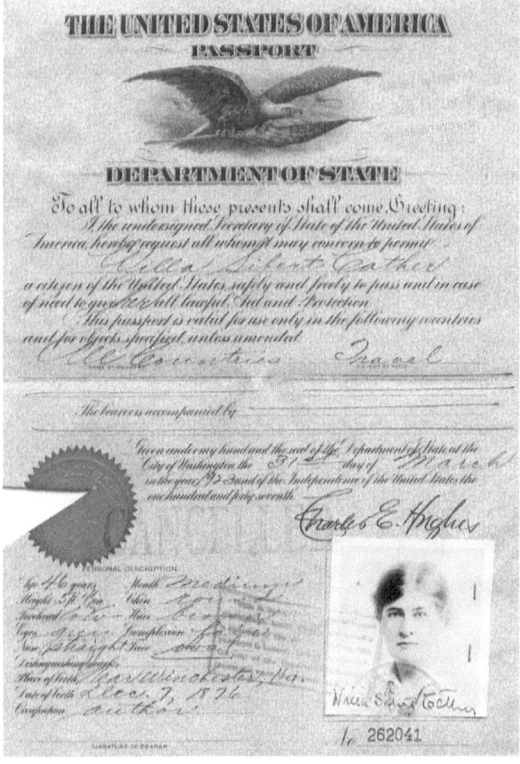

18. & 19. Indefatigable travelers. (*above*) Wharton's 1927 passport. Courtesy Lilly Library, Indiana University, Bloomington, Indiana. (*left*) Cather's 1923 passport. OBJ-50-063, James and Angela Southwick Collection, Willa Cather Foundation Special Collections and Archives, National Willa Cather Center, Red Cloud, Nebraska.

Like Wharton's letter about returning *"dahin,"* this one expresses a certain disbelief, a feeling that some places, despite their existence on maps, were more mythical than real. It was as if the Kingdom of Art had suddenly materialized and she were able to travel there.

Both Wharton and Cather embraced the growing distinction between mere "tourists" and genuine "travelers" that had established itself by the late 1800s. Commercial tourism had become an established fact in the nineteenth century; Karl Baedeker began publishing his authoritative travel guides in the 1830s, and Thomas Cook ran his first organized tour in 1841.[14] One indirect result of the new ease and popularity of travel was that those who considered themselves serious "travelers" began to distinguish themselves from the increasingly common groups of "tourists" traveling together in guided tours. The availability of guidebooks also changed the landscape for those writing about travel. Whereas earlier travel writers had focused on major sites, later travel writers "wanted to write of areas for which guide-books could not be purchased."[15]

Wharton and Cather thought of themselves as true travelers. Wharton "exert[ed] time and effort to move … off the beaten path and away from scenes suggested by the guidebooks," as Gary Totten has observed; Cather did the same.[16] During an 1891 trip to Venice, Wharton happily contrasted her own experience of "gliding peacefully over the Lagoon" with that of "the thousands of Cook's tourists with which Venice swarms … all crowding in to St. Mark's for the Easter services."[17] In *A Motor-Flight through France* Wharton exalted, "The motor-car has restored the romance of travel."[18] Although such a statement may seem incomprehensible today, in an age in which train travel was the norm, the novelty of automobile travel allowed motorists "the delight of taking a town unawares, stealing on it by back ways," and rediscovering "some silhouette hidden for half a century or more."[19] Wharton's travels in Italy also made good use of the motor car, allowing her to visit previously inaccessible sites, even when this meant—as it once did (as she related afterward)—that her automobile had to be lowered down a mountain by ropes, with her chauffeur, Cook, "steering down the vertical descent, and twenty men hanging on to a *funa* [rope] that, thank the Lord, *didn't break.*"[20]

As Lee notes, "Wharton makes a point of distinguishing her knowledgeable travels from those of the usual American tourists."[21] Even during World War I, Wharton gloried in getting to sites near the front that were generally inaccessible to the nonmilitary public; a 1915 letter, for instance, expresses her thrill at having seen "Ypres, which no one is allowed to go to."[22] Her travelogue *In Morocco* opens by remarking that "To step on board a steamer in a Spanish port, and three hours later to land in *a country without a guide-book*, is a sensation to rouse the hunger of the repletest sight-seer."[23]

Cather also enjoyed the sense of exploration that came with independent travel, sometimes substituting her favorite literary readings for guidebooks. Like James's passionate pilgrim, she saw England through the lens of literature, viewing Chester's Hawarden Castle through the work of the English historical novelist Maurice Hewlett.[24] In Shropshire, she wrote, "We threw away our guide books and have blindly followed the trail of the Shropshire Lad."[25] Her excitement about Le Lavandou, the small French town on the Mediterranean where she experienced a sense of near-perfect happiness, stemmed partly from her sense of discovery. Like Wharton exalting at being in "a country without a guide-book," Cather explains that "We came to Lavandou chiefly because we could not find anyone who had ever been here.... No books have ever been written about Lavandou, no music or pictures ever came from here."[26] For the true traveler, what better recommendation could there be? Surely Cather's moment of unaccountable happiness in an unknown, unexplored place (which, she asserts, "does not exist on the ordinary map of France") is a precursor to other off-the-map moments of happiness that her characters experience unexpectedly, even paradoxically.[27] One of the most memorable of these is in *The Professor's House*, when Tom Outland, despite his devastating rupture with Roddy Blake, experiences euphoria and a sense of possession on the Blue Mesa. "I had my happiness unalloyed.... It was my high tide," he says, adding, "Happiness is something one can't explain."[28] Another is the inexplicable happiness Claude Wheeler feels in *One of Ours* despite the epidemic devastating his fellow soldiers as they cross the Atlantic: "He awoke every morning with that sense of freedom and going forward, as if the world were growing bigger each day and he were growing with it."²⁹ In such moments Cather, Tom, and Claude are all off the ordinary map of the everyday world, off even the tourist's map, creating their own individual maps of places that matter to them, and they are heady with the experience.

But if Wharton and Cather shared a love of travel, they also shared something less exhilarating: a fear of rootlessness or homelessness, a fear that extends deep into their fiction. The tension between the love of travel and the need for a rooted existence is conveyed beautifully in the 1956 poem "Questions of Travel," by the American poet Elizabeth Bishop. The poem's departure point is the speaker's remark that the landscape she is observing has "too many waterfalls," suggesting that the most beautiful of voyages may lead to fatigue and surfeit; as it continues, she offers a meditation on the relationship between travel and home, asking whether travel is mere "childishness" and whether it is wiser to remain home, "dream[ing]" of other places without attempting to realize those dreams.³⁰

Bishop (1911–79) was well qualified to ask such questions, as her life spanned places as disparate as Worcester, Massachusetts, her birthplace; Nova Scotia; Europe; and Brazil. Although a generation younger than Cather and Wharton, she articulates in "Questions of Travel" a tension that is central to the work of both fiction writers: the pull between the desire to travel and see the world, and the desire for home.³¹ The poem ends with the traveler questioning again whether she should have simply stayed home, "*wherever that may be*?" (emphasis in original). These questions haunt the work of Wharton and Cather. Where should one travel, and should we travel at all? "*Wherever that may be*" implies other, even more disturbing questions: Where *is* home? Do I have any home at all?

Like Bishop, Wharton and Cather moved a number of times, losing, as Bishop puts it in her poem "One Art," not only "loved houses" but "cities" and even "continents."³² Wharton's and Cather's childhoods were marked by displacement; both experienced displacement again as adults. After World War I, the changes engendered by population movements and the rapid rise of the automobile left Wharton and

Cather alienated from cities they had once been excited to settle in. In 1920 Wharton wrote to a friend that "Paris is simply awful—a kind of continuous earthquake of motor busses, trams, lorries, taxis & other howling & swooping & colliding engines, with hundreds of thousands of U.S. citizens rushing about in them."[33] In a 1929 letter, Cather expressed similar frustration with daily life in New York: "One does have to come back to cities for some things.... But as soon as I get back here, I get rather used up. The old New York of ten years ago wouldn't tire me, but the present New York—words fail me!"[34] Two years earlier she had lost a beloved home when impending demolition forced her to move from her residence of fifteen years at 5 Bank Street.[35]

Their lives as women who had moved far from family and friends also created difficulties. Despite their deliberate choice of such lives, both suffered a sense of personal diaspora, expressing sadness that their favorite people were often hundreds or thousands of miles away. In 1902, for instance, Wharton wrote to Daisy Chanler, "I look back on those few hours with you as a kind of oasis in an uncommonly sandy summer. How I wish things didn't so persistently arrange themselves to keep us in different places!"[36] A few years later she was writing to Berenson, "Why are the few, the very few, nice people in the world always at the antipodes—each, that is, at a different one?"[37] Until the end of her life, her letters would express such feelings. Cather's letters too are full of thoughts of absent friends and relatives. In 1910 she told her brother Roscoe, "I could write to you better if I could see you once again. This long stretch of time and distance takes the starch out of one."[38] The distances separating people she loved remained a burden. In 1930 both Isabelle Hambourg and Cather's mother were seriously ill. Writing from Hambourg's home near Paris, Cather remarked to her mother, "It is very sad for me that the two people I love best in the world get sick thousands of miles apart."[39] Travel could be wonderful, but personal diaspora was painful.

The sense of displacement and the need for home created a powerful and poignant counterpoint to Wharton's and Cather's love of travel, and many of their works quietly portray the tension between the two. As we saw before, Wharton's earliest published story, "Mrs.

Manstey's View," is inflected by travel—Mrs. Manstey's long-ago trip to Europe—and by distance: her daughter's migration to California. Wharton's most fully articulated statement of the problem of rootlessness is in *The House of Mirth* and merits a return to that novel. In the penultimate chapter of the novel her protagonist, Lily Bart, lies on what is about to become her deathbed. Although she has dreaded the "material poverty" into which she has inexorably fallen, Lily now realizes there is something worse:

> It was the clutch of solitude at her heart, the sense of being swept like a stray uprooted growth down the heedless current of the years . . . the feeling of being something rootless and ephemeral, mere spin-drift. . . . And as she looked back she saw that there had never been a time when she had had any real relation to life. Her parents too had been rootless. . . . She herself had grown up without any one spot of earth being dearer to her than another: there was no centre of early pieties, of grave endearing traditions, to which her heart could revert and from which it could draw strength.[40]

Lily dies alone in a boarding house, a place that is a dismal reminder not only of her poverty but of her homelessness, which Wharton identifies as Lily's lack of connection to "any one spot of earth," a failure to connect to place. Both "rootless" and "uprooted" (her parents too were "rootless"), she is a plant that has never had a chance to establish itself in earth; instead she is like "spin-drift," seafoam, blown about by the winds. She has never formed bonds with a specific place, bonds that would have made that place "dearer to her than another," a place "to which her heart could revert." In short, a home.

Lily's death in a boarding house only makes evident what has been the case all along: the fact that Lily is homeless throughout the novel, a situation that, as Judith Fryer observed, "deprives her of something fundamentally human."[41] Lily's homelessness has been disguised from the reader, and perhaps from Lily herself, by the form it has taken, that of the privileged procession from one luxurious location to another, from her beautiful bedroom at the Trenors' estate to her stateroom on the Dorsets' yacht. Yet these resting places are all temporary and revocable, a reality that Lily experiences when Bertha Dorset humiliatingly kicks her off the yacht in Nice and Lily is left without a place to spend the night. Nor, as we have seen, is Lily's room at Mrs. Peniston's really her own. Through Lily, Wharton connects homelessness with statelessness: "The being to whom no four walls mean more than any others, is . . . expatriate everywhere."[42]

If Lily has never had a home because of her parents' transient existence, she too is transient, using travel as an escape from her problems. This is one of the many reasons travel is attractive: "It triggers the thrill of escape, from the constriction of the daily, the job, the boss, the parents . . . [and] from the traveler's domestic identity."[43] But Lily's attempt to escape is of a different order, an effort to evade the series of unhappy events that have followed one upon another with an inexorable and cruel logic—Trenor's near assault, Selden's failure to propose, and Rosedale's unwelcome proposal—all of which, ironically, emerge from her success as Mrs. Reynolds at the Brys' *tableaux vivants*. Little wonder, then, that Lily jumps at the unexpected invitation from Bertha to join her on a Mediterranean cruise. In a further ironic turn, what has made Lily realize that Selden is not going to propose to her is a notice in the evening paper that he has sailed for Havana.[44] Mistakenly believing that Lily is having an affair with Trenor, he is doing exactly what Lily is doing: traveling to escape from personal problems. Far from being an adventure, travel may be simply a disguise for homelessness and an attempt, pleasantly distracting but ultimately futile, to flee from problems.

Yet *The House of Mirth* does not simplistically endorse any conventional idea of home, as has sometimes been argued.[45] With the exception of the portrayal of the home of the working girl Nettie Struther near the novel's end, the opposite seems more accurate: at almost every turn Wharton "destabilize[s] domesticity,"[46] deconstructing any conventional concept of "home." The room Lily occupies in the boarding house is neither more nor less a home than her room at Mrs. Peniston's; it is simply another room she is futilely attempting to make her own. Among literary definitions of "home," surely Robert Frost's "The Death of the Hired Man" is one of the grimmest. In this poem, in which a husband and wife discuss "what you mean by home" and whether they should allow a man who previously worked for them to spend his final days there, two definitions are offered. The husband defines home as "the place where, when you have to go there, / They have to take you in," while his wife counters, somewhat more generously, "I should have called it / Something you somehow haven't to deserve."[47] These stark, antisentimentalized definitions of "home" suggest how grim Lily's situation is. Mrs. Peniston disowns Lily because she thinks Lily does not deserve even a room in her home; Lily has a room in the boarding house only because she has paid for it. Lily Bart has no place where, if she went there, they would have to take her in.

In *Lucy Gayheart*, published thirty years after *The House of Mirth*, Cather echoes Lily's reflections on the need "for one spot of earth being dearer to her than another" in the reflections of the musician Clement Sebastian. After the death of a friend Sebastian broods: "Life had so turned out that now, when he was nearing fifty, he was without a country, without a home, without a family, and very nearly without friends.... He had missed the deepest of all companionships, a relation with the earth itself, with a countryside and a people. That relationship, he knew, cannot be gone after and found; it must be long and deliberate, unconscious."[48] Unlike Lily Bart, Clement Sebastian has financial resources and significant success. Yet the terms in which he thinks resemble hers remarkably: Lily reflects on a life in which "one spot of earth" might be a "centre of early pieties, of grave endearing traditions,"[49] Clement on "a relation with the earth itself, with a countryside and a people." Both think of such a place as something that one would have known from early childhood and with which one would have begun a relationship before one was even conscious of doing so. In these passages Wharton and Cather anticipate the observations of geographers like Yi-Fu Tuan, who "has often expressed his belief that all of us carry with us throughout our adult life the landscape in which we lived our early lives.... Our real 'home' lies in this internal landscape ... [which] makes us 'whole' in ways that can scarcely be imagined by those persons whose fragmented view of the world ... reflects the rootlessness inseparable from the peripatetic nature of modern life."[50]

It is Lily's failure to achieve her goals that fosters her reflections; paradoxically, it is Clement's success that generates his. Both his personal life and his musical career mean that he has associations with many places. His wife and his accompanist are both English, and what would conventionally be called his "home" is in England; he has adopted a French boy and has a house in Chantilly, near Paris; he has sung throughout Europe and the United States; he fondly recalls a vacation to the French Alps in young adulthood. He was, in fact, born in Chicago but "had left it at eighteen and had lived abroad most of the time since;"[51] he has no sense of Chicago or the United States as "home." His life has been as glamorously itinerant as Lily's but also as rootless. "Surely a man couldn't congratulate himself upon a career which had led to such results," he thinks.[52]

Even before the scene in which Sebastian reflects on his rootlessness, Cather has suggested the relationship between travel, rootlessness, and mortality. Lucy receives a note from Sebastian canceling an appointment, "as he had to attend the funeral services of a friend."[53] Checking the newspaper, Lucy finds that "a French singer, returning from California, had died in her hotel last night after an illness of only twenty-four hours. There would be a funeral service for her at eleven o'clock in the small Catholic church near her hotel. Afterwards her body would be sent back to France."[54] The neutrality of the newspaper language (which Cather echoes) simultaneously understates and suggests the constant motion of travel: a singer has crossed the Atlantic from France to the United States, then traveled the width of North America to California, a train journey of several days. Having crossed half the continent again, from California to Chicago, she dies suddenly in an anonymous hotel in a city strange to her; services will be conducted in that city, and her remains will be shipped eastward, across half a continent and then an ocean, before resting in her home country. It is a strange, grim itinerary. When Lucy follows Sebastian into the church where the service is being held, she sees on his face an expression that seems distressed disproportionately even for the circumstances: "It was a terrible look; anguish and despair, and something like entreaty."[55] Lucy wonders, "Had this woman been a very dear friend? Or was it death itself that seemed horrible to him—death in a foreign land, in a hotel, far from everything one loved?"[56] (Wharton too may have been haunted by such thoughts. Writing of the sudden death of an English friend in a hotel in New York City in 1929, she remarked, "His death must have been terribly lonely. Even his few friends in N.Y. were probably all scattered"; in 1935 her sister-in-law Minnie Jones would die suddenly in a London hotel and be buried in England.)[57] Sebastian's own death by drowning in Italy's Lake Como, far from any of the places he might call home, pulled down by a man whom he has called his friend, is no less pathetic than Lily Bart's death in a boarding house. Like Lily, he becomes—almost literally—spindrift upon the waters.

Yet Sebastian's rootlessness and miserable death do not point to a simple message to "stay close to home" any more than Lily Bart's do. In both *Lucy Gayheart* and *The House of Mirth* most of the characters who stay closest to home—Lucy's sister Pauline, Harriet Arkwright (Harry's wife), and Milton Chase in *Lucy Gayheart*, Mrs. Peniston and Percy Gryce in *The House of Mirth*—are limited and judgmental, people who stay home not out of love for "one spot of earth" but because they fear the wider world or lack the curiosity and imagination to wish to encounter it. Even characters who have what Lily and Sebastian imagine to be home, a particular place with deep and lifelong associations, do not find there the consolation that Lily and Sebastian might expect.

Cather subtly but systematically uses the word "home" at key moments in the three books that comprise *Lucy Gayheart* to suggest the complex, contradictory meanings of "home." The opening paragraph of Book I tells us that the residents of Haverford, Nebraska, remember Lucy as "a slight figure always in motion; dancing or skating, or walking swiftly with intense direction, like a bird flying home."[58] Though the story is being told in retrospect, with Lucy as a figure in the past, this is, for the reader, the beginning of the story; it subtly associates Lucy with the idea of home. As the novel proceeds, however, the reader finds that in spite of the lovely opening figure of Lucy as "a bird flying home," much of her story is about her desire not to return home but to get away from home. It is bitterly ironic that as her own story ends at the conclusion of Book II, when she drowns in the Platte River while ice skating, a wagon is said to be "taking Lucy Gayheart home"[59]—it is the place she has tried so hard to escape. (Cather's subtle artistry is evident in the contrast between the lightness and speed of the opening image—that of a bird flying, a motion characteristic of Lucy—and the slow heaviness of the wagon that brings her body home, a contrast that conveys nearly subconsciously the inertia of Lucy's dead body.) At the end of Book III, in which, twenty-five years later, Harry Gordon reflects on Lucy and his own life, he looks at the footprints the thirteen-year-old Lucy had made in the cement sidewalk outside her own house—steps that are not "like a bird flying home," as in the novel's first paragraph, but that are, on the contrary, "running away"—the novel's final words.[60] Built into the very structure of the novel, then, is an extended meditation on what home means, or fails to mean.

Lucy is, of course, the central character in this meditation. She has exactly what Clement Sebastian and Lily Bart lack, a "spot of earth" that is "dear," a home, a family, and "a relation with the earth itself." Yet the novel hints at how little this may matter or, perhaps, how easy it is to idealize such concepts. During the summer in Chicago that Lucy dedicates to her music, she thinks of her home town, Haverford: "She loved her own little town, but it was a heart-breaking love, like loving the dead who cannot answer back."[61] When she leaves Chicago after Sebastian's death, she feels "that if once she got home she wouldn't suffer so much," but this proves "an illusion."[62] What she finds is that she feels anything but at home: "When she looked about her at this house where she had grown up, she felt so alien that she dreaded to touch anything."[63] What she had thought of as "home" is not homelike; she thinks of it as merely a building, as "this house where she had grown up." Not only is she not happy to be there, but she feels "alien" within the house: "Even in her own bed she lay tense."[64] If one's room is, especially for an adolescent, the core of one's home, surely the bed is the nucleus of that core; even there Lucy cannot find comfort. Further, her room affords her little privacy; she knows that her sister Pauline, whose room is next to hers, can hear her cry or even "turn over in bed."[65] Only when she is in the old orchard—which the practical Pauline plans to cut down so that she can plant more profitable crops—does she feel safe. It is here that she goes to remember Clement Sebastian, to "repeat lines from some of Sebastian's songs, trying to get exactly his way of saying the words," and sometimes to cry.[66] In the orchard she has what Sebastian and Lily long for, a connection to "one spot of earth [that is] dearer to her than another." Yet by itself it is not enough to constitute a home.

Although Lucy is the central character in the novel's challenge to the concept of "home," she is not the only one. Through brief depictions of the consciousness of Lucy's sister, Pauline, Cather further questions the concept of home. Before encountering these passages in the novel, the reader may well see Pauline as difficult, unsympathetic, and overbearing—a negative contrast to the sympathetic Lucy. But Cather deepens and complicates her depiction of Pauline, making her a sympathetic and "real" character—one of the hallmarks of great fiction for both Cather and Wharton. Cather's development of Pauline also allows the reader to see the complexity of the dynamics of this three-person family, further challenging the cozy resonance of "home." When their mother died, when Pauline was eighteen and Lucy was six, Pauline took on a mother's role toward Lucy; like some other Cather characters, including Augusta in *The Professor's House* and Alexandra Bergson in *O Pioneers!*, Pauline sacrifices her own self-interest, indeed her own future, for the benefit of others—others who fail to appreciate or even to perceive that sacrifice. Pauline had been proud, in an almost maternal way, of Lucy until her younger sister reached adolescence; then she began to notice that people treated Lucy and herself very differently, with Lucy being treated always as the one having special talents, while Pauline was treated as someone for whom anything would do.[67] Enviously Pauline thinks of Lucy as the "parlour cat"—the one who gets all the petting—and herself as the "kitchen cat," the one who does useful things like catching mice.[68] Cather captures the complexity of this relationship in a single sentence: "In her own way Pauline loved her sister, though there had been moments when she certainly hated her."[69] Within the family, however, Pauline cannot express her negative emotions. Even when she is irritated with Lucy, she resolutely presents a cheerful manner.

Perhaps more than Pauline herself, the reader knows what is going on beneath Pauline's stoically positive surface. Although she seems harshly practical, Pauline is so moved by her sister's tears when the first tree in the orchard is being cut down that she too becomes teary-eyed. Though she does not really understand why Lucy is so upset, she orders the project postponed. (Readers are later told that the orchard was never cut down; perhaps this is Pauline's tribute to her dead sister.) Although Pauline's manner toward Lucy is sometimes blunt, she cares about her sister and wants her to be happy—for instance, giving her sister a cup of coffee and sending her to her room to rest when Lucy is agitated about the orchard. Surprisingly the "practical" Pauline feels a certain admiration for her sister's stoical silence when she hears Fairy Blair's version of Lucy's grief over Sebastian's death. Cather notes that "Pauline was a much more complex person than her sister."[70] Lucy is oblivious to all of this, thinking of Pauline simply as a "good" person and assuming that "good people were usually fussy and a little tiresome."[71] The reader is asked to see further than Lucy does and to understand that even Pauline, the sister who keeps the home together and the family running, is far from finding her own home a warm and loving place.

The tensions within this outwardly calm family bring to mind Cather's comment that even within a "'happy family... every individual... is clinging passionately to his individual soul, and is in terror of losing it in the general family flavour.'"[72] Beneath its relatively calm surface, the Gayheart family is locked into a set of tensions and unexamined assumptions about themselves and each other. Lucy resents what she sees as Pauline's harshness and lack of sympathy (though she can hardly expect sympathy, as she never tells Pauline what happened in Chicago). Mr. Gayheart, as the father of the family, is nominally responsible for the family's material well-being. Yet he brings in little money from his watch repair business, has no mind to check on the tenant farmers living on his properties, and decides without consulting Pauline that it is fine to spend the considerable amount of money required to send Lucy to Chicago for her music. Pauline resents her father's improvidence, as well as the fact that he and Lucy take for granted her willingness to shoulder the whole responsibility for the family's physical and financial well-being. The situation is compounded by Mr. Gayheart's assumption that Pauline, whom he sees as "a girl of good common sense [who] must see that Lucy was different," is perfectly happy staying home and caring for everything, even while he secretly fears her—and lavishes affection on Lucy.[73] Much of his leisure time he spends not at home but in his shop, a pattern that will be repeated later in the story by Harry Gordon. Underlying the tense dynamics of the Gayheart home is the unarticulated sadness of a wife and mother who died young and of two little boys, born between Pauline and Lucy, who died in childhood.

If this is "home"—a home whose complex dynamics echo those of families in other Cather and Wharton fictions—one might ask, who needs it? If homelessness is bad, so too, at least in this vision, is home. Yet Cather portrays and acknowledges the number of factors in this family (or any family) that are beyond their own control, from the early deaths of Mrs. Gayheart and the two little boys to the wish of characters like Pauline to work hard and preserve at least the appearance—to themselves as well as to their neighbors—of an amicable and loving family. In this Pauline is like Wharton's May Welland Archer in *The Age of Innocence*, whose goal as a wife and mother is to preserve her family as a "loving and harmonious household" in, she assumes, a world of similarly happy families. Yet May's ability to preserve this illusion is the result of both her "hard bright blindness" and "a kind of innocent family hypocrisy" through which Newland and their children allow May to preserve her ignorance.[74] Such "innocent family hypocris[ies]" are common in the fictional families of both authors.

It is Harry Gordon, Haverford's town sophisticate, who has the novel's last word on "home" and the idea of the hometown. Harry is not so much a true hybrid, like Father Latour, as a crossover character: while in Haverford he is quite the sophisticate, in larger places he is cautious not to appear provincial, carefully "wear[ing] exactly what well-dressed men in Chicago were wearing" and ordering champagne with dinner.[75] Still Harry chooses to live in Haverford, bringing his wife Harriet Arkwright there from the larger city of Omaha. Yet his home in Haverford is hardly homelike. Harry marries Harriet in a fit of pique after Lucy has refused his blunt proposal; within a week of their marriage he regrets it. He and Harriet build a handsome house, but it is formal and "chill"; it is not surprising that Harry "fit[s] up" a part of the old bank building "as a study and private office.... Almost stealthily, he had made it more comfortable, and ... spent more and more time there."[76] He is making himself a more homelike home, one that is his alone.

Like Lily Bart, Newland Archer, and others, Harry uses travel to escape home; he "often went to Denver for the weekend, 'driving like the devil,'"[77] sometimes talking aloud to himself of his unhappiness about Lucy. Like Claude Wheeler, Harry uses World War I as a way to escape an unhappy marriage through travel legitimized, even ennobled, by international conflict. "Like many other men whose lives were dull or empty," the narrator relates, "Harry Gordon 'threw himself,' as the phrase went, enthusiastically into war work."[78] Harry is motivated not by the cause but by his desperation to escape his "dull or empty" life. Only after eight months in France is he able to settle down into a calmer, more responsible life, including a better relationship with his wife. The house they share, if it never becomes a home (it is described as a "big, slippery-floored many-bathroomed house"), is at least "not so chill as it used to be."[79] Harry is a pendulum man, epitomizing the to-and-fro of mobility: he is able to return home only because of his frequent flights from it.

It is to Harry that Cather gives the novel's last reflection on home. As a public, wealthy, and important man, his sense of "home" is wider than Lucy's. He thinks in terms not only of particular houses but of towns, and asks himself, "What was a man's 'home town,' anyway, but the place where he had had disappointments and had learned to bear them?"[80] Surely as a definition of "home," this approaches in bleakness Frost's "where, when you have to go there, they have to take you in." In the end, although Lucy was trying so hard to "run away" from Haverford, she too learned, or tried to learn, to bear her disappointments there. Yet her situation may suggest an even bleaker definition of home. In some situations, home may be the place you have to run away from.

In the popular assessment of Wharton and Cather, it is Wharton who is the fatalist, Cather who is the optimist. Yet the two authors run very, very close together in their querying of "home," as well as in their grim portrayals of marriage, so long seen as the basis of "home." Surely one reason Lily Bart is not attracted to marriage is because the prospects seem so bleak; her erstwhile friends, Bertha Dorset and Judy Trenor, both manipulate their husbands, who are themselves unsympathetic and manipulative. Nor are the marriages in *Lucy Gayheart* models of happiness. Although Clement Sebastian and his wife were once happy, by the time Lucy meets him, he and his wife "were both better off when they had the Atlantic between them."[81] Harry Gordon's marriage to Harriet Arkwright is "barren in every sense."[82] The novel's sole portrait of a happy marriage, that of the Auerbachs, is uncongenial to Lucy as a model; she rebels against Professor Auerbach's advice that she marry Gordon and settle down, a recommendation, in effect, that she become like the very domestic Mrs. Auerbach. The Auerbachs are an admirable couple but do not reflect what Lucy wants from her life.

As in many other novels of this period,[83] unhappy marriages appear with startling regularity in the works of both authors, and Cather's comments on marriage sometimes seem to gloss works by Wharton. In a letter to Zoë Akins when Akins married for the first time at age forty-six, Cather wrote that "marriage is always a gamble.... The worst thing is to be bored to death by a smiling, pale personality"[84]—the perfect summary of Newland Archer's dulling marriage to May Welland in *The Age of Innocence*. Wharton rarely portrays marriages that are satisfactory for both partners, a situation recalling Jim Burden's reflection near the end of *My Ántonia*. Noting that Ántonia's husband, Anton Cuzak, had "a fine life, certainly, but it wasn't the kind of life he had wanted to live," Jim "wonder[s] whether the life that was right for one was ever right for two!"[85] Anton's name is the shorter, masculine version of Ántonia's, perhaps suggesting that he is secondary to her. (By the same token Harry Gordon's wife, Harriet, has a name that is the feminine, diminutive version of his own.) Given the narrator's hint in the introduction that Jim Burden's "brilliant marriage" is not a happy one,[86] Jim's journey to visit Ántonia is sometimes interpreted as a trip undertaken to escape the restrictions of marriage and the novel itself, ostensibly a memoir by Jim, as a mental escape from his wife.

For Wharton characters as well, travel is valued as a potential escape from an unhappy marriage. When Ellen Olenska remarks in *The Age of Innocence* that "every form of travel had its hardships," Newland "abruptly return[s] that he thought them all of no account compared with the blessedness of getting away."[87] Ethan Frome dreams of escaping a suffocating home and marriage by fleeing to the West with Mattie; Newland Archer tells his wife that he would like "to go away.... On a long trip, ever so far off—away from everything— ... [to] India—or Japan."[88] The excuse of travel is, as they both know, a socially acceptable way of escaping the "smiling, pale personality" to whom he is chained, or even of seeking Ellen's companionship in Paris. May counters his proposal in the terms in which he has couched it, saying, "As far as that? But I'm afraid you can't, dear.... Not unless you'll take me with you."[89] This would, of course, be no escape at all. Although it says a great deal for Newland's character that he stays with May when she reveals that she is pregnant (he is rewarded by a son who is his "born comrade"),[90] the marriage saps him. In the novel's epilogue, set after May's death, Newland has "lost the habit of travel."[91] In a Wharton novel this means a great deal: he has lost the habit of adventure, exploration, even enthusiasm for life. He sees "into what a deep rut he had sunk. The worst of doing one's duty was that it apparently unfitted one for doing anything else."[92] The life that was "right for one"—in this case, for May Welland Archer—was not "right for two."

Although Wharton and Cather may have shared the fears of their characters, they were in many ways luckier than the fictions they created. Lily felt herself rootless; Wharton described herself as "a rooted possessive person."[93] Lily is homeless; Wharton was, quite literally, a homemaker, investing time, energy, and capital in creating her houses and gardens. She sometimes spoke of her homes as if they were physically part of her. After the strenuous years of World War I, when she was able to settle into Sainte Claire, she wrote to a friend that she was "thrilled to the spine,... as if I were going to get married—to the right man at last!"[94] If her homes protected her, she also protected them. In 1934 she declined an honorary degree from Columbia University partly because of civil unrest that threatened her property, explaining to Minnie, "If I am on the spot I can count on every kind of protection.... I feel about my houses as a crab must about its carapace."[95] For all her love of travel, she was also happy to return home. In 1896, after an extended trip to Europe, she wrote Bahlmann that she was delighted to return home to Newport: "I can't tell you how lovely the house & place looked after our long absence, & how good my bed felt after Hotel [*sic*] mattresses for over eight months! . . . It is so nice getting shaken down & hugging the books & getting a nod & smile from the pictures every time one passes them."[96] Over three decades later she would express the same dynamic, first describing a wonderful trip she had just completed and then expressing how lovely it was to be home: "And yet Hyères is best, & I was childishly glad to get back!"[97]

Like Wharton, Cather sometimes expressed a joyous, even physical sense of home. En route from Red Cloud to New York in 1921, she wrote Fisher that "I wish I could like any spot in the world as well as the Divide between the Platte and the Republican [Rivers]—but I can't, so there! The place that just makes your 'tummy' turn over inside you when you go back to it or leave it, is your place."[98] A year later, back in Nebraska for her parents' golden wedding anniversary, she wrote, "It's always a joy to be back here—I get more thrills to the square mile out of this cornfield country than I can out of any other country in the world"; in this letter, Nebraska is referred to casually twice as "home."[99]

Yet, as Joseph Urgo has written, while it is possible to visit all the places Cather lived, it is not easy to "answer the question 'Where was Willa Cather's home?'"[100] Although Cather lived in New York City for the majority of her adult life, the extent to which she felt "at home" there is unclear. It may even be misleading to say that she lived *in* New York from 1906 to 1947; she traveled so often and so extensively, spending months at a time in places as various as Pittsburgh, New Hampshire, Grand Manan Island, and Europe, that it would be difficult to calculate how much of that time she actually spent there. New York was the center of American cultural life in Cather's eyes, and early on it had the glamor she captured in "Paul's Case,"[101] yet she was critical of it nearly from the time of her arrival. As early as January 1907 she was writing that New York "is as big and raw and relentless as ever. . . . Hideous literature is produced as fast as the presses can grind it out. . . . The new conductor of the Philharmonic, and the opera are the only things that save my soul from death."[102] While she waxed ecstatic about her new apartment at 5 Bank Street in a 1912 letter to Sergeant, she ended by remarking, "Your card [from London] makes me restless. I want to be in London. There's no place like it!"[103] In many ways New York was a place to conduct business, "to see my dentist, oculist, lawyer, etc. One does have to come back to cities for some things."[104]

For five years after she had to move out of her Bank Street apartment in 1927, Cather's base in New York was the Grosvenor Hotel. She hated having no permanent address in this period, describing it as an "awful way to live!" in a letter she wrote that year.[105] Yet in September 1932, when she was about to return to New York to look for a new place to live, she remarked to Zoë Akins, "I almost hope I won't find an apartment!"[106] When she relocated to 570 Park Avenue at the end of the year, it was partly because she deeply needed a place she could call her own: "I simply have to have a dwelling place and my own books and things about me. Then I can travel in comfort and not feel like a tramp."[107] The phrase "dwelling place" seems so deliberately chosen, suggesting not "home" but a pied-à-terre. Yet Cather found such a place necessary; she had, in Janis Stout's phrase, a "need for secure at-homeness."[108] Moreover, a permanent address served as a base for further travel. As Stout has written, Cather "shape[d] her adult life as a series of volitional departures on journeys of emergence, discovery, and self-fulfillment *even while maintaining a powerful homing urge*"; Cather was "both an incessant traveler and a homebody"—a phrase that applies equally to Wharton.[109] Cather's feelings about the city remained deeply ambivalent. Only sixteen days before her death in April 1947, she wrote the novelist Sigrid Undset that "New York has become the most foolish city in the world—to live in. . . . Every American now seems to want to live in New York City, drink cocktails and wear outrageous clothes," adding, "I hope to escape from New York before very long."[110] Yet there is no doubt that the two apartments she shared with Edith Lewis were, as Melissa Homestead has demonstrated, home in every sense. First at 5 Bank Street, and later at 570 Park, Cather, Lewis, and their cook and housekeeper Josephine Bourda formed a happy and stable household where they also welcomed friends and relatives.[111] A letter Cather wrote to Irene Miner Weisz shortly after her move to 570 Park reassured her worried friend that she had a home again: "This I want you to know, dear, that I have a home, that it looks like a glorified Bank Street, and that we have Josephine back! The old original Josephine . . . with all her bubbling Southern nature still in force, and a better cook than ever!"[112]

Nevertheless, "home" remained a complex proposition for Cather. A decade after her move to New York she wrote sadly of the breakup of the McClung household in Pittsburgh, where she had not only lived with the family but had returned on many occasions to write even after moving to New York, remarking, "The loss of a home like that leaves one pretty lonely and miserable."[113] Emotionally the "place that ma[d]e" Cather's "'tummy' turn over" remained Nebraska, and she frequently refers to Red Cloud as "home." Returning to Pittsburgh from Nebraska a year after she had left Red Cloud, she wrote to Mariel Gere, "I will not be away from Nebraska another year. Of what use are money and success if one is not happy? And I can not be happy so far away from home."[114] Yet she never moved back to Red Cloud. If it was the place she most often thought of as "home," perhaps this was possible only because she had traveled away from it—only because she had escaped, as Thea Kronborg escapes from Moonstone and as Lucy Gayheart escapes, at least temporarily, from Haverford. In some ways her poem "Going Home (Burlington Route)" may best capture her feelings for home. "How smoothly the trains run beyond the Missouri; / Even in my sleep I know when I have crossed the river," it begins.[115] This sense of being in transit, not of being in the place thought of as "home" but of heading in that direction, combines travel and home, perhaps providing the best of both states. The poem ends as it begins, still in motion, with Cather describing the train's "wheels turn[ing] as if they were glad to go; . . . Singing and humming . . . / As if they, too, were going home."[116] *Going* home may be more satisfactory, even, paradoxically, more homelike, than *being* home.

LIVING IN A BROKEN WORLD

Questions of travel and home, of place and culture, were challenged and complicated by the war years. Wharton in particular had witnessed the vast difference between her own chosen travel and expatriation, and the plight of thousands of refugees from the war zones, forced to leave their homes. Like others of their generation, Wharton and Cather could not anticipate the extent to which the war would change the world in which they had grown up and established themselves as writers, nor the profound disillusionment that would result from the war that was supposed to have ended all wars. Siegfried Sassoon acknowledged the end of the Edwardian era in the title of his memoir, *Good-bye to All That*; in *A Room of One's Own* Virginia Woolf observed that the war had subtly changed everything, even poetry, with difficult, unmelodious modern poetry replacing the beautiful lyricism of Tennyson and Rosetti. It would take a poet a generation younger, Philip Larkin, to summarize much of this feeling in the famous line from his poem "MCMXIV": "Never such innocence again." After the war, even travel writing, a genre typically positive in tone, would reflect "a certain world-weariness, springing from disillusionment with European civilisation and dismay at its impact on the rest of the world."[117]

Wharton and Cather were, like so many millions of others, deeply relieved, even jubilant, when the war ended on November 11, 1918. Yet both gradually realized that they had been overly optimistic; the profound destruction of World War I had fundamentally changed the world they knew. As Wharton wrote, there would be no simple "return . . . to the world we had so abruptly passed out of four years earlier."[118] Wharton was living in a devastated country and still deeply involved in a range of charities whose work would continue for many years after the war. Cather was also a witness to the damage the war had wrought. During her 1920 visit to Paris she continued to admire the beauty of the city, but she also saw "recently crippled veterans . . . sunning themselves" in the Luxembourg Gardens.[119] She saw further evidence of the war's destruction when she visited her cousin's grave in Villers Tournelle. Travel was difficult, as "the railroads in that region are very much disorganized. In that demolished district there are now no hotels and no places to spend the night."[120] Wharton gradually realized that "the world I had grown up in and been formed by had been destroyed in 1914";[121] for Cather too the sense of decided change came slowly, but finally definitively.

"The world broke in two in 1922 or thereabouts," she wrote in 1936.[122] The actual moment of realization, if indeed there was such a moment, may have been impossible to pin down, but for Cather, as for Wharton, a vast gulf divided the prewar world from the postwar world. Wharton wrote in her memoir, "The compact world of my youth has receded into a past from which it can only be dug up in bits by the assiduous relic-hunter"; in her preface to *Not under Forty*, Cather wrote that after the rift caused by the war, "the persons and prejudices recalled in these sketches slid back into yesterday's seven thousand years."[123] Both allied themselves with the past, with Wharton claiming that her memoir was of interest primarily because she spoke of a world now "extinct" and Cather counting herself as one of "the backward."[124]

The postwar world held much that distressed them. If they had hoped that American doughboys might bring French culture back to the United States, they must have been disappointed. France itself, though still identifiably French, was devastated; the United States, far from weaning itself from the Gilded Age materialism, plunged into the yet more materialistic 1920s. The war and postwar years were also a period of increasing personal losses for both Wharton and Cather. During the war Wharton had suffered not only the deaths of French and American friends who were directly involved but also the loss of Henry James, Anna Bahlmann, and her friend Egerton Winthrop, all in 1916; "the friends I love best have been taken from me," she wrote.[125] The losses accumulated after the war; her lifelong friend Walter Berry died in 1927, with Wharton at his bedside. In a 1933 letter, when her longtime maid Elisa was dying and Gross, her housekeeper, had become "quite mindless," she wrote that "The strain on my heart-strings (I mean the metaphorical ones) is severe, for since Walter's death I've been incurably lonely *inside*, & these two faithful women kept the hearth-fire going."[126]

Cather too suffered significant losses. Her cousin had died in the war; she was also saddened by deaths in the 1918 flu pandemic, by which Red Cloud was hit hard. In December of that year she wrote, "It's cruel how many boys have died.... Before I left Red Cloud we had seven funerals in one week for boys who were sent home from Camp Dodge, Iowa."[127] The postwar years brought personal losses as well. Her father died in March 1928, her mother in August 1931. In 1932 she wrote Zoë Akins after the sudden death of Akins's husband, "It's a brutal fact, Zoe [sic], that after one is 45, it simply rains death, all about one, and after you've passed fifty, the storm grows fiercer.... Death just becomes a deep, be-numbing fact in one's life."[128] She encountered more of that storm in 1938, when her brother Douglass died unexpectedly in June and her cherished friend Isabelle McClung Hambourg in October.[129] "With Douglass and Isabelle both gone out of my life, I scarcely know how I shall go on," she wrote.[130]

The energy and exuberance of Wharton's and Cather's earlier lives were checked by these losses. Shortly before Christmas 1916 Wharton had written, "One can carry one's load without the aid of joy—but it's a long cold road."[131] Wharton's "without the aid of joy" anticipates Cather's Godfrey St. Peter, who, in *The Professor's House*, realizes that he must learn to "live without delight."[132] It is difficult for him to accept such a prospect: "Theoretically he knew that life is possible, may even be pleasant, without joy, without passionate griefs. But it had never occurred to him that he might have to live like that."[133] At the novel's conclusion he is setting out on the "long cold road" Wharton described. It is only a few steps further to a new awareness and acknowledgment of pain in Wharton's and Cather's later works. In Cather's fine 1931 story "Old Mrs. Harris," Grandma Harris tells her grandchildren as they watch their cat die an agonizing death, "Everything that's alive has got to suffer"; in Wharton's *The Gods Arrive*, published a year later, Vance Weston's grandmother tells him on her deathbed, "Maybe we haven't made enough of pain—been too afraid of it. Don't be afraid of it."[134] In these works pain plays a role in the individual's "coming to moral and emotional maturity,"[135] as Avril Horner and Janet Beer observe.

Wharton died in 1937; Cather lived another decade, during which the horrors of World War II would deepen her sense of living in a broken world. In 1944 she wrote letter to her old friend Viola Roseboro:

> I have been thinking of you in connection to the death of the world—the death of the world you loved so well, and roamed about it so much. Oh, I am so glad you did roam about—roamed as far as Con-

stantinople and saw the Saint Sophia—which I shall never see. What a grand old sailor you were!—just drinking your fill of the beautiful old world which we thought would last forever. Why should the beautiful cities that were a thousand years a-making tumble down on our heads <u>now, in our short lifetime?</u>[136]

The war was not only destroying the beautiful cities of Europe but was also causing displacement on an unprecedented scale. In the same letter Cather states plainly the danger of uprootedness that she had illustrated in Clement Sebastian. While *One of Ours* presented war-related travel as an adventure (at least for Claude), during World War II Cather saw military service as disruptive:

> These young people are all uprooted and some of them quite lost. None of the young people are doing what they wanted to do, or prepared themselves to do, or were already accomplishing with great happiness. Two young professors of Amherst . . . write me from the mud of Guadalcanal. My dearest young niece only knows of her husband that he is commanding an airplane carrier "somewhere in the Pacific". I feel bitterly because so many of the boys from my own little town in Nebraska have been shunted out to those terrible Pacific Islands, where the hardships are so much greater than they can be anywhere in Europe.[137]

The context of international warfare surely influenced Cather's loss of interest in travel. In a 1945 letter to Carrie Sherwood she states, "I am not exaggerating . . . when I confide to you that I would rather go home to Red Cloud than to any of the beautiful cities in Europe where I used to love to go."[138]

Despite the grim challenges of the postwar world, Wharton and Cather continued to find meaning in life, including relishing their memories of travel and planning further trips. Wharton explained in a 1930 letter: "One of my many ways of missing Walter [Berry] is to recall one of those improvised dashes in pursuit of architecture for which he was always ready, & relive some of the golden wander-weeks we used to have, from Cape Cod to Capa—Finisterre!—Well, it's all so much hoarded treasure, that moth & rust can't corrupt."[139] The year after moving to 570 Park Avenue, Cather was able to reclaim the pleasure of travel, writing to Fisher that train travel still evoked a sense of childhood joyousness: "When I get on a Santa Fe train now and swing west to the coast, I often waken in my berth with that glorious feeling I had in childhood, the certainty of countless miles of empty country and open sky and wind and night on every side of me. It's the happiest feeling I ever have."[140] Just as both left incomplete novels at the time of their deaths, so both had unfulfilled travel plans. In April 1937, increasingly weak, Wharton wrote Berenson, "I had made the most elaborate plans—or dreamed the most elaborate dreams—about getting to you by delicious slow stages . . . ; but instead I've had to be content with lingering here, fighting one tidal wave of fatigue after another, & occasionally getting in a little work on 'The Buccaneers.'" She adds, "[I] shall now look forward to calling on you next November"—a trip that she would never make.[141] In a letter written shortly after Cather's death, her niece Virginia Cather Brockway mentioned that "Aunt Willie . . . was making hopeful plans. . . . She would ask Edith [Lewis] how she would feel about packing up and going to California right away. And they were planning to go to Maine as Aunt Willie was most anxious to get back to work."[142]

Travel and the experience of beauty it offered remained central to Wharton and Cather, not as separate elements of life but because they were deeply interrelated. Even in the postwar world, or perhaps especially in that world, beauty mattered because it "quicken[ed] the sense of life, giving it new shape and direction," serving as "its own reward," to return to Nehamas.[143] Beauty also offered a gateway to larger or transcendent truths, as Plato had claimed; this included the beauty and sense of continuity Wharton and Cather both found in Europe's great Catholic churches. Although neither converted to Roman Catholicism, both were drawn to it after the war.[144] Many Americans felt the same: "When World War I shook their confidence in the old order and heightened the need for moral foundations beyond social and temporal ones, Americans found authenticity in European structures and assurance in Roman Catholic practices," as Carol Singley observes.[145] The war years further blurred the lines between religion and art for both authors. Early in her career Cather had portrayed art as a demanding god; in *The Professor's House* Godfrey St. Peter tells his students, "Art and religion (they are the same thing, in the end, of course) have given man the only happiness he has ever had," as both provide a "gorgeous drama" that allows people to "believ[e] in the mystery and importance of their own little individual lives."[146] Wharton never made such decided statements either in her own voice or through her characters, yet she too "believed in the close connection of literature and faith"; her rational skepticism about the church as a younger adult was, as Singley points out, "modified by her developing consciousness—stirred at Amiens, Chartres, Beauvais—of the aesthetic and historical importance of Christianity over the centuries of European civilization."[147] For both, art could lead to a religious feeling, while the experience of sublime religious spaces could engender feelings of wonder and awe like those stirred by great art.

In parallel passages, one from Cather's *One of Ours* and the other from Wharton's *The Gods Arrive*, the authors describe moments in which young American men, both raw midwesterners, unexpectedly receive intimations of wonder and awe through religious architecture. As we saw in chapter 5, Claude experiences a moment of profound connection between the past and the present, the immediate and the infinite, in Rouen's Church of St. Ouen as the sun streams through the church's stained glass and its bell reverberates. In *The Gods Arrive*, Vance has a similar experience. In a town fifty miles from Paris whose name Vance does not even know, he takes shelter in a church during a thunderstorm. Although he had earlier been unable to appreciate Chartres Cathedral in any meaningful way, and although he is not in search of a spiritual or aesthetic experience, he has both in this unnamed church. Except for "a cluster of candles before a distant shrine," the church is dark; Vance is waiting "absently" for the storm to pass "when a flash illuminated the walls of glass, and celestial fields of azure and rose suddenly embowered him. In another instant all was dark, ... then the incandescence began again. ... Vance sat among these bursts of glory and passages of darkness as if alternate cantos of the Paradiso and the Inferno were whirling through him."[148] As the reference to Dante suggests, this is an experience both literary and religious; it becomes one of his "secreted treasures,"[149] like Claude's experience in St. Ouen.

Claude and Vance are young men who have grown up with only a tenuous connection to Christianity and to long-established ideals of beauty; both, in these purely accidental moments, achieve a profound experience of beauty that, though not conventionally religious, connects them "to history, culture, and tradition."[150] These scenes resemble each other to such an extent that it is hard not to wonder whether Wharton had read Cather's Pulitzer Prize–winning novel and drawn on it, consciously or not, for the experience of her own midwesterner in France. Her description of Vance as "put[ting] the whole of himself into" a scene in his novel and reflecting that "his self had come out of Euphoria, been conceived and fashioned there, made of the summer heat on endless wheat-fields, the frozen winter skies,"[151] also echoes Cather's work, most notably *My Ántonia*'s reflections on "what it is like to spend one's childhood in little towns like these, buried in wheat and corn," with their "burning summers" and "blustery winters."[152] Another strikingly parallel passage suggests the authors' deep affinities and their need for something beautiful and enduring in a broken world. In *Death Comes for the Archbishop*, Cather wrote of a Santa Fe church bell whose "full, clear" notes evoke Rome, Jerusalem, and the past for Father Latour; in *Hudson River Bracketed*, Vance's first intimation of a richer, deeper world is the sound of the bell in Euphoria's Catholic church: "That solemn reverberation, like the note of Joshua's trumpet, had made the walls of the present fall, and ... [he] had reached back for the first time into the past."[153]

THE CULTURE OF PLACE

In the novels on which they were working at the time of their deaths, Wharton's *The Buccaneers* and Cather's "Hard Punishments," the authors articulated for a final time their sense of the profound importance of the connection between place and culture, while also suggesting the crucial roles of imagination and wonder. *The Buccaneers* focuses on the adventures of a group of *nouveau riche* American girls who, failing to make their way into the inner sanctum of New York high society, set their sights on England, where aristocrats are charmed by the beauty and energy of the young Americans and attracted by their fathers' fortunes. The novel has elicited a wide range of responses; it has been called "arguably the most charming novel Edith Wharton ever wrote," a work in which Wharton "celebrate[s] American openness and energy"; it has also, with equal credibility, been summarized as "a harsh exposure of society marriage as a form of prostitution and gambling, ... sex as a threat and a bargain, marital sadism and neglect, and ... prejudice and racism."[154] In this complex work the central figure is the youngest of the girls, Annabel ("Nan") St. George, who, as the most imaginative and least ambitious of them, nevertheless makes the "best" marriage, to Ushant, the Duke of Tintagel, the most eligible bachelor in England by rank and wealth. But the Duke proves a cold figure; overly concerned about fortune hunters, his main reason for marrying the unworldly Nan seems to be that she does not fully appreciate how eligible he is. A mechanistic figure, he never gains the slightest appreciation of Nan's warm, sympathetic, and imaginative nature.

While readings of the novel are disparate, the work itself comes into focus "if readers see [it] through Wharton's interest in place," as Suzanne Jones has written.[155] It is through Nan that Wharton conveys the centrality of place and culture, and the necessity of imagination to perceive this. Virginia St. George, Nan's older sister, marries well, but she lacks the imagination to appreciate much of the world she is entering; Virginia "sees *literally*," while Nan "sees *imaginatively*."[156] When she and Nan visit the stately and historic Allfriars, Virginia sees the dining room only as "a big room with cracks in the ceiling, and bits of plaster off the walls."[157] Nan says nothing in response. "She knew that Virginia's survey of the world was limited to people, the clothes they wore, and the carriages they drove in. Her own universe was so crammed to bursting with wonderful sights and sounds that ... Nan sometimes felt a shamefaced pity for her. It must be cold and lonely, she thought, in such an empty colourless world as her sister's."[158] When Nan attempts to share her more imaginative view of the world, telling Virginia that she "like[s] to imagine all those people on the walls, in their splendid historical dresses, walking about in the big rooms," Virginia only tells her to "shut up" and that she is "too old for baby-talk."[159] Nan may be shy, but she has an inner life her sister has no inkling of: "Her imagination rushed out to the beauties of the visible world; and the decaying majesty of Allfriars moved her strangely."[160]

Nan's imagination and love of beauty provide her some consolation once she realizes the emptiness and emotional abusiveness of her marriage to the duke. In Longlands, his ancestral home, the sitting room that has always been designated "the Duchess's room" automatically becomes "hers." Like Lily in "her" room at her Aunt Peniston's, however, Nan does not feel that the room is hers in any meaningful way; when she removes some of the lesser artwork to make it more congenial to her, she is told firmly that everything must be returned to its original place. Mercifully the room is also home to a number of paintings by Correggio. One evening, while Nan is showing the room to the young Englishman Guy Thwarte, he becomes "absorbed" in the "world of sylvan loves and revels" in the Correggios, as Nan has on a number of occasions.[161] (One is reminded of Cather's Paul, lost in front of paintings of Paris or Venice.) Guy comments to Nan that the paintings, which he has seen by daylight on an earlier occasion, are "even more magical" at night. She replies, "I often come here when it's getting dark, and sit among them without making a sound. Perhaps some day, if I'm very patient, I'll tame them, and they'll come down to me...."[162] Knowing how devoid of imagination Ushant is, Guy wonders how he responds to such remarks. But he only says, "They must make up to you for a great deal," to which Nan agrees; their shared appreciation of the paintings brings them together.[163] In this they demonstrate Nehamas's observation: the nonexistence of a standard definition of beauty means that those who do find the same things beautiful are drawn into community.

Indeed this is an experience that Nan and Guy have already had. Earlier in the novel, before her marriage, Nan visited Honourslove, the Thwartes' home in the Cotswolds; based on the historic Stanway,[164] Honourslove moves Nan deeply. She immediately finds the place "warm, cared-for, exquisitely intimate."[165] In spite of her usual self-consciousness, she feels "herself suddenly at ease" and senses Guy's "latent passion for every tree and stone of the beautiful old place."[166] Such a feeling is "new" to her as an American, "a dweller in houses without histories," yet it "is exquisitely familiar to her imagination."[167] When the others in the group—her more practical sister and their friends—go inside, Nan and Guy remain on the terrace to admire the "magic hour" at the end of the day. When Guy tells her that he has Honourslove "in my bones," the usually quiet Nan responds by telling him about her sense of "the *beyondness* of things," and they agree that they "understand" each other: they "*are* beyond," Guy confirms.[168] When Nan suddenly reverts to her usual self-consciousness and "stammer[s]" the conventional phrase, "It's a beautiful view," Guy replies, "It all depends on who looks at it."[169] His answer too may be conventional, but it makes a deeper point: their shared appreciation of beauty has brought them into community, with "each seeing the other in every line of the landscape."[170]

Unlike her sister and their friends, Nan is not particularly attracted to the social whirl of London. Rather, she is, like Wharton, drawn to something she finds in England's historic homes and landscapes, a sense of a deep connection to the past and thus to something larger than herself.[171] When she and Virginia hear the house at Allfriars creaking in the night, the supposedly down-to-earth Virginia is alarmed. But to Nan the house's night sounds recall the estate's history; she feels as if she were hearing "the long murmur of the past breaking on the shores of a sleeping world."[172] Once Nan realizes that her marriage will never be anything but miserable, she hopes to find consolation in the sense of the past she feels in England. Although she thinks of returning to the United States, she recalls "the thinness of the mental and moral air in her own home; the noisy quarrels about nothing, the paltry preoccupations," and realizes that she would rather stay in England, the "atmosphere" of which "had gradually filled her veins and penetrated to her heart."[173] Echoing James's compendium of European cultural offerings absent from the United States, Nan reflects that "life in England had a background, layers and layers of rich deep background, of history, poetry, old traditional observances, beautiful houses, beautiful landscapes, beautiful ancient buildings. . . . Would it not be possible . . . to create for one's self a life out of all this richness, a life which should somehow make up for the poverty of one's personal lot?"[174]

Through Nan, Wharton depicts the confluence of place, culture, beauty, a sense of home, and a grounding sense of a deep connection to the past that both consoles her for a difficult present and gives her strength, even hope. Godfrey St. Peter tell his students that art and religion are really one; Wharton illustrates this in the architecture of Honourslove, which evokes a feeling akin to reverence in Guy. In fact Guy employs a religious lexicon when he thinks of his family's connection to Honourslove: the place itself is "the first and last article of the family creed."[175] Guy's attachment to the estate illustrates the sense of home Wharton had delineated in *The House of Mirth*: the need for an attachment to a particular "spot of earth" that is "a centre of early pieties, of grave endearing traditions."[176] Although Guy leaves Honourslove for several years—a period that Wharton calls an "exile"—it is only to earn the money required to save the estate. Upon his return Guy feels his connection to the place anew, sensing the "kinship between himself and the soil. . . . What a power there was in these accumulated associations."[177] Even among the remains of his ancestors in the family chapel he feels at home, seeing the very tombs and effigies as being "kept warm by each other's nearness."[178]

Cather's final, unfinished novel, "Hard Punishments," similarly depicts the confluence of place, culture, and beauty. The novel is set in Avignon, a city with which Cather fell in love on her first visit and where, like Nan at Honourslove, she first saw "a life rooted in the centuries."[179] She and Edith Lewis returned in 1935, and in the Palace of the Popes they experienced a transcendent moment. Lewis recalled, "As we wandered through the great chambers of white, almost translucent stone, alone except for a guide, this young fellow suddenly stopped still in one of the rooms and began to sing, with a beautiful voice. It echoed down the corridors and under the arched ceilings like a great bell sounding—but sounding from some remote past; its vibrations seemed laden, weighted down with the passions of another age—cruelties, splendours, lost and unimaginable to us in our time."[180] This, she implies, was the genesis of "Hard Punishments." In the surviving fragments of the novel (at Cather's behest most of the novel was destroyed; only two short scenes remain), Cather captures a great deal of "the passions of another age." In *A Motor-Flight through France* Wharton had written, "A great Gothic cathedral... has sheltered such a long succession of lives, given collective voice to so many inarticulate and contradictory cravings, seen so much that was sublime and terrible, or foolish, pitiful and grotesque, that it is like some mysteriously preserved ancestor of the human race."[181] The cruel and the splendid, the terrible and the sublime: Wharton and Cather shared the same sense of human history and its embodiment in such edifices.

"Hard Punishments" focuses on three characters, all of whom are suffering: an elderly, nearly blind priest, and two boys who have suffered the "hard punishments" of the title. One has had his tongue torn out for blasphemy; the other's hands are useless, the result of his punishment for minor theft.[182] Although Cather's medieval Avignon, based closely on Thomas Okey's 1911 history of the city,[183] is a place where barbaric punishments are meted out, it is also, like Wharton's Honourslove, an embodiment of beauty and continuity capable of generating consolation through a sense of reverence and awe. In writing of Gothic cathedrals, Wharton also stated that their "supreme gift" was "the rousing of the sense of reverence";[184] this is exactly the feeling Cather evokes in "Hard Punishments."

In the final surviving scene of this work, Cather uses Father Ambrose's perspective to describe a Christmas mass in the chapel of the Palace of the Popes as he admires "the lights from many candles he could see—bright points in darkness and about each a haze like a halo."[185] In this work in progress Cather left two words in some instances (apparently undecided which suited her purposes best), but the direction of the scene is clear. As the text continues, the priest "closed his eyes and shut off even such poor sight as he had, to rest the more wholly upon the music and the beautiful words. And in the cadence of the priest he seemed to feel/sense the feeling (awe) of the close-packed crowd around him,—like a heart beating under his hand."[186] Cather goes beyond mere piety, emphasizing, like Wharton, the importance of imagination and the ability to wonder. More emphatically than any earlier passage, this one conveys Cather's lifelong sense of art, beauty, and culture as analogous to religion. Through Ambrose, Cather evokes a sense of reverence and wonder. "All about him he could feel something more beautiful than light or music ... the kindling of emotion, faith, belief, imagination ———— which is itself a miracle."[187] This series of nouns, with Cather perhaps equating them, perhaps implying a progression, is important; however one interprets them, the inclusion of "imagination," the final word, is significant. Moreover, the concept of imagination leads to further reflections, with Ambrose thinking, "Was there ... anything in all the universe, anything so wonderful as wonder—wonderment? That thing which the beautiful or the noble calls up in all human creatures not utterly base. That wave of emotion which is both exaltation and humility, humbleness and triumph—triumph over we know not what."[188] Of all Cather's statements on the importance of beauty, this final scene, set in the chapel at Avignon, is perhaps the most important, as well as the most akin to Wharton's sense of the beautiful: *this* moment in *this* particular place generates a sense of wonder. Cather's repetition of this word in three forms—"wonderful," "wonder," and "wonderment"—conveys its crucial importance. It is this feeling that will allow Ambrose and the two boys, who are praying near him, to continue on with their lives, not as maimed beings, but as "living soul[s]."[189]

Through Father Ambrose, Cather delves into some other reflections as well, some of them perhaps surprising. He wonders, for instance, about extraterrestrial life: "Were there in the systems of stars, other creatures who could feel the heavens with the heart?"[190] Yet more unconventionally, he wonders whom God himself, the creator of all the wonderment Ambrose admires, worships: "Surely the Creator of it all could not rejoice and wonder as did men—that would be self worship—whom did God worship? That was a frightful thought—for without the power to worship, to be humbled and exalted in admiration, any being would be a stone, a blindness and dumbness in eternity."[191] Together with Cather's earlier reflection that any "human creature not utterly base" will be moved to wonder by the beautiful and the noble, this passage emphasizes the importance of wonder. For Wharton and

Cather, beauty was central because it brought people to a state of admiration, reverence, "wonderment"; lacking the imagination to feel these, human life is base, and without it, in Father Ambrose's reflections, God himself "would be a stone, a blindness and dumbness." The works of both authors convey the importance of imagination and the ability to wonder again and again throughout their *oeuvres*.

In *The Buccaneers* and "Hard Punishments," Wharton and Cather added one final dimension to the idea of the culture of place and the place of culture. In Honourslove and the Palace of the Popes they depict locations where "culture" and "place" are synonymous, even identical. "Honourslove" is continuous with its geographic location, including not only the house but the surrounding area, of which Guy knows every detail: "Red Farm, where the famous hazel copse was, Ausprey with its decaying Norman church, Little Ausprey with the old heronry at the Hall, Odcote, Sudcote . . .—all were thick with webs of memory for the youth whose people had so long been rooted in their soil."[192] Similarly, the Palace of the Popes, as Cather had described it from her first visit there, is integrally linked to its location, the "sheer precipice" of natural stone "crowned by the great palace of the popes."[193] For the settings of their final works, Wharton and Cather chose places where the place of culture and the culture of place were identical and where human history and natural history were integrally linked. If both settings are associated with pain, they are also associated with beauty. In a broken world, the connection to places that had "seen so much that was sublime and terrible," that had witnessed both "cruelties" and "splendours," suggested the possibility of a life that would continue, somehow, into the future.

In their lives, letters, and fictions Cather and Wharton were harbingers of the sense of rootlessness and exile that has become so common in the late twentieth and early twenty-first centuries, as well as of an increasing sense of transnationalism. In the introduction to his collection *Reflections on Exile*, Edward Said wrote in 2000 that "The greatest single fact of the past three decades has been, I believe, the vast human migration attendant upon war, colonialism and decolonization, economic and political revolutions.... Exiles, émigrés, refugees, and expatriates uprooted from their lands must make do in their surroundings."[194] If the experience of exile has, as Said maintains, "still to find its chroniclers," he acknowledges that the "door [was] first tried by [Joseph] Conrad."[195] Certainly many of the uprooted characters whom Wharton and Cather describe are a relatively fortunate lot; they are largely expatriates, people who have chosen to leave their homelands, rather than exiles, forced out and unable to return home. Cather refers to her French missionaries Latour and Vaillant as "exiles—happy ones" in the French-inflected home they make for themselves in the Southwest, and certainly the wanderings of many Wharton characters are, if not entirely chosen, still a kind of privilege. Yet for many of them, as for their more truly exiled characters who, for one reason or another, cannot go home again, "homes are always provisional," in Theodor Adorno's words.[196] Wharton's and Cather's rootless or uprooted characters are the precursors of so many characters in today's fiction, like those created by Jhumpa Lahiri, who often live on an "unaccustomed earth," to use the title of one of her story collections—people who work to create meaningful lives for themselves in unaccustomed places. (Lahiri takes her title from Hawthorne, who was also much concerned with the relation between place and culture.) If in one way they are citizens of multiple cultures, in another they are sometimes insufficiently rooted in any one place or culture. If belonging to multiple cultures can be a blessing, it can also, as Lisa Suhair Majaj has written, mean that one is constantly pulled between cultures.[197] Yet Lahiri's characters, like so many of Wharton's and Cather's characters and like the writers themselves, successfully transplant themselves to a new environment, or to new environments. For them "home" may be multiple places rather than a single place; they may be living with "a new geographical consciousness of a decentered or multiply-centered world,"[198] in Said's phrase. After the war Wharton felt both of her houses as homes; for Cather, New York City, Red Cloud, Grand Manan, and perhaps Jaffrey, New Hampshire, were all "home" in some way.

It is unfortunate that neither Cather nor Wharton was able to read Bishop's "Questions of Travel." While Bishop's poem expresses melancholy rootlessness, it also expresses the good that comes from such a life: What would one have given up if one had not traveled? Although the poem begins with a sense of fatigue, as it progresses, Bishop turns her eye to details like the ones Cather and Wharton might have observed, and the tone changes to reflection and appreciation. Noting that the place she is visiting is characterized by both "the crudest wooden footwear" and birdcages that are "whittled fantasies," Bishop ponders the link between them, remarking, "Surely it would have been a pity / not to have seen" such things, which have in turn led her to reflect.[199]

Thoughtful travel leads not only to the appreciation of details the average tourist might overlook but to pondering that never would have happened otherwise. The philosopher Blaise Pascal had claimed in his *Pensées* "that all human misery comes from one thing alone, being unable to sit quietly in a room"; Bishop closes her poem with a nod to this observation, asking whether the desire to travel is driven by "*lack of imagination*"—or whether Pascal might have been "*not entirely right / about just sitting quietly in one's room?*"[200] Both Wharton and Cather knew Pascal's famous *Pensées*;[201] as wanderers in the Land of Letters and the Kingdom of Art, they pondered the relationship not only between real and imagined places but also between geographic and intellectual adventures. In *The Age of Innocence* Newland Archer reflects that most of the "real things" in his life have happened in his library; in "Coming, Aphrodite!" Cather wrote that her painter, Don Hedger, "would have more tempestuous adventures sitting in his dark studio" than the singer Eden Bower "would find in all the capitals of Europe."[202] Yet Archer is limited by his limited travel, and Hedger benefits by long trips abroad. Perhaps in this matter Pascal was "not entirely right." If travel always "has its discomforts," as the Countess Olenska remarks, it also has its rewards. For both authors "stay[ing] at home" would never have been acceptable. What if Wharton had stayed quite literally "tethered in native pastures, even if it reduce her to a back-yard in New York," as Henry James had recommended for the benefit of her fiction, or if Cather had never left Virginia—which, although it was "tranquil and ordered and serene," was also "smothering... factitious and unreal"—or had not escaped the small town that she loved but found stifling?[203]

Bishop's speaker wonders whether "lack of imagination" leads people to travel; Wharton and Cather suggest that the opposite is the case—that imagination leads to travel, and that travel in turn enhances the ability to imagine and wonder.

This study began with Cather's observation that "geography is a terribly fatal thing sometimes" and with Wharton's objection to reading biographies of those who had led "starved existences," lives led in places lacking any "dust of ideas in the air." Wharton's and Cather's own lives, like their works, demonstrate over and over the importance of the culture of place and of the place of culture, the need for a more nourishing existence. As we saw in the introduction, "culture" construed broadly refers to "the way distinct communities construct meanings for the individual lives that unfold within them."[204] If Cather and Wharton challenged the idea of home in their fictions, their lives suggest the importance of creating a place with an individual culture that is beautiful, consoling, and hope-giving, and that thus allows the construction of meaning. In some ways neither ever found the ideal place to live. Both lived far from friends and family members they would have loved to have seen more often; Wharton found green havens outside Paris and in southern France, while Cather had to put up with an increasingly noisy New York City. Yet, to return to an earlier moment in this study, each was able to achieve exactly what their 1905 characters longed for. Lily wanted not just a room of her own but a beautiful mansion of her own; circumscribed by social rules, she is unable to achieve this, while Wharton, not because of but in spite of her marriage, achieved not one but two such homes. Similarly, for the last fifteen years of her life, Willa Cather—perched high on Park Avenue, surrounded by beauty and often by flowers—realized the life that was, for Paul, only a temporary reality, one he was sure could never be his.

Having suffered from heart attacks and strokes, Wharton underwent a slow decline in her last years; she spent her final months in Pavillon Colombe, among her gardens. Yet she remained hopeful. In October 1936 she wrote to Mary Berenson, "I wish I knew what people mean when they say they find 'emptiness' in this wonderful adventure of living, which seems to me to pile up its glories like an horizon-wide sunset as the light declines. I'm afraid I'm an incorrigible life-lover and life-wonderer & adventurer."[205] She qualifies this, adding, "Bodily suffering strikes at the roots of all these joys"; still, the "life-wonderer" prevailed. Only a few months before her death in August 1937, severely restricted by a series of heart attacks she had suffered over many years, she wrote to Bernard Berenson, "I'm used to invalidism now, & find it full of oases & hidden springs."[206] Her friend Elisina Tyler, who was with her for the last weeks of her life, reported that far from taking the good fortune of her life for granted, Wharton expressed a deep gratitude for being able to end it in a place of such beauty: "I might just be an old woman taking the air on a bench in a public garden, with the children knocking their hoops into my skirts—and why was so much beauty given to me instead?"[207]

Cather lived a decade longer than Wharton, suffering many losses. Yet in 1932 she sounded a note of optimism not unlike Wharton's, writing at the end of her condolence letter to Zoë Akins that "Personal life is rather a failure, <u>always</u>; biologically so. But something rather nice does happen in the mind itself as one grows older. If it hasn't begun with you yet, keep your courage, <u>it will happen</u>. A kind of golden light comes as a compensation for many losses. You'll see!!"[208] Her letters from later years did not always express the same optimism, and yet the hopeful note reemerges. At the end of a 1943 letter to Fisher she expressed deep sadness, even despair, about the effects of the war: "What is there to say about anything that is happening now? There is no spot on the earth's surface that one can rest one's mind against any more."[209] Commenting that she had been ill, she wrote, "Slowly one comes to life again—but one wonders why, when most of the world one loved is being destroyed and so many of the friends one loved have been destroyed." Yet she has added an enthusiastic postscript: "Isn't Churchill a great old boy? Isn't England a great old land?"[210]

Although Cather's death came suddenly and unexpectedly, she had suffered for some time from what she described as an inability to withstand too much excitement or agitation, even pleasant excitement; she needed to remain in her own safe and quiet haven.[211] The small individual community of her home with Edith Lewis was a beautiful one, decorated with artwork old and new, including prints by Piranesi and new artwork by Lewis's friend Achsah Brewster.[212] Even while the destruction of beauty on a large scale during World War II was heartbreaking, Cather remained intensely appreciative of small, beautiful things, like the violets sent by her brother Roscoe for Christmas in 1944 or the "deep rose" cyclamen sent her shortly after New Year by Zoë Akins.[213] In her 1932 letter to Akins she urged her friend to "get the most you can out of your house and mind and thoughts."[214] The nouns are central. House, mind, thoughts; even those who inhabited the Kingdom of Art needed physical homes as well. If "a place is a locality or a physical environment, a space which human beings have converted into a meaningful habitation" as well as a "cultural landscape" and a place that reflects the "inner landscape of the mind,"[215] Wharton and Cather created places, individual cultural spaces, that embodied the central importance of beauty in their lives.

Chapter 1 opened by noting that Wharton and Cather never met and by speculating on how such a meeting might have gone, suggesting that, in spite of the common interests they shared, it would have been neither a dismal failure nor a grand success. Yet imagining them more specifically in each other's homes may suggest other possibilities. It is, in fact, not so difficult to imagine Cather in either of Wharton's homes, with their spacious rooms and beautiful gardens. Both the Pavillon Colombe and Sainte Claire were in places meaningful to Cather. Sainte Claire, in Hyères, was just a few miles west of Le Lavandou, where Cather had described herself as gloriously happy, writing admiringly of the beautiful views of the Mediterranean, views that Wharton's home also took in. As Cather also loved Paris and northern France, the Pavillon Colombe would have been equally pleasant to her; her extended stay in 1923 with Jan and Isabelle Hambourg at their home in Ville d'Avray, just west of Paris, would have deepened her sense of being at home in this part of France. A photograph from one visit to the Hambourgs shows Cather on the front steps of their home; Cather's pose at the doorway, like the photograph of Wharton posed in the doorway of the Pavillon Colombe (one of the last photographs taken of her), suggests belonging (figs. 20 and 21). Remarkably similar photos of Wharton and Cather dining on the terraces of French homes also suggest their shared affinity for France and French culture (figs. 22 and 23).

Cather had learned relatively early in her career that she was not, after all, Edith Wharton, and ought not to attempt to write Wharton's novels. But she would have found much to admire in the older woman's arrangement of her homes and gardens, and in Wharton's deep love of beauty and her appreciation of France's farms and gardens. In northern France, Wharton wrote, "Agriculture has mated with poetry instead of banishing it," and one sees "the higher beauty of land developed, humanized, brought into relation to life and history"—a contrast to the American landscape, "the raw material with which the greater part of our own hemisphere is still clothed."[216] Although the last remark may seem harsh, it recalls Cather's descriptions of Nebraska as "not a country at all, but the material out of which countries are made"[217] and of parts of New Mexico as a "country still waiting to be made into a landscape."[218] Cather had a tolerance, even a love, of such landscapes that Wharton lacked. Yet Cather's descriptions of gardens like the Kohlers' in *The Song of the Lark* and of the garden-like farms of Ántonia Cuzak and Alexandra Bergson demonstrate that she shared Wharton's love of beautiful and carefully tended gardens. Wharton's sense of agriculture "mat[ing] with poetry" in France, her sense that "every field has a name, a history, a distinct place of its own,"[219] is first cousin of Alexandra Bergson's sense of the "Genius of the Divide" in *O Pioneers!*, her belief that her prosperous farm is not so much the result of her own skills but rather the product of the collaboration between human endeavor and the land itself. It is, after all, easy to imagine the two women strolling through the beautiful gardens at Pavillon Colombe or the stunning Mediterranean garden at Sainte Claire and conversing about their love of place.

Wharton, for her part, might have been equally impressed by a visit to Cather's Park Avenue apartment, perhaps impressed by the address itself, but far more with the solid quietness of the building, which Cather had carefully tested before signing a lease.[220] Then there was the beauty with which Cather and Lewis had furnished it, including their selection of artwork; Wharton might well have paused before the portrait

20. & 21. At home in France. (*left*) Cather in the doorway of the home of Isabelle and Jan Hambourg, Ville d'Avray, France, just west of Paris, 1923. Philip L. and Helen Cather Southwick Collection, Archives and Special Collections, University of Nebraska–Lincoln Libraries. (*right*) Wharton in her doorway at the Pavillon Colombe, St. Brice-sous-Forêt, just north of Paris, 1937. Courtesy Lilly Library, Indiana University, Bloomington, Indiana.

of George Sand, a writer she also admired.[221] She would have enjoyed the flowers with which they often adorned their apartment; in his recollection of dining with Cather and Lewis on one occasion, Truman Capote recalled not only "beautifully bound books lin[ing] all walls of the living room" but "flowers everywhere—masses of winter lilac, peonies, and lavender-colored roses."[222] And then there would have been the sharing of the French delicacies Josephine Bourda would have provided for them. Like Cather, Wharton would have appreciated the apartment as a quiet and beautiful refuge from the increasingly noisy city below. Bending the rules of time and space a bit further, we can imagine Wharton laughing appreciatively at Cather's 1947 remark that

22. & 23. "Good eating and good talk." (*top*) Cather (right) dining al fresco with Jan and Isabelle Hambourg at their home in Ville d'Avray, 1923. Philip L. and Helen Cather Southwick Collection, Archives and Special Collections, University of Nebraska–Lincoln Libraries. (*bottom*) Wharton dining al fresco on the terrace at Sainte Claire, 1920s. From left: Robert Norton, Walter Berry, Wharton, Gaillard Lapsley. Edith Wharton Collection, Yale Collection of American Literature, Beinecke Rare Book and Manuscript Library.

New York had become "the most foolish city in the world—to live in. . . . Every American now seems to want to live in New York City, drink cocktails and wear outrageous clothes," or agreeing with her remark that the city "was big and raw and relentless."[223] After all, neither author was essentially a city person, and both might have wanted to escape to what Wharton once called a "green woody *walky* place."[224] Yet it was also essential to have a home. Particularly in a difficult world it was crucial to have "a dwelling place and [one]'s own books and things,"[225] a home that reflected the best gleanings of travel while also providing a safe and beautiful center to which one could return. Such a place could not, perhaps, solve the larger issues of American culture. But it could give one a place where one could reflect and write about such matters and, in thoughtful ways, ask readers to consider them.

NOTES

INTRODUCTION

1. Tuttleton, Lauer, and Murray, *Edith Wharton*, 295.
2. Quoted in Nettels, "Wharton and Trollope," 7.
3. Berendt, "Regionalism," 160.
4. Eeckhout, "Why Would the Spatial Be So Special?," 24–26.
5. Joseph Murphy, "The Genius Revisited," 4.
6. Eeckhout, "Why Would the Spatial Be So Special?," 21–24.
7. Bakhtin, "Forms of Time," 84.
8. Robert T. Tally Jr., "Translator's Preface," in Westphal, *Geocriticism*, xi.
9. Bakhtin, "Forms of Time," 84, 85.
10. Said, "Culture and Imperialism," 84.
11. Quoted in Barrows, "Introduction," 3.
12. Warf and Arias, *The Spatial Turn*, 1; emphasis in original.
13. Mahoney and Katz, *Regionalism*, x.
14. Cather, *My Ántonia*, 7.
15. Schama, *Landscape and Memory*, 3.
16. Cather, Postcard to Elsie Cather, June 11, 1908.
17. Barber, *The Map Book*, 7.
18. Many works by Native American authors reflect a deep awareness of the history of specific places. Well-known examples include Momaday's *The Way to Rainy Mountain* and Silko's *Ceremony*.
19. Dimock, *Through Other Continents*, 1.
20. Dimock, *Through Other Continents*, 2.
21. Welty, "Place in Fiction," 116.
22. Kowalewski, "Contemporary Regionalism," 8.
23. Proulx, "Dangerous Ground," 7.
24. S. Lewis, "American Scene in Fiction," 142.
25. S. Lewis, "American Scene in Fiction," 142.
26. Welty, "Place in Fiction," 118.
27. Bradbury, *The Atlas of Literature*, 152.

28. Glotfelty, "Introduction," xix, xxiii.
29. See also Reynolds, "Willa Cather's Case," 85.
30. MacDonald, "Introduction," 2–3.
31. Dawson, *Making Peace with the Past?*, 55–56.
32. Warf and Arias, *The Spatial Turn*, 1; E. K. Brown, "Homage to Willa Cather," 85.
33. Gómez Reus, "'Remember Spain!'"; Simour, "The White Lady Travels." On social geography, see Griffith, *The Color of Democracy*, 25–26, and Orgel, "Introduction," xii–xiii.
34. Wharton, *A Son at the Front*, 18.
35. Wharton, *The Letters of Edith Wharton*, 553.
36. Wharton to B. Berenson, February 22, 1930, BB.
37. James, *Hawthorne*, 34.
38. Millington, "Where Is Cather's Quebec?," 24.
39. Millington, "Where Is Cather's Quebec?," 24.
40. Pater, "Conclusion," 841. For Pater's influence on Cather, see Watson and Moseley, *Willa Cather and Aestheticism*, 7–9. For Wharton and Pater, see Benstock, *No Gifts from Chance*, 282, and Orlando, *Edith Wharton and the Visual Arts*, 138.
41. Pater, "Conclusion," 841.
42. Pater, "Conclusion," 840.
43. Nehamas, *Only a Promise of Beauty*, 3.
44. Nehamas, *Only a Promise of Beauty*, 3.
45. Nehamas, *Only a Promise of Beauty*, 3.
46. Nehamas, *Only a Promise of Beauty*, 144.
47. Nehamas, *Only a Promise of Beauty*, 2.
48. Nehamas, *Only a Promise of Beauty*, 77, 138.
49. Wharton, "Talk to American Soldiers," 264.
50. Cather, *The World and the Parish*, 2:510, 512.
51. Quoted in Ross, "A Gathering of Orchestras," 76.
52. Hadju, "Who Needs the NEA and NEH?"
53. Brooks, "The Essential John McCain."
54. Wharton, *The Letters of Edith Wharton*, 424.
55. Appiah, "Presidential Address 2017," 517.
56. Gopnik, *Paris to the Moon*, 167.
57. Appiah, "Presidential Address 2017," 518.
58. Lorde, "Poetry Is Not a Luxury"; Walker, *In Search of Our Mothers' Gardens*, and Walker, "Everyday Use."
59. Chast, *Going into Town*, 115.
60. Appiah, "Presidential Address 2017," 515.

1. THE "ARISTOCRAT" AND THE PIONEER

1. Wharton to Gaillard Lapsley, July 18, 1928, Wharton MSS, Box 60, YCAL.
2. On Wharton as gardener, see Lee, *Edith Wharton*, 531–35, 558–64, and Bratton, *Yrs. Ever Affly*, esp. xli–xlv.
3. Quoted in Tuttleton, Lauer, and Murray, *Edith Wharton*, 295, and O'Connor, *Willa Cather*, 84, 96.
4. Quoted in Tuttleton, Lauer, and Murray, *Edith Wharton*, 295.
5. Quoted in Tuttleton, Lauer, and Murray, *Edith Wharton*, 294.
6. Quoted in Tuttleton, Lauer, and Murray, *Edith Wharton*, 294, 295.
7. Quoted in Tuttleton, Lauer, and Murray, *Edith Wharton*, 295.
8. On Wharton's aristocratic friends, see Benstock, *Women of the Left Bank*, 39–45; Wegener, "'Rabid Imperialist'"; Wharton, "Life and I," 202.
9. Quoted in O'Connor, *Willa Cather*, 88–89.
10. O'Connor, *Willa Cather*, 40, 88.
11. Quoted in O'Connor, *Willa Cather*, 84.
12. The term "West" is still used broadly. In *A Companion to the Regional Literatures of America*, Crow notes that his volume contains chapters on "the Great Plains, the Southwest, the Rocky Mountain West, and California, which from an Eastern perspective might blur into one generalized West" (3).
13. See Porter, *On the Divide*, and Thacker, "'As the Result of Many Solicitations.'"
14. Cather, *The Selected Letters of Willa Cather*, 105.
15. Jewell and Stout, "Introduction," xiii.
16. Wharton, *A Backward Glance*, 44.
17. Woodress, *Willa Cather*, 19, 43.
18. Wharton, *A Backward Glance*, 10, 11.
19. Wharton, *A Backward Glance*, 8–10.
20. Woodress, *Willa Cather*, 12, 15.
21. Wharton, *A Backward Glance*, 11, 10.
22. Woodress, *Willa Cather*, 13.
23. Woodress, *Willa Cather*, 13.
24. Woodress, *Willa Cather*, 13.
25. DeSanctis, "Retracing Willa Cather's Steps in the South of France."
26. Quoted in Lee, *Edith Wharton*, 145.
27. Tóibín, "The Custom of the Country"; "Julian Fellowes."
28. The Mount, https://www.edithwharton.org/2013site/wp-content/uploads/2013/01/LancomeFrenchTouchLipsticks.pdf.
29. Wharton, *The Age of Innocence*, 347.
30. Woodress, *Willa Cather*, 245.
31. Lawrence, *The School of Femininity*, 248.
32. Lawrence, *The School of Femininity*, 256, 258.

33. Lawrence, *The School of Femininity*, 357.
34. Lawrence, *The School of Femininity*, 357, 364.
35. Cather, *The Selected Letters of Willa Cather*, 570.
36. Auchincloss, *Pioneers and Caretakers*, 3.
37. Auchincloss, *Pioneers and Caretakers*, 20, 97–121.
38. Woodress, *Willa Cather*, 182.
39. O'Brien, *Willa Cather*, 81–82.
40. Welsch and Welsch, *Cather's Kitchens*, xvii.
41. Reynolds, "The Politics of Cather's Regionalism," 3.
42. See John J. Murphy, "Comprising Realism"; Clarke, "Modernist Domesticity"; Meyer, "Contamination, Modernity, Health, and Art in Edith Wharton and Willa Cather." Major studies comparing Wharton and Cather include Nettels, *Language and Gender in American Fiction*; Williams, *Not in Sisterhood*; Thompson, *Influencing America's Tastes*; Griffith, *The Color of Democracy*; and Sherman, *Sacramental Shopping*. Excluding dissertation abstracts, the MLA Bibliography shows 144 different books and articles that have treated both Wharton and Cather between 1975 and August 2017.
43. Jewell and Stout, "Introduction," xiii.
44. Showalter, *A Jury of Her Peers*, 270.
45. Green, *The Other Americans in Paris*, 3.
46. Woodress, *Willa Cather*, 183, 187.
47. For a complete list of Cather's publications in *McClure's Magazine*, see Crane, *Willa Cather*, 231–34 and 243–47.
48. Benstock, *No Gifts from Chance*, 326.
49. "An American Pioneer," 30.
50. Van Doren, "Contemporary American Novelists: Edith Wharton," 40–41.
51. Van Doren, "Contemporary American Novelists: Willa Cather," 93.
52. Information on publications and reviewers was compiled from Garrison, *Edith Wharton*; Crane, *Willa Cather*; Tuttleton, Lauer, and Murray, *Edith Wharton*; and O'Connor, *Willa Cather*.
53. Cather, *The Selected Letters of Willa Cather*, 410.
54. Benstock, *No Gifts from Chance*, 414.
55. Lee, *Edith Wharton*, 636; Woodress, *Willa Cather*, 422.
56. Lee, *Edith Wharton*, 636; Woodress, *Willa Cather*, 498.
57. Cather, "148 Charles Street," 69. O'Brien also remarks on the near misses between Cather and James (*Willa Cather*, 308–9).
58. Wharton, *A Backward Glance*, 189.
59. Jewett, *Letters of Sarah Orne Jewett*, 248, 249.
60. Cather, *The Selected Letters of Willa Cather*, 118.
61. Wharton, *A Backward Glance*, 293.
62. E. K. Brown, "Edith Wharton," 100.

63. Both Wharton's *The Letters of Edith Wharton* and Jewett's *Letters of Sarah Orne Jewett* include letters to Norton.
64. Wharton, *The Letters of Edith Wharton*, 65.
65. Carlin, "Cather's Jewett," 171, 177.
66. Carlin, "Cather's Jewett," 184–85.
67. In this study, Dorothy Canfield is referred to as such before her 1907 marriage to John Fisher; thereafter, as Dorothy Canfield Fisher.
68. Woodress, *Willa Cather*, 159.
69. Woodress, *Willa Cather*, 159–60; Lee, *Willa Cather*, 60. Cather's encounter with Housman is mentioned in Parker's recent *A. E. Housman*, but it is not recounted in biographies of Housman, including Richards's *Housman*, Haber's *A. E. Housman*, or Graves's *A. E. Housman*. It figured largely in Cather's memory but apparently not in his. Also contributing to the rift between Cather and Canfield was their conflict in 1905 over a story Cather had written, "The Profile," which included an unflattering depiction of a mutual friend. See Madigan, "Willa Cather in Paris."
70. Thacker, "'One Knows It Too Well to Know It Well,'" 306.
71. Quoted in R. W. B. Lewis, *Edith Wharton*, 440.
72. Lee, *Edith Wharton*, 409.
73. Benstock, *No Gifts from Chance*, 366; Lee, *Edith Wharton*, 614.
74. Wharton to Lapsley, December 8, 1929, Wharton MSS, Box 60, YCAL.
75. Wharton to Lapsley, May 1, 1936, Wharton MSS, Box 60, YCAL.
76. Twain and Cyril Clemens were "third cousins, twice removed" (Rasmussen, *Mark Twain*, 77).
77. Wharton to Lapsley, August 8, 1936, MSS 42, Box 60, YCAL.
78. Cather, *The Selected Letters of Willa Cather*, 491, 492; Stout, *A Calendar of the Letters of Willa Cather*, Letter #1323, 196.
79. Stout, *A Calendar of the Letters of Willa Cather*, Letter #1336, 199.
80. Both authors also took titles from a series of woodcuts made in the early 1500s, Hans Holbein the Younger's "Dance of Death," which dramatically show a skeletal Death figure stopping a wide range of people, from peasants to aristocrats, in the midst of life. Wharton took the title of her late story "After Holbein" from the series, as Cather did for her novel *Death Comes for the Archbishop* (Cather, "On *Death Comes for the Archbishop*," 11).
81. Benstock, *No Gifts from Chance*, 382.
82. Benstock, *No Gifts from Chance*, 383; Wharton, *The Letters of Edith Wharton*, 481.
83. Benstock and Lee refer to a story that Fitzgerald "threw himself at [Wharton's] feet in homage" in the Scribner's office in New York during her 1923 visit to the United States, but both mention that the story is undocumented (Benstock, *No Gifts from Chance*, 382; Lee, *Edith Wharton*, 604).
84. Woodress, *Willa Cather*, 351.

85. On Cather's and Akins's friendship, see Woodress, *Willa Cather*; see also Kreizenbeck, *Zoë Akins*; Benstock, *No Gifts from Chance*, 410.
86. Kreizenbeck, *Zoë Akins*, 181.
87. The online Calendar of Letters at the Willa Cather Archive shows six letters from Cather to Lewis, dating from 1921 through 1944. Wharton's *The Letters of Edith Wharton* includes three letters from Wharton to Lewis.
88. Wharton, *The Letters of Edith Wharton*, 445; Lee, *Edith Wharton*, 591; Benstock, *No Gifts from Chance*, 364.
89. Wharton, *The Letters of Edith Wharton*, 448.
90. Wharton, *The Letters of Edith Wharton*, 445.
91. S. Lewis, *The Man from Main Street*, 171.
92. S. Lewis, *The Man from Main Street*, 180, 266, 188.
93. Lee, *Edith Wharton*, 624.
94. Cather, *The Selected Letters of Willa Cather*, 302.
95. Cather, *The Selected Letters of Willa Cather*, 544.
96. Quoted in Nettels, "Edith Wharton's Correspondence with Zona Gale," 232.
97. Quoted in Nettels, "Edith Wharton's Correspondence with Zona Gale," 212.
98. Williams, *Not in Sisterhood*, 5.
99. Nettels, "Edith Wharton's Correspondence with Zona Gale," 209.
100. Cather, "The Novel Démeublé," 41–42.
101. Quoted in Nettels, "Edith Wharton's Correspondence with Zona Gale," 225.
102. On Edel's friendship with Brown, see Edel, "Editor's Foreword," xxx. On his friendship with Wharton, see his "Summers in an Age of Innocence."
103. The Dorothy Canfield Collection, UVM, includes two letters from Edel to Fisher (July 23, 1952, and July 31, 1956) indicating that he stayed with her at least once, in 1952. Edel also thanks Fisher extensively for her assistance in his acknowledgments in E. K. Brown, *Willa Cather* (344).
104. Lee, *Edith Wharton*, 471; Washington, *Dorothy Canfield Fisher*, 87–88, 89.
105. Washington, *Dorothy Canfield Fisher*, 85.
106. Quoted in Madigan, *Keeping Fires Night and Day*, 89–90.
107. Cather, "My First Novels," 93.
108. Quoted in O'Connor, *Willa Cather*, 38.
109. Quoted in O'Connor, *Willa Cather*, 40–41.
110. Wharton, *The House of Mirth*, 3.
111. Cather, *Alexander's Bridge*, 4.
112. James, "Daisy Miller," 8. On the narrative and thematic links among "Daisy Miller," *The House of Mirth*, and *A Lost Lady*, see Olin-Ammentorp, "Daisy, Lily, and Marian."
113. Wharton, *The House of Mirth*, 7.
114. Cather, *Alexander's Bridge*, 4–5.
115. Wharton, *The House of Mirth*, 14.

116. Waid, "Burying the Regional Mother," 43.
117. Sergeant, *Willa Cather*, 72–73.
118. Sergeant, *Willa Cather*, 73.
119. Sergeant papers, MSS 3, Box 11, YCAL.
120. Cather to Fisher, October 14 [1926], UVM.
121. Perkins to Cather, August 25, 1937, Princeton.
122. Cather to Perkins, n.d. [October 1937], Princeton.
123. Cather, *The Selected Letters of Willa Cather*, 647.
124. Harris, "Explanatory Notes," 726.
125. Wharton, *Ethan Frome*, 36–37.
126. Cather, *One of Ours*, 279.
127. Wharton, *Ethan Frome*, 185.
128. Wharton, *Ethan Frome*, 185.
129. Cather, *O Pioneers!*, 236.
130. Cather, *O Pioneers!*, 241.
131. Cather, *Lucy Gayheart*, 648; Wharton, *Ethan Frome*, 32.
132. Cather to Greenslet, October 23, 1916, Harvard.
133. Greenslet to Cather, October 27, 1916, Harvard.
134. Quoted in Rosowski, "Historical Essay," 213.
135. Cather, *The Selected Letters of Willa Cather*, 302.
136. Wharton, *The Letters of Edith Wharton*, 124.
137. Cather to Sherwood, May 14, 1929, NWCC.
138. Cather, *The Selected Letters of Willa Cather*, 416.
139. Cather, *The Selected Letters of Willa Cather*, 309.
140. Williams, *Not in Sisterhood*, 37.
141. Bloom, *The Anxiety of Influence*, 14.
142. Gilbert and Gubar, *The Madwoman in the Attic*, 49; emphasis in original.
143. Thacker, "'One Knows It Too Well to Know It Well,'" 306.
144. Quoted in Skaggs, *Axes*, xiii.
145. Byatt, "Telescope, Microscope, Window." Personal notes.
146. Cather, *The Professor's House*, 257.
147. Wharton, *The House of Mirth*, 255.
148. Wharton, *The House of Mirth*, 235–36; emphasis added.
149. Wharton, *The House of Mirth*, 413.
150. Cather, *Lucy Gayheart*, 26.
151. Cather, "Before Breakfast," 156.
152. Cather, "The Old Beauty," 18.
153. Cather, "The Old Beauty," 17, 21.
154. Cather, "The Old Beauty," 9.
155. Cather, "The Old Beauty," 24–25.
156. Cather, "The Old Beauty," 25; ellipsis in original.

157. Cather, "The Old Beauty," 52.
158. Wharton, *The Age of Innocence*, 347, 349.
159. Woodress, *Willa Cather*, 195.
160. Cather, *The Selected Letters of Willa Cather*, 666.
161. This analysis is based on the reviews included in Tuttleton, Lauer, and Murray, *Edith Wharton*, and O'Connor, *Willa Cather*.
162. Quoted in Tuttleton, Lauer, and Murray, *Edith Wharton*, 335.
163. Quoted in Tuttleton, Lauer, and Murray, *Edith Wharton*, 329.
164. Wharton, *The Letters of Edith Wharton*, 445.
165. Quoted in O'Connor, *Willa Cather*, 140.
166. Wharton to Lapsley, July 18, 1928, MSS 42, Box 60, YCAL.
167. Other than *A Lost Lady*, it is difficult to ascertain which Cather works Wharton might have read. Neither the Ramsden Catalog, which lists the books Wharton bequeathed to Colin Clark (Lee, *Edith Wharton*, 672), nor her library at The Mount (which is composed primarily of the Clark collection) includes any Cather titles. An undated inventory of the books in Wharton's library at her home in St. Brice does not include any Cather titles ("Liste des Livres à Jean-Marie," i.e., Pavillon Colombe, MSS 42, Box 50, YCAL). There does not appear to be any catalog of the volumes bequeathed to her godson William Tyler. These books, stored in London, were destroyed in the Blitz in 1940. But as they consisted primarily of volumes of "art, archaeology and history" (Lee, *Edith Wharton*, 671), it is unlikely that they included works by Cather.
168. Wharton, *A Backward Glance*, 206.
169. Powers, *Henry James and Edith Wharton*, 270.
170. Woodress, *Willa Cather*, 180.
171. Wharton, *The Writing of Fiction*, 109. See also her "A Reconsideration of Proust," 182.
172. Wharton, *The Letters of Edith Wharton*, 491; Lee, *Edith Wharton*, 182.
173. Lee, *Edith Wharton*, 620.
174. Wharton, *The Letters of Edith Wharton*, 491. As of April 2018, Wharton's phrase was still used to advertise Loos's *Gentlemen Prefer Blondes* on the Penguin and Liveright editions of the novel.
175. Wharton, *French Ways and Their Meaning*, 16.
176. Lee, *Edith Wharton*, 602; Woodress, *Willa Cather*, 339.
177. Weir, *Eleanor of Aquitaine*, notes that Berengaria, who was from the royal family of Navarre, journeyed extensively throughout her life, accompanying Richard on his crusade to Acre and visiting locations in current-day Italy, France, and England.

2. LAND OF LETTERS, KINGDOM OF ART

1. Wharton, *A Backward Glance*, 119.
2. Slote, *The Kingdom of Art*, 417.

3. Slote, "First Principles," 31.
4. Cather, *The World and the Parish*, 2:511; Wharton, *A Backward Glance*, 356.
5. Wharton, "Life and I," 188–89.
6. Rosowski, *The Voyage Perilous*, 22.
7. Quoted in Rosowski, *The Voyage Perilous*, 21.
8. Lee, *Edith Wharton*, 678, 86.
9. See Sullivan, "Willa Cather's German Connections," 320–21.
10. In *The Writing of Fiction*, Wharton calls "Balzac, Tolstoi, Thackeray, George Eliot" the "great writers" (76). She expresses admiration for Flaubert in "The Criticism of Fiction" (124), "Visibility in Fiction" (169), and elsewhere. On Cather's admiration of Balzac, see Cather, *Willa Cather in Europe*, 113–14; on Balzac and Flaubert, see Cather, "A Chance Meeting," 23–25.
11. Wharton, *French Ways and Their Meaning*, chapter 4.
12. Wharton, *The Writing of Fiction*, 36.
13. Cather, *Willa Cather in Europe*, 113, and Cather, "The Best Stories of Sarah Orne Jewett," 49.
14. Cather, *The Selected Letters of Willa Cather*, 613; Woodress, *Willa Cather*, 51.
15. Cather, *The Selected Letters of Willa Cather*, 362.
16. Cather, *The Selected Letters of Willa Cather*, 596.
17. Wharton, "Visibility in Fiction," 169.
18. Wharton, "Visibility in Fiction," 167, 169.
19. Quoted in Slote, *The Kingdom of Art*, 46, 48.
20. Benstock, *No Gifts from Chance*, 142.
21. E. K. Brown, "Edith Wharton," 95.
22. Wharton, *The Letters of Edith Wharton*, 91.
23. Wharton, *The Letters of Edith Wharton*, 88, 71.
24. Lee, *Edith Wharton*, 212–21.
25. E. K. Brown calls "The Marriage of Phaedra" the "most Jamesian" of the stories in *The Troll Garden* (*Willa Cather*, 117); Lee singles out "Flavia and Her Artists" (*Willa Cather*, 74).
26. E. K. Brown, *Willa Cather*, xix, 143.
27. Lee, *Willa Cather*, 208, 217.
28. Nettels, "Willa Cather and the Example of Henry James," 193.
29. Nettels, "Willa Cather and the Example of Henry James," 216.
30. Nettels, "Willa Cather and the Example of Henry James," 189.
31. John J. Murphy, "Kindred Spirits," 225, 227, 236.
32. Wharton, *A Backward Glance*, 190.
33. Nettels, "Willa Cather and the Example of Henry James," 214. See also John J. Murphy, "Kindred Spirits," 235, 236.
34. On the influence of Turgenev, see Edel, *Henry James*, 237–38. On the influence of the French novelists, see Powers, *Henry James and the Naturalist Movement*.

35. Powers, *Henry James and the Naturalist Movement*, 20–23, 21.
36. Powers, *Henry James and the Naturalist Movement*, 40.
37. Wharton, "Permanent Values in Fiction," 175.
38. Cather, "The Novel Démeublé," 40.
39. Cather, "Light on Adobe Walls," 125.
40. James, "The Art of Fiction," 55, 53, 58.
41. James, "The Art of Fiction," 58.
42. Powers, *Henry James and the Naturalist Movement*, 26.
43. Cather, "On the Art of Fiction," 101.
44. Cather, "On the Art of Fiction," 102.
45. Cather, "The Novel Démeublé," 36.
46. Cather, "The Novel Démeublé," 36–37.
47. Wharton, *The Writing of Fiction*, 11.
48. Wharton, *The Writing of Fiction*, 14.
49. Cather, "The Novel Démeublé," 39–40; cf. Wharton, "Visibility in Fiction," 168.
50. Wharton, *The Writing of Fiction*, 42.
51. Wharton, *The Writing of Fiction*, 71.
52. Cather, "The Novel Démeublé." 41–42.
53. Cather, "The Novel Démeublé," 43.
54. Cather, *The World and the Parish*, 1:479.
55. Wharton, *The Writing of Fiction*, 61–62.
56. Cather, "The Novel Démeublé," 36.
57. Wharton, *The Writing of Fiction*, 58, 39.
58. Cather, "The Best Stories of Sarah Orne Jewett," 47, 48.
59. Wharton, *The Writing of Fiction*, 43.
60. Wharton, *The Writing of Fiction*, 19; cf. 117.
61. Wharton, "Tendencies in Modern Fiction," 173.
62. Wharton, "Tendencies in Modern Fiction," 173.
63. Quoted in Bohlke, *Willa Cather in Person*, 78.
64. Quoted in Bohlke, *Willa Cather in Person*, 78.
65. Quoted in Bohlke, *Willa Cather in Person*, 78.
66. Quoted in Nettels, "Edith Wharton's Correspondence with Zona Gale," 213.
67. Quoted in Nettels, "Edith Wharton's Correspondence with Zona Gale," 214.
68. Cather, *The Selected Letters of Willa Cather*, 666.
69. Wharton, *The Letters of Edith Wharton*, 461.
70. Wharton, *The Writing of Fiction*, 50.
71. Wharton, *The Writing of Fiction*, 48.
72. Wharton, *The Writing of Fiction*, 50.
73. Cather, "The Novel Démeublé," 40.
74. Cather, "The Novel Démeublé," 42.
75. Wharton, *The Writing of Fiction*, 13.

76. Wharton, *The Writing of Fiction*, 50. Wharton's relationship to modernism has been much discussed. For a good summary, see Haytock, "Modernism."
77. Wharton, *The Letters of Edith Wharton*, 451.
78. Cather, *The Selected Letters of Willa Cather*, 321.
79. Swift, "Cather, Freudianism, and Freud."
80. Quoted in Bohlke, *Willa Cather in Person*, 58. Cather was interested enough in Freudian principles applied to literature that she read one book on the topic, Joseph Collins's 1923 *The Doctor Looks at Literature* (Rosowski, *The Voyage Perilous*, 142). Cather mentions Collins's book in her letter of February 27, 1924 (Cather, *The Selected Letters of Willa Cather*, 355).
81. Cather, "On *Death Comes for the Archbishop*," 9.
82. Wharton, *The Writing of Fiction*, 70.
83. Kim, "Edith Wharton and Epiphany," 152.
84. Millington, "Where Is Cather's Quebec?," 38, and Millington, "Willa Cather's Two Modernisms," 52.
85. Wharton, *A Backward Glance*, 48; Cather, "The Novel Démeublé," 35, and Cather, "Escapism," 28.
86. For parodies of Wharton as the lady with the lorgnette, see Abel Faivre's rather cruel cartoon of Wharton visiting the front during World War I (Olin-Ammentorp, *Edith Wharton's Writings from the Great War*, 17) and Sergeant's word portrait of Wharton, quoted in chapter 1.
87. E. K. Brown, *Willa Cather*, 68.
88. Showalter, *A Jury of Her Peers*, 270.
89. Cather, *The World and the Parish*, 1:275, 276–77.
90. Wharton, *A Backward Glance*, 65.
91. Cather, *The World and the Parish*, 1:276.
92. Wharton, *A Backward Glance*, 65–66.
93. Wharton, *A Backward Glance*, 66–67.
94. Eliot, "Silly Novels by Lady Novelists," 2.
95. Eliot, "Silly Novels by Lady Novelists," 3.
96. Nettels, *Language and Gender in American Fiction*, 6.
97. Nettels, *Language and Gender in American Fiction*, 6.
98. Nettels, *Language and Gender in American Fiction*, 6, 7; emphasis in original.
99. Nettels, *Language and Gender in American Fiction*, 7.
100. Williams, *Not in Sisterhood*, 2.
101. Showalter, *A Jury of Her Peers*, 271.
102. Lee, *Willa Cather*, 30.
103. Wharton, *A Backward Glance*, 44.
104. Wharton, *A Backward Glance*, 29.
105. Wharton, *A Backward Glance*, 29–30.
106. Wharton, *A Backward Glance*, 44.

107. Wharton, "Life and I," 192.
108. Cather, *The Selected Letters of Willa Cather*, 88.
109. Quoted in Bohlke, *Willa Cather in Person*, 10.
110. Wharton, *A Backward Glance*, 44–45.
111. Wharton, "Life and I," 202.
112. Cather, *The Selected Letters of Willa Cather*, 25.
113. Cather, *The Selected Letters of Willa Cather*, 25.
114. Cather, *The Selected Letters of Willa Cather*, 27.
115. Cather, *The Selected Letters of Willa Cather*, 28.
116. Cather, *The Selected Letters of Willa Cather*, 29.
117. Woodress, *Willa Cather*, 117.
118. Wharton, "Mrs. Manstey's View," 2.
119. Wharton, "Mrs. Manstey's View," 2.
120. Wharton, "Mrs. Manstey's View," 3.
121. Wharton, "Mrs. Manstey's View," 11.
122. Wharton, "Mrs. Manstey's View," 11.
123. Wharton, "Friends," 197.
124. Wharton, "Friends," 197.
125. Wharton, "Friends," 197.
126. Wharton, "Friends," 197–98.
127. Wegener notes the consonance of "Schoolroom Decoration" and *The Decoration of Houses* (*Edith Wharton*, 61).
128. Wharton, "Schoolroom Decoration," 57–58.
129. Wharton, "Schoolroom Decoration," 58.
130. Wharton, "Schoolroom Decoration," 59.
131. Cather, "A Wagner Matinée," 246–47.
132. Cather, "The Sculptor's Funeral," 254.
133. Cather, "The Sculptor's Funeral," 267.
134. Cather, "The Sculptor's Funeral," 263, 262.
135. Woodress, "Historical Essay," 373.
136. Woodress, *Willa Cather*, 156.
137. Goldman-Price, *My Dear Governess*, 72.
138. Cather, *The Selected Letters of Willa Cather*, 490.
139. Cather, *The Selected Letters of Willa Cather*, 490.
140. Goldman-Price, *My Dear Governess*, 65.
141. Goldman-Price, *My Dear Governess*, 51.
142. Goldman-Price, *My Dear Governess*, 51.
143. Wharton, *The Letters of Edith Wharton*, 100.
144. Wharton, *The Letters of Edith Wharton*, 483.
145. Cather, *The Selected Letters of Willa Cather*, 63.
146. Cather, *The Selected Letters of Willa Cather*, 63.

147. Cather, *The Selected Letters of Willa Cather*, 110.
148. Cather, *The Selected Letters of Willa Cather*, 429.
149. Wharton, *The House of Mirth*, 314–15.
150. Cather, *The Professor's House*, 252.
151. Cather, *The Selected Letters of Willa Cather*, 20.
152. Cather, *The Selected Letters of Willa Cather*, 169.
153. Wharton, *The Letters of Edith Wharton*, 59.
154. Cather, "My First Novels," 93.
155. Benstock, *No Gifts from Chance*, 124; Lee, *Edith Wharton*, 100.
156. Quoted in Stouck, "Historical Essay," 283.
157. Quoted in Powers, *Henry James and Edith Wharton*, 34.
158. Jewett, *Letters of Sarah Orne Jewett*, 248.
159. S. Lewis, "The American Scene in Fiction," 142.
160. Cather, *Lucy Gayheart*, 26–27.
161. Cather, *Lucy Gayheart*, 27.
162. Wharton, *The Age of Innocence*, 358.
163. Wharton, *The Age of Innocence*, 101.
164. Cather, *Lucy Gayheart*, 175–76.
165. Wharton, *The Age of Innocence*, 335.
166. Cather, "Old Mrs. Harris," 112.
167. Warf and Arias, *The Spatial Turn*, 1; emphasis in original.

3. NEW YORK CITY

1. See Wharton, *A Backward Glance*, 88; Benstock, *No Gifts from Chance*, 44; Lee, *Edith Wharton*, 61.
2. Lee, *Edith Wharton*, 128.
3. Keep, *History of the New York Society Library*, 369.
4. Wharton's father, George Frederic Jones, is listed as a member in the *New York Society Library List of Shareholders*, n.p., 1914.
5. King, *Books and People*, 208.
6. Skaggs, "Introduction," 14; emphasis in original.
7. John J. Murphy, "From Cornfield to the Big Apple Orchard," 21.
8. Lee, *Edith Wharton*, 60.
9. Wharton, *New Year's Day*, 9.
10. Benstock, *No Gifts from Chance*, 44; see also Wharton's letter from the Washington Square address (Goldman-Price, *My Dear Governess*, 61). Woodress, *Willa Cather*, 190.
11. Woodress, *Willa Cather*, 190.
12. See Bender, *The Unfinished City*, 6–7, and Folpe, *It Happened on Washington Square*, 6.
13. Wharton, *New Year's Day*, 6.

14. Wharton, *The Age of Innocence*, 50, 27.
15. For Wharton's chronology, see Emsley, "Appendix A," 410–11.
16. Folpe, *It Happened on Washington Square*, 5.
17. Cather, "Coming, Aphrodite!," 9, 11.
18. Cather, "Coming, Aphrodite!," 24.
19. Cather, "Coming, Aphrodite!," 25.
20. Wharton, *The House of Mirth*, 14, 426.
21. Wharton, *The House of Mirth*, 87.
22. Wharton, *The House of Mirth*, 488–89.
23. Cather, "Paul's Case," 224; Cather, *My Mortal Enemy*, 551.
24. Lee, *Edith Wharton*, 16.
25. Wharton, *The House of Mirth*, 258; Cather, *My Mortal Enemy*, 552.
26. Woodress, *Willa Cather*, 186; R. W. B. Lewis, *Edith Wharton*, 173.
27. Lee, *Edith Wharton*, 207.
28. Wharton, *A Backward Glance*, 1–3.
29. Goldman-Price, *My Dear Governess*, 113.
30. Goldman-Price, *My Dear Governess*, 114.
31. Wharton, *The Letters of Edith Wharton*, 313.
32. Wharton, *The Letters of Edith Wharton*, 222.
33. Goldman-Price, *My Dear Governess*, 152.
34. Woodress, *Willa Cather*, 189.
35. Cather, *The Selected Letters of Willa Cather*, 102; see Woodress, *Willa Cather*, 189. See also John J. Murphy, "From Cornfield to the Big Apple Orchard," 21.
36. E. Lewis, *Willa Cather Living*, 74.
37. Steffensen-Bruce, *Marble Palaces*, 12.
38. Steffensen-Bruce, *Marble Palaces*, 12, 13.
39. Steffensen-Bruce, *Marble Palaces*, 12.
40. Brownell, *French Traits*, 291.
41. The Met, http://www.metmuseum.org/about-the-museum/history-of-the-museum/main-building.
42. Lee, *Edith Wharton*, 22.
43. Cather, *My Mortal Enemy*, 544.
44. Quoted in Tuttleton, Lauer, and Murray, *Edith Wharton*, 112, 119.
45. Ammons, *Edith Wharton's Argument with America*, 34.
46. Robinson, "The Traffic in Women"; Duvall, "The Futile and the Dingy," 161.
47. Quoted in Tuttleton, Lauer, and Murray, *Edith Wharton*, 124, 127.
48. Quoted in Tuttleton, Lauer, and Murray, *Edith Wharton*, 115.
49. Robinson, "The Traffic in Women," 355.
50. Wharton, *The House of Mirth*, 303.
51. Auchincloss, "Edith Wharton and Her New Yorks," 35.
52. Quoted in O'Connor, *Willa Cather*, 34, 32.

53. Quoted in O'Connor, *Willa Cather*, 100–101, 115.
54. Quoted in O'Connor, *Willa Cather*, 99, 105.
55. Quoted in O'Connor, *Willa Cather*, 104–5.
56. Summers, "'A Losing Game in the End,'" 110–11; Carpenter, "Why Willa Cather Revised 'Paul's Case,'" 597, 599.
57. Stout, "Between Two Wars," 95; Porter, "Life Is Very Simple," 152.
58. Ku, "'A Boy under Ban of Suspension,'" 84.
59. O'Brien, *Willa Cather*, 283.
60. Ammons, *Edith Wharton's Argument with America*, 3.
61. Wharton, "Schoolroom Decoration," 58–59.
62. Wharton, *The Decoration of Houses*, 173.
63. Wharton, *The Decoration of Houses*, 174.
64. Wharton, *The Letters of Edith Wharton*, 84.
65. On Wharton's interest in Emerson, see Singley, *Edith Wharton*, esp. 19–20, 23.
66. Emerson, "The Rhodora."
67. Sergeant, *Willa Cather*, 67; cf. Woodress, *Willa Cather*, 180.
68. Cather, "A Wagner Matinée," 244.
69. Cather, "A Gold Slipper," 139.
70. Cather, "A Gold Slipper," 148.
71. Cather, "A Gold Slipper," 161.
72. Rosowski, *The Voyage Perilous*, x.
73. S. Lewis, *The Man from Main Street*, 5.
74. Lee, *Edith Wharton*, 22.
75. Wharton, *A Backward Glance*, 6.
76. See Marchand, "Object Lessons," 8.
77. Wharton to Bernard Berenson, February 20, 1921, BB; Cather, *The Selected Letters of Willa Cather*, 375.
78. Glennon, "The Custom of Main Street," 49.
79. Singley, *Edith Wharton*, 21, 22.
80. Singley, *Edith Wharton*, 25.
81. Slote, "First Principles," 43, 44.
82. Cather, "Paul's Case," 215.
83. Wharton, *The Letters of Edith Wharton*, 99.
84. Lee, *Edith Wharton*, 96.
85. Goldman-Price, *My Dear Governess*, 114.
86. Cather, *My Mortal Enemy*, 50.
87. Cather, *My Mortal Enemy*, 51.
88. Cather, "Escapism," 27.
89. Quoted in Steffensen-Bruce, *Marble Palaces*, 95.
90. Pater, "Conclusion," 840.
91. Carpenter, "Why Willa Cather Revised 'Paul's Case,'" 591.

92. Nehamas, *Only a Promise of Beauty*, 81, 77, 138.
93. Abrams's note; selections from Arnold, *Culture and Anarchy*, Norton Anthology of English Literature, 1430.
94. M. Arnold, *Culture and Anarchy*, 110.
95. E. K. Brown, *Willa Cather*, 77; Moorhead, quoted in E. K. Brown, *Willa Cather*, 77.
96. Lears, "From Salvation to Self-Realization," 3.
97. Wharton, *The House of Mirth*, 7.
98. Cather, "Paul's Case," 209, 211.
99. Wharton, *The House of Mirth*, 176.
100. Wharton, *The House of Mirth*, 110.
101. Wharton, *The House of Mirth*, 528.
102. Wharton, *The House of Mirth*, 528.
103. Wharton, *The House of Mirth*, 487.
104. Cather, "Paul's Case," 209.
105. Cather, "Paul's Case," 208.
106. Cather, "Paul's Case," 209.
107. Cather, "Paul's Case," 214.
108. Cather, "Paul's Case," 221–22.
109. Wharton, *The House of Mirth*, 512–13.
110. Wolff, *A Feast of Words*, 110–11, 117.
111. R. W. B. Lewis, *Edith Wharton*, 155; see Duvall, "The Futile and the Dingy."
112. Cather, "Paul's Case," 233; Wharton, *The House of Mirth*, 242.
113. Cather, "Paul's Case," 224.
114. Cather, "Paul's Case," 222, 228.
115. Cather, "Paul's Case," 223.
116. Cather, "Paul's Case," 228.
117. Cather, "Paul's Case," 224.
118. Wharton, *The House of Mirth*, 39–40.
119. Wasserman, "Is 'Paul's Case' a Case?," 125.
120. Cather, "Paul's Case," 221.
121. Edel, "Homage to Willa Cather," 202.
122. Page, "The Theatricality of 'Paul's Case,'" 555, 556.
123. Cather, "Paul's Case," 226, 227.
124. Cather, *Lucy Gayheart*, 100.
125. Wharton, *The House of Mirth*, 211. On Lily's *tableau*, see also Orlando, *Edith Wharton and the Visual Arts*, 59–74.
126. Wharton, *The House of Mirth*, 216.
127. Gubar, "'The Blank Page' and Issues of Female Creativity," 248; Wharton, *The House of Mirth*, 216.
128. Wharton, *The House of Mirth*, 220.

129. Wharton, *The House of Mirth*, 39.
130. Wharton, *The House of Mirth*, 412.
131. Wharton, *The House of Mirth*, 35.
132. Wharton, *The Custom of the Country*, 207.
133. Wharton, *A Backward Glance*, 6.
134. Wharton, *The Custom of the Country*, 254; Cather, "Paul's Case," 212.
135. Cather, "Paul's Case," 214.
136. Cather, "Paul's Case," 214.
137. Thoreau, *Walden*, 3.
138. On business, culture, and gender, see Banta, "Men, Women, and the American Way," esp. 22–24.
139. James, *The American Scene*, 64–65.
140. James, *The American Scene*, 65.
141. Wharton, *The House of Mirth*, 128.
142. Cather, "Paul's Case," 213.
143. Wharton, *The House of Mirth*, 86.
144. Wharton, *The House of Mirth*, 86.
145. See, for instance, Wolff, *A Feast of Words*, 125; Dimock, "Debasing Exchange."
146. Nehamas, *Only a Promise of Beauty*, 91.
147. Nehamas, *Only a Promise of Beauty*, 62–63.
148. Nehamas, *Only a Promise of Beauty*, 63; emphasis added.
149. Wharton, *The House of Mirth*, 464, 474.
150. Wharton, *The House of Mirth*, 515.
151. Cather, "Paul's Case," 229–30.
152. Cather, "Paul's Case," 233.
153. Cather, "Paul's Case," 234.
154. Cather, "Paul's Case," 234.
155. Wharton, *The House of Mirth*, 38.
156. Wharton, *The House of Mirth*, 77.
157. Wharton, *The House of Mirth*, 114.
158. Wharton, *The Letters of Edith Wharton*, 177.
159. Pater, "Conclusion," 837.
160. Cather, *The Selected Letters of Willa Cather*, 614.
161. Wharton, *A Backward Glance*, 207.
162. Nehamas, *Only a Promise of Beauty*, 132.
163. Wharton, *The House of Mirth*, 10.
164. On Lily Bart's surname suggesting "barter," see, for instance, Ammons, *Edith Wharton's Argument with America*, 34.
165. Lee, *Willa Cather*, 46.
166. Banta, "Introduction," vii.
167. Wharton, *The House of Mirth*, 9; Cather, "Paul's Case," 234.

168. Wasserman, "Is 'Paul's Case' a Case?," 126. Singley also connects Lily and Bartleby to "a long line of naysayers" (*Edith Wharton*, 73).
169. Edel, "Homage to Willa Cather," 202.
170. Wharton, *The Letters of Edith Wharton*, 388.
171. Cather, "Paul's Case," 206.
172. Cather, *The Selected Letters of Willa Cather*, 614.
173. Cather, *The Selected Letters of Willa Cather*, 614.
174. Cather, "Coming, Aphrodite!," 61.
175. Wharton, *A Son at the Front*, 45.
176. Cather, "Coming, Aphrodite!," 60, 61.
177. Wharton, *A Son at the Front*, 45.
178. Wharton, *The House of Mirth*, 108.
179. Cather, "Coming, Aphrodite!," 61.
180. Cather, "Coming, Aphrodite!," 60; Wharton, *A Son at the Front*, 45.
181. Cather, "Coming, Aphrodite!," 61.
182. Cather, "Coming, Aphrodite!," 61.
183. Cather, "Coming, Aphrodite!," 62.
184. Wharton, *A Son at the Front*, 46.
185. Wharton, *A Son at the Front*, 45.
186. Wharton, *A Son at the Front*, 5.
187. Cather, "Coming, Aphrodite!," 10.
188. For Daudet's influence on Wharton, see Lee, *Edith Wharton*, 306, 576; for Daudet's influence on Cather, see Woodress, *Willa Cather*, esp. 127, and Durrans, *The Influence of French Culture on Willa Cather*.
189. Daudet, *Artists' Wives*, 5.
190. Daudet, *Artists' Wives*, 8–9.
191. Cather, "Coming, Aphrodite!," 5–6.
192. Wharton, *A Son at the Front*, 43.
193. Wharton, *A Son at the Front*, 43–44.
194. Wharton, *A Son at the Front*, 44.
195. Wharton, *A Son at the Front*, 44.
196. Wharton, *The Age of Innocence*, 68.
197. Wharton, *The Age of Innocence*, 71.
198. Wharton, *The Age of Innocence*, 201.
199. Wharton, *False Dawn*, 135, 143.
200. Cather, *One of Ours*, 552.

4. THE WEST

1. Benstock, *No Gifts from Chance*, 155.
2. R. W. B. Lewis, *Edith Wharton*, 172.
3. Benstock, *No Gifts from Chance*, 155; Lee, *Edith Wharton*, 206.

4. R. W. B. Lewis, *Edith Wharton*, 172.
5. Quoted in Lee, *Edith Wharton*, 206.
6. Totten, "Imagining the American West," 3, 5.
7. Wharton, *The Marne*, 60–61.
8. Wharton, *The Custom of the Country*, 147.
9. Wharton, *The Marne*, 60.
10. The reviewer for *The Nation* (October 30, 1913) states that Apex City is in Arizona; this is "corrected" to "Indiana" by Tuttleton, Lauer, and Murray (*Edith Wharton*, 208). R. W. B. Lewis states that Apex is in Kansas (*Edith Wharton*, 348); Benstock locates it in Illinois (*No Gifts from Chance*, 284), while Baym et al., the editors of *The Norton Anthology of American Literature, Shorter 8th Ed.*, vol. 2, place Apex in Ohio (499). It is impossible to determine which state Apex City is in, although it is clearly east of Nebraska. Moffatt mentions that after a train ride, he and Undine were "made one at Opake, Nebraska"; Undine recalls riding the "Limited" as it "plunged into the sunset," clearly going west (Wharton, *The Custom of the Country*, 467, 556). Thus Iowa, Illinois, Indiana, and Ohio are all possibilities. Wharton's "Chronology" for *The Custom of the Country* does not mention which state Apex City is in (Emsley, "Appendix A," 410–15).
11. See Griffith, *The Color of Democracy*, 167.
12. S. Lewis, "The American Scene in Fiction," 142.
13. S. Lewis, "The American Scene in Fiction," 143.
14. Cather, *The Selected Letters of Willa Cather*, 546.
15. Cather, *The Selected Letters of Willa Cather*, 547.
16. Cather, *The Selected Letters of Willa Cather*, 208.
17. Reed, *Harold von Schmidt Draws and Paints the Old West*, 1–30.
18. Quoted in O'Connor, *Willa Cather*, 89.
19. Cather, "My First Novels," 94.
20. Cather, "My First Novels," 94.
21. Griffith, *The Color of Democracy*, 166.
22. Boardman, "Western American Literature and the Canon," 45.
23. "Bunner Sisters" was written in 1893 but not published until 1916 (Benstock, *No Gifts from Chance*, 69–70).
24. Wharton, "Bunner Sisters," 215, 214.
25. Wharton, *Ethan Frome*, 142, 143.
26. Wharton, *Ethan Frome*, 143.
27. Wharton, *The House of Mirth*, 258, 379.
28. Wharton, *The House of Mirth*, 440.
29. Moseley, "Explanatory Notes," 696–97.
30. See Olin-Ammentorp, "Thea at the Art Institute."
31. Moore, "Chicago's Cliff Dwellers and *The Song of the Lark*," 107–8.

32. Rich, "Chauncey McCormick," 62, 66.
33. See also Totten, "Imagining the American West," 6.
34. Thacker, *The Great Prairie Fact and the Literary Imagination*, 146, 147.
35. Cather, *The Selected Letters of Willa Cather*, 150.
36. Cather, *The Selected Letters of Willa Cather*, 150.
37. Cather, *The Selected Letters of Willa Cather*, 414
38. Cather, *My Mortal Enemy*, 559.
39. See Egli, "Early Western Literary Women": "Paradoxically, while there was an overwhelming national enthusiasm for western expansion and a desire for images of the life in the West, there was . . . a widening chasm between East and West" (83). Egli ties this partly to "the literature each was producing" (83).
40. Quoted in B. Brown, "Reading the West," 3.
41. B. Brown, "Reading the West," 4.
42. Turner, "The Significance of the Frontier," 39.
43. Turner, "The Significance of the Frontier," 39.
44. Cowley, "Foreword," 9, 10.
45. Cowley, "Foreword," 12, 13.
46. Rahv, "Paleface and Redskin," 1.
47. Rahv, "Paleface and Redskin," 2.
48. Rahv, "Paleface and Redskin," 2.
49. See Fetterley and Pryce, *Writing Out of Place*, and Howard, *Form and History in American Literary Naturalism*.
50. Howells, quoted in Campbell, *Resisting Regionalism*, 3.
51. Campbell, *Resisting Regionalism*, 1.
52. Norris, quoted in Campbell, *Resisting Regionalism*, 1.
53. Norris, "A Plea for Romantic Fiction," 76.
54. For an astute reading of Wharton's relationship to the naturalists, see chapter 6 in Campbell, *Resisting Regionalism*. See also Pizer's landmark essay "The Naturalism of Edith Wharton's *House of Mirth*."
55. Quoted in Tuttleton, Lauer, and Murray, *Edith Wharton*, 295.
56. Quoted in O'Connor, *Willa Cather*, 55.
57. Quoted in O'Connor, *Willa Cather*, 55.
58. Quoted in O'Connor, *Willa Cather*, 88–89.
59. Quoted in O'Connor, *Willa Cather*, 81.
60. Quoted in O'Connor, *Willa Cather*, 81.
61. Quoted in O'Connor, *Willa Cather*, 84.
62. Quoted in O'Connor, *Willa Cather*, 96.
63. Quoted in O'Connor, *Willa Cather*, 91.
64. Woolf, "American Fiction," 111.
65. James, *Hawthorne*, 34.
66. Woolf, "American Fiction," 112.

67. Woolf, "American Fiction," 117.
68. Quoted in Lee, *Edith Wharton*, 611.
69. Wharton, "The Great American Novel," 152.
70. Wharton, "Tendencies in Modern Fiction," 173.
71. Wharton, "Tendencies in Modern Fiction," 172.
72. Wharton, "Tendencies in Modern Fiction," 151.
73. Cather, *The Selected Letters of Willa Cather*, 613.
74. Wharton, *The Selected Letters of Willa Cather*, 91.
75. Mitchell, *Westerns*, 95.
76. Wharton to Lapsley, February 2, 1929, MSS 42, Box 60, F 1719; quotations are from the editor's letter that Wharton forwarded to Lapsley.
77. Wharton, "Writing a War Story," 248; final ellipsis in the original.
78. Wharton, *The Letters of Edith Wharton*, 577.
79. Wharton, *The Letters of Edith Wharton*, 577.
80. Cather, "My First Novels," 93.
81. Cather, *The Selected Letters of Willa Cather*, 355–56.
82. Cather, *The Selected Letters of Willa Cather*, 356.
83. Egli, "Early Western Literary Women," 83.
84. Stout, *Picturing a Different West*, 4–24.
85. Cather, *The Selected Letters of Willa Cather*, 183.
86. Cather, *The Selected Letters of Willa Cather*, 272.
87. Quoted in O'Connor, *Willa Cather*, 238.
88. Cather, *The Selected Letters of Willa Cather*, 211.
89. Quoted in Tuttleton, Lauer, and Murray, *Edith Wharton*, 204, 208, 210.
90. Wilson, "Justice to Edith Wharton," 24.
91. R. W. B. Lewis, *Edith Wharton*, 350.
92. Wharton, *The Custom of the Country*, 208.
93. Wolff, *A Feast of Words*, 237.
94. Cather, *The Song of the Lark*, 196.
95. Quoted in O'Connor, *Willa Cather*, 61–62, 63.
96. Quoted in O'Connor, *Willa Cather*, 62.
97. Wharton, "The Great American Novel," 152.
98. See, for instance, Wharton, *The Writing of Fiction*, 36.
99. Cather, "The Best Stories of Sarah Orne Jewett," 49.
100. Wharton, *A Backward Glance*, 55.
101. Cather, "Nebraska," 238.
102. Cather, "Nebraska," 238.
103. Wharton, *A Backward Glance*, 6.
104. See, for instance, Ammons, *Edith Wharton's Argument with America*, 107; Wolff, *A Feast of Words*, 224, 230; Benstock, *No Gifts from Chance*, 283.
105. Benstock, *No Gifts from Chance*, 283.

106. Wharton, *A Backward Glance*, 55; Cather, "Nebraska," 238.
107. Wharton, *A Backward Glance*, 41; Cather, *The World and the Parish*, 1:336.
108. Bohlke, *Willa Cather in Person*, 3, 5.
109. Wharton, *A Backward Glance*, 53.
110. Goldman-Price, *My Dear Governess*, 32, 100, 150, 157.
111. Reynolds, "Willa Cather's Case," 90.
112. Adams, *The Education of Henry Adams*, 1067.
113. *The Virginian*, quoted in Mitchell, *Westerns*, 105.
114. Mitchell, *Westerns*, 105.
115. Rahv, "Paleface and Redskin," 1.
116. Rosowski, *The Voyage Perilous*, 69.
117. "Why, *everything!*" (*The Custom of the Country*, 96); "I only want impossible things" (*The Song of the Lark*, 269); "young people" (*The Song of the Lark*, 241); they "will always get on better with men" (*The Song of the Lark*, 307); "I can't wait" (*The Song of the Lark*, 402); "My child" (*The Custom of the Country*, 96); "She is very much interested" (*The Song of the Lark*, 307); "an ulterior motive" (*The Song of the Lark*, 348).
118. Adams, *The Education of Henry Adams*, 1070.
119. Cather, *The Song of the Lark*, 307, 452.
120. Adams, *The Education of Henry Adams*, 1070, 1071.
121. Cather, "Coming, Aphrodite!," 37.
122. Rosowski, *The Voyage Perilous*, 69.
123. Cather, *The Song of the Lark*, 517–18.
124. Love, *New Americans*, 131.
125. Cather, *The Song of the Lark*, 499, 501.
126. Cather, "Coming, Aphrodite!," 74.
127. Wharton, *The Custom of the Country*, 53.
128. Wharton, *The Custom of the Country*, 57.
129. Wharton, *The Custom of the Country*, 54.
130. Wharton, *The Custom of the Country*, 286.
131. Wharton, *The Custom of the Country*, 52, 53.
132. Wharton, *The Custom of the Country*, 55, 56.
133. James, "Daisy Miller," 19.
134. Cather, *The Song of the Lark*, 75.
135. Cather, *The Song of the Lark*, 71.
136. Cather, *The Song of the Lark*, 71.
137. Cather, *The Song of the Lark*, 293.
138. Cather, *The Song of the Lark*, 476.
139. Cather, *The Song of the Lark*, 476.
140. Wharton, *The Custom of the Country*, 184; emphasis in original.
141. Wharton, *The Custom of the Country*, 184.

142. Cather, *The Song of the Lark*, 349–50.
143. Trilling, "The Princess Casamassima," 58. See also Olin-Ammentorp, "Girls from the Provinces."
144. Trilling, "The Princess Casamassima," 59.
145. Trilling, "The Princess Casamassima," 59.
146. Trilling, "The Princess Casamassima," 60.
147. Trilling, "The Princess Casamassima," 60.
148. Cather, *The Song of the Lark*, 44.
149. Trilling, "The Princess Casamassima," 59.
150. Wharton, *The Custom of the Country*, 57.
151. Wharton, *The Custom of the Country*, 51; emphasis in original.
152. Cather, *The Song of the Lark*, 195.
153. Cather, *The Song of the Lark*, 182.
154. Wharton, *The Custom of the Country*, 34–35, 18.
155. Wharton, *The Custom of the Country*, 31–32, 9.
156. Wharton, *The Custom of the Country*, 5, 7.
157. Wharton, *The Custom of the Country*, 65; emphasis in original.
158. Cather, *The Song of the Lark*, 242.
159. Love, *New Americans*, 109.
160. Cather, *The Song of the Lark*, 331.
161. Wharton, *The Custom of the Country*, 123.
162. Wharton, *A Backward Glance*, 6.
163. Wharton, *A Backward Glance*, 6.
164. Wharton, *The Custom of the Country*, 558.
165. Wharton, *The Custom of the Country*, 561.
166. Wharton, *The Custom of the Country*, 545.
167. Love, *New Americans*, 109.
168. Love, *New Americans*, 110.
169. Cather, *The Song of the Lark*, 503.
170. Cather, *The Song of the Lark*, 505.
171. Wharton, *The Custom of the Country*, 548, 549.
172. Wharton, *The Custom of the Country*, 550.
173. Wharton, *The Custom of the Country*, 550.
174. Wharton, *The Custom of the Country*, 552.
175. Wharton, *The Custom of the Country*, 554.
176. Wharton, *The Custom of the Country*, 254.
177. Griffith, *The Color of Democracy*, 45.
178. Wharton, *The Custom of the Country*, 455.
179. Cather, *The Song of the Lark*, 531–32.
180. Cather, *The Song of the Lark*, 532.
181. Cather, *The Song of the Lark*, 539.

182. Cather, *The Song of the Lark*, 538.
183. Cather, *The Song of the Lark*, 618; emphasis added.
184. Cather, *The Song of the Lark*, 618.
185. Wharton, *The Glimpses of the Moon*, 181.
186. Wharton, *The Glimpses of the Moon*, 70.
187. Wharton, *The Glimpses of the Moon*, 71.
188. Lee, *Edith Wharton*, 613.
189. Wharton, *The Glimpses of the Moon*, 58.
190. Wharton, *The Glimpses of the Moon*, 58. Wharton's use of the term "over-education" deserves an essay in itself.
191. Wharton, *The Glimpses of the Moon*, 238–39.
192. Wharton, *The Glimpses of the Moon*, 290, 292.
193. Wharton, *The Glimpses of the Moon*, 290.
194. Wharton, *The Glimpses of the Moon*, 290.
195. Wharton, *Hudson River Bracketed*, 16, 28.
196. Wharton, *Hudson River Bracketed*, 4.
197. Lee, *Edith Wharton*, 625.
198. Wharton, *Hudson River Bracketed*, 6.
199. Wharton, *Hudson River Bracketed*, 6.
200. Wharton, *Hudson River Bracketed*, 7.
201. Bratton, *Yrs. Ever Affly*, 117, 33.
202. Quoted in Tuttleton, Lauer, and Murray, *Edith Wharton*, 494.
203. Wharton, *Hudson River Bracketed*, 17.
204. Wharton, *Hudson River Bracketed*, 15.
205. Wharton, *Hudson River Bracketed*, 17.
206. Wharton, *Hudson River Bracketed*, 12.
207. Quoted in Tuttleton, Lauer, and Murray, *Edith Wharton*, 467, 470.
208. Haytock, *Edith Wharton and the Conversations of Literary Modernism*, 170, 171; Horner and Beer, *Edith Wharton*, 115. For an excellent overview of twentieth-century criticism of the novel, see Thompson, *Influencing America's Tastes*, 106–7.
209. Wharton, *Hudson River Bracketed*, 73, 176.
210. Wharton, *Hudson River Bracketed*, 184.
211. Wharton, *Hudson River Bracketed*, 64.
212. Wharton, *Hudson River Bracketed*, 342.
213. Cather, *The Selected Letters of Willa Cather*, 217.
214. Wharton, *Hudson River Bracketed*, 66.
215. Wharton, *Hudson River Bracketed*, 59.
216. Horner and Beer, *Edith Wharton*, 102.
217. Wharton, *Hudson River Bracketed*, 436.
218. Quoted in Horner and Beer, *Edith Wharton*, 85.
219. Goldman-Price, *My Dear Governess*, 15.

220. Goldman-Price, *My Dear Governess*, 270, 271.
221. Goldman-Price, *My Dear Governess*, 272.
222. Goldman-Price, *My Dear Governess*, 272.
223. Goldman-Price, *My Dear Governess*, 272.
224. Wharton, *The Letters of Edith Wharton*, 374.
225. Lee, *Edith Wharton*, 438, 439.
226. Rosowski, *The Voyage Perilous*, 74.
227. Cather, *The Selected Letters of Willa Cather*, 218.
228. Cather, *The Selected Letters of Willa Cather*, 218.
229. Cather, *The Selected Letters of Willa Cather*, 666.
230. Cather, *The Selected Letters of Willa Cather*, 454.
231. Cather, *The Selected Letters of Willa Cather*, 503.
232. Wharton, *The Letters of Edith Wharton*, 411.
233. Wharton, *The Letters of Edith Wharton*, 281.
234. Wharton, *A Backward Glance*, 49.
235. Wharton, *A Backward Glance*, 51; emphasis in original.
236. Wharton, *A Backward Glance*, 50.
237. Wharton, *A Backward Glance*, 50.
238. Mencken, *The American Language*, 707.
239. Wharton, *A Backward Glance*, 50.
240. Wharton, *A Backward Glance*, 50.
241. Wharton, *A Backward Glance*, 49 (emphasis in original), 51.
242. Wharton, *A Backward Glance*, 51.
243. Wharton, *A Backward Glance*, 52, 53.
244. Wharton, *The Letters of Edith Wharton*, 455.
245. Wharton, *The Letters of Edith Wharton*, 471.
246. Goldman-Price, *My Dear Governess*, 32.
247. Goldman-Price, *My Dear Governess*, 98.
248. "Pow-wow." *American Heritage Dictionary*, 4th ed.
249. Wharton, *The Letters of Edith Wharton*, 391.
250. Wharton, *The Letters of Edith Wharton*, 406.
251. Cather, "Nebraska," 238.
252. Ryan, "Introduction," 5–6. For fascinating discussions of Twain in a wide cultural context, see Ryan and McCullough, *The Cosmopolitan Mark Twain*.
253. Edel, *Henry James*, 607; R. W. B. Lewis, *Wharton*, 94, 168.
254. Adams, *The Education of Henry Adams*, 1002.

5. THE IDEA OF FRANCE

1. Benstock, *No Gifts from Chance*, 19.
2. Wharton, *A Backward Glance*, 33–34.
3. Benstock, *No Gifts from Chance*, 271.

4. Wharton, *A Backward Glance*, 40.
5. Goldman-Price, *My Dear Governess*, 66.
6. Lee, *Edith Wharton*, 265.
7. Lee, *Edith Wharton*, 96; Cather, *The World and the Parish*, 1:151.
8. Lee, *Edith Wharton*, 274.
9. Lee, *Edith Wharton*, 278.
10. Reminiscences of A. Baccon-Gibod, MSS 42, Box 62, YCAL.
11. Lee, *Edith Wharton*, 524, 539.
12. Lee, *Edith Wharton*, 61; Goldman-Price, *My Dear Governess*, 59–60.
13. Woodress, *Willa Cather*, 160.
14. Woodress, *Willa Cather*, 160.
15. Woodress, *Willa Cather*, 160.
16. E. K. Brown, *Willa Cather*, 269.
17. Woodress, *Willa Cather*, 83; Washington, *Dorothy Canfield Fisher*, 17–18, 88–89.
18. Prenatt, "Negotiating Authority," 70–71.
19. Cather, *Willa Cather in Europe*, 94.
20. See Woodress, *Willa Cather*, 161.
21. Woodress, *Willa Cather*, 324; Lee, *Edith Wharton*, 503.
22. Benstock, "Landscapes of Desire," 29.
23. Woodress, *Willa Cather*, 156, 163.
24. Woodress, *Willa Cather*, 160–62.
25. E. Lewis, *Willa Cather Living*, 158; Cather, "A Chance Meeting," 12.
26. James, *A Little Tour in France*, 18.
27. Goldman-Price, *My Dear Governess*, 87–88.
28. Cather, *Willa Cather in Europe*, 174–75.
29. Goldman-Price, *My Dear Governess*, 231.
30. Cather, *Willa Cather in Europe*, 135–39.
31. Cather, *Willa Cather in Europe*, 135.
32. E. K. Brown, *Willa Cather*, 104.
33. Cather, *Willa Cather in Europe*, 158–59, 157.
34. Wharton, *The Letters of Edith Wharton*, 436.
35. Cather, *Willa Cather in Europe*, 157.
36. Wharton, *The Letters of Edith Wharton*, 434. Wharton alludes to Dante, *Paradiso*, Canto XXX, line 52.
37. Wharton, *A Motor-Flight through France*, 57, 59.
38. Wharton, *The Letters of Edith Wharton*, 278, 279.
39. Cather, *Death Comes for the Archbishop*, 286.
40. Lee, *Edith Wharton*, 525.
41. Benstock, *Women of the Left Bank*, 13.
42. Beach, *Shakespeare and Company*, 20.
43. Beach, *Shakespeare and Company*, 60. See also Benstock's *Women of the Left Bank*.

44. Palleau-Papin, "Slowly, but Surely," 542–44.
45. Benstock, *No Gifts from Chance*, 238, 250.
46. Wharton, *The Letters of Edith Wharton*, 233.
47. Benstock, *No Gifts from Chance*, 318.
48. Woodress, *Willa Cather*, 339.
49. Benstock, *No Gifts from Chance*, 403, 453; Wharton, *The Letters of Edith Wharton*, 358.
50. Sergeant, *Willa Cather*, 98. On Cather and cubism, see Prenatt, "'Intrigued by the Cubist.'" On Cather and modern art, see also the essays by Stout, Aksakalova, and Middleton in Watson and Moseley, *Willa Cather and Aestheticism*.
51. Lee, *Edith Wharton*, 307.
52. See Garrison, *Edith Wharton*, for publication details. For Wharton's poetry, see also Wharton, *Selected Poems*.
53. See Cather, *April Twilights and Other Poems*.
54. Nettels, "'The Bravest Act of His Life,'" 46.
55. Lee, *Edith Wharton*, 305.
56. Benstock, *No Gifts from Chance*, 246; Lee, *Edith Wharton*, 306; Asselineau, "Edith Wharton," 357.
57. Asselineau, "Edith Wharton," 356.
58. Blazek, "Wharton and France," 276.
59. Asselineau, "Edith Wharton," 358–59.
60. Asselineau, "Edith Wharton," 362.
61. Lee, *Edith Wharton*, 305.
62. Woodress, *Willa Cather*, 161.
63. Gervaud, "Willa Cather and France," 69.
64. Cather, "A Chance Meeting," 5.
65. Cather, *Death Comes for the Archbishop*, 289.
66. Cather, *The Song of the Lark*, 335.
67. Palleau-Papin, "Slowly, but Surely," 539.
68. Cather, *The Selected Letters of Willa Cather*, 546–48. See also Palleau-Papin, "The Translation in the Closet," and Madigan, "Translating the Southwest."
69. Quoted in Palleau-Papin, "Slowly, but Surely," 546.
70. Palleau-Papin, "The Hidden French in Willa Cather's English," 47, 51.
71. Palleau-Papin, "The Hidden French in Willa Cather's English," 54.
72. Cf. Palleau-Papin, "The Hidden French in Willa Cather's English," 53.
73. Palleau-Papin, "The Hidden French in Willa Cather's English," 53.
74. Chénetier, "Sorbonne Keynote Address," 39.
75. Chénetier, "Sorbonne Keynote Address," 39.
76. Gopnik, "Introduction," xiii.
77. Quoted in McCullough, *The Greater Journey*, 9.
78. McCullough, *The Greater Journey*, 47.

79. McCullough, *The Greater Journey*, 65.
80. Stowe, *Sunny Memories of Foreign Lands*, 392.
81. Stowe, *Sunny Memories of Foreign Lands*, 392.
82. McCullough, *The Greater Journey*, 218.
83. Brownell, *French Traits*, 7.
84. Goldman-Price, *My Dear Governess*, 114.
85. Wharton, *French Ways and Their Meaning*, 39–40.
86. Wharton, quoted in Benstock, "Landscapes of Desire," 28.
87. Ferguson, *Accounting for Taste*, 170.
88. Ferguson, *Accounting for Taste*, 201.
89. Cather, *The Selected Letters of Willa Cather*, 65.
90. Cather, *The Selected Letters of Willa Cather*, 65.
91. Cather, *The Selected Letters of Willa Cather*, 65.
92. Cather, *The Selected Letters of Willa Cather*, 66.
93. Gopnik, "Introduction," xvi.
94. Gopnik, "Introduction," xx.
95. Cather, *The Selected Letters of Willa Cather*, 293.
96. Cather, *The Selected Letters of Willa Cather*, 291.
97. Cather, *The Selected Letters of Willa Cather*, 291–92.
98. Gopnik, "Introduction," xx.
99. Lee, *Edith Wharton*, 462.
100. Chapter 6, "The New French Woman," was originally published in the *Ladies' Home Journal* (Garrison, *Edith Wharton*, 457).
101. Benstock, *No Gifts from Chance*, 348.
102. Durrans, *The Influence of French Culture on Willa Cather*, 248.
103. Gervaud, "Willa Cather and France," 80.
104. Quoted in Sergeant, *Willa Cather*, 145.
105. For Sergeant in wartime France, see Prenatt, "Negotiating Authority."
106. Sergeant, *French Perspectives*, vii.
107. Wharton, *French Ways and Their Meaning*, 18–19.
108. Wharton, *French Ways and Their Meaning*, 89.
109. Wharton, *French Ways and Their Meaning*, 93.
110. Wharton, *French Ways and Their Meaning*, 93.
111. Coolidge, "Address to the American Society of Newspaper Editors."
112. Wharton, *French Ways and Their Meaning*, 107–8.
113. Wharton, *French Ways and Their Meaning*, 108.
114. Wharton, *French Ways and Their Meaning*, 108.
115. Wharton, *French Ways and Their Meaning*, 109; emphasis in original.
116. Wharton, *French Ways and Their Meaning*, 111.
117. Wharton, *French Ways and Their Meaning*, 69.
118. Wharton, *French Ways and Their Meaning*, 69–70.

119. Wharton, *French Ways and Their Meaning*, 71.
120. Wharton, *French Ways and Their Meaning*, 40.
121. Quoted in Bohlke, *Willa Cather in Person*, 70.
122. Quoted in Bohlke, *Willa Cather in Person*, 70.
123. Quoted in Bohlke, *Willa Cather in Person*, 70.
124. Quoted in Bohlke, *Willa Cather in Person*, 71.
125. Olin-Ammentorp, *Edith Wharton's Writings from the Great War*, 22; cf. Lee, *Edith Wharton*, 456–57.
126. Wharton, *The Letters of Edith Wharton*, 373, 380.
127. For the most detailed account of Wharton's wartime charities, see Price, *The End of the Age of Innocence*.
128. Lee, *Edith Wharton*, 483.
129. Quoted in Price, *The End of the Age of Innocence*, 148.
130. Wharton to Norton, May 5, 1917, MSS 42, Box 40, YCAL.
131. Wharton, *A Backward Glance*, 359–60.
132. Stout, "Between Two Wars," 72.
133. Cather, *The Selected Letters of Willa Cather*, 195, 196.
134. Cather, *The Selected Letters of Willa Cather*, 219.
135. Lee, *Edith Wharton*, 473.
136. Cather, *The Selected Letters of Willa Cather*, 196–97.
137. Cather, *The Selected Letters of Willa Cather*, 196–97.
138. Cather, "Roll Call on the Prairies," 30.
139. Wharton, *The Book of the Homeless*, xx; emphasis in original.
140. Cather, *The Selected Letters of Willa Cather*, 197.
141. Cather, *The Selected Letters of Willa Cather*, 240.
142. Cather, *The Selected Letters of Willa Cather*, 240.
143. Cather, *The Selected Letters of Willa Cather*, 244; Wharton to Adele [Mrs. James A.] Burden, October 15, 1917, MSS 42, Box 64, YCAL.
144. Jewell, "Willa Cather's Shifting Perspectives on the Great War."
145. See also Jewell, "Willa Cather's Shifting Perspectives on the Great War," 15.
146. Cather, *The Selected Letters of Willa Cather*, 255–56.
147. Cather, *The Selected Letters of Willa Cather*, 258.
148. "Allies Push Germans Back."
149. Cather, *The Selected Letters of Willa Cather*, 259.
150. Cather, *The Selected Letters of Willa Cather*, 260.
151. Cather, *The Selected Letters of Willa Cather*, 260.
152. Cather, *The Selected Letters of Willa Cather*, 327, 198.
153. Woodress, *Willa Cather*, 67; Washington, *Dorothy Canfield Fisher*, 20.
154. Cather, *The Selected Letters of Willa Cather*, 241.
155. Price, *The End of the Age of Innocence*, 123.
156. Price, *The End of the Age of Innocence*, 122.

157. Price, *The End of the Age of Innocence*, 122.
158. Harris, "Historical Essay," 652.
159. See Wharton, *The Letters of Edith Wharton*, for her correspondence with Chapman; Benstock, *No Gifts from Chance*, 378.
160. Quoted in Chapman, *Victor Chapman's Letters from France*, 41.
161. Wharton, *The Letters of Edith Wharton*, 406; Cather, *The Selected Letters of Willa Cather*, 294.
162. Wharton, *The Letters of Edith Wharton*, 407.
163. Cather, *One of Ours*, 514.
164. Cather, *The Selected Letters of Willa Cather*, 293–94.
165. Wharton, *The Letters of Edith Wharton*, 407.
166. Cather, *The Selected Letters of Willa Cather*, 294.
167. Harris, "Explanatory Notes," 790.
168. Woodress, *Willa Cather*, 311.
169. Cather, *The Selected Letters of Willa Cather*, 296.
170. Benstock, *No Gifts from Chance*, 316.
171. See Wharton to Theodore Roosevelt, July 23, 1918, Theodore Roosevelt Papers. Courtesy of the Library of Congress Manuscript Division and the Theodore Roosevelt Center at Dickinson State University. www.theodorerooseveltcenter.org/Research/Digital-Library/Record?libID=o146915. Accessed April 24, 2018.
172. Benstock, *No Gifts from Chance*, 342.
173. Lee, *Edith Wharton*, 501.
174. Wharton, *The Letters of Edith Wharton*, 409.
175. Wharton to Theodore Roosevelt, July 23, 1918, Theodore Roosevelt Papers.
176. Wharton to Thomas Rhinelander, April 23, 1919, MSS 42, Box 64, YCAL.
177. Olin-Ammentorp, *Edith Wharton's Writings from the Great War*, 65.
178. Quoted in Tuttleton, Lauer, and Murray, *Edith Wharton*, 267.
179. "Echoes and Shadows," 56; *Times Literary Supplement*, quoted in Tuttleton, Lauer, and Murray, *Edith Wharton*, 269.
180. Wharton, *The Marne*, 8–9.
181. Olin-Ammentorp, *Wharton's Writings from the Great War*, 65–78.
182. Cather, *The Selected Letters of Willa Cather*, 318; Wharton, *A Backward Glance*, 369.
183. Haytock, *Edith Wharton and the Conversations of Literary Modernism*, 129; Sensibar, "'Behind the Lines,'" 249.
184. Stout, *Willa Cather*, 176.
185. For an excellent summary of critical responses to *One of Ours*, see Harris, "Historical Essay," 654–67. For distinctions between Claude's and Cather's views, see, for instance, Harris, "Pershing's Crusaders," esp. 85–88.
186. Wharton, *A Son at the Front*, 40–41.

187. Cather, *One of Ours*, 277–78.
188. Cather, *One of Ours*, 279.
189. Cather, *The Selected Letters of Willa Cather*, 293.
190. Cather, *One of Ours*, 425.
191. Cather, *One of Ours*, 425.
192. Cather, *One of Ours*, 446.
193. Cather, *One of Ours*, 447.
194. Cohen, "Culture and the 'Cathedral,'" 184, 185.
195. Cather, *One of Ours*, 450, 452.
196. Harris, "Claude Wheeler's Visit," 6.
197. Cather, *Lucy Gayheart*, 100.
198. Wharton, *French Ways and Their Meaning*, v.
199. Wharton, *A Son at the Front*, 66, 67.
200. Cather, *One of Ours*, 455, 457.
201. Cather, *One of Ours*, 458.
202. Cather, *One of Ours*, 459.
203. Wharton, *French Ways and Their Meaning*, chapter 6; Cather, *One of Ours*, 461.
204. Wharton, *Fighting France*, 114; Cather, *One of Ours*, 507.
205. Cather, *One of Ours*, 507.
206. Cather, *One of Ours*, 508.
207. Cather, *One of Ours*, 509.
208. Cather, *One of Ours*, 509.
209. Cather, *One of Ours*, 535.
210. Cather, *One of Ours*, 548.
211. Cather, *One of Ours*, 552.
212. Cather, *One of Ours*, 550.
213. Cather, *One of Ours*, 551.
214. Cather, *One of Ours*, 543.
215. Smith, Audoin-Rouzeau, and Becker, *France and the Great War*, 79.
216. Smith, Audoin-Rouzeau, and Becker, *France and the Great War*, 79.
217. Smith, Audoin-Rouzeau, and Becker, *France and the Great War*, 42.
218. Smith, Audoin-Rouzeau, and Becker, *France and the Great War*, 3.
219. Wharton, *A Son at the Front*, 18.
220. Wharton, *A Son at the Front*, 19.
221. Sensibar, "'Behind the Lines,'" 249–50.
222. Wharton, *A Son at the Front*, 32.
223. Smith, Audoin-Rouzeau, and Becker, *France and the Great War*, note, "The French army had suffered some 329,000 deaths in August and September 1914, . . . the most deadly period of the war" (40). The year 1915 was also one of horrific losses (79–81). On the American arrival in France, see Keegan, *The First World War*, 372–75 and 407–11.

224. Wharton, *A Son at the Front*, 70.
225. Wharton, *A Son at the Front*, 121; Keegan, *The First World War*, 5–6, 421.
226. Quoted in Smith, Audoin-Rouzeau, and Becker, *France and the Great War*, 28.
227. Wharton, *A Son at the Front*, 220.
228. Wharton, *A Son at the Front*, 326.
229. Wharton, *A Son at the Front*, 326.
230. Wharton, *A Son at the Front*, 126.
231. Wharton, *A Son at the Front*, 374–75.
232. Wharton, *A Son at the Front*, 376.
233. Smith, Audoin-Rouzeau, and Becker, *France and the Great War*, 111.
234. Cather, *One of Ours*, 553.
235. Cather, *One of Ours*, 552.
236. Cather, *One of Ours*, 539.
237. Cather, *One of Ours*, 500–501.
238. Wharton, *A Son at the Front*, 366; emphasis in original.
239. Wharton, *A Son at the Front*, 405.
240. Haytock, *Edith Wharton and the Conversations of Literary Modernism*, 124.
241. Wharton, *A Son at the Front*, 400.
242. Wharton, *A Son at the Front*, 400.
243. Cather, *One of Ours*, 605.
244. Cather, *One of Ours*, 145–46.
245. Cather, *One of Ours*, 146.
246. Cather, *One of Ours*, 604.
247. Cather, *One of Ours*, 604.
248. In a companion speech delivered during the war, Wharton also made an effort to explain American behavior to a French audience. The *Times Literary Supplement* published an extended excerpt, translated and edited by Virginia Ricard, on February 14, 2018 (Wharton, "America at War").
249. Wharton, "Talk to American Soldiers," 264.
250. Wharton, "Talk to American Soldiers," 263.
251. Wharton, "Talk to American Soldiers," 270, 271.
252. Cather, *One of Ours*, 534–35.
253. Lee, *Edith Wharton*, 281.
254. Quoted in Bohlke, *Willa Cather in Person*, 118.
255. Quoted in Woodress, *Willa Cather*, 455.
256. Quoted in Woodress, *Willa Cather*, 455.
257. Madigan, "'An Artist in Her Way.'"
258. Cather, *The Selected Letters of Willa Cather*, 306.
259. Lee, *Edith Wharton*, 281.
260. Cather, *One of Ours*, 535.
261. Stout, *Willa Cather*, 237.

262. P. Smith, "Achaeans, Americanos, Prelates and Monsters," 103.
263. P. Smith, "Achaeans, Americanos, Prelates and Monsters," 103.
264. Stout, *Willa Cather*, 240, 241.
265. Wegener, "'Rabid Imperialist,'" 788.
266. Wharton, *In Morocco*, 13–14.
267. Cather, *Death Comes for the Archbishop*, 37.
268. Cather, *Death Comes for the Archbishop*, 56.
269. Cather, *Death Comes for the Archbishop*, 61.
270. Cather, *Death Comes for the Archbishop*, 70.
271. Cather, *Death Comes for the Archbishop*, 223, 261.
272. Cather, *Death Comes for the Archbishop*, 44–45.
273. Cather, *Death Comes for the Archbishop*, 273.
274. Cather, *Shadows on the Rock*, 227.
275. Wharton, *French Ways and Their Meaning*, 22.
276. Cather, *Death Comes for the Archbishop*, 41.
277. Cather, *Death Comes for the Archbishop*, 185.
278. Cather, *Death Comes for the Archbishop*, 271–72.
279. Cather, *Death Comes for the Archbishop*, 272.
280. Cather, *Death Comes for the Archbishop*, 37.
281. Cather, *Death Comes for the Archbishop*, 28.
282. Cather, *Death Comes for the Archbishop*, 28.
283. Cather, *Death Comes for the Archbishop*, 35.
284. Cather, "On *Death Comes for the Archbishop*," 5–6.
285. Cather, *Death Comes for the Archbishop*, 253, 254.
286. Cather, *Death Comes for the Archbishop*, 253.
287. Cather, *Death Comes for the Archbishop*, 240.
288. Cather, *Death Comes for the Archbishop*, 240.
289. Cather, *Death Comes for the Archbishop*, 253, 254.
290. Cather, *Death Comes for the Archbishop*, 255.
291. Cather, *Death Comes for the Archbishop*, 256.
292. Cather, *Death Comes for the Archbishop*, 254.
293. Cather, "On *Death Comes for the Archbishop*," 7.
294. Cather, *Death Comes for the Archbishop*, 253.
295. Cather, *Death Comes for the Archbishop*, 282.
296. Cather, *Death Comes for the Archbishop*, 107.
297. Wharton, "Talk to American Soldiers," 271.
298. Wharton, "Talk to American Soldiers," 270–71; emphasis added.
299. Lopez, "Learning to Like *Chili Colorado*," 87.
300. Cather, *Death Comes for the Archbishop*, 241.
301. Cather, *Death Comes for the Archbishop*, 241.
302. Cather, *Death Comes for the Archbishop*, 241.

303. Cather, *Death Comes for the Archbishop*, 242.
304. Bhushan, "Becoming Cosmopolitan," 19.
305. Cather, "On *Death Comes for the Archbishop*," 9; emphasis added.
306. Cather, *Death Comes for the Archbishop*, 283.
307. Bhabha, "The Commitment to Theory," 25; emphasis in original.
308. Bhabha, "The Commitment to Theory," 38; emphasis in original.
309. Bhushan, "Becoming Cosmopolitan," 20.
310. Cather, *Death Comes for the Archbishop*, 143.
311. Cather, *Death Comes for the Archbishop*, 108.
312. Cather, *Death Comes for the Archbishop*, 277.
313. Cather, *Death Comes for the Archbishop*, 208.
314. Cather, *Death Comes for the Archbishop*, 287.
315. Cather, *Death Comes for the Archbishop*, 37, 288.
316. P. Smith, "Achaeans, Americanos, Prelates and Monsters," 104.
317. See, for instance, Reynolds, *Willa Cather in Context*.
318. Cather, *Death Comes for the Archbishop*, 14.
319. Cather, *Death Comes for the Archbishop*, 207.
320. Appiah, "Presidential Address 2017," xv, 5.
321. Cather, *Death Comes for the Archbishop*, 306.
322. Quoted in Bohlke, *Willa Cather in Person*, 71–72.
323. Cather, "The Novel Démeublé," 40.
324. Cather, *Death Comes for the Archbishop*, 306.
325. Cather, *Death Comes for the Archbishop*, 307.
326. Quoted in Tuttleton, Lauer, and Murray, *Edith Wharton*, 273.
327. Cather's endorsement of French civilization in *Shadows on the Rock* is much more limited, mentioning the brutality of French history, particularly in the reign of Louis XIV. "Continental France, not the Huron villages, provides the book's most striking instances of savagery" (Millington, "Where Is Cather's Quebec?," 32). See also Olin-Ammentorp, "Willa Cather's 'Individual Map' of Paris," 11.
328. Gervaud, "Willa Cather and France," 66.
329. Cather, *The Professor's House*, 152.
330. Glennon, "The Big Bribes," 18; Blazek, "Wharton and France," 282.
331. Woodress, *Willa Cather*, 372.
332. Goldman-Price, *My Dear Governess*, 251, 252.
333. Quoted in Benstock, *No Gifts from Chance*, 431.
334. Cather, *The Selected Letters of Willa Cather*, 296.

6. QUESTIONS OF TRAVEL AND HOME

1. Hamera and Bendixen, "Introduction," 8.
2. See Fussell, "Introduction," 13; Carr, "Modernism and Travel," 73; Hulme and Youngs, "Introduction," 8; Roberson, "American Women and Travel Writing," 223.

3. Wharton, *A Backward Glance*, 61.
4. Wharton, *A Backward Glance*, 29–43.
5. Wharton, *A Backward Glance*, 31.
6. Goldman-Price, *My Dear Governess*, 54.
7. Wharton, *The Letters of Edith Wharton*, 296.
8. Wharton, *A Backward Glance*, 177.
9. Travel summaries for 1902 and 1903 are based on the Willa Cather Geographic Chronology of the Willa Cather Archive, http://cather.unl.edu/geochron/.
10. Cather, *The Selected Letters of Willa Cather*, 361.
11. E. K. Brown, *Willa Cather*, 40–41.
12. Cather, *The Selected Letters of Willa Cather*, 105.
13. Cather, *The Selected Letters of Willa Cather*, 105.
14. Carr, "Modernism and Travel," 70; Hulme and Youngs, "Introduction," 7.
15. Carr, "Modernism and Travel," 79.
16. Totten, "The Dialectic of History and Technology," 31.
17. Goldman-Price, *My Dear Governess*, 94.
18. Wharton, *A Motor-Flight through France*, 1.
19. Wharton, *A Motor-Flight through France*, 1.
20. R. W. B. Lewis, *Edith Wharton*, 319; emphasis in original.
21. Lee, *Edith Wharton*, 93.
22. Wharton, *The Letters of Edith Wharton*, 357.
23. Wharton, *In Morocco*, 1; emphasis in original.
24. Cather, *Willa Cather in Europe*, 19.
25. Cather, *The Selected Letters of Willa Cather*, 63.
26. Cather, *Willa Cather in Europe*, 154–55, 157.
27. Cather, *Willa Cather in Europe*, 155.
28. Cather, *The Professor's House*, 250, 252.
29. Cather, *One of Ours*, 412.
30. Bishop, "Questions of Travel," 75.
31. See also Janis Stout, who observes that the work of many women writers demonstrates "a tension between the urge to break out, to shake the dust from one's feet, and an equally powerful homing urge, an urge to construct and maintain and to value relational ties" (*Through the Window, Out the Door*, x).
32. Bishop, "One Art," 167.
33. Wharton, *The Letters of Edith Wharton*, 432.
34. Cather, *The Selected Letters of Willa Cather*, 423.
35. Woodress, *Willa Cather*, 412.
36. Wharton, *The Letters of Edith Wharton*, 69.
37. Wharton, *The Letters of Edith Wharton*, 209.
38. Cather, *The Selected Letters of Willa Cather*, 130.
39. Cather, *The Selected Letters of Willa Cather*, 428.

40. Wharton, *The House of Mirth*, 515–16.
41. Fryer, *Felicitous Space*, 88.
42. Wharton, *The House of Mirth*, 239–40.
43. Fussell, "Introduction," 13.
44. Wharton, *The House of Mirth*, 289.
45. See Boydston, "'Grave Endearing Traditions.'"
46. Clarke, "Modernist Domesticity," 190.
47. Frost, "The Death of the Hired Man," 43.
48. Cather, *Lucy Gayheart*, 83.
49. Wharton, *The House of Mirth*, 516.
50. Berendt, "Regionalism," 151.
51. Cather, *Lucy Gayheart*, 84.
52. Cather, *Lucy Gayheart*, 83.
53. Cather, *Lucy Gayheart*, 56.
54. Cather, *Lucy Gayheart*, 56–57.
55. Cather, *Lucy Gayheart*, 57.
56. Cather, *Lucy Gayheart*, 57–58.
57. Wharton, *The Letters of Edith Wharton*, 523; Lee, *Edith Wharton*, 742.
58. Cather, *Lucy Gayheart*, 5.
59. Cather, *Lucy Gayheart*, 212.
60. Cather, *Lucy Gayheart*, 242.
61. Cather, *Lucy Gayheart*, 144.
62. Cather, *Lucy Gayheart*, 184.
63. Cather, *Lucy Gayheart*, 164.
64. Cather, *Lucy Gayheart*, 164.
65. Cather, *Lucy Gayheart*, 165.
66. Cather, *Lucy Gayheart*, 165.
67. Cather, *Lucy Gayheart*, 179.
68. Cather, *Lucy Gayheart*, 180.
69. Cather, *Lucy Gayheart*, 177.
70. Cather, *Lucy Gayheart*, 178.
71. Cather, *Lucy Gayheart*, 181.
72. Cather, "Katherine Mansfield," 135–36.
73. Cather, *Lucy Gayheart*, 180, 169–70.
74. Wharton, *The Age of Innocence*, 348.
75. Cather, *Lucy Gayheart*, 104.
76. Cather, *Lucy Gayheart*, 221, 219.
77. Cather, *Lucy Gayheart*, 232.
78. Cather, *Lucy Gayheart*, 220–21.
79. Cather, *Lucy Gayheart*, 221.
80. Cather, *Lucy Gayheart*, 242.

81. Cather, *Lucy Gayheart*, 84.
82. Cather, *Lucy Gayheart*, 227.
83. See, for instance, Haytock, *Wharton and the Conversations of Literary Modernism*; Clarke, "Modernist Domesticity."
84. Cather, *The Selected Letters of Willa Cather*, 471.
85. Cather, *My Ántonia*, 355.
86. Cather, *My Ántonia*, x.
87. Wharton, *The Age of Innocence*, 336.
88. Wharton, *The Age of Innocence*, 342.
89. Wharton, *The Age of Innocence*, 342.
90. Wharton, *The Age of Innocence*, 350.
91. Wharton, *The Age of Innocence*, 350.
92. Wharton, *The Age of Innocence*, 351.
93. Quoted in Lee, *Edith Wharton*, 548.
94. Wharton, *The Letters of Edith Wharton*, 417.
95. Wharton, *The Letters of Edith Wharton*, 577.
96. Goldman-Price, *My Dear Governess*, 167.
97. Wharton, *The Letters of Edith Wharton*, 545.
98. Cather to Fisher, November 5, 1921, UVM.
99. Cather, *The Selected Letters of Willa Cather*, 332.
100. Urgo, "The Cather Thesis," 37.
101. Cather, *The Selected Letters of Willa Cather*, 614.
102. Cather, *The Selected Letters of Willa Cather*, 102.
103. Cather, *The Selected Letters of Willa Cather*, 169.
104. Cather, *The Selected Letters of Willa Cather*, 423.
105. Cather, *The Selected Letters of Willa Cather*, 396.
106. Cather, *The Selected Letters of Willa Cather*, 472.
107. Cather, *The Selected Letters of Willa Cather*, 477.
108. Stout, *Through the Window, Out the Door*, 66.
109. Stout, *Willa Cather*, 26, 28; emphasis in original.
110. Cather, *The Selected Letters of Willa Cather*, 671.
111. Homestead, "Willa Cather, Sarah Orne Jewett, and the Historiography of Lesbian Sexuality," 22–27.
112. Cather to Weisz, January 19, 1933, Midwest MS Cather-Weisz, Newberry.
113. Cather, *The Selected Letters of Willa Cather*, 224.
114. Cather, *The Selected Letters of Willa Cather*, 46.
115. Cather, "Going Home," 148.
116. Cather, "Going Home," 148–49.
117. Carr, "Modernism and Travel," 81.
118. Wharton, *A Backward Glance*, 362–64.
119. Woodress, *Willa Cather*, 310.

120. Cather, *The Selected Letters of Willa Cather*, 294.
121. Wharton, *A Backward Glance*, 369–70.
122. Cather, "Prefatory Note," n.p.
123. Wharton, *A Backward Glance*, 7; Cather, "Prefatory Note," n.p.
124. Wharton, *A Backward Glance*, 7; Cather, "Prefatory Note," n.p.
125. Wharton, *The Letters of Edith Wharton*, 379.
126. Wharton, *The Letters of Edith Wharton*, 561; emphasis in original.
127. Cather, *The Selected Letters of Willa Cather*, 264.
128. Cather, *The Selected Letters of Willa Cather*, 474.
129. Woodress, *Willa Cather*, 479.
130. Cather, *The Selected Letters of Willa Cather*, 557.
131. Wharton, *The Letters of Edith Wharton*, 385.
132. Cather, *The Professor's House*, 282.
133. Cather, *The Professor's House*, 282.
134. Cather, "Old Mrs. Harris, 118; Wharton, *The Gods Arrive*, 409. Kim also comments on Wharton's emphasis on pain in this novel ("Edith Wharton and Epiphany," 166).
135. Horner and Beer, *Edith Wharton*, 113–14.
136. Cather, *The Selected Letters of Willa Cather*, 631; emphasis in original.
137. Cather, *The Selected Letters of Willa Cather*, 631.
138. Cather, *The Selected Letters of Willa Cather*, 647.
139. Wharton to Bernard Berenson, August 20, 1930, BB.
140. Cather, *The Selected Letters of Willa Cather*, 484.
141. Wharton, *The Letters of Edith Wharton*, 604.
142. Cather, *The Selected Letters of Willa Cather*, 675.
143. Nehamas, *Only a Promise of Beauty*, 77, 138.
144. On Wharton's attraction to Catholicism in later life, see Lee, *Edith Wharton*; Benstock, *No Gifts from Chance*; and Singley, *Edith Wharton*. On Cather, see Woodress, *Willa Cather*, esp. 409–11; John J. Murphy, "Building the House of Faith"; and Stout, "Faith Statements and Nonstatements."
145. Singley, *Edith Wharton*, 188.
146. Cather, *The Professor's House*, 69, 68.
147. Singley, *Edith Wharton*, 206; R. W. B. Lewis, *Edith Wharton*, 510.
148. Wharton, *The Gods Arrive*, 82.
149. Wharton, *The Gods Arrive*, 83.
150. Horner and Beer, *Edith Wharton*, 82.
151. Wharton, *The Gods Arrive*, 387.
152. Cather, *My Ántonia*, ix.
153. Cather, *Death Comes for the Archbishop*, 45; Wharton, *Hudson River Bracketed*, 323.
154. Benstock, *No Gifts from Chance*, 460; Glennon, "Toward a Brighter Vision," 98; Lee, *Edith Wharton*, 726.

155. Jones, "The 'Beyondness of Things,'" 8.
156. Jones, "The 'Beyondness of Things,'" 15; emphasis in original.
157. Wharton, *The Buccaneers*, 252.
158. Wharton, *The Buccaneers*, 252–53.
159. Wharton, *The Buccaneers*, 253.
160. Wharton, *The Buccaneers*, 253.
161. Wharton, *The Buccaneers*, 404.
162. Wharton, *The Buccaneers*, 404; ellipsis in original.
163. Wharton, *The Buccaneers*, 404.
164. Lee, *Edith Wharton*, 731.
165. Wharton, *The Buccaneers*, 256.
166. Wharton, *The Buccaneers*, 256.
167. Wharton, *The Buccaneers*, 256.
168. Wharton, *The Buccaneers*, 257; emphasis in original.
169. Wharton, *The Buccaneers*, 258.
170. Wharton, *The Buccaneers*, 258.
171. Horner and Beer, *Edith Wharton*, 138.
172. Wharton, *The Buccaneers*, 254.
173. Wharton, *The Buccaneers*, 425.
174. Wharton, *The Buccaneers*, 425.
175. Wharton, *The Buccaneers*, 227.
176. Wharton, *The House of Mirth*, 515–16.
177. Wharton, *The Buccaneers*, 387.
178. Wharton, *The Buccaneers*, 388.
179. E. K. Brown, *Willa Cather*, 104.
180. E. Lewis, *Willa Cather Living*, 190.
181. Wharton, *A Motor-Flight through France*, 10–11.
182. Woodress, *Willa Cather*, 493.
183. Woodress, *Willa Cather*, 493.
184. Wharton, *A Motor-Flight through France*, 10.
185. Cather, "Hard Punishments," 5.
186. Cather, "Hard Punishments," 5.
187. Cather, "Hard Punishments," 5.
188. Cather, "Hard Punishments," 5.
189. Cather, "Hard Punishments," 5.
190. Cather, "Hard Punishments," 5.
191. Cather, "Hard Punishments," 5.
192. Wharton, *The Buccaneers*, 229.
193. Cather, *Willa Cather in Europe*, 137.
194. Said, "Introduction," xiv.
195. Said, "Introduction," xiv.

196. Adorno, quoted in Said, "Introduction," xxii.
197. See Majaj, "Boundaries."
198. Said, *Reflections on Exile*, 471.
199. Bishop, "Questions of Travel," 75, 74.
200. Translation of Pascal from Bishop, *Elizabeth Bishop*, 935; Bishop, "Questions of Travel," 75; emphasis in original.
201. R. W. B. Lewis, *Edith Wharton*, 86; John J. Murphy, "Explanatory Notes," 279.
202. Wharton, *The Age of Innocence*, 344; Cather, "Coming, Aphrodite!," 37.
203. Benstock, *No Gifts from Chance*, 188; E. Lewis, *Willa Cather Living*, 12, 13.
204. Millington, "Where Is Cather's Quebec?," 24.
205. Wharton, *The Letters of Edith Wharton*, 598.
206. Wharton, *The Letters of Edith Wharton*, 604.
207. Quoted in Lee, *Edith Wharton*, 748–49.
208. Cather, *The Selected Letters of Willa Cather*, 474.
209. Cather, *The Selected Letters of Willa Cather*, 617.
210. Cather, *The Selected Letters of Willa Cather*, 617.
211. See Cather, *The Selected Letters of Willa Cather*, 624–25.
212. "Willa Cather Foundation Art Collection," 15.
213. Cather, *The Selected Letters of Willa Cather*, 640, 641.
214. Cather, *The Selected Letters of Willa Cather*, 474.
215. MacDonald, "Introduction," 2–3; Dawson, *Making Peace with the Past?*, 55–56.
216. Wharton, *A Motor-Flight through France*, 5.
217. Cather, *My Ántonia*, 7.
218. Cather, *Death Comes for the Archbishop*, 100.
219. Wharton, *A Motor-Flight through France*, 5.
220. Woodress, *Willa Cather*, 447.
221. Woodress, *Willa Cather*, 448; Lee, *Edith Wharton*, 224.
222. Capote, "Willa, Truman," n.p.
223. Cather, *The Selected Letters of Willa Cather*, 671, 102.
224. Wharton, *The Letters of Edith Wharton*, 303.
225. Cather, *The Selected Letters of Willa Cather*, 477.

BIBLIOGRAPHY

ARCHIVAL SOURCES

BB. Biblioteca Berenson, Villa I Tatti—Harvard University Center for Italian Renaissance Studies; courtesy of the President and Fellows of Harvard College.
Harvard. bMS Am 1925 (341), Houghton Library, Harvard University.
Newberry. Midwest MS Cather-Weisz, Newberry Library, Chicago.
NWCC. Willa Cather Foundation Special Collections and Archives, National Willa Cather Center, Red Cloud, Nebraska.
Princeton. Archives of Charles Scribner's Sons (C0101), Manuscripts Division, Department of Rare Books and Special Collections, Princeton University Library.
UVM. Dorothy Canfield Collection, Special Collections, University of Vermont Library.
WCCF. Willa Cather Collection, Cather Foundation, Red Cloud, Nebraska.
YCAL. Yale Collection of American Literature, Beinecke Rare Book and Manuscript Library.

PUBLISHED SOURCES

Abrams, M. H., ed. *The Norton Anthology of English Literature*, 5th ed., vol. 2. New York: W. W. Norton, 1986.
Adams, Henry. *The Education of Henry Adams*. [1907.] In *Henry Adams: Novels, Mont Saint Michel, The Education*, 715–1181. New York: Library of America, 1983.
"Allies Push Germans Back on 28-Mile Front." *New York Times*, July 19, 1918, http://0-search.proquest.com.library.lemoyne.edu/hnpnewyorktimes/docview/100139719/fulltextPDF/295CDB48693340A6PQ/2?accountid=27881.
"American Authors Who Have Set Art Above Popularity." *Vanity Fair* 15, no. 5 (January 1921): 55.
"An American Pioneer—Willa Cather." *Vanity Fair*, July 1927, 30.
Ammons, Elizabeth. *Edith Wharton's Argument with America*. Athens: University of Georgia Press, 1980.
Appiah, Kwame. "Presidential Address 2017." PMLA 132, no. 3 (May 2017): 513–25.

Arnold, Marilyn. "Poses of the Mind, Paeans of the Heart: Cather's Letters of Life in the Provinces." In *Cather: Family, Community, and History*, edited by John J. Murphy, 3–17. Provo UT: Brigham Young University Humanities Publications Center, 1990.

Arnold, Matthew. *Culture and Anarchy*. Edited by Jane Garnett. Oxford: Oxford University Press, 2006.

Asselineau, Roger. "Edith Wharton—She Thought in French and She Wrote in English." In Joslin and Price, *Wretched Exotic*, 355–63.

Auchincloss, Louis. "Edith Wharton and Her New Yorks." In Howe, *Edith Wharton*, 32–42.

——. *Pioneers and Caretakers: A Study of Nine American Women Novelists*. Minneapolis: University of Minnesota Press, 1961.

Bailey, Colin. *Building the Frick Collection*. New York: Frick Collection and Scala Publishers, 2006.

Bakhtin, M[ikhail] M. "Forms of Time and of the Chronotope in the Novel." In *The Dialogic Imagination: Four Essays*, 84–258. Translated by Caryl Emerson and Michael Holquist. Austin: University of Texas Press, 1981.

Banta, Martha. "Introduction." In *The House of Mirth*, by Edith Wharton, vii–xxxi. Oxford: Oxford University Press, 1994.

——. "Men, Women, and the American Way." In *The Cambridge Companion to Henry James*, edited by Jonathan Freedman, 21–39. Cambridge: Cambridge University Press, 1998.

Barber, Peter, ed. *The Map Book*. New York: Walker and Company, 2005.

Barrows, Adam. "Introduction: Time and Literature after the Spatial Turn." In *Time, Literature, and Cartography after the Spatial Turn*, 1–31. New York: Palgrave Macmillan, 2016.

Baym, Nina, et al., eds. *The Norton Anthology of American Literature, Shorter 8th Ed.*, vol. 2. New York: Norton, 2012.

Beach, Sylvia. *Shakespeare and Company*. New York: Harcourt, Brace, 1959.

Bender, Thomas. *The Unfinished City: New York and the Metropolitan Idea*. New York: New Press, 2002.

Benstock, Shari. "Landscapes of Desire: Edith Wharton and Europe." In Joslin and Price, *Wretched Exotic*, 19–42.

——. *No Gifts from Chance: A Biography of Edith Wharton*. New York: Scribner's, 1994.

——. *Women of the Left Bank: Paris, 1900–1940*. Austin: University of Texas Press, 1986.

Berendt, Stephen. "Regionalism and the Realities of Naming." In Mahoney and Katz, *Regionalism and the Humanities*, 150–65.

Bhabha, Homi. "The Commitment to Theory." In *The Location of Culture*, 19–39. London: Routledge, 1994.

Bhushan, Nalini. "Becoming Cosmopolitan: The European Encounter with the New World in *Death Comes for the Archbishop.*" *Willa Cather Newsletter and Review* 58, no. 2 (Winter 2015): 18–22.

Bishop, Elizabeth. *Elizabeth Bishop: Poems, Prose, and Letters.* New York: Library of America, 2008.

———. "One Art." In Bishop, *Elizabeth Bishop,* 166–67.

———. "Questions of Travel." In Bishop, *Elizabeth Bishop,* 74–75.

Blazek, William. "Wharton and France." In Rattray, *Edith Wharton in Context,* 275–84.

Bloom, Harold. *The Anxiety of Influence: A Theory of Poetry.* New York: Oxford University Press, 1973.

Boardman, Kathleen. "Western American Literature and the Canon." In *Updating the Literary West,* 44–69.

Bohlke, L. Brent. *Willa Cather in Person: Interviews, Speeches, and Letters.* Lincoln: University of Nebraska Press, 1986.

Boydston, Jeanne. "'Grave Endearing Traditions': Edith Wharton and the Domestic Novel." In *Faith of a (Woman) Writer,* edited by Alice Kessler-Harris and William McBrien, 31–40. New York: Greenwood Press, 1988.

Bradbury, Malcolm, ed. *The Atlas of Literature.* London: De Agostini, 1996.

Bratton, Daniel, ed. *Yrs. Ever Affly: The Correspondence of Edith Wharton and Louis Bromfield.* East Lansing: Michigan State University Press, 2000.

Brooks, David. "The Essential John McCain." *New York Times,* October 19, 2017, https://www.nytimes.com/2017/10/19/opinion/the-essential-john-mccain.html?_r=0).

Brown, Bill. "Reading the West: Cultural and Historical Backgrounds." In *Reading the West: An Anthology of Dime Westerns,* edited by Bill Brown, 1–40. Boston: Bedford, 1997.

Brown, E. K.. *Edith Wharton: Étude Critique.* Paris: Librairie E. Droz, 1935.

———. "Edith Wharton: The Art of the Novel." In Howe, *Edith Wharton,* 95–102.

———. "Homage to Willa Cather." In Slote and Faulkner, *The Art of Willa Cather,* 185–204.

———. *Willa Cather: A Critical Biography.* Completed by Leon Edel, 1953. Lincoln: University of Nebraska Press, 1987.

Brownell, William Crary. *French Traits: An Essay in Comparative Criticism.* [1888.] New York: Scribner's, 1895.

Byatt, A. S. "Telescope, Microscope, Window—Willa Cather's Distance from Her Text." Plenary address, Willa Cather International Seminar, June 26, 2007.

Campbell, Donna. *Resisting Regionalism: Gender and Naturalism in American Fiction, 1885–1915.* Athens: Ohio University Press, 1997.

Capote, Truman. "Willa, Truman. Truman, Willa." *Vanity Fair,* November 2006, https://www.vanityfair.com/news/2006/11/capote-200611.

Carlin, Deborah. "Cather's Jewett: Relationship, Influence, and Representation." In Kaufman and Millington, *Cather Studies 10*, 169–88.

Carpenter, David. "Why Willa Cather Revised 'Paul's Case': The Work in Art and Those Sunday Afternoons." *American Literature* 59, no. 4 (December 1987): 590–608.

Carr, Helen. "Modernism and Travel, 1880–1940." In *The Cambridge Companion to Travel Writing*, edited by Peter Hulme and Tim Youngs, 70–86. Cambridge: Cambridge University Press, 2013.

Carter, Erica, James Donald, and Judith Squires, eds. *Space and Place: Theories of Identity and Location*. London: Lawrence and Wishart, 1993.

Cather, Willa. *Alexander's Bridge*. [1912.] Edited by Tom Quirk and Frederick Link. Lincoln: University of Nebraska Press, 2007.

———. *April Twilights and Other Poems*. Edited by Robert Thacker. New York: Knopf, 2013.

———. "Before Breakfast." In *The Old Beauty and Others*, 141–66. New York: Knopf, 1948.

———. "The Best Stories of Sarah Orne Jewett." In Cather, *Willa Cather on Writing*, 47–59.

———. "The Best Years." In Cather, *Willa Cather: Stories, Poems, and Other Writings*, 728–57.

———. "A Chance Meeting." In Cather, *Not under Forty*, 3–42.

———. "Coming, Aphrodite!" In Cather, *Youth and the Bright Medusa*, 3–74.

———. *Death Comes for the Archbishop*. Edited by John J. Murphy, Charles Mignon, Frederick Link, and Kari Ronning. Lincoln: University of Nebraska Press, 1999.

———. "Eric Hermannson's Soul." In *Early Stories of Willa Cather*, edited by Mildred R. Bennett, 187–216. New York: Dodd, Mead, 1957.

———. "Escapism." In Cather, *Willa Cather on Writing*, 18–29.

———. "Going Home (Burlington Route)." In Cather, *April Twilights and Other Poems*, 148–49.

———. "A Gold Slipper." In Cather, *Youth and the Bright Medusa*, 139–67.

———. "Hard Punishments." In John J. Murphy, "Toward Completing a Triptych: The 'Hard Punishments' Fragments." *Willa Cather Newsletter and Review* 55, no. 2 (Fall 2011): 2–8.

———. "Katherine Mansfield." In Cather, *Not under Forty*, 123–47.

———. "Light on Adobe Walls." In Cather, *Willa Cather on Writing*, 123–26.

———. *A Lost Lady*. [1923.] Edited by Susan Rosowski, Kari Ronning, Charles Mignon, and Frederick Link. Lincoln: University of Nebraska Press, 1997.

———. *Lucy Gayheart*. [1935.] Edited by David Porter. Lincoln: University of Nebraska Press, 2015.

———. *My Ántonia*. [1918.] Edited by Charles Mignon, Kari Ronning, and James Woodress. Lincoln: University of Nebraska Press, 1994.

———. "My First Novels (There Were Two)." In Cather, *Willa Cather on Writing*, 91–97.
———. *My Mortal Enemy*. In Cather, *Willa Cather: Stories, Poems, and Other Writings*, 531–81.
———. "Nebraska: The End of the First Cycle." *The Nation*, September 5, 1923, 236–38.
———. "Neighbor Rosicky." [1930.] In Cather, *Obscure Destinies*, 5–61.
———. *Not under Forty*. [1936.] Lincoln: University of Nebraska Press, 1988.
———. "The Novel Démeublé." [1922.] In Cather, *Willa Cather on Writing*, 35–43.
———. *Obscure Destinies*. [1932.] Edited by Kari Ronning, Frederick Link, and Mark Kamrath. Lincoln: University of Nebraska Press, 1998.
———. "The Old Beauty." In *The Old Beauty and Others*, 3–72. New York: Knopf, 1948.
———. "Old Mrs. Harris." In Cather, *Obscure Destinies*, 63–157.
———. "On *Death Comes for the Archbishop*." In Cather, *Willa Cather on Writing*, 3–13.
———. "148 Charles Street." [1936.] In Cather, *Not under Forty*, 52–75.
———. *One of Ours*. [1922.] Edited by Richard Harris, Frederick Link, and Kari Ronning. Lincoln: University of Nebraska Press, 2006.
———. "On the Art of Fiction." In Cather, *Willa Cather on Writing*, 101–4.
———. *O Pioneers!* [1913.] Edited by Susan Rosowski, Charles Mignon, Kathleen Danker, and David Stouck. Lincoln: University of Nebraska Press, 1991.
———. "Paul's Case." [1905.] In Cather, *Youth and the Bright Medusa*, 199–234.
———. "Peter." In *Willa Cather's Collected Short Fiction, 1892–1912*, edited by Virginia Faulkner, 541–43. Lincoln: University of Nebraska Press, 1970.
———. Postcard to Elsie Cather from Rome, June 11, 1908. In *Complete Letters of Willa Cather*, edited by Andrew Jewell et al., #1855. Willa Cather Archives, Love Library, University of Nebraska, Lincoln. cather.unl.edu. Accessed April 24, 2018.
———. "Preface to the 1932 Jonathan Cape Edition [of *The Song of the Lark*]." In Cather, *The Song of the Lark*, 617–18.
———. "Prefatory Note." In Cather, *Not under Forty*.
———. *The Professor's House*. [1925.] Edited by James Woodress, Kari Ronning, and Frederick Link. Lincoln: University of Nebraska Press, 2002.
———. "Roll Call on the Prairies." *Red Cross Magazine*, July 1919, 27–31.
———. "The Sculptor's Funeral." [1905.] In Cather, *Youth and the Bright Medusa*, 249–73.
———. *The Selected Letters of Willa Cather*. Edited by Andrew Jewell and Janis Stout. New York: Knopf, 2013.
———. *Shadows on the Rock*. [1931.] Edited by John J. Murphy, David Stouck, and Frederick Link. Lincoln: University of Nebraska Press, 2005.
———. *The Song of the Lark*. [1915.] Edited by Ann Moseley and Kari Ronning. Lincoln: University of Nebraska Press, 2012.

———. *The Troll Garden*. [1905.] In *Early Novels and Stories*, 1–131. New York: Library of America, 1987.

———. "A Wagner Matinée." [1904.] In Cather, *Youth and the Bright Medusa*, 235–47.

———. *Willa Cather: Stories, Poems, and Other Writings*. New York: Library of America, 1992.

———. *Willa Cather in Europe: Her Own Story of the First Journey*. Edited by George Kates. Lincoln: University of Nebraska Press, 1988.

———. *Willa Cather on Writing*. Foreword by Stephen Tennant. Lincoln: University of Nebraska Press, 1988.

———. *The World and the Parish: Willa Cather's Articles and Reviews, 1893–1902*, 2 vols. Edited by William Curtin. Lincoln: University of Nebraska Press, 1970.

———. *Youth and the Bright Medusa*. [1920.] Edited by Mark Madigan, Frederick Link, Charles Mignon, Judith Boss, and Kari Ronning. Lincoln: University of Nebraska Press, 2009.

Chapman, Victor. *Victor Chapman's Letters from France, with Memoir by John Jay Chapman*. New York: Macmillan, 1917.

Chast, Roz. *Going into Town: A Love Letter to New York*. New York: Bloomsbury, 2017.

Chénetier, Marc. "Sorbonne Keynote Address: Shadows of a Rock: Translating Willa Cather." In Murphy, Palleau-Papin, and Thacker, *Cather Studies 8*, 23–45.

Clarke, Deborah. "Modernist Domesticity: Reconciling the Paradox in Edith Wharton, Willa Cather, and Nella Larsen." In *History of the Modern Novel*, edited by Gregory Clark, 190–208. New York: Cambridge University Press, 2015.

Cohen, Debra. "Culture and the 'Cathedral': Tourism as Potlatch in *One of Ours*." In Trout, *Cather Studies 6*, 184–204.

Coolidge, Calvin. "Address to the American Society of Newspaper Editors, Washington, D.C." January 17, 1925, http://www.presidency.ucsb.edu/ws/?pid=24180. Accessed August 8, 2018.

Cowley, Malcolm. "Foreword: The Revolt against Gentility." [1937.] In *After the Genteel Tradition: American Writers, 1910–1930*, edited by Malcolm Cowley. Carbondale: Southern Illinois University Press, 1967.

Crane, Joan. *Willa Cather: A Bibliography*. Lincoln: University of Nebraska Press, 1982.

Cronon, William. *Changes in the Land: Indians, Colonists, and the Ecology of New England*. New York: Hill and Wang, 1983.

Crow, Charles. *A Companion to the Regional Literatures of America*. Malden MA: Blackwell Publishing, 2003.

Daudet, Alphonse. *Artists' Wives*. Translated by Laura Ensor. New York: Turtle Point, 2009.

Dawson, Graham. *Making Peace with the Past? Memory, Trauma and the Irish Troubles*. Manchester: Manchester University Press, 2007.

DeSanctis, Marcia. "Retracing Willa Cather's Steps in the South of France." *Literary Hub*, August 18, 2017, http://lithub.com/retracing-willa-cathers-steps-in-the-south-of-france/.

Dimock, Wai Chee. "Debasing Exchange: Edith Wharton's *The House of Mirth*." PMLA 100, no. 5 (October 1985): 783–92.

———. *Through Other Continents: American Literature across Deep Time*. Princeton NJ: Princeton University Press, 2006.

Durrans, Stéphanie. *The Influence of French Culture on Willa Cather: Intertextual References and Resonances*. Lewiston NY: Mellen, 2007.

Duvall, J. Michael. "The Futile and the Dingy: Wasting and Being Wasted in *The House of Mirth*." In *Memorial Boxes and Guarded Interiors: Edith Wharton and Material Culture*, edited by Gary Totten, 159–83. Tuscaloosa: University of Alabama Press, 2007.

Dwight, Eleanor. *Edith Wharton: An Extraordinary Life*. New York: Abrams, 1994.

"Echoes and Shadows." *The Nation* 108, no. 2793 (January 11, 1919): 56–57.

Edel, Leon. "Editor's Foreword." [1953.] In *Willa Cather: A Critical Biography*, by E. K. Brown, xxvii–xxxiv. Lincoln: University of Nebraska Press, 1987.

———. *Henry James: A Life*. New York: Harper and Row, 1985.

———. "Homage to Willa Cather." In Slote and Faulkner, *The Art of Willa Cather*.

———. "Summers in an Age of Innocence: In France with Edith Wharton." *New York Times Book Review*, June 1991, 3, 44, 46.

Edmiston, Susan, and Linda Cirino. *Literary New York: A History and Guide*. Boston: Houghton Mifflin, 1976.

Eeckhout, Bart. "Why Would the Spatial Be So Special? A Critical Analysis of the Spatial Turn in American Studies." In *Ambassadors: American Studies in a Changing World*, edited by Massimo Bacigalupo and Gregory Dowling, 19–37. Rapallo, Italy: Azienda Grafica Busco Edizioni, 2006.

Egli, Ida Rae. "Early Western Literary Women." In *Updating the Literary West*, 82–98.

Eliot, George. "Silly Novels by Lady Novelists." In *Silly Novels by Lady Novelists*, 1–34. London: Penguin, 2010.

Emerson, Ralph. "The Rhodora." https://quod.lib.umich.edu/a/amverse/BAD1982.0001.001/1:5.15?rgn=div2;view=fulltext.

Emsley, Sarah. "Appendix A: Edith Wharton's Outline and Notes for *A Custom of the Country*." In *The Custom of the Country*, by Edith Wharton, 410–15. Edited by Sarah Emsley. Toronto: Broadview Editions, 2008.

Ferguson, Priscilla Parkhurst. *Accounting for Taste: The Triumph of French Cuisine*. Chicago: University of Chicago Press, 2004.

Fetterley, Judith, and Marjorie Pryce. *Writing out of Place: Regionalism, Women, and American Literary Culture*. Urbana: University of Illinois Press, 2003.

Fisher, Dorothy. *The Brimming Cup*. New York: Harcourt Brace, 1921.

———. "A Little Kansas Leaven." In *Home Fires in France*, 132–72. New York: Henry Holt, 1918.

Folpe, Emily. *It Happened on Washington Square*. Baltimore: Johns Hopkins University Press, 2002.

Frost, Robert. "The Death of the Hired Man." In *Robert Frost: Collected Poems, Prose, and Plays*, 40–45. New York: Library of America, 1995.

Fryer, Judith. *Felicitous Space: The Imaginative Structures of Edith Wharton and Willa Cather*. Chapel Hill: University of North Carolina Press, 1986.

Fussell, Paul. "Introduction." In *The Norton Book of Travel*, 13–17. New York: W. W. Norton, 1987.

Gale, Zona. *Miss Lulu Bett and Selected Stories*. Edited by Barbara H. Solomon and Eileen Panetta. New York: Anchor, 2005.

Garrison, Stephen. *Edith Wharton: A Descriptive Bibliography*. Pittsburgh: University of Pittsburgh Press, 1990.

Gervaud, Michel. "Willa Cather and France: Elective Affinities." In Slote and Faulkner, *The Art of Willa Cather*, 65–81.

Gilbert, Sandra, and Susan Gubar. *The Madwoman in the Attic: The Woman Writer and the Nineteenth-Century Literary Imagination*. New Haven CT: Yale University Press, 1979.

Glennon, Jenny. "The Big Bribes: Jewelry, American Taste, and Globalization in Wharton's Twenties Novels." *Edith Wharton Review* 27, no. 1 (Spring 2011): 17–23.

———. "The Custom of Main Street: Wharton, Sinclair Lewis, and Middle-Class Taste." *Edith Wharton Review* 30, no. 1 (Spring 2014): 45–59.

———. "Toward a Brighter Vision of 'American Ways and Their Meaning': Edith Wharton and the Americanization of Europe after the First World War." In *American Writers in Europe: 1850 to the Present*, edited by Ferda Asya, 97–114. Basingstoke, UK: Palgrave, 2013.

Glotfelty, Cheryll. "Introduction: Literary Studies in an Age of Environmental Crisis." In *The Ecocriticism Reader: Landmarks in Literary Ecology*, edited by Cheryll Glotfelty and Harold Fromm, xv–xxxvii. Athens: University of Georgia Press, 1996.

Goldman-Price, Irene, ed. *My Dear Governess: The Letters of Edith Wharton to Anna Bahlmann*. New Haven CT: Yale University Press, 2012.

Gómez Reus, Teresa. "'Remember Spain!' Edith Wharton and the Book She Never Wrote." *English Studies: A Journal of English Language and Literature* 98, nos. 1–2 (February–April 2017): 175–93.

Gopnik, Adam. "Introduction." In *Americans in Paris*. New York: Library of America, 2004.

———. *Paris to the Moon*. New York: Random House, 2001.

Graves, Richard. *A. E. Housman, the Scholar-Poet*. New York: Scribner's, 1980.

Green, Nancy. *The Other Americans in Paris: Businessmen, Countesses, Wayward Youth, 1880–1941*. Chicago: University of Chicago Press, 2014.
Griffith, Jean. *The Color of Democracy in Women's Regional Writing*. Tuscaloosa: University of Alabama Press, 2009.
Gubar, Susan. "'The Blank Page' and Issues of Female Creativity." *Critical Inquiry* 8, no. 2 (Winter 1981): 243–63.
Haber, Tom. *A. E. Housman*. New York: Twayne, 1967.
Hadju, David. "Who Needs the NEA and NEH?" *The Nation*, April 7, 2017, https://www.thenation.com/article/who-needs-the-nea-and-neh/.
Hamera, Judith, and Alfred Bendixen, eds. "Introduction." In *The Cambridge Companion to American Travel Writing*, edited by Alfred Bendixen and Judith Hamera, 1–9. Cambridge: Cambridge University Press, 2009.
Harris, Richard. "Claude Wheeler's Visit to the Church of St. Ouen." *Willa Cather Newsletter and Review* 59, no. 3 (Spring 2017): 6–7.
———. "Explanatory Notes." In Cather, *One of Ours*, 613–75.
———. "Historical Essay." In Cather, *One of Ours*, 677–797.
———. "Pershing's Crusaders: G. P. Cather, Claude Wheeler, and the AEF Soldier in France." In Murphy, Palleau-Papin, and Thacker, *Cather Studies 8*, 74–90.
Hawthorne, Nathaniel. "The Artist of the Beautiful." In *Nathaniel Hawthorne's Tales*, 2nd ed., 198–218. Edited by James McIntosh. New York: Norton, 2012.
Haytock, Jennifer. *Edith Wharton and the Conversations of Literary Modernism*. New York: Palgrave Macmillan, 2008.
———. "Modernism." In Rattray, *Edith Wharton in Context*, 364–73.
Homestead, Melissa. "Willa Cather, Sarah Orne Jewett, and the Historiography of Lesbian Sexuality." In Kaufman and Millington, *Cather Studies 10*, 3–37.
Homestead, Melissa, and Guy Reynolds, eds. *Cather Studies 9: Willa Cather and Modern Cultures*. Lincoln: University of Nebraska Press, 2011.
Horner, Avril, and Janet Beer. *Edith Wharton: Sex, Satire, and the Older Woman*. Basingstoke, UK: Palgrave McMillan, 2011.
Housman, A. E. *A Shropshire Lad*. [1896.] New York: Dover, 1990.
Howard, June. *Form and History in American Literary Naturalism*. Chapel Hill: University of North Carolina Press, 1985.
Howe, Irving, ed. *Edith Wharton: A Collection of Critical Essays*. Englewood Cliffs NJ: Prentice-Hall, 1962.
Howells, William Dean. *Indian Summer*. Boston: Ticknor, 1886.
———. *Italian Journeys*. [1868.] Boston: Houghton Mifflin, 1872.
———. *Venetian Life*. [1866.] Boston: Riverside Press, 1907.
Hulme, Peter, and Tim Youngs, eds. "Introduction." In *The Cambridge Companion to Travel Writing*, edited by Peter Hulme and Tim Youngs, 1–13. Cambridge: Cambridge University Press, 2002.

James, Henry. *The American Scene*. [1907.] Introduction by Leon Edel. Bloomington: Indiana University Press, 1968.

———. "The Art of Fiction." In *Henry James: Literary Criticism: Essays on Literature, American Writers, English Writers*, edited by Mark Wilson and Leon Edel, 44–65. New York: Library of America, 1984.

———. "Daisy Miller." [1878.] In *Henry James: Major Stories and Essays*, 3–60. New York: Library of America, 1999.

———. *Hawthorne*. [1879.] Ithaca NY: Cornell University Press, 1997.

———. *Italian Hours*. In *Henry James: Collected Travel Writings*, 279–619. New York: Library of America, 1993.

———. *A Little Tour in France*. In *Henry James: Collected Travel Writings*, 1–277. New York: Library of America, 1993.

———. "A Passionate Pilgrim." In *Henry James: Complete Stories, 1864–1874*, 543–611. New York: Library of America, 1999.

———. *Washington Square*. [1880.] Baltimore: Penguin, 1968.

Jewell, Andrew. "Willa Cather's Shifting Perspectives on the Great War." *Willa Cather Newsletter and Review* 59, no. 3 (Spring 2017): 14–18.

Jewell, Andrew, and Janis Stout. "Introduction." In *The Selected Letters of Willa Cather*, edited by Andrew Jewell and Janis Stout, vii–xvi. New York: Knopf, 2013.

Jewett, Sarah Orne. *Letters of Sarah Orne Jewett*. Edited by Annie Fields. Boston: Houghton Mifflin, 1911.

Jones, Suzanne W. "The 'Beyondness of Things' in *The Buccaneers*: Vernon Lee's Influence on Edith Wharton's Sense of Place." *Symbiosis: A Journal of Anglo-American Literary Relations* 8, no. 1 (April 2004): 7–30.

Joslin, Katherine, and Alan Price, eds. *Wretched Exotic: Essays on Edith Wharton in Europe*. New York: Peter Lang, 1993.

"Julian Fellowes: 'Abbey' Owes Much to Wharton." *Berkshire Eagle*, February 20, 2013, http://www.berkshireeagle.com/ci_22625329/julian-fellowes-abbey-owes-much-wharton.

Kaufman, Anne, and Richard Millington, eds. *Cather Studies 10: Willa Cather and the Nineteenth Century*. Lincoln: University of Nebraska Press, 2015.

Kazin, Alfred. *A Writer's America: Landscape in Literature*. New York: Knopf, 1988.

Keegan, John. *The First World War*. New York: Knopf, 1999.

Keep, Austin. *History of the New York Society Library*. [1908.] Boston: Gregg Press, 1972.

Kim, Sharon. "Edith Wharton and Epiphany." *Journal of Modern Literature* 30, no. 3 (Spring 2006): 150–75.

King, Marion. *Books and People: Five Decades of New York's Oldest Library*. New York: Macmillan, 1954.

Kipling, Rudyard. *Puck of Pook's Hill*. London: MacMillan, 1927.

Kowalewski, Michael. "Contemporary Regionalism." In *A Companion to the Regional Literatures of America*, edited by Charles L. Crow, 7–24. Malden MA: Blackwell Publishing, 2003.

Kreizenbeck, Alan. *Zoë Akins: Broadway Playwright*. Westport CT: Praeger, 2004.

Ku, Chung-Hao. "'A Boy under Ban of Suspension': Renouncing Maturity in Willa Cather's 'Paul's Case.'" *Modern Fiction Studies* 61, no. 1 (Spring 2015): 69–89.

Larkin, Philip. "MCMXIV." 1964, http://www.poetrybyheart.org.uk/poems/mcmxiv/. Accessed September 22, 2017.

Lawrence, Margaret. *The School of Femininity*. New York: Stokes, 1936.

Lears, T. J. Jackson. "From Salvation to Self-Realization." In *The Culture of Consumption: Critical Essays in American History, 1880–1980*, edited by Richard W. Fox and T. J. Jackson Lears. New York: Pantheon Books, 1983.

Lee, Hermione. *Edith Wharton*. New York: Knopf, 2007.

———. *Willa Cather: Double Lives*. New York: Vintage, 1989.

Lewis, Edith. *Willa Cather Living: A Personal Record*. Lincoln: University of Nebraska Press, 2000.

Lewis, R. W. B. *Edith Wharton: A Biography*. New York: Harper and Row, 1975.

Lewis, Sinclair. "The American Fear of Literature." In S. Lewis, *The Man from Main Street*, 3–17.

———. "The American Scene in Fiction." In S. Lewis, *The Man from Main Street*, 142–47.

———. *The Man from Main Street: A Sinclair Lewis Reader*. Edited by Harry Maule and Melville Cane. New York: Random House, 1953.

———. "Minnesota, the Norse State." In S. Lewis, *The Man from Main Street*, 273–83.

Loos, Anita. *Gentlemen Prefer Blondes*. [1925.] In *"Gentlemen Prefer Blondes" and "But Gentlemen Marry Brunettes."* Introduction by Regina Barraca. New York: Penguin, 1998.

Lopate, Phillip, ed. *Writing New York: A Literary Anthology*. New York: Library of America, 1998.

Lopez, Esther M. "Learning to Like *Chili Colorado*: Constructing Culture in *Death Comes for the Archbishop*." *Willa Cather Newsletter and Review* 54, no. 2 (Fall 2010): 85–89.

Lorde, Audre. "Poetry Is Not a Luxury." In *Sister Outsider: Essays and Speeches*, 36–39. Freedom CA: Crossing Press, 1984.

Love, Glen. *New Americans: The Westerner and the Modern Experience in the American Novel*. Lewisburg PA: Bucknell University Press, 1982.

Lutwack, Leonard. *The Role of Place in Literature*. Syracuse NY: Syracuse University Press, 1984.

MacDonald, Mary, ed. "Introduction." In *Experiences of Place*, edited by Mary MacDonald, 1–17. Cambridge MA: Harvard University Press, 2003.

Madigan, Mark J. "'An Artist in Her Way': An Homage to Joséphine Bourda." *Willa Cather Newsletter and Review* 58, no. 3 (Spring 2016): 26–30.

———, ed. *Keeping Fires Night and Day: Selected Letters of Dorothy Canfield Fisher*. Columbia: University of Missouri Press, 1993.

———. "Translating the Southwest: The 1940 Translation of *Death Comes for the Archbishop*." In *Willa Cather at the Modernist Crux*, edited by Ann Moseley, John J. Murphy, and Robert Thacker, 214–26. Lincoln: University of Nebraska Press, 2017.

———. "Willa Cather in Paris: The Mystery of a Torn Photograph." In Murphy, Palleau-Papin, and Thacker, *Cather Studies 8*, 62–73.

Mahoney, Timothy, and Wendy Katz, eds. *Regionalism and the Humanities*. Lincoln: University of Nebraska Press, 2008.

Majaj, Lisa Suhair. "Boundaries: Arab/American." In *Food for Our Grandmothers: Writings by Arab-American and Arab-Canadian Feminists*, edited by Joanna Kadi, 65–86. Boston: South End Press, 1994.

Malpas, J. E. *Place and Experience: A Philosophical Topography*. Cambridge: Cambridge University Press, 1999.

"Mapping a Writer's Worlds: A Geographic Chronology of Willa Cather's Life." Willa Cather Archives, http://cather.unl.edu/geochron/.

Marchand, Mary. "Object Lessons: Wharton's *The Custom of the Country* and the New Connoisseurship." *Edith Wharton Review* 17, no. 1 (Spring 2011): 1–10.

McCullough, David. *The Greater Journey: Americans in Paris*. New York: Simon and Schuster, 2011.

Mencken, H. L. *The American Language*. Edited by Raven McDavid Jr. New York: Knopf, 1977.

Meyer, Susan. "Contamination, Modernity, Health, and Art in Edith Wharton and Willa Cather." In Kaufman and Millington, *Cather Studies 10*, 97–115.

Millington, Richard. "Where Is Cather's Quebec? Anthropological Modernism in *Shadows on the Rock*." In Thacker and Peterman, *Cather Studies 4*, 23–44.

———. "Willa Cather's Two Modernisms." *Letterature d'America* 33, no. 155 (2013): 41–56.

Mitchell, Lee C. *Westerns: Making the Man in Fiction and Film*. Chicago: University of Chicago Press, 1996.

Moers, Ellen. *Literary Women*. Garden City NY: Doubleday, 1976.

Momaday, N. Scott. *The Way to Rainy Mountain*. Albuquerque: University of New Mexico Press, 1969.

Moore, Michelle. "Chicago's Cliff Dwellers and *The Song of the Lark*." In Homestead and Reynolds, *Cather Studies 9*, 93–113.

Moseley, Ann. "Explanatory Notes." In Cather, *The Song of the Lark*, 619–809.

Murphy, John J. "Building the House of Faith: 'Hard Punishments,' the Plan and the Fragments." In John J. Murphy, *Willa Cather and the Culture of Belief*, 202–27.

———. "Compromising Realism to Idealize a War: Wharton's *The Marne* and Cather's *One of Ours*." *American Literary Realism* 33, no. 2 (Winter 2001): 157–67.

———. "Explanatory Notes." In Cather, *Death Comes for the Archbishop*, 381–512.

———. "From Cornfield to the Big Apple Orchard: New York as School for Cather and Her Critics." In Skaggs, *Willa Cather's New York*, 21–42.

———. "Kindred Spirits: Willa Cather and Henry James." In Kaufman and Millington, *Cather Studies 10*, 223–42.

———, ed. *Willa Cather and the Culture of Belief*. Provo UT: Brigham Young University Press, 2002.

Murphy, John J., Françoise Palleau-Papin, and Robert Thacker, eds. *Cather Studies 8: Willa Cather: A Writer's Worlds*. Lincoln: University of Nebraska Press, 2010.

Murphy, Joseph. "The Genius Revisited: Willa Cather and the Spirit of Place." *Willa Cather Newsletter and Review* 54, no. 1 (Summer 2010): 4–11.

Nehamas, Alexander. *Only a Promise of Beauty: The Place of Beauty in a World of Art*. Princeton NJ: Princeton University Press, 2007.

Nettels, Elsa. "'The Bravest Act of His Life': Cather, Claude, and the Disadvantages of a Prairie Childhood." In Murphy, Palleau-Papin, and Thacker, *Cather Studies 8*, 46–61.

———. "Edith Wharton's Correspondence with Zona Gale: 'An Elder's Warm Admiration and Interest.'" *Resources for American Literary Study* 24, no. 2 (1988): 207–34.

———. *Language and Gender in American Fiction: Howells, James, Wharton and Cather*. Charlottesville: University Press of Virginia, 1997.

———. "Wharton and Trollope: 'The Way We Live Now' in 'The House of Mirth.'" *Edith Wharton Review* 22, no. 2 (Fall 2006): 6–9.

———. "Willa Cather and the Example of Henry James." In Kaufman and Millington, *Cather Studies 10*, 189–222.

———. "Youth and Age in the Old and New Worlds: Willa Cather and A. E. Housman." In Thacker and Peterman, *Cather Studies 4*, 284–93.

New York Society Library List of Shareholders, Officers, Benefactors and Its History with Illustrations. New York: New York Society Library, 1914.

Norris, Frank. "A Plea for Romantic Fiction." In *The Literary Criticism of Frank Norris*, edited by Donald Pizer, 75–78. Austin: University of Texas Press, 1964.

O'Brien, Sharon. *Willa Cather: The Emerging Voice*. New York: Oxford University Press, 1987.

O'Connor, Margaret. *Willa Cather: The Contemporary Reviews*. Cambridge: Cambridge University Press, 2001.

Olin-Ammentorp, Julie. "Daisy, Lily, and Marian: Cather Revises James and Wharton." *Letterature d'America* 33, no. 144 (2013): 57–76.

———. *Edith Wharton's Writings from the Great War*. Gainesville: University Press of Florida, 2004.

———. "Girls from the Provinces: Wharton's Undine Spragg and Cather's Thea Kronborg." In *Edith Wharton's The Custom of the Country: A Reassessment*, edited by Laura Rattray, 127–42. London: Pickering and Chatto, 2010.

———. "Thea at the Art Institute." In Homestead and Reynolds, *Cather Studies 9*, 182–203.

———. "Willa Cather's 'Individual Map' of Paris." *Willa Cather Newsletter and Review* 58, no. 2 (Winter 2015): 4–11.

———. "Willa Cather's *One of Ours*, Edith Wharton's *A Son at the Front*, and the Literature of the Great War." In Murphy, Palleau-Papin, and Thacker, *Cather Studies 8*, 125–47.

Orgel, Stephen, ed. "Introduction." In *The Custom of the Country*, by Edith Wharton, vii–xxiii. Oxford: Oxford University Press, 2008.

Orlando, Emily. *Edith Wharton and the Visual Arts*. Tuscaloosa: University of Alabama Press, 2007.

Page, Philip. "The Theatricality of 'Paul's Case.'" *Studies in Short Fiction* 28, no. 4 (Fall 1991): 553–57.

Palleau-Papin, Françoise. "The Hidden French in Willa Cather's English." In Thacker and Peterman, *Cather Studies 4*, 45–65.

———. "Slowly, but Surely: Willa Cather's Reception in France." *Studies in the Novel* 45, no. 3 (Fall 2013): 538–58.

———. "The Translation in the Closet: Willa Cather and Marguerite Yourcenar." *Willa Cather Newsletter and Review* 58, no. 2 (Winter 2015): 50–55.

Parker, Peter. *A. E. Housman: Into the Heart of England*. London: Little, Brown, 2016.

Patell, Cyrus, and Bryan Waterman, eds. *The Cambridge Companion to the Literature of New York*. Cambridge: Cambridge University Press, 2010.

Pater, Walter. "Conclusion." *Studies in the History of the Renaissance*. [1873.] In *Norton Anthology of Theory and Criticism*, edited by Vincent Leitch, 839–41. New York: W. W. Norton, 2001.

Peterman, Michael, and Robert Thacker. "Introduction: Gazing Down from Cap Diamant: Cather's Canadian and Old World Connections." In Thacker and Peterman, *Cather Studies 4*, 1–6.

Pizer, Donald. "The Naturalism of Edith Wharton's *The House of Mirth*." *Twentieth Century Literature* 41, no. 2 (Summer 1995): 241–48.

Pollack, Sheldon, Homi Bhabha, Carol Breckenridge, and Dipesh Chakrabarty. "Cosmopolitanisms." In *Cosmopolitanism*, edited by Dipesh Chakrabarty, Homi Bhabha, Sheldon Pollack, and Carol Breckenridge, 1–14. Durham NC: Duke University Press, 2002.

Porter, David. "'Life Is Very Simple—All We Have to Do Is Our Best!': Willa Cather and the Brewsters." In *Willa Cather: New Facts, New Glimpses, Revisions*, edited by John J. Murphy and Merrill Skaggs, 141–57. Madison NJ: Fairleigh Dickinson University Press, 2008.

———. *On the Divide: The Many Lives of Willa Cather*. Lincoln: University of Nebraska Press, 2008.

Powers, Lyall H., ed. *Henry James and Edith Wharton: Letters, 1900–1915*. New York: Scribner's, 1990.

———. *Henry James and the Naturalist Movement*. East Lansing: Michigan State University Press, 1971.

Prenatt, Diane. "'Intrigued by the Cubist': Cather, Sergeant, and Auguste Chabaud." *Willa Cather Newsletter and Review* 59, no. 2 (Fall/Winter 2016): 2–9.

———. "Negotiating Authority: Elizabeth Shepley Sergeant's World War I Memoir." *Studies in the Humanities* 41, nos. 1–2 (March 1915): 69–99.

Price, Alan. *The End of the Age of Innocence*. New York: St. Martin's, 1996.

Proulx, Annie. "Dangerous Ground: Landscape in American Fiction." In Mahoney and Katz, *Regionalism and the Humanities*, 6–25.

Quirk, Tom. "Historical Essay." In Cather, *Alexander's Bridge*, 135–94.

Rahv, Philip. "Paleface and Redskin." In *Image and Idea: Twenty Essays on Literary Themes*, 1–6. London: Weidenfeld and Nicolson, 1957.

Rasmussen, R. Kent. *Mark Twain A–Z: The Essential Guide to His Life and Writing*. New York: Oxford University Press, 1995.

Rattray, Laura, ed. *Edith Wharton in Context*. Cambridge: Cambridge University Press, 2012.

Reed, Walt. *Harold von Schmidt Draws and Paints the Old West*. Flagstaff AZ: Northland Press, 1972.

Reynolds, Guy. "The Politics of Cather's Regionalism: Margins, Centers and the Nebraskan Commonwealth." March 2003, http://digitalcommons.unl.edu/cgi/viewcontent.cgi?article=1000&context=englishtalks.

———. *Willa Cather in Context*. New York: St. Martin's, 1996.

———. "Willa Cather's Case: Region and Reputation." In Mahoney and Katz, *Regionalism and the Humanities*, 79–94.

Rich, Daniel. "Chauncey McCormick: Some Recollections." *Art Institute of Chicago Quarterly* 48, no. 4 (November 15, 1954): 61–67.

Richards, Grant. *Housman, 1897–1936*. London: Oxford, 1941.

Roberson, Susan. "American Women and Travel Writing." In *The Cambridge Companion to American Travel Writing*, edited by Alfred Bendixen and Judith Hamera, 214–27. Cambridge: Cambridge University Press, 2009.

Robinson, Lillian. "The Traffic in Women: A Cultural Critique of *The House of Mirth*." In *Case Studies in Contemporary Criticism*, edited by Shari Benstock, 340–58. Boston: St. Martin's, 1994.

Romines, Ann, ed. *Willa Cather's Southern Connections: New Essays on Cather and the South*. Charlottesville: University Press of Virginia, 2000.

Rosowski, Susan. "Historical Essay." In Cather, *A Lost Lady*, 177–233.

———. *The Voyage Perilous: Willa Cather's Romanticism*. Lincoln: University of Nebraska Press, 1986.

Ross, Alex. "A Gathering of Orchestras." *New Yorker*, April 17, 2017, https://www.newyorker.com/magazine/2017/04/17/a-gathering-of-orchestras-in-dc.

Ryan, Ann. "Introduction: Mark Twain and the Cosmopolitan Ideal." In Ryan and McCullough, *The Cosmopolitan Mark Twain*, 1–20.

Ryan, Ann, and Joseph McCullough, eds. *The Cosmopolitan Mark Twain*. Columbia: University of Missouri Press, 2008.

Said, Edward. "Culture and Imperialism." In Said, *Reflections on Exile and Other Essays*.

———. "Introduction." In Said, *Reflections on Exile and Other Essays*.

———. *Reflections on Exile and Other Essays*. Cambridge MA: Harvard University Press, 2000.

Sandburg, Carl. "Chicago." *Poetry* 3, no. 6 (March 1914). https://www.poetryfoundation.org/poetrymagazine/poems/12840/chicago.

Sassoon, Siegfried. *Goodbye to All That*. New York: Cape and Smith, 1930.

Schama, Simon. *Landscape and Memory*. New York: Knopf, 1995.

Sensibar, Judith. "'Behind the Lines' in Edith Wharton's *A Son at the Front*: Re-Writing a Masculinist Tradition." In Joslin and Price, *Wretched Exotic*, 241–56.

Sergeant, Elizabeth. *French Perspectives*. Boston: Houghton Mifflin, 1916.

———. *Willa Cather: A Memoir*. Lincoln: University of Nebraska Press, 1953.

Sherman, Sarah. *Sacramental Shopping: Louisa May Alcott, Edith Wharton, and the Spirit of Modern Consumerism*. Durham: University of New Hampshire Press, 2013.

Shively, Steven. "The Compatibility of Art and Religion for Willa Cather." In *Cather Studies 11: Willa Cather at the Modernist Crux*, edited by Ann Moseley, John J. Murphy, and Robert Thacker, 19–42. Lincoln: University of Nebraska Press, 2017.

Showalter, Elaine. *A Jury of Her Peers: American Women Writers from Anne Bradstreet to Annie Proulx*. New York: Knopf, 2009.

Silko, Leslie. *Ceremony*. New York: Penguin, 2006.

Simour, Lhoussain. "The White Lady Travels: Narrating Fez and Spacing Colonial Authority in Edith Wharton's *In Morocco*." *Hawwa: Journal of the Middle East and the Islamic World* 7 (2009): 39–56.

Singley, Carol. *Edith Wharton: Matters of Mind and Spirit*. Cambridge: Cambridge University Press, 1995.

Skaggs, Merrill McGuire. *Axes: Willa Cather and William Faulkner*. Lincoln: University of Nebraska Press, 2007.

———. "Introduction." In Skaggs, *Willa Cather's New York*, 13–16.

———, ed. *Willa Cather's New York: New Essays on Cather and the City*. Madison NJ: Fairleigh Dickinson University Press, 2000.

Slote, Bernice. "First Principles: The Kingdom of Art." In Slote, *The Kingdom of Art*, 31–112.

———, ed. *The Kingdom of Art: Willa Cather's First Principles and Critical Statements, 1893–1896*. Lincoln: University of Nebraska Press, 1966.
Slote, Bernice, and Virginia Faulkner, eds. *The Art of Willa Cather*. Lincoln: University of Nebraska Press, 1974.
Smith, Leonard, Stéphane Audoin-Rouzeau, and Annette Becker. *France and the Great War, 1914–1918*. Cambridge: Cambridge University Press, 2003.
Smith, Patricia. "Achaeans, Americanos, Prelates and Monsters: Willa Cather's *Death Comes for the Archbishop* as a New World Odyssey." In *Padre Martinez: New Perspectives from Taos*, edited by E. A. Mares, 101–24. Taos NM: Millicent Rogers Museum, 1988.
Solnit, Rebecca, and Joshua Jelly-Schapiro. *Nonstop Metropolis: A New York City Atlas*. Berkeley: University of California Press, 2016.
Steffensen-Bruce, Ingrid. *Marble Palaces, Temples of Art: Art Museums, Architecture, and American Culture, 1890–1930*. Lewisburg PA: Bucknell University Press, 1998.
Stouck, David. "Historical Essay." In Cather, *O Pioneers!*, 283–303.
Stout, Janis. "Between Two Wars in a Breaking World: Willa Cather and the Persistence of War Consciousness." In Trout, *Cather Studies 6*, 70–91.
———, ed. *A Calendar of the Letters of Willa Cather*. Lincoln: University of Nebraska Press, 2002.
———. "Faith Statements and Nonstatements in Willa Cather's Personal Letters." In John J. Murphy, *Willa Cather and the Culture of Belief*, 7–27.
———. *Picturing a Different West: Vision, Illustration, and the Tradition of Cather and Austin*. Lubbock: Texas Tech University Press, 2007.
———. *Through the Window, Out the Door: Women's Narratives of Departure, from Austin and Cather to Tyler, Morrison, and Didion*. Tuscaloosa: University of Alabama Press, 1998.
———. *Willa Cather: The Writer and Her World*. Charlottesville: University Press of Virginia, 2000.
Stowe, Harriet Beecher. *Sunny Memories of Foreign Lands*, vol. 2. Boston: Phillips, Sampson, 1854.
Sullivan, Peter. "Willa Cather's German Connections: 'Uncle Valentine' and Wertherian Wandering." In Thacker and Peterman, *Cather Studies 4*, 319–29.
Summers, Claude. "'A Losing Game in the End': Aestheticism and Homosexuality in 'Paul's Case.'" *Modern Fiction Studies* 36, no. 1 (Spring 1990): 103–19.
Swift, John. "Cather, Freudianism, and Freud." In *Cather Studies 7: Willa Cather as Cultural Icon*, edited by Guy Reynolds. Lincoln: University of Nebraska Press, 2007. https://cather.unl.edu/cs007_swift.html.
Swift, John, and Joseph Urgo. *Willa Cather and the American Southwest*. Lincoln: University of Nebraska Press, 2002.
Teasdale, Sara, ed. *The Answering Voice: One Hundred Love Lyrics by Women*. Boston: Houghton Mifflin, 1917.

Thacker, Robert. "'As the Result of Many Solicitations': Ferris Greenslet, Houghton Mifflin, and Cather's Career." *Studies in the Novel* 45, no. 3 (Fall 2013): 369–86.

———. *The Great Prairie Fact and the Literary Imagination*. Albuquerque: University of New Mexico Press, 1989.

———. "'One Knows It Too Well to Know It Well': Willa Cather, A. E. Housman, and *A Shropshire Lad*." In Kaufman and Millington, *Cather Studies 10*, 300–327.

Thacker, Robert, and Michael Peterman, eds. *Cather Studies 4: Willa Cather's Canadian and Old World Connections*. Lincoln: University of Nebraska Press, 1999.

Thompson, Stephanie. *Influencing America's Tastes: Realism in the Works of Wharton, Cather and Hurst*. Gainesville: University Press of Florida, 2002.

Thoreau, Henry David. *Walden and Resistance to Civil Government*, 2nd ed. Edited by William Rossi. New York: W. W. Norton, 1992.

Tóibín, Colm. "The Custom of the Country." Photographs by Annie Leibovitz. *Vogue*, September 2012, 810–27.

Totten, Gary. "The Dialectic of History and Technology in Edith Wharton's *A Motor-Flight through France*." *Studies in Travel Writing* 17, no. 2 (2013): 133–44.

———. "Edith Wharton's Wild West: Undine Spragg and Dakota Divorce Culture." *Edith Wharton Review* 31, nos. 1–2 (2015): 93–96.

———. "Imagining the American West in Wharton's Short Fiction." *Journal of the Short Story in English* 58 (2012): 1–13.

Trilling, Lionel. "The Princess Casamassima." In *The Liberal Imagination: Essays on Literature and Society*, 57–92. Garden City NY: Doubleday, 1957.

Trout, Steven, ed. *Cather Studies 6: History, Memory, and War*. Lincoln: University of Nebraska Press, 2006.

Tuan, Yi-Fu. *Topophilia: A Study of Environmental Perception, Attitudes, and Values*. Englewood Cliffs NJ: Prentice-Hall, 1974.

Turner, Frederick. "The Significance of the Frontier." In *Frontier and Section: Selected Essays of Frederick Jackson Turner*, 37–62. Introduction by Ray Billington. Englewood Cliffs NJ: Prentice-Hall, 1961.

Tuttleton, James, Kristin Lauer, and Margaret Murray. *Edith Wharton: The Contemporary Reviews*. Cambridge: Cambridge University Press, 1992.

Updating the Literary West. Western Literature Association, sponsor. Fort Worth: Texas Christian University Press, 1997.

Urgo, Joseph. "The Cather Thesis: The American Empire of Migration." In *The Cambridge Companion to Willa Cather*, edited by Marilee Lindemann, 35–50. Cambridge: Cambridge University Press, 2005.

Van Doren, Carl. "Contemporary American Novelists: Willa Cather." *The Nation* 113, no. 2925 (July 27, 1921): 92–93.

———. "Contemporary Novelists: Edith Wharton." *The Nation* 112, no. 2897 (January 12, 1921): 40–41.

Veblen, Thorstein. *The Theory of the Leisure Class.* [1899.] New York: Modern Library, 1934.

Waid, Candace. "Burying the Regional Mother: Faulkner's Road to Race through the Visual Arts." *Faulkner Journal* 23, no. 1 (Fall 2007): 37–92.

———. *Edith Wharton's Letters from the Underworld: Fictions of Women and Writing.* Chapel Hill: University of North Carolina Press, 1991.

Walker, Alice. "Everyday Use." In *In Love and Trouble.* New York: Harcourt Brace, 1973.

———. *In Search of Our Mothers' Gardens: Womanist Prose.* San Diego: Harcourt Brace, 1983.

Warf, Barney, and Santa Arias. *The Spatial Turn: Interdisciplinary Perspectives.* London: Routledge, 2009.

Washington, Ida. *Dorothy Canfield Fisher: A Biography.* Shelburne VT: University Press of New England, 1982.

Wasserman, Loretta. "Is 'Paul's Case' a Case?" *Modern Fiction Studies* 36, no. 1 (Spring 1990): 121–29.

Watson, Sarah, and Ann Moseley, eds. *Willa Cather and Aestheticism: From Romanticism to Modernism.* Madison NJ: Fairleigh Dickinson University Press, 2012.

Weatherby, H. L., and George Core, eds. *Place in American Fiction: Excursions and Explorations.* Columbia: University of Missouri Press, 2004.

Wegener, Frederick, ed. *Edith Wharton: The Uncollected Critical Writings.* Princeton NJ: Princeton University Press, 1996.

———. "'Rabid Imperialist': Edith Wharton and the Obligations of Empire in Modern American Fiction." *American Literature* 72, no. 4 (2000): 783–812.

Weir, Alison. *Eleanor of Aquitaine: A Life.* New York: Ballantine, 1999.

Welsch, Roger, and Linda Welsch. *Cather's Kitchens: Foodways in Literature and Life.* Lincoln: University of Nebraska Press, 1987.

Welty, Eudora. "Place in Fiction." [1956.] In *The Eye of the Story: Selected Essays and Reviews,* 116–33. New York: Vintage, 1979.

Westphal, Bertrand. *Geocriticism: Real and Fictional Spaces.* [2007.] Translated by Robert T. Tally Jr. New York: Palgrave Macmillan, 2011.

Wharton, Edith. *The Age of Innocence.* [1920.] New York: Scribner's, 1968.

———. "America at War." Speech delivered February 18, 1918. Translated by Virginia Ricard. *Times Literary Supplement,* February 14, 2018, https://www.the-tls.co.uk/articles/public/america-at-war-wharton/. Accessed April 16, 2018.

———. *A Backward Glance.* [1934.] New York: Scribner's, 1964.

———. *The Book of the Homeless.* [1916.] New York: Cosimo, 2005.

———. *The Buccaneers.* [1938.] In *"Fast and Loose" and "The Buccaneers,"* 119–479. Edited by Viola Winner. Charlottesville: University Press of Virginia, 1993.

———. "Bunner Sisters." In *Edith Wharton: Collected Stories, 1911–1937,* 166–246. New York: Library of America, 2001.

———. "The Children of Flanders Rescue Committee." [1915.] In Olin-Ammentorp, *Edith Wharton's Writings from the Great War*, 251–52.

———. "The Criticism of Fiction." [1914.] In Wegener, *Edith Wharton*, 120–29.

———. *The Custom of the Country*. [1913.] New York: Scribner's, 1956.

———. *The Decoration of Houses*. With Ogden Codman Jr. [1897.] New York: W. W. Norton, 1978.

———. *Ethan Frome*. [1911.] New York: Scribner's, 1921.

———. *False Dawn*. New York: Appleton, 1924.

———. *Fast and Loose*. In *"Fast and Loose" and "The Buccaneers,"* 1–111. Edited by Viola Winner. Charlottesville: University Press of Virginia, 1993.

———. *Fighting France: From Dunkerque to Belfort*. New York: Scribner's, 1919.

———. *French Ways and Their Meaning*. New York: Appleton, 1919.

———. "Friends." [1900.] In *The Collected Short Stories of Edith Wharton*, vol. 1, edited by R. W. B. Lewis, 197–214. New York: Scribner's, 1968.

———. *The Glimpses of the Moon*. New York: Appleton, 1922.

———. *The Gods Arrive*. [1932.] London: Virago, 1987.

———. "The Great American Novel." [1927.] In Wegener, *Edith Wharton*, 151–58.

———. *The House of Mirth*. New York: Scribner's, 1905.

———. *Hudson River Bracketed*. [1929.] New York: Scribner's, 1957.

———. *In Morocco*. [1920.] Hopewell NJ: Ecco, 1996.

———. *Italian Backgrounds*. New York: Scribner's, 1905.

———. *Italian Villas and Their Gardens*. [1904.] New York: Da Capo, 1988.

———. *The Letters of Edith Wharton*. Edited by R. W. B. Lewis and Nancy Lewis. New York: Scribner's, 1988.

———. "Life and I." In *The Unpublished Writings of Edith Wharton*, vol. 2, 185–204. Edited by Laura Rattray. London: Pickering and Chatto, 2009.

———. *The Marne*. New York: Appleton, 1918.

———. *A Motor-Flight through France*. [1908.] Introduction by Mary Suzanne Schriber. DeKalb: Northern Illinois University Press, 1991.

———. "Mrs. Manstey's View." [1891.] In *Edith Wharton: Collected Stories 1891–1910*, 1–11. New York: Library of America, 2001.

———. *New Year's Day*. New York: Appleton, 1924.

———. "Permanent Values in Fiction." [1934.] In Wegener, *Edith Wharton*, 175–79.

———. "A Reconsideration of Proust." [1934.] In Wegener, *Edith Wharton*, 179–83.

———. "Schoolroom Decoration." [1897.] In Wegener, *Edith Wharton*, 57–61.

———. *Selected Poems*. Edited by Louis Auchincloss. New York: Library of America, 2005.

———. *A Son at the Front*. New York: Scribner, 1923.

———. "Talk to American Soldiers." In Olin-Ammentorp, *Edith Wharton's Writings from the Great War*, 261–72.

———. "Tendencies in Modern Fiction." [1934.] In Wegener, *Edith Wharton*, 170–74.

———. *The Valley of Decision*. New York: Scribner's, 1902.

———. "Visibility in Fiction." [1929.] In Wegener, *Edith Wharton*, 163–69.

———. "Writing a War Story." [1919.] In *Edith Wharton: Collected Short Stories, 1911–1937*, 247–60. New York: Library of America, 2001.

———. *The Writing of Fiction*. [1925.] New York: Simon and Schuster, 1997.

White, E. B. *Here Is New York*. New York: Harper, 1949.

"Willa Cather Foundation Art Collection." *Willa Cather Review* 60, no. 4 (Fall 2017): 13–18.

Williams, Deborah. "Hiding in Plain Sight." *Willa Cather Pioneer Memorial Newsletter* 43, no. 2 (Fall 1999): 25–31.

———. *Not in Sisterhood: Edith Wharton, Willa Cather, and Zona Gale: The Politics of Female Authorship*. New York: Palgrave, 2001.

Wilson, Edmund. "Justice to Edith Wharton." In Howe, *Edith Wharton*, 19–31.

Wister, Owen. *The Virginian: A Horseman of the Plains*. [1902.] Introduction by Thomas McGuane. Lincoln: University of Nebraska Press, 1992.

Wolff, Cynthia Griffin. *A Feast of Words: The Triumph of Edith Wharton*, 2nd ed. New York: Oxford University Press, 1995.

———. "Lily Bart and the Beautiful Death." *American Literature* 46, no. 1 (March 1974): 16–40.

Woodress, James. "Historical Essay." In Cather, *My Ántonia*, 369–401.

———. *Willa Cather: A Literary Life*. Lincoln: University of Nebraska Press, 1987.

Woolf, Virginia. "American Fiction." [1925.] In *Collected Essays*, vol. 2, 111–21. New York: Harcourt, 1967.

———. *A Room of One's Own*. [1929.] New York: Harcourt Brace Jovanovich, 1991.

INDEX

Page numbers in italics refer to illustrations.

Ácoma people, 251–52
Adams, Henry, 168, 169, 170, 192
adaptation to place, 242, 250–53, 295
Adorno, Theodor, 295
A. E. Housman (Parker), 309n69
aesthetics, 4, 15–17, 119–20, 128; in Cather's letters, 88, 95, 135; of food and conversation, 208–9, 245–46; literary, 50–51, 73; and place, 11, 88–89, 90–94, 196; religion and, 286–87, 292–93; as suspect, 124–25, 136; in Wharton's letters, 21, 94–95, 96, 119–20, 135, 197–98. *See also* art; beauty
"After Holbein" (Wharton), 309n80
The Age of Innocence (Wharton), 83, 108, 112; art in, 143–44; fatality of place in, 13; France in, 201; and the "individual map," 98–99; *Lucy Gayheart* and, 99–100; New York aristocracy in, 109, 157; Pulitzer for, 42, 48, 50; reception of, 27–28, 157; resolution of, 65; success of, 122; Vernon Parrington on, 27–28; women in, 35, 62, 143, 274, 277
Akins, Zoë, 48, 283, 298, 299
Alaska, 150
Alexander's Bridge (Cather), 52–53; Henry James influencing, 75; H. L. Mencken on, 29, 158; Paris in, 203;
as "studio piece," 97; Wharton influencing, 53–54, 59
The Ambassadors (James), 76
ambition, 168–69, 171–74, 176, 177, 181, 212
"America at War" (Wharton), 336n248
American Ambulance, 51
"American Authors Who Have Set Art Above Popularity," 39–40, 41
American culture, 2, 18, 20, 303; as "Americanizing," 254; "aristocracy" in, 27–28, 31, 109, 174; beauty disregarded in, 20–21, 112–13, 119–21, 124–25, 137–38, 206–8; vs. European culture, 19, 112–13, 153–54, 211–14, 226–32, 240–42; indifference to history in, 8, 185–86; as lacking, 13–14, 20–21, 212–13, 230–31, 290; as money making, 115, 130–31, 143, 211–13, 246, 255; pioneers in, 145; purity and, 155; realism vs. naturalism in, 28, 29, 154–58; regionalism in, 3, 9, 29, 37–38, 191–92; war novels critiquing, 226–39; in the West, 151–52; western shift in, 157–60; women in, 51, 131, 138, 156, 169–70. *See also* the West
American literature. *See* literature
The American Scene (James), 131
Ammons, Elizabeth, 116, 119
Anderson, Sherwood, 159

The Answering Voice (Teasdale), 39
anxiety of authorship, 59–60
anxiety of influence, 52–53, 59–60
Apex City, 147, 177–78, 180–81, 323n10
Appiah, Kwame Anthony, 21–22, 251, 253–54
April Twilights (Cather), 106, 202–3
Archer, Isabel, 94
Archer, May Welland, 274, 276, 277
Archer, Newland, 34; library of, 296; marriage of, 276–77; New York and, 13, 99–100, 143–44; Paris and, 98–99
architecture, 113; American, 185, 247–50; as art, 207, 209; reverence inspired by, 186–87, 198, 228, 290–91, 292–93
Arias, Santa, 6, 12, 100–101
Arkwright, Harriet, 61–62, 270, 274, 276
Arles (France), 196, 197
Armajillo, Ramón, 244
Arnold, Matthew, 14, 21, 124–25
art: as afterthought, 121; as amoral, 76–77; vs. amusement, 79; for art's sake, 15–16; vs. capitalism, 20, 118–19, 122–24, 125, 137–44, 211–13; capitalism funding, 115, 118–19, 121–22, 151–52; ecstasy and, 15–16, 66, 137; as everyday, 209; French language as, 205; modernist, 73, 199, 201; not appreciated, 207; as performance, 128; physical sensation in, 81; and pragmatism, 137–44; religion replaced by, 123, 210, 285–86; as selection, 77–78, 81; slowness of, 80; success in, 138–39, 143, 164, 165, 170–72, 179; as suspect, 16; temptations of, 72–73; visual, as paradigm, 76
"The Artist of the Beautiful" (Hawthorne), 131
artists: debt of, to France, 234; escaping the West, 179–80; wives of, 137–44

Artists' Wives (Daudet), 142
"The Art of Fiction" (James), 77
Asselineau, Roger, 204
Atlas of Literature (Bradbury), 7
"Atrophy" (Wharton), 204
Auchincloss, Louis, 36, 117
Audoin-Rouzeau, Stéphane, 232, 335n223
Austen, Jane, 40, 74, 84, 85
Auvergne (France), 195, 198–99, 246, 247, 252
Avignon (France), 196, 197, 203, 291–93

Babbitt (S. Lewis), 49, 182
A Backward Glance (Wharton), 13–14, 30–31, 70, 145, 161; epigrams of, 73; language in, 188–89; the *nouveaux riches* in, 176; title of, 48; World War I in, 215, 282
Bahlmann, Anna, 113, 186–87, 282
Bakhtin, Mikhail, 5–6
Bakst, Léon, 201, 202
Baltazar, Fray, 251–52
Balzac, Honoré de, 74, 313n10
Banta, Martha, 136, 137
Barber, Peter, 7
Bart, Lily, 34, 35, 53–54, 60–61, 64, 134; as artist, 128, 129, 135–36; beauty of, 63, 131; critics' views of, 116–17; death of, 132–33, 266; and money, 61, 110–11, 115–17, 129–30, 134; on New York, 105, 112, 125; normalcy resisted by, 136–37, 322n168; rootlessness of, 266–68, 275–76, 297; on success, 139–40; ugliness suffered by, 125, 126; western acquaintances of, 150–51
Bartley, Winifred, 53, 54
Baym, Nina, 323n10
Beamish, Chetty, 64
beauty: aging and, 63–64; in American culture, 20–21, 112–13, 119–21, 124–25,

137–38, 206–8; community created by, 289–90; cost of, 129–30, 248–49; in *Death Comes for the Archbishop*, 246–48, 287; decline in status of, 16; definitions of, varying, 124; devaluation of, 125; duty to create, 240, 249–50; dying for lack of, 115–16, 119, 132–34; vs. economic concerns, 115–19, 122–24, 129–31, 134–35, 137–44, 211–12; as elitist, 21; of France, 197–98, 206–11, 228, 240, 245, 300; gender and, 131–32; hatred of, 121; human need for, 90–94, 115–20, 132–35, 137, 207–8; morality and, 16, 92; mortality and, 15; in "Mrs. Manstey's View," 90–91; pain and, 294; of place, 4, 88–92, 291–93, 298, 300; in the postwar world, 285–86; of the prairie, 120, 152, 180, 183; as promise of happiness, 132; public support of, 119; religion replaced by, 123, 285–86; skin deep, 68; as suspect concept, 4, 21, 124–25; and temperament, 135; in time, 293; travel and, 285; wars destroying, 281, 298, 299; of women, 62–64; wonder evoked by, 19, 292–94; and worship, 293–94. *See also* aesthetics; art

Becker, Annette, 232, 335n223

Beer, Janet, 283

Beers, Edith, 149

"Before Breakfast" (Cather), 62

Belgium, invasion of, 216

Belknap, Troy, 224–25

Benstock, Shari, 12, 166, 196, 309n83; on Apex City, 323n10; on Henry James, 74–75; on intellectual honesty, 210

Berengaria (ship), 69

Berengaria, Queen, 69, 312n177

Berenson, Bernard, 123, 137

Bergson, Alexandra, 34, 35, 132

Bergson, Emil, 57

Bergson, Henri, 168

Berry, Walter, 282, 284, 302

"The Best Years" (Cather), 147

Bhabha, Homi, 251

Bhushan, Nalini, 250–51

Birdseye, Nellie, 111–12

Bishop, Elizabeth, 264, 295–97; "One Art," 264; "Questions of Travel," 264, 295–97

Bloom, Harold, 31–32, 33, 59

Boas, Franz, 15

Bogan, Louise, 241

"The Bohemian Girl" (Cather), 39

The Book of the Homeless (Wharton), 201, 216, 224

Bourda, Josephine, 241, 279–80, 301

Bourdieu, Pierre, 16

Bourget, Paul, 194, 199

Bourne, Randolph, 29, 158

Bowen, Charles, 164

Bower, Eden, 138–41, 142–43, 144, 170, 296

Boynton, H. W., 65–66, 163, 165

Bradbury, Malcolm, 7, 9

Brandeis, Louis, 65

Brant, Julia, 138–41, 142–43, 144, 226

Brewster, Achsah, 299

The Brimming Cup (Fisher), 51

Brockway, Virginia Cather, 285

Bromfield, Louis, 182

Brown, E. K., 12, 44, 51, 75, 313n25

Brownell, William Crary, 114, 208

Bryant, William Cullen, 114

The Buccaneers (Wharton), 19, 106, 285, 287–91

"Bunner Sisters" (Wharton), 146, 149–50, 323n23

Burden, Jim, 6–7, 56, 276

Byatt, A. S., 60

California, Cather on, 152

Cameron, Elizabeth, 218

Campbell, Donna, 156, 157
Campton, George, 13, 237, 238–39
Campton, John, 138–41, 142–43, 144, 225; criticism of, 225, 232, 234; debt of, to France, 234; Fortin-Lescluze and, 228–29, 235. See also *A Son at the Front* (Wharton)
Canfield, Dorothy. See Fisher, Dorothy Canfield
capitalism: American culture as, 115, 130–31, 143, 211–13, 246, 255; vs. art, 20, 118–19, 122–24, 125, 137–44, 211–13; art funded by, 115, 118–19, 121–22, 151–52
Capote, Truman, 301
Carlin, Deborah, 45
cartography. See maps and mapping
Cather, Charles, 282–83
Cather, Douglass, 283
Cather, G. P., 196, 217, 218, *219*, 281
Cather, Jasper, 31
Cather, Mary, 265, 283
Cather, Willa, *41*, *43*, *71*, *301*, *302*; A. E. Housman and, 45, 46–48, *47*, 96, 309n69; aesthetics in letters of, 88, 95, 135; and American culture, 209–10, 213–14; American identity of, 241, 257; ancestors of, 31; art loved by, 120–21, 137, 201, 299, 300–301; burial of, 32; childhood displacement of, 88, 264; as critic, 83–85; critics of, on place, 12, 29–30; decline and death of, 285, 298–99; distancing of, from Wharton, 59, 65, 162; energy of, 166, *167*; on fatal geography, 1, 12, 13, 93–94, 297; finances of, 122; 5 Bank Street home of, 8, 106, 265, 279; and France, 19, 195–98, 208–11, 213–14, 241; French language and, 204–6; French values shared by, 210–11, 257; homes of, 257, 278–80, 295, 296–97, 298–99, 300–303; illustrators of, 148; insecurities of, 25–26, 45; on kingdom of art, 70, 90; Léon Bakst and, 201, *202*; loneliness of, 265; on military service, 217, 222, 284; on New York, 265; New York homes of, 10–11, 69, 106–9, 112–15, 278–80, 300–303; passport of, *261*; in Pittsburgh, 71, 72, 90, 121, 125, 280; as populist, 27, 29–30; postwar losses of, 282–83; on Rome, 7, 30, 260; Sarah Orne Jewett and, 44, 45, 60, 74, 98, 165; on Sigmund Freud, 82, 315n80; Sinclair Lewis and, 49–50, 310n87; social class of, 30, 31, 36–37, 38–39; on suicide, 89, 94, 116, 127, 133; translators of, 147–48, 205; travels of, 96, 195–97, 241, 260–64, 278–79, 284–85; travel writing of, 94, 203; as western writer, 29, 155–56, 157–58; Wharton and, literary connections between, 17–18, 38, 39–52, 58–59, 68–69; Wharton compared to, 65–66; Wharton reading, 58, 66–67, 68, 312n167; Wharton's influence on, 52–65; World War II and, 283–84, 298; writers admired by, 73–74, 84, 313n10
Cather, Willa, works of: *Alexander's Bridge*, 29, 52–54, 59, 75, 97, 158, 203; *April Twilights*, 106, 202–3; "Before Breakfast," 62; "The Best Years," 147; "The Bohemian Girl," 39; "A Chance Meeting," 204; "Cherbourg," 203; "Coming, Aphrodite!," 18, 109–10, 137, 138–41, 171, 201; *Death Comes for the Archbishop*, 19, 35, 42, 82, 83, 147–48, 198–99, 203, 205–6, 242–48, 249, 250–55, 287, 309n80; "Eleanor's House," 75; "Flavia and Her Artists," 75; "Going Home (Burlington Route)," 280; "A Gold Slipper," 121; "Grandmither, Think Not I Forget,"

39; "Hard Punishments," 19, 203, 287, 291–94; "The Hawthorn Tree," 39; *A Lost Lady*, 48, 58, 60, 61, 66–67, 100; *Lucy Gayheart*, 57–58, 61–62, 98, 99–100, 268–75; "The Marriage of Phaedra," 75; *My Ántonia*, 6–7, 29, 39–40, 55–56, 148, 158, 166, 287; "My First Novels (There Were Two)," 52, 97, 162; *My Mortal Enemy*, 60, 108, 109, 111, 112, 123, 152; "Nebraska: The End of the First Cycle," 145, 183; *Not under Forty*, 282; "The Novel Démeublé," 50, 77–78, 79; *Obscure Destinies*, 179; "The Old Beauty," 62–64; *The Old Beauty and Others*, 62; "Old Mrs. Harris," 73, 100, 283; *One of Ours*, 42, 56, 58, 66, 97, 132, 144, 193, 214, 218, 220, 222, 224–32, 236–40, 255, 256, 263–64, 284, 286, 287; "On the Art of Fiction," 77; *O Pioneers!*, 29, 34, 39, 48, 97, 98, 132, 148–49, 157, 162–63, 166; "Paul's Case," 18, 39, 105, 108, 111, 112, 115–18, 122–34, 136–37, 297; "Peter," 93–94, 119; *The Professor's House*, 60–61, 83, 96–97, 122, 203, 256, 263, 283; "The Profile," 309n69; "The Sculptor's Funeral," 39, 93; *Shadows on the Rock*, 83, 203, 206, 245, 255, 338n327; *The Song of the Lark*, 18, 34, 73, 76, 111, 122, 149, 151, 179–80, 187–88, 190, 300; "Sunday on the Seine," 203; "Then Back to Ancient France Again," 202; *The Troll Garden*, 67, 72, 313n25; "A Wagner Matinée," 92–93, 117, 121; *Youth and the Bright Medusa*, 117
Cather Childhood Home, 32
Cather's Kitchens (Welsch and Welsch), 37
Catlin, George, 153
Central Park, 111–12
Ceremony (Silko), 305n18

Cézanne, Paul, 201
"A Chance Meeting" (Cather), 204
Changes in the Land (Cronon), 7
Chanler, Daisy, 218
Chapman, John Jay, 220
Chapman, Victor, 218, 220
characters: aliveness of, 74, 165; Cather's, happiness of, 34–35; Cather's, Margaret Lawrence on, 35–36; cultural criticism via, 226; economic concerns of, 53–54, 60–61; vs. incident, 77; visibility of, 74; Wharton's, frustration of, 34, 35, 40
"Chartres" (Wharton), 202
Chast, Roz, 21
Chelles, Raymond de, 176
Chénetier, Marc, 206
"Cherbourg" (Cather), 203
Chicago IL: culture in, 151–52; as "Hog Butcher for the World," 151; in *Lucy Gayheart*, 98, 128, 269, 271; in *Song of the Lark*, 151–52, 164, 172, 174
The Children (Wharton), 83
"Chriemhild of Burgundy" (Wharton), 202
chronotope, 5, 6
churches and cathedrals, 285–87; of Auvergne, 198–99, 247; bells of, 215, 287; Chartres Cathedral, 286; Grace Church, 112; of Jean-Marie Latour, 247–49, 252; Palace of the Popes, 197, 247, 291–92, 294; St. Ouen, 228; St. Trophime, 197; ugly, 246, 247
"civilization," frontier undoing, 153–54
Clark, Colin, 312n167
class privilege, 21
Clemens, Cyril, 46–48, 47, 309n76
Collins, Joseph, 315n80
colonialism, 242–44, 250, 255
"Coming, Aphrodite!" (Cather), 18, 109–10, 137, 138–41, 171, 201

"Coming Home" (Wharton), 97, 202
A Companion to the Regional Literatures of America (Crow), 9, 307n12
Conrad, Joseph, 295
"Contemporary American Novelists" (Van Doren), 40
Cooper, James Fenimore, 153
Core, George, 9
Cortissoz, Royal, 201
cosmopolitanism, 251, 253–54, 295
The Country of the Pointed Firs (Jewett), 54, 55
creative writing schools, 80
Cronon, William, 7
Crow, Charles, 9, 307n12
culture: adaptation to, 242; and business, 131–32; and class privilege, 21; definitions of, 14–15; destabilization of, 83; "high," 15, 20; as necessity, 137; old vs. new, 16–17; in the West, 151–52. *See also* American culture; France and French culture
Culture and Anarchy (Arnold), 14
The Custom of the Country (Wharton), 18, 109, 184, 189, 242; beauty in, 122; Central Park in, 111; elitism in, 146–47; France in, 201; geography in, 147, 323n10; Henry James on, 67; money making in, 130, 149, 212; the West in, 146–47, 177–78, 184, 187, 191, 323n10. *See also* Spragg, Undine
Cuzak, Anton, 276
Cuzak, Ántonia, 56, 276

The Daemon Knows (Bloom), 31–32, 33
"Daisy Miller" (James), 53, 171
"Dance of Death" (Holbein), 309n80
Dante Alighieri, 198, 286–87, 330n36
Dastrey, Paul, 235, 236
Daudet, Alphonse, 142
Davril, René, 235

Dawson, Graham, 11
death: beauty and, 15; in postwar years, 282–83; ugliness leading to, 115–16, 119, 132–34
Death Comes for the Archbishop (Cather), 19, 35, 83, 242; Americanness in, 244–46, 249, 250, 254, 255; beauty in, 246–48, 287; "civilization" in, 244–45; colonialism in, 242–44, 250, 255; France and French language in, 198–99, 203, 205–6, 255; Howells Medal won for, 42; Mexican and Native characters in, 242–43, 244, 245–47, 251–52, 253, 254–55; politics in, 254–55; quietness of, 82; title of, 309n80; translation of, 147–48, 205
"The Death of the Hired Man" (Frost), 267–68, 275
The Decoration of Houses (Wharton and Codman), 92, 119, 136, 316n127
de Couçy, Gabrielle Longstreet, 62, 63–64
de Courcy, Olive, 220, 229–30
deep landscape novels, 9
de la Ramée, Marie Louise, 84–85
de Noailles, Anna, 199
de Tranlay, Marquise, 235–36
Detroit MI, 146
Dewey, John, 168
d'Humières, Robert, 222
dialect and slang, 159, 163, 189–90
Dimock, Wai-Chee, 8, 186
dislocation, 17, 87–94
displacement, war causing, 264–65, 284
A Distinguished Provincial in Paris (Balzac), 173
Dorset, Bertha, 267, 276
Dos Passos, John, 237–38
Dreiser, Theodore, 151
du Breuil de Saint-Germain, Jean, 222

Dumas, Alexandre, 202
Durrans, Stéphanie, 210–11
Duvall, J. Michael, 116
Dwight, Eleanor, 12

East-West divide, 152–54, 179, 184, 324n39; as energy-sensibility divide, 168, 184–85; English perspective on, 158–60; gender and, 156, 162–63; as oversimplification, 191–92; perpetuation of, 154; and realism-naturalism divide, 154–56, 157–58, 160; and women's fiction, 156–58
East-West hybridity, 176–77, 184–86
ecocriticism, 10
Edel, Leon, 51, 128, 310n103
Edith Wharton (Lee), 37, 51. *See also* Lee, Hermione
Edith Wharton (R. W. B. Lewis), 36. *See also* Lewis, R. W. B.
Edith Wharton: Étude Critique (Brown), 51. *See also* Brown, E. K.
Edith Wharton's Argument with America (Ammons), 116, 119
Egli, Ida Rae, 162, 324n39
"Eleanor's House" (Cather), 75
Eliot, George, 84, 85–86, 313n10
Eliot, T. S., 47, 47
Emerson, Ralph Waldo, 120, 136, 137
energy, 165–69, 175–76, 180; Cather and, 152, 192, 250, 259, 283; language and, 190; western, 155–56, 165–66, 168, 175–80, 184, 250; Wharton on, 175–76, 177–78, 184, 288
English language, 80–81, 83, 188–89. *See also* dialect and slang; fiction
environmental history, 7
epiphany, Wharton's use of, 83
Ethan Frome (Wharton), 17, 44, 157; Cather influenced by, 54–58; escape in, 150, 277; origins of, 204; western Massachusetts in, 13, 147; the West in, 150
Eugenie, Empress, 194
Euphoria IL, 181, 182, 287
Europe: Americans experiencing history of, 8; frontier vs., 153–54; literature mediating, 95–97; World War I and, 280–82; World War II and, 259, 283–84, 299. *See also* France and French culture
exile, 252, 294–95
expatriates, 234, 241, 295
Experiences of Place (MacDonald), 11

False Dawn (Wharton), 144
Farmer, Gladys, 132
Fast and Loose (Wharton), 201
fatality of place, 1, 12, 13–14, 68, 93–94, 297
Faubourg St. Germain (Paris), 194
Faulkner, William, 60
Faust (Goethe), 73
A Feast of Words (Wolff), 36
Felicitous Space (Fryer), 38, 266
Ferguson, Priscilla, 208
Ferrand, Beatrix, 106
Ferrand, Bishop, 253
Feuillerat, Albert, 199
fiction: aliveness of characters in, 74, 165; "American," perceptions of, 159–60; dialect and slang in, 159, 163, 189–90; external narrators in, 55–56; "manly," 86; theater as analogue for, 79; "women's," 84–87. *See also* literature
Fields, Annie, 42, 44
Fifth Avenue (New York), 112
Fifth Avenue Hotel (New York), 107, 108–9
Fighting France (Wharton), 201, 230
Fisher, Dorothy Canfield, 218, 309n67; A. E. Housman and, 45, 96; *The Brimming Cup*, 51; Cather and, friendship of, 51, 204; Cather and,

Fisher, Dorothy Canfield (*continued*)
rift between, 45, 309n69; France and, 195, 204; *Her Son's Wife*, 55; Leon Edel and, 51, 310n103; "A Little Kansas Leaven," 52; Wharton and, 51–52
Fisher, Lily, 172, 179
Fitzgerald, F. Scott, 48, 67–68, 309n83
Flaubert, Gustave, 77
"Flavia and Her Artists" (Cather), 75
flowers, 26, 127, 128, 297, 301
flu epidemic, 222, 224, 282
food and culinary appreciation, 208, 209
Forain, Jean-Louis, 232, 233
Forrester, Marian, 60, 61
Foucault, Michel, 4
France and French culture, 19, 193–257, 300; Americans learning from, 193, 239–40; beauty of, 197–98, 206–11, 228, 240, 245, 300; brutal history of, 338n327; Cather sharing values of, 210–11, 257; and financial ambition, 211–12; as idealized, 239, 255–57; imperialism of, 243; Paris's place in, 197; United States contrasted with, 206–24; values of, 198, 209–14, 229, 230–31, 235–37, 240–41. *See also* Paris
Franklin, Benjamin, 136, 137, 208
French language in Wharton and Cather texts, 203–6
French naturalists, 17, 73–74, 76
French Perspectives (Sergeant), 211
French Traits (Brownell), 208
French Ways and Their Meaning (Wharton), 68, 201, 332n100; French values in, 198, 210, 211–12, 239–40; money in, 211–13; Puritanism in, 208; reception of, 255; wartime in, 228
Frenside, George, 184
Freud, Sigmund, 82, 315n80
"Friends" (Wharton), 91
Frome, Ethan, 13, 34, 35, 56, 147

the frontier, 120–21, 153–54, 155–56
Frost, Robert, 86, 267–68, 275
Fryer, Judith, 38, 266
Fullerton, Morton, 188

Gale, Zona, 42, 50–51, 80–81
gardens, 26, 252, 277, 300
Garland, Hamlin, 50
Gayheart, Jacob, 273–74
Gayheart, Lucy, 98, 99, 128, 131, 269–71, 272–73
Gayheart, Pauline, 270, 271, 272–74
gender: East-West divide and, 156, 162–63; roles, 131–32; and "women's fiction," 84–87. *See also* women
genius loci, 5
gentility as literary subgenre, 154–55, 156–57
Gentlemen Prefer Blondes (Loos), 68, 312n174
geocriticism, 5. *See also* geography; place; space
Geocriticism (Westphal), 5
geography: as fatal, 1, 12, 13–14, 68, 93–94, 297; language and, 205; literature as, 17, 70–101; social, 12–13
Gerhardt, David, 229, 236–37
Gervaud, Michel, 204, 255–56
Gide, André, 204
Gilbert, Sandra, 59–60
the Gilded Age, success in, 129–32
Glennon, Jenny, 122
The Glimpses of the Moon (Wharton), 180–81, 201
Glotfelty, Cheryll, 10
"Goblin Market" (Rosetti), 72
God, 293–94
The Gods Arrive (Wharton), 18, 181, 191; pain in, 283, 342n134; reception of, 182; wonder in, 286–87
"Going Home (Burlington Route)" (Cather), 280

The Golden Bowl (James), 147
Goldman-Price, Irene, 95
"A Gold Slipper" (Cather), 121
Good-bye to All That (Sassoon), 281
Gopnik, Adam, 21, 206, 209
Gordon, Harry, 61–62, 99, 131, 271, 274–75, 276
"Grandmither, Think Not I Forget" (Cather), 39
Graves, Richard, 309n69
"The Great American Novel" (Wharton), 159
The Great Gatsby (Fitzgerald), 48, 256
Greek myths, 193
Green, Nancy, 39
Greenslet, Ferris, 58
Grenfell, Henry, 62
Grenfell, Margaret, 62
Grey, Zane, 163
Grout, Caroline Franklin, 204–5
Gryce, Percy, 129–30, 132, 270
Gubar, Susan, 59–60

Haber, Tom, 309n69
Hallelujah MO, 181
Hambourg, Isabelle McClung, 45, 196, 204, 265, 280, 283, 299, 302
Hambourg, Jan, 299, 302
"Hard Punishments" (Cather), 19, 203, 287, 291–94
Harris, Richard, 56, 228
Hatch, Norma, 150–51
Haverford NE, 98, 99; Harry Gordon in, 274–75; Lucy Gayheart in, 270, 271, 275; and Wharton's New York, 99–100
Hawthorne, Nathaniel, 131, 295
"The Hawthorn Tree" (Cather), 39
Healy, George, 207
Hebraism vs. Hellenism, 124–25
Hedger, Don, 110, 138–41, 142–43, 144, 296

Henshawe, Myra, 60, 61, 123
Her Son's Wife (Fisher), 55
Hewlett, Maurice, 263
Hicks, Coral, 180–81
high modernism, 81–82
history: American indifference to, 8, 185–86; natural, 294; of place, 289–91, 292, 300, 305n18
Holbein, Hans the Younger, 309n80
home, 112, 250, 264–80, 291, 299, 303; attachment to, 289–90, 291; definitions of, 267–68; escaping, 275–77, 280; in *House of Mirth*, 266–68, 270; language and, 203; literature as, 17, 70, 72, 87, 90, 299; in *Lucy Gayheart*, 268–75; in multiple places, 295; need for, 19, 128, 264, 265–68, 279, 291; as provisional, 295; returning to, 277–78; travel anchored by, 258, 264, 278, 279, 295–97, 303
homelessness, 216, 264, 266–67, 274, 280–81, 295
Homestead, Melissa, 279
honors, 26, 42, 43, 48–49, 50, 59, 161, 218
Honourslove (estate), 289–90, 291, 292, 294
Horner, Avril, 283
hothouse flowers, 119–20, 127, 128
The House of Mirth (Wharton), 17, 18, 34, 39, 105; beauty in, 115–17, 124, 125, 135–37; economic concerns in, 53–54, 61–62, 110–11, 115–17, 122, 129–31; flowers in, 127, 128; France in, 201; home and homelessness in, 266–68, 270; new wealth in, 123, 150–51; and "The Old Beauty," 62–64; and "Paul's Case," 18, 115–18; play based on, 146; reviewers on, 116–17, 136; setting of, 97, 98, 112; success in, 139–40; travel and literature linked in, 96; the West in, 150–51

Housman, A. E., 73; Cather and, 45, 46–48, 47, 96, 309n69; Wharton and, 45–47, 47

Howells, William Dean, 86, 156

Hudson River Bracketed (Wharton), 18, 147, 181–86; reception of, 182, 183–84; "spirit of the pioneers" in, 191

Hudson River Valley, 13

Hugo, Victor, 96

hybridity, 251, 252–53, 295

Hyères (France), 26, 195, 197–98, 278, 299

identity: American, 9, 21, 153, 157, 241; hybridity and, 251; travel and, 267

imagination, 288–89; aesthetic, 128, 129; as miracle, 293; place influencing, 10; travel and, 296–97; wonder and, 292–93, 294

Indian Summer (Howells), 94

"individual map," 98–101

In Morocco (Wharton), 94, 243, 263

"Inquiétude" (Forain), 232, 233

intellectual honesty, 210–11

International Mark Twain Society, 46–47

Italian Backgrounds (Wharton), 94

Italian Hours (James), 94

Italian Villas and Their Gardens (Wharton), 94

Ives, Burton, 139, 140, 141

Jaffrey NH, 95

James, Henry, 14, 67, 74–75, 155; *The Ambassadors*, 76; *The American Scene*, 131; "The Art of Fiction," 77; Cather admiring, 42, 44, 73; Cather influenced by, 52, 53, 59, 75–76; "Daisy Miller," 53, 171; death of, 204, 282; on fiction, 77; *The Golden Bowl*, 147; influences on, 76; *Italian Hours*, 94; on lack of American culture, 159, 290; *A Little Tour in France*, 94, 197; on The Mount, 32; *The Portrait of a Lady*, 94; *The Princess Casamassima*, 173; travel writing of, 94; *Washington Square*, 109; Wharton admiring, 73; Wharton critiqued by, 296; Wharton critiquing, 76; Wharton frustrated with, 67; Wharton's friendship with, 42, 44, 97–98, 260; writing advice of, 97–98

James, William, 168

Jazz Age, 256

Jefferson, Thomas, 207

Jelly-Schapiro, Joshua, 7

Jewell, Andrew, 217

Jewett, Rutger, 161

Jewett, Sarah Orne: Cather and, 44, 45, 60, 74, 98, 165; on literature, 80; Wharton and, 44–45; writing advice of, 98

Jones, George Frederic (Wharton's father), 317n4

Jones, Mary Cadwalader (Minnie), 106, 270

Jones, Mary Mason, 114

Jones, Suzanne, 288

Joslin, Katherine, 12

Joyce, James, 81

A Jury of Her Peers (Showalter), 38

Kansas City MO, 186–87

Kazin, Alfred, 9

Kennedy, John F., 20

"Kerfol" (Wharton), 201

Kim, Sharon, 83, 342n134

The Kingdom of Art (Slote), 1, 70

Kingsley, Charles, 72

Kipling, Rudyard, 7

Knopf, Alfred, 58

Kowalewski, Michael, 9

Kronborg, Thea, 34, 192; beauty of, 169–70; as competitive, 172; and domesticity, lack of interest in, 172–

73; music and, 151; in New York culture, 176–77; as pioneer, 163–80, 191; as provincial, 173–74, 175; readers' love of, 165; ruthlessness of, 170–71; West embodied by, 168–69, 175. *See also* Spragg, Undine

landscape: French vs. American, 300; inner, 11–12, 268; knowledge of, 9, 147–48
Landscape and Memory (Schama), 7
language: Cather on, 187–88; English, 80–81, 83, 188–89; French, 203–6; provincial, 174, 175, 187–88; slang, 159, 189–90
Lansing, Nick, 180–81
Lansing, Susy, 180–81
Lapsley, Gaillard, 46, 302
Larkin, Philip, 281
Latour, Jean-Marie, 35, 198, 205–6, 242–55; beauty and, 246–49, 250; cathedral of, 247–49, 252; changing, 250–51; as "happy exile," 295; hybrid identity of, 244, 251, 252–54
Lauer, Kristin, 323n10
Lawrence, D. H., 81
Lawrence, Margaret, 35–36
Lee, Hermione, 309n83; on American language, 187; on Cather, 36, 37, 51, 75, 313n25; on dislocation, 87; on Paris, 201; on Wharton, 12, 51, 187, 201, 263, 309n83
Le Lavandou (France), 197–98, 263, 299
"Les Metteurs en Scène" (Wharton), 204
Lewis, Edith, 114, 241, 279, 285, 291, 298, 299, 300, 301
Lewis, R. W. B., 12, 36, 75; on Apex City's location, 323n10; on Lily Bart, 116; on Undine Spragg, 164; on Wharton's western travels, 146

Lewis, Sinclair, 9, 159, 190; on art in America, 121; *Babbitt*, 49, 182; Cather and, 49–50, 310n87; on knowledge of place, 147; *Main Street*, 49, 50; Vance Weston and, 182; Wharton and, 48–49, 67–68, 189, 310n87
"Life and I" (Wharton), 72, 88
Linstrum, Carl, 132
Literary Women (Moers), 36
literature: American, set outside United States, 159–60; American, Virginia Woolf on, 158–60; Europe mediated through, 95–97; as home, 17, 70, 72, 87, 90, 299; space-time in, 6; spatial turn in, 5, 7–10, 191; as a vocation, 70; western, 156–59, 162–63, 324n39; "women's," 84–85, 156, 162–63
"A Little Kansas Leaven" (Fisher), 52
A Little Tour in France (James), 94, 197
Llona, Victor, 205
Long Beach CA, 152
Longstreet, Gabrielle. *See* de Couçy, Gabrielle Longstreet
Loos, Anita, 68, 312n174
Lopez, Esther, 250
A Lost Lady (Cather), 48, 58, 60, 61, 66–67, 100
Love, Glen, 175, 177
Lucy Gayheart (Cather), 57–58, 61–62, 98; and *The Age of Innocence*, 99–100; home and homelessness in, 268–75; orchard in, 271–72, 273
Lujon, Manuel, 244

MacDonald, Mary, 11
Madame de Treymes (Wharton), 201
Madison Square Garden (New York), 115
Main Street (S. Lewis), 49, 50
Majaj, Lisa Suhair, 295
Mann, Thomas, 47, 47

Manon Lescaut (Prévost), 68
Mansfield, Katherine, 35
maps and mapping, 7, 21–22, 98–101, 107, 200
The Marne (Wharton), 146, 201, 214, 217, 224–25, 255
marriage: artists', 137–44; as barter, 116, 165, 288; Cather on, 276; as prostitution, 288; as undesirable, 173; as unhappy, 149, 150, 176, 184–85, 274–77; of Wharton, 194
"The Marriage of Phaedra" (Cather), 75
Marvell, Paul, 178
Marvell, Ralph, 170, 175, 178, 184
Massachusetts, western, 13, 147
materialism: and art, 121–24, 213–14; of the Jazz Age, 256, 259, 282; of westerners, 183
Maupassant, Guy de, 77
McClung, Isabelle. *See* Hambourg, Isabelle McClung
McClure's Magazine, 39, 107, 109
McCormick, Chauncey, 151–52
McCullough, David, 207
"MCMXIV" (Larkin), 281
Mediterranean coast (France), 197–98
Mencken, H. L., 29, 39–40, 41, 52–53, 158
Mérimée, Prosper, 77–78
Merrick, Harvey, 93
Metropolitan Museum (New York), 114, 124
the Midwest, 153–54, 160, 181–83, 187, 286–87
Millington, Richard, 15, 83
Miss Lulu Bett (Gale), 50
"Miss Mary Pask" (Wharton), 201
"A Misunderstanding" (Daudet), 142
Mitchell, Lee, 168
modernism, 73, 83, 199, 201
Moers, Ellen, 36
Moffatt, Elmer, 122, 149, 177–78, 184

Momaday, N. Scott, 305n18
money: culture and, 21, 115, 123–24, 137–38, 151–52, 211–13; vs. freedom, 137–38, 140; making, 115, 130–31, 143, 211–13, 246, 255; old vs. new, 123, 166, 176; success as, 122, 130, 137, 140–41, 143, 213
Moonstone CO, 151, 172, 179–80, 187
morality: beauty and, 16, 92; Puritan, 124–25; truth and, 76
Morpeth, Paul, 129
Morse, Samuel, 207
Morse, Victor, 218, 220
A Motor-Flight through France (Wharton), 94, 195, 198, 201, 262, 292
The Mount (Wharton's home), 32, 112, 312n167
"Mrs. Manstey's View" (Wharton), 90–91, 119, 149, 265–66
Murphy, John J., 76, 106
Murray, Margaret, 323n10
music: Cather enjoying, 89, 114, 115; in "A Gold Slipper," 121; in "Hard Punishments," 292–93; in *The House of Mirth*, 111; in *Lucy Gayheart*, 98, 268, 269; in *One of Ours*, 231; in "The Sculptor's Funeral," 93; in *The Song of the Lark*, 151, 164, 176; in "A Wagner Matinée," 92–93; Wharton enjoying, 73
Mussolini, Benito, 46–47, 47
My Ántonia (Cather), 6–7, 287; critics on, 29, 39–40, 148, 158; *The Swiss Family Robinson* in, 166; Wharton influencing, 55–56
"My First Novels (There Were Two)" (Cather), 52, 97, 162
My Mortal Enemy (Cather), 60, 108, 109; art and wealth in, 123; Central Park in, 111; Fifth Avenue in, 112; the West in, 152

National Endowment for the Arts, 20

National Endowment for the Humanities, 20

naturalism: Cather on, 160; vs. realism, 28, 29, 154–58, 160; in Wharton's fiction, 157

Nebraska: Cather praising, 166; Cather's first impression of, 88, 92; as Cather's home, 10, 32, 89–90, 98, 152, 278, 280; emptiness of, 226–27; European culture and, 30; harshness of, 93–94, 300; World War I and, 216

"Nebraska: The End of the First Cycle" (Cather), 145, 183

Nehamas, Alexander, 16, 88, 124, 285, 289

Nettels, Elsa, 75–76, 86

New Criticism, 4–5

New Hampshire, 42, 95, 278, 295

New Mexico, 242–43, 253, 254, 255, 300

Newport RI, 89, 92, 168, 278

New York NY, 18, 105–44; art displays in, 112–13, 114, 118, 123, 124, 208; artificiality in, 110–11; capitalism and art in, 115, 118–19, 137, 143–44, 206; Cather's homes in, 10–11, 69, 106–9, 112–15, 278–80, 300–303; change in, 8, 176; chronology of, 114–15; as foolish, 303; money-making culture of, 115, 118, 123, 206, 210; mythic status of, 115; Newland Archer and, 13, 99–100; vs. Paris, 114; social class in, 30–31, 109–11, 174–75; Wharton-Cather intersections in, 107, 108–12; Wharton's dislike of, 87–88, 112–13

New York Society Library, 106, 317n4

Nonstop Metropolis (Solnit and Jelly-Schapiro), 7

Norris, Frank, 156

Norton, Charles Eliot, 123

Norton, Robert, 302

Norton, Sara (Sally), 44, 119–20, 208, 214–15

Notre-Dame de Paris (Hugo), 96

Not under Forty (Cather), 282

the *nouveaux riches*, 123, 150–51, 166, 176, 287–88

"The Novel Démeublé" (Cather), 50, 77–78, 79

O'Brien, Sharon, 36, 37, 118, 308n57

Obscure Destinies (Cather), 179

Okey, Thomas, 292

"The Old Beauty" (Cather), 62–64

The Old Beauty and Others (Cather), 62

The Old Maid (Wharton), 48

"Old Mrs. Harris" (Cather), 73, 100, 283

Old New York (Wharton), 83, 144

Olenska, Ellen, 98–99, 100, 143, 276, 296

"One Art" (Bishop), 264

One of Ours (Cather), 66, 97, 193, 225–32, 239–40; Cather on, 58; *Ethan Frome* influencing, 56; excitement of travel in, 263–64; France in, 214, 224–32, 239–40, 255, 286, 287; idealism of, 220, 236–37; inspiration for, 218, 220, 222; money in, 132, 144, 193; publication of, 256; Pulitzer Prize for, 42; values in, 144, 193, 214, 263–64; wonder in, 228, 286, 287; World War I in, 193, 225–28, 229–32, 236–37, 238, 284

Only a Promise of Happiness (Nehamas), 16, 132

"On the Art of Fiction" (Cather), 77

O Pioneers! (Cather), 29, 34, 39; financial failures in, 132; reception of, 157, 162–63; setting of, 97, 98, 148–49; *The Swiss Family Robinson* in, 166; title of, 48

Orchard, Zeb, 251

"The Other Two" (Wharton), 157

Ottenburg, Fred, 122, 149, 173

Ouida (Marie Louise de la Ramée), 84–85
Outland, Tom, 263

pain, 283, 294, 298, 342n134
Palace of the Popes (Avignon), 197, 247, 291–92, 294
"Paleface and Redskin" (Rahv), 155–56
Palleau-Papin, Françoise, 205
Paris, 193–97, 201, 203, 209–10; American artists in, 206–7; American soldiers in, 220–21, 239–40; cemeteries of, 203; Fourth of July parades in, 220–21; mapping Wharton and Cather in, 199, *200*; Newland Archer and, 98–99; postwar, 265, 281
Parker, Peter, 309n69
Parrington, Vernon, 27–28, 29, 157
Pascal, Blaise, 296
Pater, Walter, 15–16, 124, 135
"Paul's Case" (Cather), 18, 39, 105, 108, 297; beauty and economics in, 115–16, 117–18, 122–25, 128–29, 130–32, 136–37; critics on, 117–18, 136; flowers in, 127, 128; and *House of Mirth*, 18, 115–18; New York in, 105, 111, 112; normalcy resisted in, 136–37; Pittsburgh in, 118, 133, 134; suicide in, 116, 133; ugliness in, 126–27
Pavillon Colombe, 25–26, 71, 194–95, 297–98, 299, *301*
Peixotto, Ernest, 148
Pensées (Pascal), 296
Père Goriot (Balzac), 173
Perkins, Maxwell, 55
Pershing, John J., 47, *47*, 218
"Peter" (Cather), 93–94, 119
Phillips, David Graham, 162–63
pioneers: spirit of, 145, 166, 191; as vanished people, 183; women as, 163–80
Pioneers and Caretakers (Auchincloss), 36

Piranesi, Giovanni Battista, 299
Pittsburgh PA: arts in, 90, 121, 125; Cather in, 71, 72, 90, 121, 125, 280; "lords of," 122, 130–31, 134, 166; Paul (character) in, 118, 133, 134; "Presbyterianism" in, 125
Pizer, Donald, 157
place, 258–303; as aesthetic conception, 11; author's knowledge of, 9; as axis of organization, 3; beauty of, 4, 88–92, 291–93, 298, 300; as character, 97; characters' relationships to, 98–101; consciousness and, 253–55; definitions of, 6–7, 11, 14, 299; elitism concerning, 146–47; fatality of, 1, 12, 13–14, 68, 93–94, 297; ignorance of, 147–48; "individual maps" of, 98–101; layers of history in, 8; as multi-dimensional, 11, 148; mythology and, 7; opportunity and, 1; and placing, 14; prestige of, 37–38; in regional American literature, 9; social maps of, 100; time and, 5–6, 114–15; trivializing of, 4–5, 6. *See also* geography; home; space; the spatial turn; travel
Place in American Fiction (Weatherby and Core), 9–10
placelessness, 21–22, 294–95. *See also* exile; homelessness
Plato, 16, 285
pleasure, 90–91, 135, 208–9
poetry, 72, 120, 151, 259, 267–68, 295–96; of A. E. Housman, 45–46, 48, 96; of Cather, 39, 48, 202–3, 280; Cather's criticism of, 83–84; of Elizabeth Bishop, 264, 295–96; postwar, 281; of Walt Whitman, 48; of Wharton, 48, 202
Popple, Claude Walsingham, 175
The Portrait of a Lady (James), 94

Powers, Lyall H., 76
prairie: beauty of, 120, 152, 180, 183; grimness of, 92–93, 120–21
"Presbyterianism," 125, 134
Prévost, Antoine-François, 68
Price, Alan, 12
The Princess Casamassima (James), 173
The Professor's House (Cather), 60–61, 83, 96–97, 256; happiness in, 263, 283; Paris in, 203; success of, 122
"The Profile" (Cather), 309n69
Protestantism, 125, 134, 208, 209
Proulx, Annie, 9
Proust, Marcel, 67
provincialism, 173–77, 226
Pruneville NE, 181
psychology, 82, 315n80
Puck of Pook's Hill (Kipling), 7
Pulitzer Prize, 1, 26, 42, 48, 50, 287
Puritanism, 124–25, 168, 169, 170, 207–8, 210
Puvis de Chavannes, Pierre, 82

"Questions of Travel" (Bishop), 264, 295–97

Rahv, Philip, 155–56, 168
The Rainbow (Lawrence), 81
"Rambouillet" (Wharton), 202
Ramsden Catalog, 312n167
Rascoe, Burton, 66
"real" Americans, 153–54, 157–60
realism, 73, 82; gender and, 156; vs. naturalism, 28, 29, 154–58, 160
Red Cloud NE, 32, 195, 280, 284
The Reef (Wharton), 52, 201, 242
Reflections on Exile (Said), 294–95
Reinhart, Charles Stanley, 20
religion: aesthetic importance of, 286–87, 292–93; art replacing, 123, 210, 285–86; Protestantism, 125, 134, 208, 209; Roman Catholicism, 285; work ethic and, 125
reverence, 186–87, 198, 210, 228, 290–94
Reynolds, Guy, 37
Reynolds, Joshua, 129
Rhinelander, Newbold, 222, 223, 224
"The Rhodora" (Emerson), 120
Ricard, Virginia, 336n248
Richards, Grant, 46, 309n69
Robinson, Lillian, 116
The Roman and the Teuton (Kingsley), 72
Roman Catholicism, 285
the Romantics, 120, 141–42
Rome, 7, 30, 260
A Room of One's Own (Woolf), 281
Roosevelt, Archie, 218, 219, 222
Roosevelt, Quentin, 218, 219, 222, 224
Roosevelt, Theodore, 218, 224
Roosevelt, Theodore, Jr., 218, 219
rootlessness, 264–75, 294–96; death and, 266–68, 269–70, 271; and uprootedness, 266, 284, 294–96
Roseboro, Viola, 283–84
Rosedale, Simon, 61, 129–30, 267
Rosetti, Christina, 72
Rosowski, Susan, 72, 121, 168, 170
Rouen (France), 228, 286
Ruskin, John, 16

Sadilek, Francis, 94
Said, Edward, 6, 294–95
Sainte Claire le Château (Wharton's home), 195, 197–98, 277, 299, 302
Saint-Gaudens, Augustus, 115
Sand, George, 84, 301
Sandburg, Carl, 151
Sand City KS, 93
San Francisco CA, 152
Sassoon, Siegfried, 281
Scales, Buck, 244
Schama, Simon, 7

The School of Femininity (Lawrence), 35–36
"Schoolroom Decoration" (Wharton), 92, 119, 316n127
"The Sculptor's Funeral" (Cather), 39, 93
Seabury, Henry, 62, 63–64
Sebastian, Clement, 98, 99, 268–70, 271, 272, 276
Selden, Lawrence, 53–54, 132, 134, 139–40, 267
"Senlis" (Wharton), 202
Sentimental Education (Flaubert), 173
Sergeant, Elizabeth Shepley, 54–55, 195–96, 201; *French Perspectives*, 211; *Shadow-Shapes*, 211
setting. *See* place
Shabata, Frank, 57
Shabata, Marie, 57
Shadow-Shapes (Sergeant), 211
Shadows on the Rock (Cather), 83, 203, 206, 245, 255, 338n327
Showalter, Elaine, 38, 84, 86–87
A Shropshire Lad (Housman), 96, 263
"The Significance of the Frontier" (Turner), 120
Silko, Leslie Marmon, 305n18
Silly Novels by Lady Novelists (Eliot), 85–86
Silver, Mattie, 56, 57, 277
Simmons, Ronald, 222, 224
Singley, Carol, 285, 286, 322n168
Sister Carrie (Dreiser), 151
Skaggs, Merrill McGuire, 2
Slote, Bernice, 1, 70, 72
Smith, Jeremiah (Cather's ancestor), 31
Smith, Leonard, 232, 335n223
Smith, Patricia, 242–43
social class, 30–34, 100; of characters, 34; language and, 189; literary ranking and, 36–37; moving between, 173–77

Solnit, Rebecca, 7
A Son at the Front (Wharton), 13, 201, 214, 256; artist's wife in, 137, 138–41; death in, 235; and France, 224–31, 232–39; language in, 190; reception of, 65–66
The Song of the Lark (Cather), 18, 34, 73; art and beauty in, 122, 149, 151, 300; Central Park in, 111; epilogue to, 179; Henry James influencing, 76; language in, 187–88, 190; preface to, 179–80. *See also* Kronborg, Thea
Sorel, Edward, 31–32, 33
Southwest, American, 147–48, 167, 205, 242–55, 295
space: definition of, 6–7; liminal, 229–30, 251, 252; vs. place, 5, 6–7; time and, 5–6, 39. *See also* geography; place; the spatial turn
Spanish flu, 222, 224, 282
the spatial turn, 4–14
The Spatial Turn (Warf and Arias), 6
Spear, Halo, 184–85
Spragg, Undine, 18, 68, 109, 111, 146–47; beauty of, 169, 171; as competitive, 171; critics on, 164–65; as destructive, 175, 176, 177; as pioneer, 163–80; as provincial, 173–75; ruthlessness of, 170, 172, 184; as victim, 164–65; West embodied by, 168–69, 175. *See also* Kronborg, Thea
Stein, Gertrude, 199
Stevens, Ebenezer (Wharton's ancestor), 31
Stewart, Pamela, 11
St. George, Nan, 288–90
St. George, Virginia, 288–89
St. Louis MO, 150
Stout, Janis, 215, 279, 339n31
Stowe, Harriet Beecher, 76, 207
St. Peter, Godfrey, 256, 283, 286, 291

St. Peter, Lillian, 60–61
Strathern, Andrew, 11
success: and art, 138–43, 164, 165, 170–72, 179; in the Gilded Age, 129–32; as money, 122, 130, 137, 140–41, 143, 213
suffering. *See* pain
suicide: Cather considering, 89; in Cather's fiction, 94, 116, 127, 133; in Wharton's fiction, 34, 55, 57, 116, 170, 184
Summer (Wharton), 39, 182
"Sunday on the Seine" (Cather), 203
The Swiss Family Robinson (Wyss), 166

"Talk to American Soldiers" (Wharton), 193, 239–40, 249–50, 336n248
Tally, Robert, Jr., 5
Tarrant, Lewis, 184
"taste," 4, 213
Teasdale, Sara, 39
Templeton, Vickie, 73, 100
"Tendencies in Modern Fiction" (Wharton), 159–60
Thacker, Robert, 60
Thackeray, William Makepeace, 74, 87, 313n10
"Then Back to Ancient France Again" (Cather), 202
Thomas, Theodore, 151
Thoreau, Henry David, 131, 138
Three Musketeers (Dumas), 202
Thwarte, Guy, 289–90, 291, 294
time: beauty located in, 293; to enjoy life, 212–13; passage of, 78; place and, 5–6, 114–15
Toklas, Alice, 199
Tolstoy, Leo, 73, 74, 78, 313n10
Topophilia (Tuan), 5
Totten, Gary, 146, 262
transcendence, 228, 291
the Transcendentalists, 120

translation: of Cather's work, 147–48, 205; hybridity as, 251; Wharton providing, 204
transnationalism, 294–95
travel, 19, 259; by car, 262; as escape from personal problems, 267, 275, 276–77; home and, 258–303, 339n31; literary experiences and, 95–97; mapless, 263–64; promise of, 295–96; rootlessness and, 264–67, 269; vs. tourism, 262–64; by train, 285; Wharton on, 94–96, 97, 258, 262–63, 276–77, 284–85; World War I and, 275; World War II and, 283–84
travel writing, 94, 195, 203, 260–62, 281
Treaty of Guadalupe Hidalgo, 242
Trenor, Gus, 61, 64, 131, 267
Trenor, Judy, 276
Trilling, Lionel, 173
The Troll Garden (Cather), 67, 72, 313n25
Tuan, Yi-Fu, 5, 168
Turner, Frederick Jackson, 120, 153–54
Tuttleton, James, 323n10
Twain, Mark, 37, 46–47, 178, 191, 309n76
Twelve Poems (Wharton), 202
Twenty-Third Street, Manhattan, 105, 107, 108, 109
Twilight Sleep (Wharton), 83
Tyler, Elisina, 46, 298
Tyler, William, 312n167

ugliness: of American life, 160, 239, 240, 246, 247, 249; of churches, 246, 247; of New York City, 87–88, 112–13, 125–26; suffering, 92–93, 117, 119, 125–26; Wharton on, 87–88, 91–92, 113, 119–20, 125, 160–61
Ulysses (Joyce), 81
Urgo, Joseph, 278
Ushant, Duke of Tintagel, 288, 289

Vaillant, Joseph, 198, 242, 244–46, 247–48, 250–51, 295
The Valley of Decision (Wharton), 97, 147
Van Doren, Carl, 40, 58
Vanity Fair (magazine), 39–40, 41
Venice (Italy), 180–81
Ville d'Avray (France), 299, 301, 302
Villers Tournelle (France), 196, 222, 281
The Virginian (Wister), 160, 168, 191
von Goethe, Johann Wolfgang, 72, 73
Von Schmidt, Harold, 148

"A Wagner Matinée" (Cather), 92–93, 117, 121
war. *See* World War I; World War II
War and Peace (Tolstoy), 74
Warf, Barney, 6, 12, 100–101
Warlick, Hinda, 146, 147
Washington Square (New York), 107, 109–10
Washington Square (James), 109
The Way to Rainy Mountain (Momaday), 305n18
wealth. *See* the *nouveaux riches*
Weatherby, H. L., 9
Wegener, Frederick, 316n127
Weir, Alison, 312n177
Welsch, Linda, 37
Welsch, Roger, 37
Welty, Eudora, 9
the West, 18, 145–92, 307n12; Cather's fear of, 152; in Cather's fiction, 148–49, 151–52, 157, 179; culture in, 151–52; easterners' disregard for, 148–49; energy of, 155–56, 165–66, 168, 175–80, 184, 250; escaping, 179–80; as fresh start, 149–51; as masculine, 162–63; in modern United States, 154; as true America, 153–54, 158, 159, 168, 187; as unstable category, 153; in Wharton's fiction, 49, 146–47, 148, 149–51, 177–78, 180–86. *See also* East-West divide
"westerns," 18, 160; Cather on, 162–63; gender and, 162–63; as genre, 154; Wharton's low opinion of, 160–61
Weston, Vance, 18, 181–82, 183–86, 192, 286–87
Westphal, Bertrand, 5, 6
Wharton, Edith, 41, 43, 71, 301, 302; A. E. Housman and, 45–47, 47; aesthetics in letters of, 21, 94–95, 96, 119–20, 135, 197–98; on American identity, 21, 211–13; American pride of, 190; ancestors of, 31; anxiety of, for reputation, 66; as aristocrat, 27–28, 30–32, 34, 36–37, 38–39, 54; art enjoyed by, 199, 201; birthplace of, 8, 10; burial of, 28, 32, 195; Cather and, literary connections between, 17–18, 38, 39–52, 58–59, 68–69; Cather compared to, 65–66; Cather influenced by, 52–65; Cather read by, 58, 66–67, 68, 312n167; charity work of, 204, 214–15, 216, 281; childhood of, 72, 87–88, 89, 114, 145, 193–94, 259–60, 264–65; as critic, 83–84, 85–86; on criticism, 67; critics of, on place, 12–13; decline and death of, 283, 285, 297–98; East epitomized by, 155, 157, 158; energy of, 166, 167, 168; on Europe vs. United States, 87–88, 89, 112–13, 114, 211–13, 256–57; fatality of place in, 1, 13–14; finances of, 122; French imperialism and, 243; French language fluency of, 203–4; Henry James and, friendship between, 42, 44, 97–98, 260; on Italy, 94, 95, 97; loneliness of, 265; in Newport, 89, 92, 168, 278; New York City associated with, 105–6, 107; passport of, 261; post-

war losses of, 282; on postwar Paris, 265; the Romantics and, 120; Roosevelt family and, 218, 219, 222, 224; Sarah Orne Jewett and, 44–45; Sinclair Lewis and, 48–49, 67–68, 189, 310n87; social class of, 30–31, 36; suicide in fiction of, 34, 55, 57, 116, 170, 184; the Transcendentalists and, 120; translators of, 204; on traveling, 94–96, 97, 258, 262–63, 276–77, 284–85; travel writing of, 94, 195, 243; on ugliness of United States, 87–88, 91–92, 113, 119–20, 125, 160–61; on Virginia Woolf, 159; the West in fiction of, 146–47, 148, 149–51, 177–78, 180–86; writers admired by, 73–74, 313n10; younger writers and, 67

Wharton, Edith, works of: "After Holbein," 309n80; *The Age of Innocence*, 13, 27–28, 35, 42, 48, 50, 62, 65, 83, 98–99, 108, 109, 112, 122, 143–44, 157, 201, 274, 277; "America at War," 336n248; "Atrophy," 204; *A Backward Glance*, 13–14, 30–31, 48, 70, 73, 145, 161, 176, 188–89, 215, 282; *The Book of the Homeless*, 201, 216, 224; *The Buccaneers*, 19, 106, 285, 287–91; "Bunner Sisters," 146, 149–50, 323n23; "Chartres," 202; *The Children*, 83; "Chriemhild of Burgundy," 202; "Coming Home," 97, 202; *The Custom of the Country*, 18, 67, 109, 122, 130, 146–47, 149, 177–78, 184, 189, 191, 201, 212, 242, 323n10; *The Decoration of Houses*, 92, 119, 136, 316n127; *Ethan Frome*, 13, 17, 54–58, 147, 150, 157, 204, 277; *False Dawn*, 144; *Fast and Loose*, 201; *Fighting France*, 201, 230; *French Ways and Their Meaning*, 68, 198, 201, 210, 211–13, 228, 239–40, 255, 332n100; "Friends," 91; *The Gods Arrive*, 18, 181, 182, 191, 283, 286–87, 342n134; "The Great American Novel," 159; *The House of Mirth*, 17, 18, 34, 39, 53–54, 61–64, 96, 97–98, 105, 110–12, 115–18, 122–25, 127–31, 135–37, 139–40, 146, 150–51, 201, 266–68, 270; *Hudson River Bracketed*, 18, 147, 181–86, 191; *In Morocco*, 94, 243, 263; *Italian Backgrounds*, 94; *Italian Villas and Their Gardens*, 94; "Kerfol," 201; "Les Metteurs en Scène," 204; "Life and I," 72, 88; *Madame de Treymes*, 201; *The Marne*, 146, 201, 214, 217, 224–25, 255; "Miss Mary Pask," 201; *A Motor-Flight through France*, 94, 195, 198, 201, 262, 292; "Mrs. Manstey's View," 90–91, 119, 149, 265–66; *The Old Maid*, 48; *Old New York*, 83, 144; "The Other Two," 157; "Rambouillet," 202; *The Reef*, 52, 201, 242; "Schoolroom Decoration," 92, 119, 316n127; "Senlis," 202; *A Son at the Front*, 13, 18, 19, 65–66, 137, 138–41, 190, 201, 214, 224–31, 232–39, 256; *Summer*, 39, 182; "Talk to American Soldiers," 193, 239–40, 249–50, 336n248; "Tendencies in Modern Fiction," 159–60; *Twelve Poems*, 202; *Twilight Sleep*, 83; *The Valley of Decision*, 97, 147; "Writing a War Story," 161, 201; *The Writing of Fiction*, 78, 79; "Yet for One Rounded Moment," 39

Wharton, Teddy, 105, 194

Wheeler, Bayliss, 132

Wheeler, Claude, 56, 132, 144, 183, 225; criticism of, 225–26; death of, 238, 239; in France, 227–28, 229–32, 239–40, 286, 287; isolated from art, 226–27. See also *One of Ours* (Cather)

Wheeler, Evangeline, 238, 239

White, William Allen, 163

Whitman, Walt, 48, 155
"Wild West," 244–45. *See also* the West
Wilhelm Meister (Goethe), 73
Willa Cather: A Literary Life (Woodress), 36. *See also* Woodress, James
Willa Cather: Double Lives (Lee), 36, 37, 51. *See also* Lee, Hermione
Willa Cather: The Emerging Voice (O'Brien), 36, 60. *See also* O'Brien, Sharon
Williams, Deborah, 59, 86
The Willows, 185–86
Wilson, Edmund, 164
Wilson, Woodrow, 214, 216
Wincher, Nettie, 171
Winslow AZ, 152
Winterbourne, Frederick, 53
Winthrop, Egerton, 282
Wister, Owen, 160, 191
wives, artists', 137–44
Wolff, Cynthia Griffin, 36, 164
women: in American culture, 51, 131, 138, 156, 169–70; as competitive, 171–72; economic exclusion of, 131; as goddesses, 169–70; as helpless, 35; pragmatism of, 137–44; Puritanism and, 168, 169, 170; realism of, 156; Romantic assumptions about, 141–42; sexual assault of, 64; tension in writing by, 339n31; and "women's fiction," 84–87
wonder: beauty evoking, 19, 292–94; capacity for, 56, 292–93, 294, 297; churches inspiring, 286–87; need for, 21, 293–94

Woodress, James, 36, 37, 109, 195
Woolf, Virginia, 35, 158–59, 281
work ethic, American, 125, 130–31, 134, 137
World War I: American Ambulance and, 51; American neutrality in, 190, 214–15; Armistice, 215, 217–18, 281; Cather and, 196, 214, 215–18, 221, 222, 281–82; and Fourth of July parades, 220–21; French losses in, 232, 235–36, 335n223; French understanding of, 232, 236–38; and home and travel, 280–87; and postwar world, 280–87; Wharton and, 97, 190, 194–95, 214–15, 222, 223, 224, 263, 280–81. *See also One of Ours* (Cather); *A Son at the Front* (Wharton)
World War II, 283–84, 298
worship, 168, 293–94. *See also* reverence
Wretched Exotic (Joslin and Price), 12
A Writer's America (Kazin), 9
"Writing a War Story" (Wharton), 161, 201
The Writing of Fiction (Wharton), 78, 79
Wyss, Johann, 166

"Yet for One Rounded Moment" (Wharton), 39
"Young Man from the Provinces" novel, 173–77
Yourcenar, Marguerite, 147–48, 205
youth: age and, 64–65, 66; displacement experienced in, 87–94; lost, 76
Youth and the Bright Medusa (Cather), 117

Zola, Émile, 76